THE
BOOK
OF THE
MONTH

THE
BOOK
OF THE
MONTH

SIXTY YEARS OF BOOKS
IN AMERICAN LIFE

EDITED BY
AL SILVERMAN

LITTLE, BROWN AND COMPANY
BOSTON   TORONTO

Second Printing

Library of Congress Cataloging-in-Publication Data

The Book of the month.

   Contains reviews, essays, and articles which
originally appeared in the Book-of-the-Month Club
news.
   Includes index.
   1. Books—Reviews—United States.   2. American
literature—20th century—History and criticism.
3. Books and reading—United States—History—20th
century.   4. Book-of-the-Month Club.   I. Silverman,
Al.   II. Book-of-the-Month Club news.
Z1035.A1B58   1986   070.5   86-7511
ISBN 0-316-10119-2

HAL

*Published simultaneously in Canada
by Little, Brown & Company (Canada) Limited*

PRINTED IN THE UNITED STATES OF AMERICA

ACKNOWLEDGMENTS

THIS ASSIGNMENT would never have been completed without the help of certain people. I thank Julie Glucksman, who spent the summer of 1985 at the Club between terms at Harvard locating most of the material and getting intact and recognizable copies to me. Bless Marian Wolfson for seeing to it that all the finished pieces were put properly together and copied in a logical way. Thanks so much to Marissa Polino for her expert fact checking. Nell Morris's assistance when the going got tough was particularly helpful to me. I'm grateful for Charles Lee's inspiration, via his well-detailed book *The Hidden Public*, a history of the Club written at the time of its fortieth anniversary. And my fervent thanks to Nancy Evans, Maron Waxman, and Bill Zinsser for all their wise editorial advice. Finally, I would not have completed this project in time for our *sixty-fifth* anniversary, never mind our sixtieth, if it had not been for the tireless efforts of my assistant and master-of-all-trades, Winifred Osborn.

Al Silverman
April 8, 1986

CONTENTS

Introduction   xi

PROLOGUE: Ernest Hemingway
      A Book-of-the-Month Club Connection   3

DECADE ONE: *1926–1936*   11

DECADE TWO: *1937–1946*   49

DECADE THREE: *1947–1956*   93

DECADE FOUR: *1957–1966*   141

DECADE FIVE: *1967–1976*   181

DECADE SIX: *1977–1986*   251

Index   325

Books are not absolutely dead things, but do contain a potency of life in them to be as active as that soul was whose progeny they are; nay, they do preserve as in a vial the purest efficacy and extraction of that living intellect that bred them. I know they are as lively, and as vigorously productive, as those fabulous dragon's teeth; and being sown up and down, may chance to spring up armed men. And yet, on the other hand, unless wariness be used, as good almost kill a man as kill a good book. Who kills a man kills a reasonable creature, God's image; but he who destroys a good book, kills reason itself, kills the image of God, as it were in the eye. Many a man lives a burden to the earth; but a good book is the precious life-blood of a master spirit, embalmed and treasured up on purpose to a life beyond life.

JOHN MILTON, *Areopagitica*

INTRODUCTION

HARRY SCHERMAN picked a good time to start a book club. It was 1926 and Hemingway was posing for a photograph with Joyce, Eliot, and Pound at Sylvia Beach's bookstore in Paris. Scott Fitzgerald was in Paris, too, with Zelda, waiting for *The Great Gatsby*, published the previous fall, to take off.

It seemed like a good year for everyone. Calvin Coolidge said so. The stock market was booming, and nobody was poor, and only the Lost Generation seemed disillusioned. But that was O.K., too; for the Lost Generation, as the critic John K. Hutchens said, it was "creative disillusionment."

Popular art flourished in 1926 and, in some cases, became high art. Rudolph Valentino made his last film, *Son of the Sheik;* Buster Keaton starred in *Battling Butler;* Lillian Gish played Hester Prynne in a Swedish film of *The Scarlet Letter;* Ronald Colman was Beau Geste and John Barrymore was Don Juan. Martha Graham did her first dance solo at New York's 48th Street Theater, and Henry Moore's "draped figure" was undraped for the public.

It was a vital year for books, too, though not quite as exciting as 1925 had been. The literary flow that year must have persuaded Harry Scherman to undrape *his* creation. In addition to *Gatsby*, the list of novels published in the United States included Theodore Dreiser's *An American Tragedy*, John Dos Passos's *Manhattan Transfer*, Virginia Woolf's *Mrs. Dalloway*, the English translation of Thomas Mann's *Death in Venice*, Liam O'Flaherty's *The Informer*, and new novels by Ellen Glasgow and Willa Cather. Pound wrote, "It is after all a grrrreat littttttttterary period."

The *r*'s and *t*'s would have to be shortened for '26. The harvest was less rich and the poet Rilke had died. There were a lot of popular best-sellers, including Edna Ferber's *Show Boat* and Anita Loos's *Gentlemen Prefer Blondes*. There was also an array of nonfiction bestsellers that could be smuggled onto today's bestseller list and nobody would know the difference: *Diet and Health;* a new edition of *The Boston Cooking School Cookbook* by Fannie Farmer; *Why We Behave Like Human Beings; Auction Bridge Complete;* and *The Story of Philosophy* by Will Durant. In that first year of the Book-of-the-Month Club's life, only two books of the month were bestsellers: *Show Boat* and John Galsworthy's *The Silver Spoon.* Not chosen as books of the month but recommended to the charter members of the Club were *The Story of Philosophy* and *The Sun Also Rises.*

Durant and Hemingway, as no other authors, thread their way through the sixty-year history of the Book-of-the-Month Club. Today, new generations of members are buying *The Story of Philosophy* as their parents and maybe their grandparents did — more than 300,000 copies have been distributed to members since 1960 alone. And Durant's massive fifty-year undertaking, *The Story of Civilization*, accomplished in partnership with his wife, Ariel, is one of the most popular "premiums" of the Club. In book-club terminology, a premium is a book (in this case eleven books) that can be had for a minimal price by anyone willing to enroll in the club. Over the years a lot of people have been willing.

As for Hemingway, what began in 1926 remains alive in 1986. In February of 1926 Hemingway came to New York and switched publishers. Scribner's was willing to publish his novel *Torrents of Spring*, a parody of Sherwood Anderson; Hemingway's first publisher, Boni & Liveright, had turned it down. In April of that year, just as the Book-of-the-Month Club was emitting its first infant squeals, Maxwell Perkins of Scribner's was reading the manuscript of *The Sun Also Rises.* And Hemingway, the man who, the French said, had "broken the language," was on his way. In 1986, Hemingway's last, unpublished novel, *The Garden of Eden*, became a "Book of the Month."

Over the years Hemingway's effect on the Club and its members has been persuasive in various ways. In 1985 Elmore Leonard, the Raymond Chandler of our time, spoke at the Detroit Institute of Art, a lecture sponsored by the Club for its members in the Detroit area. Leonard, who established his literary reputation late in life, told of BOMC books coming into the house, beginning in 1937. His older sister had joined the

Club, and Leonard began to grab the books. He remembered reading *Out of Africa, The Yearling,* Carl Van Doren's *Benjamin Franklin, Captain Horatio Hornblower, Native Son, Darkness at Noon, The Moon Is Down* — all BOMC Selections — and, he told the audience that night, "the novel that would eventually get me started as a writer, *For Whom the Bell Tolls.*" Some years later he reread the novel, this time, he said, "to use the book as a text that would teach me how to write."

If the middle 1920s had a distinctiveness, beside prosperity, it was this: entrepreneurs of the word had captured America. DeWitt and Lila Acheson Wallace founded the *Reader's Digest* in 1922; Henry Luce and Briton Hadden started *Time* in 1923; Henry Seidel Canby became founding editor of *The Saturday Review of Literature* in 1924; Harold Ross created *The New Yorker* in 1925. And, in 1926, Harry Scherman invented the book club.

Scherman was a word man. He always believed in the power of words to change people's lives. This was a belief that turned into a vision, a vision of an organization that could reach out to a vast and varied and interested and untapped reading public.

Born in 1887 and reared in Philadelphia, Scherman quit the Wharton School at the University of Pennsylvania to come to New York to work for an advertising agency. He had a bent for advertising, particularly mail-order. He was a brilliant copywriter and idea man.

In 1914 Scherman, with Charles and Albert Boni and Maxwell Sackheim, formed the Little Leather Library. These were miniature classics bound in sheepskin. Scherman persuaded the Whitman Candy Company to enclose a book in every one-pound box of chocolate. The venture was too successful — more than 40 million copies of these miniature classics were produced and they exhausted the market. But Scherman was ready to move on. His next idea was to distribute the best *new* books being published — books that would be chosen by an independent and eminent board of literary experts, books that would be sent through the mail across the country. It would be the first such organization in the English-speaking world.

The first announcement appeared in the February 13, 1926, issue of *Publishers Weekly,* the book-publishing community's Bible then as it is now. It described a plan "to solicit subscriptions to an A-Book-a-Month program." In April of that year "A Book a Month" was launched as "The Book-of-the-Month Club." The first book was *Lolly Willowes,* a first novel by an unknown British writer, Sylvia Townsend Warner.

It was not by accident that the original board of judges should choose a new author rather than a surefire name as the Club's first Selection. As Scherman wrote years later, the Club has "provided that swift accumulation of renown which is the most valuable support and encouragement a working writer can have." The Cinderella example of Scherman's swift accumulation of renown came in 1936.

Margaret Mitchell was a writer none of the Club's judges had ever heard of. When *Gone with the Wind* came to them for discussion, the debate was lively. There were some doubts about the characterization and the quality of the writing. One judge admitted that it was "a page turner," but he wasn't sure if other readers would like it well enough to turn the pages. In the end the board felt that the book would do. The Club released *Gone with the Wind* just before its publication. Still little known, it received a polite but underwhelming reception from members. But becoming the book of the month did something for the book and the author. The following letter from Margaret Mitchell to Harry Scherman, dated June 20, 1936, ten days before publication date, explains what it meant to the author.

> Atlanta, Ga.
> June 20, 1936
>
> Dear Mr. Scherman;
>
> Thank you so much for your letter. I was very glad to get it, not only because of the flattering sentiments you expressed but because I have been wanting to write to the Book of the Month Club and did not know who to address. I wanted to thank the Editorial Board from the bottom of my heart for selecting my book. It was quite the most exciting and unexpected thing that ever happened to me, so exciting and unexpected that I did not believe it true and told no one for three days (my husband was out of town at the time and I waited for his return to discuss the matter). Then I cagily told a friend on the Atlanta Journal that Mr. Brett, Jr. of The Macmillan Company had evidently taken leave of his senses for he had written me the most remarkable letter and it did not seem possible that the Book of the Month Club had really picked me. Then my friend said that I was the So-and-soest fool she had ever heard of to know such news for three days and keep it from my own old newspaper and she rushed the news into print, accompanying it with the world's worst picture. And I quaked, thereafter, fearing there had been a mistake somewhere and that you all would denounce me as an imposter.

I had had the manuscript knocking around the house for so many years, never even trying to sell it, so when Mr. Latham bought it my excitement was naturally great. But when I heard that you all had selected it, it was too much to be borne and I went to bed and was ill, with an ice pack and large quantities of aspirin. And your letter, telling me that it was the unanimous choice, has made me so proud, that it has taken great strength of character not to go back to bed again! I thank you all, so very, very much. I have never had anything happen to me that was as nice.

I hope to come to New York sometime in the Autumn and I hope to meet and thank in person the members of the Board. Henry Seidel Canby's article about the book in the Bulletin was enough to turn a harder head than mine and Dorothy Canfield's review in the Ladies Home Journal was most flattering. . . . . I suppose I shall have to put my prejudices in my pocket and read the Russians, Tolstoi and Dostoyevsky, etc. And probably Thackeray and Jane Austen, too. Yes, I know it sounds illiterate of me but I never could read them. But when people are kind enough to mention them in the same breath with my book, I ought to be able to do more than duck my head and suck my thumb and make unintelligible sounds. Heaven knows, this "up-country" Georgia girl never expected to get in the same sentence with them!

> Sincerely,
> (signed) Margaret Mitchell
> (Mrs. John R. Marsh)
> 4 East 17th Street N. E.

The Scherman method worked from the beginning. By the time the Club turned twenty-five, in 1951, 100 million books had been sent into the nation's households. Scherman felt that less than 10 percent of that number would have made it into readers' hands if it hadn't been for his invention. But some critics worried about the standardizing effect that such a massive distribution of preselected books would have on America's reading habits. In his challenging essay "Masscult and Midcult," Dwight Macdonald criticized the Book-of-the-Month Club for what he felt was its tendency to water down and vulgarize high culture. On the other hand, Carl Van Doren said, "A good book is not made less good or less useful by being put promptly into the hands of many readers." Harry Scherman was a pragmatist, and a populist, when it came to reading. He understood that there would always be that gulf between Macdonald's High Culture and popular culture, but he also felt that the two sometimes merged and, anyway, that a bridge existed between the two and that people could walk back and forth as they chose. Which is what Book-of-the-Month Club members did then and do today.

"If you are to deal with or think about the American people en masse," Scherman wrote in 1966, "you can trust them as you trust yourself. You can trust their consuming curiosity about all the quirks and subtleties of human existence; you can trust their fascination with every colorful aspect of history; you can trust their immediate response to good humor and gaiety, but also to the most serious thought; you can trust their gracious open-mindedness, forever seeking new light upon their troubled but wonderful world. Whoever may have good evidence about that world, and whatever it may be, here is proof that the thoughtful people of this country will give him the audience he deserves."

Harry Scherman died in 1969 at the age of eighty-two. Clifton Fadiman, the senior judge of the board at the time, remembered Scherman as full of "goodness and generosity." The publisher Bennett Cerf called Harry Scherman "the happiest man I know."

"Trust them as you trust yourself." That became the philosophy of the first Editorial Board assembled by Scherman. And it is the abiding watchword of the Club to this day. But what kind of audience deserved that trust? Scherman talked about "the thoughtful people." That was close to George Saintsbury's "general congregation of decently educated and intelligent people." Those standards fit the Scherman era, but since then the world has become more complicated, and more perilous. Today, Clifton Fadiman says, members are looking for books that will satisfy "the serious American interest in self-education. They want books that explain our terrifying age honestly." The newest member of the Editorial Board, Gloria Norris, opened it up even more. "I think one reason we've kept members for so long is that we respect their possibilities."

The Club has had eighteen judges in its sixty years. Five of them — Amy Loveman, Basil Davenport, Lucy Rosenthal, David Willis McCullough, and Gloria Norris — rose from the ranks of the Club's editorial staff. These wise and learned men and women were in the forefront of the search for books that would strike their hearts and would therefore be likely to pierce the hearts of the reading public.

But when the Club was founded, Harry Scherman felt that it was important to find literary figures with established reputations for his first board. "You had to set up some kind of authority," he said, "so that the subscribers would feel that there was some reason for buying a group of books. We had to establish indispensable confidence with publishers and readers." Scherman chose well: Henry Seidel Canby, Dorothy Canfield Fisher, William Allen White, Heywood Broun, Christopher Morley. White was the editor of the *Emporia* (Kansas) *Gazette* and represented the values of middle America. The New York newspaper columnist Heywood Broun spoke for urban America. The witty and sophisticated novelist Christopher Morley looked for "what literature is most intended to be, entertainment, surprise and delight."

But the two most influential figures, as you will note by their contributions in this volume, were chairman Canby and Miss Canfield. She was a woman of high moral values and determined taste. She was also the most conscientious reader on the first board. Robert Frost sums up her character in these pages, but it can be said that her standards were exacting. A novelist herself, she tended to focus on the accuracy of image, the unity of plot, the depth of characterization. She didn't like books that seemed "soft and arranged." She looked for books that exhibited "value, truth and literary skill."

It was Canby, a Quaker, who shaped a board that acted on the Quaker system of concurrence — that is, the judges arrived at a sense of agreement about their enjoyment of a book or its importance. No concurrence, no Book of the Month. At least once, the spirit of concurrence worked against Canby. In his *American Memoir* he recalls holding out for John Steinbeck's *The Grapes of Wrath*. Alas, he couldn't get any of his colleagues to concur. More recently, in 1985, John K. Hutchens, a member of the board since 1964, a loving and gentle man with a hard-rock Montana integrity and a deep sense of balance in his judgment of books, lost his heart to a novel called *Heart of the Country* by Greg Matthews. It was about a half-breed, hunchbacked buffalo hunter, and Hutchens called it "one of the best books on the old West I've ever read." Another judge, David W. McCullough, was almost as enthusiastic. He mentioned its faults but said, "I think it's a great, strong book." But two of the other judges felt just as passionately the other way. No concurrence. The book became an Alternate, not a Selection.

Even through this debate, however, the spirit of concurrence prevailed. Clifton Fadiman once explained the process. "In all the time I have been with the Club I have never heard a judge defend *himself* —

only the book in question. Because we know that the book and author under discussion are more important, for the moment, than our prejudices, oddities, life-slants."

Harry Scherman was always proud of the system he had worked out for selecting books. But he remembered one book that got through the net — *The Caine Mutiny* — "because our first reader's reaction happened to coincide with the original *unexcitement* on the part of the publisher." He also recalled how *Darkness at Noon*, another book that arrived without the publisher's "excitement," was discovered by its first reader at the Club and passed on to the judges, who made it a Selection. Over the years, inevitably, worthy books were missed, some that were to become classics. *Man's Fate* didn't make it, nor did *Under the Volcano* or *All the King's Men*, though all of them received favorable reviews in the *News*. No Faulkner novel became a book of the month until his last book, a minor work called *The Reivers*, perhaps because one judge confessed that he always giggled when reading Faulkner. Yet many other books by little-known writers who became well known were taken, including Richard Wright's *Native Son* and *Black Boy*, Koestler's *Darkness at Noon*, Orwell's *Animal Farm* and *1984*, J. D. Salinger's *Catcher in the Rye*, and, more recently, Toni Morrison's *Song of Solomon* and John Irving's *The World According to Garp*.

Lest you think that books are picked by the Club when they become winners, you should know that manuscripts are submitted six months or more *before* publication. The Club's readers and judges don't have the benefit of hindsight. They must make their decision long before the fate of the book in the marketplace is known. Will the judges make the book a Selection? Will it become an Alternate? Will it be ignored? The readings, the reports, the debates, and the passion that a reader has for a book — these are all elements that go into the final decision. Incidentally, when we talk about "Selection," sometimes called "Main Selection," it is *the* Book of the Month, the book picked by the outside judges. An Alternate is a book that has been selected by the editorial readers who work inside.

In the early days, Selection was all. More than 50 percent of the members took the Selection. But they didn't have much choice because only one or two Alternates were offered along with the Selection. The last Selection to reach 50 percent acceptance was *Crusade in Europe* by Dwight D. Eisenhower. That was in 1948. Today the Club offers a dozen new Alternates in each issue of the *News*, along with the Selection and a backlist of 125 books, most of them quite recent. Club members, that family of intelligent book readers grown more intelligent and sophisticated in their reading tastes over the years, now make their choices from a rich variety of possibilities. So much for masscult.

When the original judges died or retired, they were replaced by others of similar stature. They included John P. Marquand, author of *The Late George Apley* and other novels about the Brahmins of Boston and its environs; John Mason Brown, the eminent drama critic of *The Saturday Review of Literature;* Paul Horgan, the novelist, critic, and historian of the West, and Gilbert Highet. Highet served from 1954 until his death in 1978. He was the most erudite of all the judges — a writer, critic, teacher, raconteur, classicist, translator, and radio commentator. He once began a lecture to his Columbia students by saying, "I was reading Toynbee this morning while shaving." He had a habit that annoyed some publishers: he would correct galleys of their books and send them back to be worked on. It was said that he could start, finish, and correct an entire galley while hanging onto a subway strap on his way home.

The current members of the board are Clifton Fadiman; John K. Hutchens; Wilfrid Sheed, the critic, novelist, essayist, baseball and cricket fan; Mordecai Richler, the Canadian novelist and saturnine humorist; David Willis McCullough; and Gloria Norris, both former editors of the Club and both writers. It is a harmonious group, still operating on the principle of concurrence.

Of all eighteen judges in the Club's history, none has had more impact than Clifton Fadiman. None has served longer. "Kip" is in his forty-second year as a judge. But it is not so much his years of service that count as how Fadiman has used those years. He is a man of high energy who looks years younger than his age. He acts even younger. He is a cultured man, one who loves books — though not uncritically — and who can't stand to be without a book to read. In his understated way he exerts a patriarchal influence on the board's deliberations. He is never without an opinion but he is also an accomplished listener. He manages to see whatever point of view a colleague might put forth, not that he always agrees with it. His own pronunciamentos are voiced with a persuasive combination of wit, authority, and, if tactically necessary, self-deprecation. Once, discussing a novel of some soap-opera dimensions, Fadiman allowed that he rather liked the book. He excused himself with these words, "I'm by far the most sentimental of us and should be watched with suspicion." Here is a sample of other judgments pronounced by Fadiman at board meetings:

- On a book about Mount Everest: "I think we should take it because it's there."
- On a contemporary novel: "It has no center. What it has is a lot of wonderful periphery."
- On a volume of William Shirer's memoirs: "One should never reach the age of eighty because by then you realize your life is not worth a good goddamn."

Here Fadiman was making a judgment on himself as an octogenarian and not on his fellow octo, William Shirer. And of course it was a judgment at odds with the facts. For Fadiman's whole life has been one both of reflection and engagement, and of constant self-scrutiny. In 1983 he wrote a letter to Gloria Norris, who was then the Club's editor-in-chief, about the novel *The Name of the Rose:*

> Clearly, I admired the book enormously. But through pride I assumed that my admiration of it followed from my superior taste and knowledge. I should know that at my age such superior taste and knowledge are shared by hundreds of thousands of my fellow Americans. The book is now a bestseller. I said, "This remarkable novel will sink without a trace." I also said, "It's the kind of book our culture will automatically reject." Unless we assume that the bestsellerdom merely reflects a kind of snobbery, we must conclude that while my judgment of the book was correct, my judgment of its appeal was ludicrously at fault. There is only one deadly sin and all the others follow from it: Pride.

The idea for this book evolved almost by accident. No Big Bang here. From time to time I had dipped into old issues of the *Book-of-the-Month Club News,* looking for a particular Selection report or a biography of an author, or trying to find out how the Club had treated a certain book. It was mostly unorganized curiosity. But each time I came away with an appetite for the past. I wanted to know more about the Club's past because that way I would know a little more about *our* past as a country. Then, in the spring of 1985, a convergence of two situations intensified my feelings.

The Club had a sixtieth anniversary coming up in 1986. What might we do to mark the occasion? How might we use our anniversary to celebrate the Club and its influence on American life over the past six decades? At about the same time, a huge manuscript came into the office, unannounced. It arrived, as Harry Scherman would have said, "with original unexcitement" from the publishers, American Heritage. It was called *A Sense of History,* and it was an anthology of fifty-four articles from the pages of *American Heritage* magazine. I first became aware of the book after I stepped out of a judges' meeting. I sit in on the board's discussions, mostly to answer any questions the judges might have about a book or an author under discussion, and to pour the wine. It had been a quiet meeting; the judges had found nothing they liked, which meant that we still had to fill one more slot in our 1985 schedule. Our executive editor, Joe Savago, stopped me in the hall.

"Don't let them get away," he said. "We think we may have found something they will like."

"What do you mean?" I said. "The meeting's over."

Our first reader of *A Sense of History* had been Larry Shapiro, a wise and conscientious editor with a marvelous feel for all kinds of books, but especially books of history, and American history in particular. Larry wrote a report on the book. All his reports are models of lucidity, and this one beamed favorably on the book. Shapiro was enthralled by many of its pieces: Wallace Stegner's memoir of his Western boyhood, David McCullough (the historian, not our judge) on Harriet Beecher Stowe, B. H. Liddell Hart on William Tecumseh Sherman, articles by Bruce Catton, Barbara Tuchman, Robert Heilbroner, John Kenneth Galbraith. Three weeks later the judges met again and concurred on *A Sense of History.* It became the Selection for December.

At about the same time, I had started to browse through back issues of the *News,* looking for ideas for our sixtieth anniversary. Suddenly I found myself going through the *News* systematically, from the first issue of April 1926 right up to the present. And the more I looked, the more I felt that a sampler from the pages of the *News* would be one way to call up the past, and maybe even tell a story of the social history of the past six decades as seen through books. Thumbing through those grand old repositories of our tradition, the yellowed paper sometimes crumbling in my hand, I felt myself transported into another world. In a strange way the experience was like one I remembered from my childhood.

I was standing on a curb on a warm Memorial Day morning in my hometown of Lynn, Massachusetts. The parade began with a battalion of police officers in their dress uniforms, white gloves gleaming as they strutted up Broad Street. Then came an open car with the Civil War survivors. They were shriveled into their blue uniforms, and two pretty young women with sashes down the front of their dresses were sitting in the car with them. Those veterans were as delicate as that paper from the *News* that broke up in my hand. But they lived! They were the last link to that profound episode of our past.

Then came the Spanish-American War veterans, a small platoon of them, some still able to walk, others riding in open cars, also with pretty escorts. Then the heart of the parade for me — the World War I veterans, proud marchers all except for those who couldn't walk because of their war wounds. I always thought of my father at that time. He was one of them; he had served in France, but he never belonged actively to any veterans' organization, and he never paraded. The only time I ever saw him in near-uniform was on one New Year's Eve. The party was at our house, and my father pulled out of the attic his steel helmet, cavorting with it. It was that evening, I'm sure, that he let me put it on my head. It was one of the few times I remembered my father so loose and free and happy. The parade intensified my feelings for my father. I was an impressionable kid then, and I loved the patriotism of the parade, which seemed to me to be pure and uncluttered, and I especially loved the pageantry.

So here I was now as a grown-up, experiencing another magical pageant, a procession of books and authors parading through time, some that began modestly and took on life through the years, others with grand reputations then that lie in mothballs today.

But it wasn't just the distant past that fascinated me. In 1972 I had gone to work for the Book-of-the-Month Club as Editorial Director, so I've had a hand in the production of the *News* since then. And looking back at those years, from 1972 to the present, I also felt good about the recent past.

Axel Rosin, Harry Scherman's son-in-law, who succeeded him as president of the company and was a dedicated standard-bearer of the Club's values, once told me: "We keep talking about the good old days but, you know, the good old days, they weren't so good." No doubt the seventies and eighties will appear the same way to the tastemakers of the nineties and beyond. But looking at sixty years of the Club's history the way I did, the way you will, in the *News*, one gets an unshakable sense of continuity.

As you browse through the pages of this personal remembrance of things past, you probably won't find a pattern to my choices. There is none. Apart from dividing the book into six sections, one for each of the six decades of the Club's life, I wasn't interested in assembling a carefully linked clockwork of activity. Even the decade breaks are artificial — what do the early prosperity years of the first decade, 1926–1936, have to do with the decade's later Depression years? Nor was I concerned about flashing the best writers past you (who are they, anyway?) or to show only the best books selected each year (who says they're the best? what about the ones that weren't taken?). The idea is to give you a feel for the material that flowed into the *News* through the years. And so you will read about *The Good Earth* and Pearl Buck; a fourteen-line review of Faulkner's *Light in August;* Dorothy Canfield's stern judgment of John O'Hara's *Appointment in Samarra;* what Fred Allen wrote about Herman Wouk, who once worked for him as a gag writer; what Randolph Churchill wrote about Evelyn Waugh; what Evelyn Waugh wrote about Nancy Mitford.

One thing that emerges from the pages of the *News*, particularly in those early years, was the fellowship that existed among writers. It was almost a daisy chain: you had E. B. White writing in the *News* about Clarence Day, and Wolcott Gibbs writing about White. There was John Gunther reporting on William Shirer's *The Rise and Fall of the Third Reich*, and Shirer writing about John Gunther. You had Norman Cousins on John Hersey, and John Hersey on Theodore White, and White on Cornelius Ryan, and Harper Lee on Truman Capote — all the way to Gore Vidal writing about himself and John le Carré telling why it took him so long to write a novel he had been thinking about for years, *A Perfect Spy.*

There also are editors and publishers writing about their authors — the great Doubleday editor Ken McCormick on Somerset Maugham; Robert Haas of Random House on Isak Dinesen; Harold Latham of Macmillan on Margaret Mitchell; Jim Silberman, then of Random House, on E. L. Doctorow. And there's the sense of discovery of new writers by our own judges: Mordecai Richler on Toni Morrison, Wilfrid Sheed on Anne Tyler, David Willis McCullough on a new writer who was eighty-eight years old when she had her book published, *". . . And Ladies of the Club. "*

You may find this collection of literary memorabilia quirky, if not downright eccentric. But that's all right if it also helps you to sort out a bracing six decades of American letters. Optimists as always, all of us who work for the Club today are looking for more for tomorrow. We are joined together to find, among the 5,000 submissions we get from publishers every year, the book that will bring us wonder and joy or help us understand this fragmented age. The find doesn't happen very often, but when it does it makes the continuing search for the Book of the Month an adventure that we never want to end.

THE
BOOK
OF THE
MONTH

PROLOGUE

Ernest Hemingway:
A Book-of-the-Month Club Connection

IF ONE WRITER can be said to have truly spanned the sixty years of the Book-of-the-Month Club, that writer would be Ernest Hemingway. In the December 1926 issue of the Club's publication, *Book-of-the-Month Club News*, there was a review of *The Sun Also Rises,* sandwiched between a review of *Tar* by Sherwood Anderson and *Preface to a Life* by Zona Gale. Referring to the novel as "the story of a lost generation," the unsigned reviewer was torn between the "technical excellence" of the book and its subject matter, "which is somewhat disagreeable" and "apparently told against it in the voting." Thus *The Sun Also Rises* did not become *the* Book of the Month even though the review acknowledged the "genius" of Hemingway's "method" as a writer.

In a 1929 review of *A Farewell to Arms,* Hemingway was noted as more than a stylistic innovator. "For the first time he makes people cry out," the reviewer stated. In 1940 *For Whom the Bell Tolls* was chosen the November Book of the Month as most of the Editorial Board's reservations about Hemingway had evaporated. Henry Seidel Canby called the book "one of the most touching and perfect love stories in modern literature." And if you want to catch a glimpse of what Hemingway was like at that time, read the piece that accompanied the Selection by Maxwell Perkins, the leading editor of the era and shepherd of many of the writers of the Lost Generation.

After *For Whom the Bell Tolls,* Hemingway was a household name for BOMC members. His books were never ignored and they all received major attention. In 1986 the connection with the Club was completed. Hemingway's supposedly last, out-of-the-trunk novel, *The Garden of Eden,* was made a Selection. A passage in that novel describes the fever of writing and in its way reveals one of the major American novelists of the past sixty years. "[He] sat down and wrote the first paragraph of the new story that he had always put off writing since he had known what a story was. He wrote it in simple declarative sentences with all of the problems ahead to be lived through and made come alive. The very beginning was written and all he had to do was go on. That's all, he said. You see how simple what you cannot do is?"

The Sun Also Rises by Ernest Hemingway

THIS novel is in a category by itself. One of the judges gave it the highest vote, and all of them placed it high among the books considered this month. If the judges had voted upon technical excellence alone, this would perhaps have been the "book-of-the-month." Its subject matter, which is somewhat disagreeable, apparently told against it in the voting. It is, however, strongly recommended by all the judges to those who are interested in the technique of writing — for seldom, in recent years, has a more skillful piece of work been done. Everyone who reads it remarks upon the genius (it is a word one finds used frequently in the critiques about the book) with which the author visualizes for the reader his scenes and characters, and special emphasis must be given to the extraordinary fidelity to type in his dialogue. "Hemingway" — says one of the members of the Committee in reporting about the book — "is a young American resident in Paris, and the novel is the story of a group of expatriates that drift and drink, chiefly drink, from Paris down to Spain and back. It is the story of a lost generation, wrecked by the war and European demoralization, but apparently not caring much, if they can get a drink. Actually there is a deep vein of pathos under the good-humored cynicism of this novel. It is a brittle world, ready to collapse into ruin or hysteria at any moment; the strain of bohemian life is just ready to snap. Many have written of the follies and poignancies of the war generation. What is most striking in Mr. Hemingway's book is not his subject but his method. He writes remarkable dialogue, crisp, witty and yet startlingly real, and his scenes — like the bull fight, and the fiesta in Spain — are brilliant."

For Whom the Bell Tolls
by Ernest Hemingway

THIS is Hemingway's best book since *A Farewell to Arms*. As that famous novel, now regarded as an American masterpiece, has been inaccurately described as a story of the Italian defeat at Caporetto in the last war, so *For Whom the Bell Tolls* will be, with equal inaccuracy, spoken of as a story of the Spanish Civil War. The scene, of course, is Spain, the time the Spanish War, the plot an attempt of a young American in the Republican forces to blow up a steel bridge at the beginning of a major attack on Segovia. But how little of this touching, and often terrible, and always engrossing, novel is included in this description.

Like *A Farewell to Arms*, this is actually the narrative of the reactions of a young man to danger, and a conflict of ideas and tense emotion. As in *A Farewell to Arms*, a love story enters, quite accidentally, and becomes a vital part of the narrative. And let me say that Hemingway, who has been celebrated for his toughness and brutality, has written in the sudden love story of Robert Jordan and his "rabbit" one of the most touching and perfect love stories in modern literature — a love story with a tragic ending which lifts rather than depresses the imagination.

The proper background for understanding a description of this fine romance is the famous series of drawings by the great Spanish artist, Goya, of a century ago, illustrating the horrors and realities of guerrilla warfare. In those celebrated prints one sees the strange Spanish peasant; cruel, yet capable of infinite loyalty; brave, because expecting suffering; ignorant of and indifferent to culture as we know it; but with an immense zest for living and an unexampled homely wisdom. These pictures show them with their fierce native emotions aroused by forces from the world outside, torturing and fighting and rescuing each other.

In the curious military world of Madrid, Russian generals and politicians (brilliant characterizations in themselves) are preparing attacks against German and Italian commanders over the mutilated body of Spain. Robert Jordan, an American teacher of Spanish on leave from his university, has enlisted in the Republican struggle. He is theoretically a Communist, because Communism at the moment is the most effective force in loyalist Spain; but actually he is a Western democrat, believing in life, liberty, and the pursuit of happiness; jut as his peasant companions, who call themselves Communists, are actually loyal only to Republicanism and agrarian reform. He is chosen for a highly dangerous mission — to go behind Franco's lines, make contact there with a band of guerrillas, and prepare at the precise and chosen moment to blow up an essential bridge. The novel at the beginning finds him already in the mountains; it ends with a chapter of exciting warfare — but its bulk lies in four short days of preparation in between.

It is exceedingly difficult to make the prospective reader of this book feel the interest and tensity of these few days, because so much that happens results from the remarkable characters with whom Jordan finds himself associated, and from his own precarious position, an outsider in almost hourly danger of death or betrayal. At the end of it all, he says that the life of this band has become his life; among these peasants are his closest friends and most dangerous enemies. Both past and future seem shadowy in comparison with this life in hiding on the mountain. And that is the way the reader feels. These striking personalities, disengaged from the Spanish type by Hemingway's unequalled power of dramatization in dialogue, become so intimate and so self-expressive under the pressure of the events, that you have lived, felt, and thought with them — a triumph for a novelist. I do not know how true they are to a Spanish type; perhaps Hemingway does not. I do know that here is a group of fully realized human beings, real beyond question, even though the story in which they are involved is a psychological romance.

There is Pilar, the matriarch, a great woman with a great and varied past — once mistress of a matador, now old and wise, foreseeing doom; brutal yet kind, with the imagination of a great artist. She is married to the drunkard, Pablo, leader of the gang, shrewdest of them all, who knows that the enterprise will ruin most of them, yet who will not finally betray them because his inner need to be brave is stronger than his reasonable fears. There is Fernando, the complete literalist, without an atom of imagination or humor, and so bravest of all. There is Anselmo, the good old man, who dreads killing, who is truly religious, who will have to kill and be killed. There is Maria, the Rabbit, escaped from a town devastated by the Fascists, still crop-headed from the tortures which clipped and burnt her scalp, after which she had been raped by the Moorish auxiliaries. A brave innocent, the almost mortal hurt to her imagination is cured by the instant love between Jordan and herself. Her story is an *andante* theme that runs through danger and beside death. There is the Gypsy, the untouchable, the eternal frivolity and self-seeking of the man incapable of ideals, to whom all these dangerous loyalties are just opportunities to trap rabbits and make off with loot.

Robert Jordan, preparing day by day for an adventure almost, but not quite, doomed to failure by a belated snowstorm and the orders to shoot the bridge by daylight, is dependent for success upon the wavering wills of these guerrillas, who must be persuaded to risk their own lives for an alien in an enterprise which they believe to be desperate, and which is desperate. Pilar is behind him, Maria comforts him, Anselmo is his friend. The rest shift and turn in a constant tension from which, as in a good play, every ounce of personality of everyone is expressed for the story.

The adventure both succeeds and fails — and this is the book, except for two interpolated scenes of a horror mitigated only because they are told of, not witnessed. The first is the account of how Pablo made the Fascists of his native town run the gauntlet. The second is Maria's story of the revenge of the Fascists upon the Reds, real and supposed, of her village — the shooting of her father and mother, when her mother who was not even a Republican died, saying: "Viva my husband, who was the mayor of this village."

War is the scene of this novel, as of pretty much everything else nowadays; but it is a magnificent romance of human nature quite apart from and above its environment of civil war.

HENRY SEIDEL CANBY

Ernest Hemingway
by Max Perkins

IN spite of Ernest Hemingway's repugnance to publicity — his first and most emphatic request to his publishers was that nothing about his personal life should be given out — he is one of those about whom legends gather; and since he is disinclined to talk about himself it is hard to disentangle truth from rumor.

But one of the earliest stories significant of his character I do know to be fact. When still a boy, but large for his age and strong, his father, yielding to his urgency, gave him as a present the price of an advertised course in boxing. You paid the ex-fighter in advance and he turned you over to a pug. In the first lesson young Hemingway got rough treatment. His nose was broken. Few returned for a second lesson, but Hemingway did, and he finished the course. It never even occurred to him that this was a racket — that you weren't supposed to come back ever.

That was in Chicago when he lived in Oak Park. Only a little later — he was certainly below sixteen — he left home, determined to take care of himself. In a surprisingly few years later he was taking care of a number of other people toward whom he thought he had loyalties. His first established job was that of reporter on the *Kansas City Star* — though if his size had not beguiled a city editor into overestimating his age by several years, he would never have got it. Before this he had shown some inclination to write, for pieces by him had appeared in his school paper, but in Kansas City he really began to learn.

Then came the World War. Even when it ended Hemingway would have been barely old enough to enlist, but he was bound to see it, and finally got into the Ambulance Service on the Italian front, later to command a section, and then to transfer to the Infantry with a lieutenant's commission. He was wounded, and in the end received as high a decoration as the Italian army gives. It is commonly thought that the war scenes in *A Farewell to Arms* came directly from that experience. They didn't. The most famous ones of all, those in the account of the Caporetto Retreat, were wholly his own creations. He wasn't there.

War is, we know, a revelation to one who can retain impressions. The book of Common Prayer says: "In the midst of life we are in death," but one could also say of war that in the midst of death we are in life. Many writers, like Tolstoy, have largely learned of life from war — for then life is quickened and intensified, and the qualities of men come sharply out. Hemingway saw it again after Versailles when, as correspondent for an American syndicate, he covered the Greco-Turkish War, and he said he learned far more of war from that, as an observer, than from the World War as a participant.

Then in Paris he turned wholly to writing, and lived for several years in poverty. This was in that post-war renaissance which so deeply affected American literature. When about 1927, he came to America, it was by way of Cuba, for economy's sake. Then he crossed to Key West, liked it, and stayed.

Hemingway became a great fisherman in those waters through which runs the deeply blue gulf stream: the fishing was needed as relief from the hardest work in the world, that in which everything is presented in final truth, where the essential quality of each thing told of is perceived and fixed. And that's why it was done — that and the need of such a man for action. Obviously his first interest was in writing, and not *his* writing only.

Once when he came to New York and Tom Wolfe was in an agony to master the material of *Of Time and the River* I asked Ernest to talk to him. No writers could have been so far apart in style and method, yet

Ernest was fully appreciative of Tom and he understood his torment in his work. I remember, at that luncheon which so encouraged Tom, Ernest told him some helpful things — always, for instance, to break off work when you "are going good." Then you can rest easily and on the next day easily resume. For such as Tom, however critical he might be of some qualities in his work, Hemingway had a deep sympathy because of Wolfe's artistic honesty — but not for the literary writers. When told of one who could not go on with his work until he found the right place to work in, he said, "There's only one place for a man to work. In his head."

Hemingway has too largely appeared as a man of force and action. He is that too and when he thought the people who were Spain were fighting for what was Spain, he gave all he could and was quite prepared to give his life. But his writings are surely enough to show what he is besides that, and what one soon learns who sees him is that he is always at his work; always aware.

DECADE ONE

1926–1936

A FIRST NOVEL *by a thirty-three-year-old British poet, a woman, was the first Main Selection of the Book-of-the-Month Club in April 1926. Lolly Willowes was the title and Sylvia Townsend Warner was the author. Henry Seidel Canby, chairman of the "members of the Selecting Committee," as the judges were then called, felt the book was probably too special and too literary and that the "proprietors" of the Club "might lose their subscribers and their collective shirts." It did not happen, though Lolly Willowes made no bestseller list. Sylvia Townsend Warner did go on to enjoy a long and respected literary career, including seven novels, twelve collections of short stories, five of poetry, and a biography of her great friend, T. H. White. In 1976, on the occasion of the Club's fiftieth anniversary, David Willis McCullough wrote to Ms. Warner to ask her recollection of that 1926 experience. She answered McCullough, who was then writing a column for the BOMC News, saying, "When I learned that the Book-of-the-Month Club had selected Lolly Willowes for its first choice I was astonished, delighted and confident that any organization daring enough to pick an unknown author would be a valuable asset to contemporary literature." Ms. Warner died two years later at the age of eighty-five.*

Lolly Willowes
or The Loving Huntsman
by Sylvia Townsend Warner

IT WILL BE of interest to our subscribers to know not only *why* the members of the Selecting Committee choose the book that is sent to subscribers each month, but *how* they arrive at their choice. The qualities that make a book readable and enjoyable are many, and qualities that will delight one person may not appeal greatly to another. It would be too much to hope that any five individuals, of different tastes, should always independently conclude that a certain book is the "best" among a great many good books. Only rarely may it be expected that a book will tower above all others so clearly that the five members of the Selecting Committee will *unanimously* agree upon it.

The object of the committee's choice is not to deliver an ultimatum as to the "best" book each month, but to find a book that will appeal most winningly and forcibly to widely differing tastes. Difference of opinion among judges is, therefore, not only inevitable but desirable, for it is clear that if ever they independently agree to recommend the same book, it will certainly possess an exceptionally high order of merit.

The method of choice decided upon, therefore, was as follows: Out of a list of about fifty current books submitted by publishers, the choice was narrowed by a process of elimination to twenty. Each one of the judges independently read these twenty books, and chose six — *ranking them in the order of their preference.* In this ranking, *Lolly Willowes* emerged with a markedly higher rating than any other. Three of the judges actually rated it first, certainly an unusual tribute in view of the many excellent books that were being considered.

The comments of the judges upon Miss Warner's book (in indicating their preferences, each one gave reasons for his choice) all seem to agree upon one point: that it is, as one of the judges wrote, "one of those wise simple books, charmingly written, that are so easy to read and so true to human nature that the reader does not at first realize how much quiet humor and how much rare life he is encountering." Another one refers to it as "an enchanting book," and another says: "It is more than a simple idyll of English country life. It is the story of a woman who seemed just like a thousand other unmarried women — a little prim, a little eccentric — but inside she was different, and there were many others who inside were different as she was, who sought self-expression in their own way, who were willing to risk their souls and even their respectabilities to get it . . . It is a simple story that changes imperceptibly and delightfully into an intriguing fantasy."

Sylvia Townsend Warner, the author of *Lolly Willowes,* heretofore has been completely unknown to American readers and has been almost so in England. This is her first book of fiction, but she has published (as might be guessed) poetry. One who met her recently described her as "not an imposing figure, but with an animation and whimsicality that springs from within and is not assumed. Her portrait makes her, 'almost as aquiline as the American eagle,' she says. She has quite the least forced humor I have met in many a day. She can and does discuss architecture and literature and music soberly, but even then there is a quality of liveliness, a sparkle, that removes any possibility of dullness. Her imagination is constantly active . . .

"She hasn't traveled abroad since childhood, but she loves to explore England, touring the country afoot. Evidently she has the instinct of an archaeologist — she speaks almost with affection of a bit of mortar, or the like, at the museum in Newcastle which bears the impression of a Roman hand.

"In writing *Lolly Willowes* she herself went out into the country as Lolly did, leaving no clue as to her whereabouts. She is evasive about a personal meeting with the devil but it may be surmised — well, who that reads 'Lolly' can believe it to be entirely a product of the imagination!"

THE STORY OF PHILOSOPHY *by Will Durant was published in 1926. Today it sells almost as mightily as it did in the beginning.* The Story of Philosophy *led to the fulfillment of a dream: Durant would write "the story of civilization." Volume I was published in 1935. "I wish to tell as much as I can," wrote Durant in the preface to that book, "in as little space as I can, of the contributions that genius and labor have made to the cultural heritage of mankind. . . . I do not need to be told how absurd this enterprise is . . . and have made it clear that no one mind, and no single lifetime, can adequately compass this task." Yet Will Durant, with the help of Ariel, his wife of sixty-eight years, worked through eleven volumes of* The Story of Civilization, *completing the last volume,* The Age of Napoleon, *when he was ninety years old.*

The Story of Philosophy by Will Durant

IF IT had not been outlawed from consideration by its price, it is quite possible that the Selecting Committee would have chosen this remarkable work as the "book-of-the-month" for its subscribers, in spite of the high merit of Mr. Galsworthy's novel. It is an exceptional book and the members of the Committee strongly recommend it to our subscribers. Philosophy, to the average person, has always been a forbidding subject. Only now and then, when a man like James or Bergson elucidates its mysteries, does it come into its own for brief periods. Professor Durant's book is apparently due to initiate another period of widespread interest in philosophy, such as William James was responsible for through his brilliant lectures. To the surprise of many people, who underestimate the underlying seriousness of mind of the American public, almost at once this book has become a "best seller."

The book is, in a way, a summary of the views of the great philosophers from Socrates to John Dewey; but it is in no sense a scholastic summary. A good deal of the best sort of biography is in it. One of the Committee gives this report of it:

"There have been dozens of histories of philosophy, in all of which there is an attempt to present the chief ideas of the great philosophers. Mr. Durant's differs from them all, and in more than merit. He has, in the first place, the ability to explain with crystal clearness and make an abstract of a great philosophic system which sacrifices neither the meaning nor the richness of the original. But best of all is his method, which must be the result of a long experience in teaching, lecturing, and studying philosophy. Philosophy cannot be 'harsh and crabbed' when it is presented first as the ripening experience of remarkable men, next as an idea, and finally as a position freely to be criticized in the light of all we know. Spinoza in these pages becomes a man again. Giants like Aristotle and Kant become human, and Voltaire, in a brilliant chapter, is a dazzling personality who quite explains the worldwide power of his thought. Only the great are discussed in this book, and this is perhaps why it seems more like a symposium of the meaning of life, made relevant to us and our time, than a historical record. It is good reading for the least philosophical of nations."

The Story of Civilization: Our Oriental Heritage by Will Durant

THIS monumental literary enterprise of Dr. Durant has pretty much the same general intention as Mr. Wells' popular *Outline of History*, but it is apparent that he will cover the subject with considerably more particularity than did Mr. Wells — and, in fairness it should be added, with a more scholarly conscience. For twenty years this has been the *magnum opus* of his dreams; for the last eight years he has been actively engaged upon it, and this present volume represents the first completed structure in the plan, carrying us down to the death of Alexander. He begins with the Orient, because, of course, Asia was the scene of the oldest civilizations, and we shall be surprised to learn, says the author — and he is right — "how much of our indispensable inventions, our economic and political organizations, our science and our literature, our philosophy and our religion, goes back to Egypt and the Orient." That the book is highly readable it is hardly necessary to report to those who have read *The Story of Philosophy;* and while Dr. Durant worked solo, he and his publishers have had its contents carefully checked by scholars in many fields, and its reliability also may therefore be counted upon. In small space like this, perhaps the best general descriptive note that can be given is that supplied by the author himself, at the very outset, in his Preface: "I wish to tell as much as I can, in as little space as I can, of the contributions that genius and labor have made to the cultural heritage of mankind — to chronicle and contemplate, in their causes, character and effects, the advances of invention, the varieties of economic organization, the experiments in government, the aspirations of religion, the mutations of morals and manners, the masterpieces of literature, the development of science, the wisdom of philosophy, and the achievement of art. I do not need to be told how absurd this enterprise is, nor how immodest is its very conception; for many years of effort have brought it to but a fifth of its completion, and have made it clear that no one mind, and no single lifetime, can adequately compass this task. Nevertheless I have dreamed that despite the many errors inevitable in this undertaking, it may be of some use to those upon whom the passion for philosophy has laid the compulsion to try to see things whole, to pursue perspective, unity and understanding through history in time, as well as to seek them through science in space."

Will Durant (1885–1981) and
Ariel Durant (1898–1981): An Appreciation
by Clifton Fadiman

IN 1926 Will Durant's *The Story of Philosophy* was published — almost hesitantly, for who cares to read about philosophy? It proved shockingly popular and has since run up an immense trade sale. The Book-of-the-Month Club alone has distributed well over 300,000 copies.

The following year was marked by a less sensational event. I got a job with Simon and Schuster, the house that has been the Durants' publisher for 55 years. During the next decade I had occasion to work with Will and even to help in a small way with the preparation of the early volumes of *The Story of Civilization*. Thus I came to know him as a friend and to admire him as a historian. Later, over the years, reviewing for BOMC many of the successive volumes, I tried hard to separate affection from judgment.

This was not easy. As a human being Will Durant was tolerant, good-humored, skeptical, nonmystical, intellectually receptive, a lover of clarity, a hater of obscurantism and a champion of the long view. He would have been at home with Voltaire and Hume, and mildly amused by the Moral Majority. He was, to use a term as perennially noble as it is now transiently traduced, a humanist.

But these personal qualities, which I admire, are precisely the qualities that animate the 11 volumes of *The Story of Civilization*, including the later volumes that also bear the name of his wife, Ariel. That is why I found it hard to separate affection from judgment.

As the years passed and the vast volumes kept appearing, my conscience was eased. Those for whom the Durants wrote have validated the seemingly impossible task to which they dedicated their energies over almost half a century. BOMC has distributed 767,789 sets of *The Story of Civilization*. Our grand total of individual Durant titles (also counting *The Story of Philosophy* and *The Lessons of History*) comes to 9,064,688. More to the point, each volume has been greeted with pleasure and, as far as such matters can be ascertained, read with profit.

This biography of civilized man was written for, but never written down to, the common reader. Scholars have faulted details and quarreled with specific interpretations. Some of them have also been made uneasy by certain gifts that the Durants, especially Will, brought to their narrative — gifts of wit, humor, vividness and, above all, lucidity. Just as some philosophers have cried down Santayana because he wrote too well, some historians have been fazed by the Durants' ability to make history dangerously readable.

The common reader, however, has not objected to readability. Hundreds of thousands, all over the world, have enjoyed what no other single book or series of books now available can give them: a leisurely large-scale, understandable narrative of the human adventure over the last 5000 years. Faithful readers of all the volumes have received something in the nature of an education, insofar as books alone can educate us.

At the Book-of-the-Month Club we take quiet pride in our association with the Durants' achievement. It is a pride quite without fatuity, for it is based on the continued good judgment, over many decades, of our members. It is you, and more than one generation of you, who have sanctioned our own admiration for the lifework of two great educators.

SINCLAIR LEWIS *dominated the bestseller lists of the 1920s. His novel* Main Street *sold 295,000 copies in 1921.* Babbitt, *published in 1922, introduced a new word into the American language.* Arrowsmith, *published in 1925, picked apart the medical profession. In 1927* Elmer Gantry *became the number one fiction bestseller of the year. In 1930 Lewis was ·the first American to win the Nobel Prize for literature.*

Elmer Gantry by Sinclair Lewis

AS EXPLAINED in our Preliminary Notice, which subscribers received a month ago, this book was given the highest vote by the entire five members of the Selecting Committee — the first time this has happened. All of the judges gave the same reason for choosing the book; it is a book which will unquestionably result in widespread controversy; it will be praised highly and condemned bitterly; it will perhaps be a topic of discussion for months, not only in pulpits and editorial columns but among intelligent people everywhere. For that reason all of the judges, voting independently, felt that it should be sent to subscribers. It is chiefly "outstanding," in other words, because of its high current interest, not so much for its literary merit. Of course, Lewis is one of the best living novelists; he knows how to tell a story as well as how to raise a social issue; but the general opinion of the judges seemed to be that *Elmer Gantry* is not quite so good writing as *Babbitt,* and that it is less novel but more interesting than *Main Street.* Dr. Canby's characterization in his final report seems to us a fair summary: "Many will be shocked by it, but everyone will wish to read it. Let it be read as special pleading by one of the most skillful reporters now alive."

THE TITLE *and the coauthors — stalwart preppies of* The New Yorker *in 1929 — tell all.*

Is Sex Necessary? Or Why You Feel the Way You Do
by James Thurber and E. B. White

IS SEX NECESSARY? *Or Why You Feel the Way You Do* is at least necessary to you, gentle reader, if you want the nip of clear December mornings after your session with July and August. It is enormously amusing and often deeply wise, but its great virtue is its saucy treatment of the turgidity of the current psychologies. It is all very well to be abreast of the times, and all of us honor our conscience by doing what we can to know what the sages know, but there's no use saying it isn't heavy going sometimes, and probably we rejoice in this antic book precisely because it releases our own thinly buried malice. Anybody who has ever tried to improve his mind for one hour will find in the "Case History of Smith," the dogs and the puzzles, a perfect rapture of liberation. The drawings of Mr. Thurber are so extremely fine that we first thought Mr. White had been rummaging for them under the desk of Clarence Day, but Mr. Day denies this flatly though enviously. He says, "You see, this fellow knows how to draw." At any rate, the drawings are wholly delightful, particularly the plates from "The Unconscious." In short, don't let this book slip by you, if you yearn for a swell time.

A NEW REALISM *in detective fiction blossomed in the 1930s. The anonymous reviewer of W. R. Burnett's* Little Caesar *wrote: "This exciting story of bootlegging, hold-ups, orgies, and cold-blooded murder is told with a literary art that is so restrained and simple as to seem not literary at all." In Dashiell Hammett's novels Book-of-the-Month Club members were introduced to "the jargon of bulls, mobsmen, speakeasy proprietors and the slang-genteel classes." William Rose Benét's 1934 review of a first novel,* The Postman Always Rings Twice, *refers to James M. Cain's prose as coming out "hot and smoking, like a plate of pork and beans."*

Little Caesar by W. R. Burnett

A DECEPTIVE book. On the surface it is the simple tabloid tale of a gun-
man, Chico, his employers and associates in the underworld of Chicago.
A clever newspaperman on the inside might, it seems, tell such a story,
if he were really on the inside, and knew these men and women as personalities, not merely as actors in crime and vice. Chico, the friendless
wop from Ohio, who cannot even speak his father's language, always
pitying and admiring his lone audacity, comes through, gets to be a boss
himself, and then, in a crash of events, has to leave it all, start again with
only his reputation to help him, and at last, in an alley, meets the bullets
that end him. But this exciting story of bootlegging, hold-ups, orgies,
and cold-blooded murder is told with a literary art that is so restrained
and simple as to seem not literary at all. Those who remember their
Merimée will be the first to recognize its excellence, for it has the same
directness, simplicity, force, as Merimée's bandit stories, and humanity,
too. These crooks of the underworld are understandable because they
live by a code of their own and in a moral atmosphere created for them.
They are good, bad, and indifferent according to their own standards —
religious, generous, loyal, faithless, too, by their own standards. If *Little
Caesar* is tabloid journalism, let us have more tabloids. But of course it
is not. If the writers of detective stories could borrow this author's art,
there would be more of their products worth recommending in these
columns.

Glass Key by Dashiell Hammett

MR. HAMMETT, we understand, was at one time an operative himself.
He knows by personal experience the methods of modern crime detection, which are neither romantic nor pretty, and the type of man likely
to engage in it — no prettier. The result is that his detective yarns have a
quality of uncompromising reality that is as far removed from the usual
pattern as anything being done in this field today. Every detective story
fan, it can be said dogmatically, should become acquainted with Mr.
Hammett. His hardboiled detectives, just a shade above the criminals
they track down and consort with — and not at all in principles but only
in astuteness — are geniune creations. They keep their mouths closed,
double-cross anybody whenever necessary, and heighten the mystery — not (one feels) just to mystify us poor readers, but because that

is the way they would operate. *Glass Key* is about a political murder, and deals incidentally with the close relations between bootlegging, crime and politics. An excellent book — not to be missed even by those who are not fans — fully up to the standard of *The Maltese Falcon*, the author's last one.

The Thin Man by Dashiell Hammett

THIS is a detective story in what might be called the Hemingway manner. It is told entirely in crisp, blunt, sometimes brutal, dialogue. It is done with remarkable skill. Mr. Hammett has perfect command of the jargon of bulls, mobsmen, speakeasy proprietors and the slang-genteel classes. His American-Greek detective, Nick Charles (real name Charlambides) is a convincing portrait. So are they all. But it is only fair to warn the sentimental lover of mystery stories against this stark, hard-drinking and coarse-talking tale. It has none of the customary picturesque padding. It comes uncomfortably close to the realities of New York murder: sordid, grim, steeped in alcohol. A powerful *tour-de-force;* not a pleasant one.

CHRISTOPHER MORLEY

The Postman Always Rings Twice by James M. Cain

JUST as a certain rapid-fire sort of acting has of recent years been developed upon the stage — the father of it all being the still sprightly and most sapient George M. Cohan, and one of its best exponents Osgood Perkins; just as the play centering about the city room of a daily newspaper, and the "talkie" centering about the hideout of a certain group of gangsters, have run a course of astonishing popularity; so the rapid-fire, tough, two-fisted novel which is usually shorter than the average because it is written by a newspaper graduate who has a compact style, at once gathers its audience. The people in such a book are supposed to be more real than other people because they are more primitive in their lust and in their anger; the milieu is supposed to be more interesting because it is a filling-station, a beanery, or a hot-dog stand. That is the kind of fiction Mr. Cain hands out, hot and smoking, like a plate of pork and beans. And, may it be said, he does his job, extremely well, almost up to the end, where he suddenly weakens, as Hemingway — for instance — never would have weakened, and his randy handy man and his glorified whore become strangely transmogrified into a modern Tristram and Iseult — which simply does not fit them at all. But Cain is intensely vivid, always holds your attention, knows how politics and shysterism defeat the law, knows how common men make love to other men's wives, how oafish brains juggle ideas of loyalty and even possess the body of the wife practically upon the dead body of the husband — as it was according to Benvenuto Cellini. If you stop to think of it, our times are not, in many ways, much better than the brutal and gory Italian Renaissance. Our times lack the grandeurs of that time, but not the bitter evil and utter callousness. Mr. Cain has written of what exists, in a manner that convinces for three-quarters of the book. His novel has already been overpraised, as would naturally happen. Nevertheless, he belongs, as a beginner, among the young Stephen Cranes and the young Frank Norrises — and how many of them have we? One looks forward to his future fiction with more than usual interest.

WILLIAM ROSE BENÉT

A TWO-VOLUME *"memorial"* edition of The Complete Sherlock Holmes *was rushed into print a month after the death of Sir Arthur Conan Doyle on July 7, 1930. The set is on the Club's active list to this day, and through the years more than 510,000 copies have been sold.*

The Complete Sherlock Holmes
(Conan Doyle Memorial Edition)
A SPECIAL EDITION IN TWO VOLUMES

SIR ARTHUR CONAN DOYLE died on July 7th last. At the regular monthly meeting of our judges which took place about ten days later, Conan Doyle's American publisher put this proposal before them — to get out a memorial edition containing all the novels and stories in which Sherlock Holmes appears — and they thought it a very desirable thing to do: not only as a fitting tribute to one of the distinguished writers of our generation, but also because they felt this was a collection pretty nearly every book reader would like to have in his library.

In England it has been possible to get the collected Sherlock Holmes stories, but never before in this country. To obtain them for his library, the American book reader would have to purchase nine separate books, not uniform. This edition, therefore, seems to fill a real need.

Each of the two volumes will contain approximately one thousand pages, one more and one a little less. A fine lightweight paper, however, will be used, so that they are no more bulky than an ordinary book. The type will be clear and readable, about the size of this. There will be an introduction by Christopher Morley — at present unwritten, or we would of course quote from it. The full contents will include four novels and fifty-six stories, arranged so far as possible, not in the order in which they were written but in a proper time sequence. The list of contents is as follows:

Volume One

A Study in Scarlet	(complete novel)
The Sign of Four	(complete novel)
Adventures of Sherlock Holmes	(12 stories)
Memoirs of Sherlock Holmes	(11 stories)

Volume Two

The Return of Sherlock Holmes	(13 stories)
The Hound of the Baskervilles	(complete novel)
The Valley of Fear	(complete novel)
His Last Bow	(8 stories)
The Case Book of Sherlock Holmes	(12 stories)

Below is Dr. Canby's report about this selection, on behalf of the judges:

"Every reader of English has read some of the Sherlock Holmes stories and many of us will want to read them again, now that their only begetter is dead, but few have read them all. It will be perhaps a surprise that the complete collection which The Book-of-the-Month Club is sending out actually fills two capacious volumes.

"Conan Doyle was not original. The tricks of the detective story — and the good detective story is full of tricks — are all present, I think, in the work of their great inventor, Edgar Allan Poe. In 'The Purloined Letter,' in 'The Mystery of Marie Roget,' and in the mystery story 'The Gold Bug,' a mystery and its solution by adroit reasoning from shrewd observation are blended with adventure. But Poe, as a writer of mystery stories, had one serious lack. He did not write enough of them. While he uses his ingenious mechanisms elsewhere he left only a few perfect examples of the type. And Poe had another deficiency. His stories are logically perfect, he was a master of terror and the mysterious; but character study, except the projection of his own personality, was beyond him. He could provide his own Dr. Watson, but the great variety of minor characters which give to the Sherlock Holmes stories an air of happenings in a familiar England, were quite beyond his powers. Sherlock Holmes himself is much more of a personality than Poe's fantastic Monsieur Dupin. Indeed I believe that these stories owe quite as much to the strongly marked personality of Holmes as to their ingenious plots. Every detective story writer since has tried to put a Holmes in his stories. None has succeeded.

"And there is still another reason why Conan Doyle has built himself such a monument in a kind of writing which usually is to the last degree ephemeral. He was, like Poe, deeply interested in science, and he had the thorough scientific training that Poe lacked. Also, like Poe, his mind was obsessed with the invisible world, and his recent leadership in attempts to communicate with the dead is well known. Now, scientific reasoning is remorselessly logical and based usually upon inductive processes in which minute observation and the most careful use of every available phenomenon is essential. Let this logic be used to solve the apparently mysterious, the possibly supernatural (as in 'The Hound of the Baskervilles' or 'The Speckled Band') and we have the ideal prescription for a mystery story. The writer is equally engrossed by mystery and by cold logic, and he is armed with the greatest of all detectors, which is science itself. But the mystery must be only apparent, the agency only possibly supernatural. Science and the invisible will not mix; the solution in a good story must always be attainable by human means. This Poe knew, and so did Doyle. Horror stories per se belong to another genre and there, too, Poe excelled, but in the mystery story the great interest, after all, lies not in the solution but in the means of reaching it. It is the nice balance between the impression of something dire and infinitely difficult which a Sherlock Holmes story always makes upon you, and the realistic working out of the attempts at solution, and the prosaic but intensely interesting explanation put at the end, which gives Doyle his eminence. No one but Poe has beaten him there, and Poe perhaps only once.

"How enviable are the first readers of these skillful and varied stories! The formula for all the tales is substantially the same, but who cares? It is a theme upon which the variations are endlessly interesting. And Sherlock Holmes himself, is, I suppose, one of those figures of myth — the demi-god — which even a prosaic age must create. He is freed from the commonplaces of life by his own disillusions; he has kept enough of the nobler emotions to be human; he has developed that power of ratiocination, which life in a scientific age requires, to a point which makes him a superman, without resort to the supernatural, though always tempting our atavistic imagination by seeming to possess it. He is the best of his kind, and it is hard to conceive of a repetition of his success unless some new creator can use the resources of the new psychology for rationalized mysteries of a new kind."

Conan Doyle once said that the commonest question asked him throughout his lifetime was whether there was a real Sherlock Holmes, and where he lived on Baker Street. Even the most experienced reader, at times, finds he has to pull himself up to realize that the master-detective was a wholly fictitious character, so much a part of our common tradition has he become. Nevertheless, as so often happens, there may be said to have been a starting-point for the conception in a real person — a professor under whom young Doyle studied at the University of Edinburgh. He mentions this in his *Memories and Adventures*, in this interesting passage:

> But the most notable of the characters whom I met was one Joseph Bell, surgeon at the Edinburgh Infirmary. Bell was a very remarkable man in body and mind. He was thin, wiry, dark, with a high-nosed acute face, penetrating gray eyes, angular shoulders, and a jerky way of walking. His voice was high and discordant. He was a very skilful surgeon, but his strong point was diagnosis, not only of disease but of occupation and character. For some reason which I have never understood he singled me out from the drove of students who frequented his wards and made me his out-patient clerk, which meant that I had to array his out-patients, make simple notes of their cases, and then show them in, one by one, to the large room in which Bell sat in state surrounded by his dressers and students. Then I had ample chance of studying his methods and of noticing that he often learned more of the patient by a few quick glances than I had done by my questions. Occasionally the results were very dramatic, though there were times when he blundered. In one of his best cases he said to a civilian patient: "Well, my man, you've served in the Army."
>
> "Ay, sir."
>
> "Not long discharged?"
>
> "No, sir."

"A Highland regiment?"

"Ay, sir."

"A non-com. officer?"

"Ay, sir."

"Stationed at Barbados?"

"Ay, sir."

"You see, gentlemen," he would explain, "the man was a re-spectful man, but did not remove his hat. They do not in the Army, but he would have learned civilian ways had he been long discharged. He has an air of authority, and he is obviously Scot-tish. As to Barbados, his complaint is elephantiasis, which is West Indian and not British." To his audience of Watsons it all seemed very miraculous until it was explained, and then it became simple enough. It is no wonder that after the study of such a character I used and amplified his methods when in later life I tried to build up a scientific detective who solved cases on his own merits and not through the folly of the criminal.

THE GOOD EARTH *topped the fiction bestseller lists for two years, 1931 and 1932, and later helped earn a Nobel Prize for Pearl Buck. Accord-ing to Henry Seidel Canby,* The Good Earth *taught the Editorial Board (no more the Selecting Committee) a lesson. In his own book,* Ameri-can Memoir, *Canby explained that popularity can come to a book that was "hitherto not widely successful with the American public," a book like* The Good Earth. *He wrote, "We began to see that there was only one safe procedure, which was to choose what we ourselves liked. If we liked a book well enough the public, whose taste was perhaps less dis-criminating but at least as sound and healthy as ours, seemed to like it also."*

The Good Earth by Pearl S. Buck

FICTION, which is our history of the present, slowly extends its bounds. Quietly and almost unnoticed, the art of skillful realism has passed be-yond our own people, beyond our own civilization, and has begun to deal with strange cultures, which we have never even tried to know from the inside, as they see themselves. The Chinese, the South Sea Islanders, the Africans are no longer merely quaint or picturesque. The novelist begins to look at them as the scientist observes them, with industrious attempts to understand and explain. He realizes that he must be born

again in his imagination before he can write of another race. And perhaps he guesses how important, now that transportation is tying all the
world together, is his effort of intuition.

Mrs. Buck is an American long resident in China. Her *The Good
Earth* is a superb example of this intuition, and in its way a unique
book. China is the mysterious cloud on the horizon for all of us. It, even
more than Russia, is the future; we know its art, we know its literature,
we know how the Chinese behave — what do we really know of China?

The Good Earth is China. In this story the West is a distant and unimportant phenomenon, and Europeans appear only vaguely and then
are to be noted for their ugliness and stupidity. Wang Lung, the hero,
knows of no desire so strong as the Chinese desire for land, which means
security; his customs are the only right customs; his misfortunes China
has always suffered; he gets rich by Chinese industry, and his happiness
is Chinese happiness. The people in this rather thrilling story are not
"queer" or "exotic," they are as natural as their soil. They are so intensely human that after the first chapter you are more interested in
their humanity than in the novelties of belief and habit. O-Lan, the first
wife, is a great character, heroic, incredibly self-sacrificing, accepting
her status of slave so willingly that the reader forgets it. When, in a superb scene, the famine drives the family southward, the Chinese tenac-
ity which holds together their morale in unspeakable hardships seems as
natural to the American reader as romantic love. You go Chinese in this
book, and after reading it can never again think of the Chinese struggle
and the Chinese people as drab, far away, and incomprehensible.

Wang Lung is a Chinese symbol of every man who has ever worked
his way up in the world. His very fingernails grip upon the land; from
the old rich lord, decaying and dissolute, he gets foot after foot of rich
rice land. Famine, war, sickness, sweep over him. He softens when he
gets rich and discovers sensuality. The play-girl Lotus, is brought home
and put ahead of the timeworn O-Lan. But he holds the land. The land
is China.

Those who suppose that the life story of a Chinese peasant will be
monotonous will have a surprise when they read this book. It did not
have to be about a strange country in order to be interesting and yet, in
reading, one wonders why it seems so much more tense and dramatic
than would be a like story laid in Dakota. The answer seems to be that
more happens in Wang Lung's neighborhood, and less can happen to
Wang Lung's self. It is the Middle Ages in which these Chinese
contemporaries of ours live. They have law and property rights, but no
sure government. Bandits and blackmailers harass them, the rag, tag and

bobtail of broken armies harrow them. When famines come they are
helpless as mice. And yet in this change and turmoil, the Chinese character is like a rock. Traits have been bred into them. Wang Lung is brutal to his wife, tyrannical with his children, superstitious, miserly,
sensual, but he has an ideal — land and a family, and a complete honesty
which makes a Puritan seem less moral than he is.

It is not necessary to question Mrs. Buck's knowledge of these Chinese people. It is guaranteed by her experience, perhaps, but what
makes it convincing is the book itself. This is surely as sympathetic and
knowledgeable a picture of Chinese life as is possible for a Westerner.
And *The Good Earth*, rather surprisingly, is a very good novel. Most
books of other races are not, no matter how vivid and interesting they
may be. But Mrs. Buck has the story-teller's gift. She sees life like a reel
unrolling, scene after scene, each exhibiting character. Ching, Cuckoo,
Lotus, the Old One, O-Lan, and Wang himself are not likely to be forgotten. They will change that impassive face with its slanting eye into
something individual and knowable for you henceforth. A Chinese famine, a Chinese looting, a Chinese uprising, a Chinese spring, will mean
something different after reading *The Good Earth*.

Our members will be interested in this quotation from a letter which
Dorothy Canfield wrote to the publishers of the book after it was chosen:

"Nobody could be more pleased than I over the choosing of *The
Good Earth*. It's a rare, fine, sterling price of work. To find such a book
among the ones sent to me by the Book-of-the-Month organization gave
me a thrill of delight. It's being able to help in the wider distribution of
such a book that makes the Book-of-the-Month work seem worthwhile
to me. . . . It's one of the few stories of Oriental life I ever read in which
all the characters seem human and understandable and possible to me, in
which my sympathies were deeply engaged as in the life of the living
people around me. Most Oriental novels, you know, are for Americans
really only curiosities, travel books of the mind, so to speak. *The Good
Earth* makes us belong to that Chinese family as if they were cousins
and neighbors."

Nobody we can find seems to know very much about Mrs. Buck —
not enough at any rate to satisfy the perfectly natural curiosity that will
grow about the writer of such a good book. All her publishers at present
can tell us is that she has always lived in China, except for the time she
spent in the United States when she was being educated. She studied at
Randolph-Macon College and at Cornell, and then, apparently very

promptly went back to become a teacher in Chinese universities. She lives in Nanking. This is her second novel, the first *East Wind: West Wind*, also being a novel about China; and she has contributed stories and articles to several magazines — in particular, *The Atlantic Monthly*, *The Nation*, and *Asia*. In a note she wrote to her publishers about her book, she said:

"What I have tried to do is not merely to portray the life of a Chinese farmer. I have tried to portray the beginning of a family, what we call here in China a 'great family.' These families almost without exception begin on the land and through some bit of luck get a start and gradually rise off the land. After two or three generations as the family leaves the land entirely, it begins to be decadent and sinks again, or rather breaks up and disintegrates. This long, wave-like motion of rise and fall of families has been characteristic of this civilization of the Orient.

"Such a portrayal I feel cannot be put into the pages of a short book — there is something almost cosmic about it. My two critics, to whom I gave the book without comment except to say I wanted it shorter and wished for their suggestions as to places to cut, felt that there was no place to cut without breaking the chain of events, each dependent on the other in the picture I have tried to make. The latter part of Wang Lung's life moves slowly because it must, for deep changes are taking place through apparently slight incidents, yet each of which has its place in the weaning of his family away from the land and the beginning of the upward rise of the wave."

HENRY SEIDEL CANBY

"FAULKNER grows in power and scope," wrote Henry Seidel Canby of this Faulkner masterpiece, Light in August. *Unfortunately not all members of the Editorial Board agreed with Canby, and Faulkner didn't achieve Selection stature with the Club until the publication of his last novel,* The Reivers.

Light in August by William Faulkner

FAULKNER grows in power and scope. This book has its terrors and its morbidities, and its theme is desertion, miscegenation, obsession with crime. But there is an unsuspected tenderness in the author's study of the poor white heroine, and a rich, sad humor in his scene, which makes one believe that the sadistic Faulkner of *Sanctuary* was only a phase. No one will read this book, or any book of Faulkner's, just to be amused, yet beside its quiet intensities, and the almost cruel fullness of life in its unfortunates, and the sombre beauty of the scenes and the ruthless logic of its life patterns, the pleasant chatty novels of surface, English "county stories," and London sophistications, seem trivial.

HENRY SEIDEL CANBY

WAH'KON-TAH *means The Great Spirit of the Osages and was the title of a* 1932 *Main Selection. The book was written by John Joseph Mathews and based on the journals of Laban J. Miles, agent for the Osage Tribe of Plains Indians. Miles also happened to be an uncle of Herbert Hoover, so Henry Seidel Canby visited the President in his last year of office to talk about his uncle.*

A Talk with President Hoover about Major Miles

A TRIBE of splendid barbarians, six feet and over, handsome in feature, eloquent in speech. An Osage of our own day, their descendant, who had used his opportunities not for white man's follies, but to get an education at Oxford. A quiet man with elements of greatness, who had been a government agent for the Osages in their heroic period, close friend of the old chiefs, and good friend of the Indians until his death only last year. A journal left by him, upon which the young Oxford Osage had built up *Wah'Kon-Tah*, one of the best studies of Indian life and imagination and the most human book on the Indian that I have ever read. This was the thread of circumstance which aroused my interest, and that of my colleagues, in Major Laban J. Miles.

It was not until later (there was no occasion for the author to mention it in the book) that I learned that this old Quaker major was an uncle of President Hoover; his favorite uncle, indeed; and that the President himself as a little boy had seen the finest of the Plains Tribes while they were still figures of saga, and had actually played, weeks in, weeks out, with their children on the lonely Osage Reservation which Mr. Mathews so quietly and so vividly describes.

A streak of Quaker runs through all our Indian relations, the President said to me, when I was privileged to talk to him about old Major Miles. It was a morning of packed business in the hard-driving White House of this Administration, but the President was willing to relax for a few minutes into memories of this Quaker major, who had been in place of a parent to him for a few years after his father's death, and a friend ever since. Mr. Hoover's voice is low and firm, and lifts only at the end of each moment of concentration in what is surely the most engaging smile of any man in public life — the smile, almost shy and confiding, of a strong, a reticent, but a friendly man.

The Major, he told me, was appointed by Carl Schurz as a result of a spasm of righteousness in Grant's second Administration when the Indian Protective Association, oganized by Quakers, had been called in to help clean up the mess into which Indian affairs had fallen. Rhodes, of Philadelphia, was president of the association at the time, and it is his son who is now Indian Commissioner, appointed by Mr. Hoover in memory of the successful tradition which he saw at work in his boyhood. These Quakers proposed Major Miles, who became a Major by the appointment, for every Indian agent was called Major.

This was in 1878, just after the President's first Indian experience when, as a child in Iowa, he played with a hundred or more Indian youngsters who were at a Quaker school in his Iowa town. When his father died, he was "passed around" a little among the relatives, and at about the age of seven came to live with his Uncle Miles on the Osage Reservation, which is the scene of *Wah'Kon-Tah*. There (the President recounted) he lived his childhood life with the children of the picturesque and often epic characters of this Indian book, went in swimming with them, played Indian games, attended Sunday School with such as would go, saw the fathers in paint and blanket and the roach and eagle feather, knew the sons intimately in spite of the barrier of language, imperfectly shared.

Exactly how long this idyllic life of a boy on the Plains lasted the President did not clearly recall, but again, later, when the Major, through some political earthquake, was temporarily retired, the President (still a lad) lived with the family at Lawrence, in Kansas. Readers of *Wah'Kon-Tah* will know that this means in an atmosphere rare in that or any day, where a man by religion a quietist had given his greatest devotion to chiefs whose profession had been fighting, and his heart and energy to the study of the imagination of another race.

The old Major lived to see the breakdown of Indian ethics and character when oil filled the country with dangerous money and much more dangerous white men: he lived long enough, also, to see in youths like Mr. Mathews, the author of *Wah'Kon-Tah*, the fruit of his own policy, that the Indian must be educated to take his place in the white man's life before it was too late.

The families were always closely associated, the President said, and the correspondence between the older man and himself was a long one. And, indeed, it seems to me there is a deeply human resemblance, more than kinship, between the quiet determination of the old man, neither overconfident nor disillusioned, in his difficult task of helping a race through the trial of readjustment, and Mr. Hoover's own character and his own record. The Major was a silent man, the author of *Wah'Kon-Tah* says, and in their troubles the Osages were often impatient, but they knew that he was a good man, and they found that he was responsible and could be trusted. Readers of the book will conclude that a blending of Indian and Quaker environment is not a bad beginning for a man destined to have a great American career.

HENRY SEIDEL CANBY

ROBERT GRAVES *died in 1985 at the age of ninety. He will be remembered for a vast body of work, stretching from essays to poetry; a popular television adaptation of* I, Claudius *brought him renewed acclaim from a new audience in the early 1980s.*

I, Claudius by Robert Graves

AN INTIMATE autobiography of that paralytic of the Julian family who became emperor by accident in that brilliant first century when the empire was all powerful in spite of the decadence of its ruling family. Graves has not written a historical romance. This is a realistic account of the life and times of a Roman who was a trained historian, and who sets down here in an autobiography the inside story that historians ought to know. The illusion is excellently kept. Claudius seems to write as a Roman, certainly he neither lives, sees, nor writes as a modern in costume, which is the practice of heroes in most historical romances. He is a cripple and a scholar at the heart of Rome who perforce is in daily contact with the managers of the time. He guesses what Augustus thinks, learns from his incredible grandmother the whole story of her poisonings with the statecraft and the patriotism that inspired them; is a Republican at heart like Augustus himself; knows the corruption, and describes it, of the times, but never doubts the Roman right to rule; faints at the blood of the amphitheatre, yet has not a single touch of humanitarianism. Indeed, this book is so like the memoirs of a modern politician or a biography of a Renaissance cardinal, and so unlike a novel of the "grandeur that was Rome," that the reader with a sweet tooth had better keep off it. This is a Rome which knows nothing of posterity but is only interested in itself. It seems a highly original book, historical in a good sense, though going far beyond verifiable detail, and to be recommended to those who like character and period study, written with historical conscience. While the story is an autobiography, not a plot, it does not lack drama nor excitement.

HENRY SEDIEL CANBY

IN *1926 Frank Nelson Doubleday, the founder of Doubleday and Company, wrote in a then unpublished manuscript: "For many years there had been no invention that I know of for selling books in a different way, until the Book-of-the-Month Club came along just a few months ago.... Here we have a totally original idea so far as I know, made possible by the fact that the people who select the books are favorably known to a large class of readers who believe that these selections are honestly made." Mr. Doubleday liked the idea so much that in 1928 he and his son Nelson Doubleday started a new book club called The Literary Guild. Mr. Doubleday, the son, wrote a biographical sketch of A. P. Herbert, whose book* Holy Deadlock *was selected by the Book-of-the-Month Club.*

A. P. Herbert

by Nelson Doubleday

ALAN HERBERT ("Peck" to his friends) lives with his wife and four children in that part of London known as Hammersmith, in an old house — in fact in two old houses — on the Thames, with a lovely garden in front which leads down to the river. He attended school at Winchester and New College, Oxford, served in the Dardanelles and France, was called to the Bar, Inner Temple, in 1918 but never practiced; for years he has been a regular contributor to *Punch,* and writes libretti for musical plays for Mr. Cochran; he sails, plays tennis, cricket and the piano, enjoys life to the full — and writes novels. Many people will have

read *The Water Gypsies*, which came about partially from his own experiences on the Thames. He has a barge about forty feet long with a
comfortable cabin and a motor that pushes it along about ten miles an
hour. One of his favorite occupations is to go up and down the Thames,
visiting all the old docks and old buildings, and talking to the stevedores
and to the sailing and steamship captains that are in and about London
town.

His photograph gives but a faint impression of what he is really like,
because his face is uncommonly mobile, and the laughter in his eyes
would make Santa Claus look like a sphinx! This perennial good humor
shows typically in his comment about himself. Some years ago, when
asked for a biographical sketch of himself, he dashed off this characteristic bit:

"I live a hideous life, and very often shave after lunch.

"I have four children and one wife. The fourth (a man-child) is extraordinarily handsome and good. All the other children are female and
very high-minded. I often sit down after breakfast each morning and try
to be funny. As the morning wears on I find the serious side of my nature gradually asserting itself with inimitable force, and by lunch-time
am ready to write a tragedy.

"My chief pursuit is sailing in the little river Thames which is at the
bottom of the garden here; I have two dinghies moored off the wall and
in the summer madly join in the yacht races of the local club. One
thrilling evening in the fall I actually won the Commodore's prize — in
the dark — at 7:30.

"I went to school at Winchester and thence to New College, Oxford. I
like dancing, but doubt if my partners rave about me. I played cricket
once this year, but don't intend to play any more as I made 55 runs
(which was top-score by 30), never having made more than 19 before,
so I feel my cricket career had better end on that glorious rate. It is true
that most of the bowlers were authors too, but there it is.

"Sailing, however, is my very real and only joy, both in the way of air
and exercise. I sail all the year round, even with snow in the boat!"

Herbert is one of those unusual fellows whose point of view seems
really governed by the need for expression of an irrepressible Irish wit,
but he is no playboy, and his humor has qualities peculiar to A. P. alone.
His one chief diversion in life, and his present book is an outgrowth of
it, is to start what he regards as reforms in the antiquated laws of
England, and his efforts in this direction have resulted in some stories
that have gone the rounds of London. On one occasion he found, in
searching some old records, that cowhide could still legally be used as

money in England, and as his next income tax was due shortly he borrowed a young heifer from a neighbor, had his back well washed, inscribed thereon his check in payment for his income tax, and hired a herd boy to lead the animal to the Bureau of Internal Revenue, and offered the check so inscribed on the heifer's back in payment of his obligation, all according to the Law of the Land. The check was refused, and he immediately wrote a letter to the London *Times* pointing out the need of modernizing and making clear what was legal tender and what was not!

On another occasion when visiting the House of Commons one night the debate was long and late. At one o'clock one of the members of the House asked him to step into the refreshment room and have a whiskey and soda. Herbert was frightfully indignant at the idea that the members of Parliament who make the laws could do their drinking at any hour of the day or night, but the man in the street, for whom the laws were made, could only do it at prescribed times. He raised a tremendous fuss in the papers about this, and it generally became the subject of talk and debate in the many clubs of London.

Aside from getting fun in baiting old laws of England that need reform, aside from the boyish joy he gets out of his barge on the river, aside from being the "funny man" on *Punch*, Herbert is a person of great charm and ready understanding. He has a host of friends in every walk of life, in London and out of it, and, in fact, seems quickly to become an intimate of everyone he knows.

ONE *of the enduring works of the past sixty years,* Man's Fate, *was reviewed modestly but not without enthusiasm by Henry Seidel Canby in 1934. "A powerful story, heroic and terrible," wrote Canby. A lesser Malraux novel,* Days of Wrath, *earned Selection status in 1936 and the accompanying portrait of Malraux by William Seabrook enabled Book-of-the-Month Club members to understand better this complex adventurer-writer.*

Man's Fate by André Malraux

A POWERFUL story, heroic and terrible, is a setting where decadence and grim virility are equally mingled. The reader will not be surprised to learn that it has made a deep impression abroad. The scene is Shanghai;

the plot begins with a murder and ends with a mass execution. The story is of the Communist conspiracy in China, which in Shanghai was put down by a corrupt general, purchased for the occasion. The characters are drawn from that strange cosmopolitan world which is beginning to be familiar even in New York. Russian zealots, Japanese zealots. Oriental sensualists sucked into the conflict, fine souls, weak souls, imperialist Frenchmen despising both their backers and their enemies — these are the personnel, and the first effect of the novel is an extraordinary picture of a mixed society that could be duplicated only in the latter days of the Roman Empire. But as the traps are set and the ring narrows and man's fate becomes obvious to zealot and epicurean alike, the real fibre of this book begins to be felt. It is not a propagandist novel, not a thesis novel at all, but rather a study of a new type of stoical heroism. No sharper contrast could be drawn than between the disintegration which is the finale of so many European novels of the day, and the scene in *Man's Fate* where the Russian gives his cyanide to his weaker Chinese comrades, and goes out to be burnt alive, saying — "After all, suppose I had been trapped in a fire."

HENRY SEIDEL CANBY

André Malraux
by William Seabrook

ABOUT 1930, "Gangster" Fels, who runs *Voilà* for Gallimard, said to me, "There's a man in Paris now you'd better meet. He's a great adventurer, and I'm not sure that he isn't also a great writer. His name is Malraux. Anyway, you'd better meet him."

I had never heard of Malraux and thought no more about it, though Fels is a tough cynic who thinks most great writers are dead. Some few weeks later I got another earful from what was then, and maybe still is, the most powerful critical group in France. Paul Morand had been giving a luncheon to Maurois, Bourdet, Cocteau, Valéry and two or three of the less fossilized old gentlemen of the Académie Française. They were speculating about who might be the "best," the most important, among the more or less new French writers. They agreed, almost unanimously, that it would probably turn out to be Malraux. This was after he had written *Les Conquérants* and *La Voie Royale*. It was before he had written *La Condition Humaine*, before he had won the Prix Goncourt — and incidentally before I had ever seen or met him. I went away to Africa without meeting him, and when I came back to Paris a year or so later, he was not in my mind.

One night in Montparnasse, I rang the bell of an old house around the corner from the Rue Delambre, to call on a not famous French friend who had been sick and in trouble. He was still in bed, with a bottle of brandy, and sitting beside the bed was a man I first took to be an American. He was of medium size, in his thirties, darkish hair, but fair, sandy complexion, clean shaven, dressed like a business man or a bank clerk, with regular, undistinguished features, neither handsome nor ugly. He was finishing a cigarette, saying nothing. He continued to say nothing until presently my sick-a-bed friend said, with the casualness of the Quartier, "Oh yes, this is Malraux — André Malraux."

We talked . . . he talked . . . about writing . . . about adventure . . . about life . . . even a little about himself. We talked until four o'clock in the morning and when I went home I had a queer, disturbed feeling such as one has after an earthquake or meeting a tiger at close quarters for the first time — a feeling that Malraux was in some deep, and perhaps tragic sense, the real thing. I felt I had been in the presence of the real thing, and it disturbed me. It was not merely what he said, though he had one of the most brilliant, searching, seeking minds I have ever encountered. It was partly his eyes, large, gray, level, keenly appraising, but sad, sometimes almost tortured, when they lighted up with tangled fire. His hands were strange too, slender yet muscular, steady yet nervous, as he laid down a glass, picked up or doused a cigarette. He seemed to be that chimeric paradox, a controlled, hair-trigger, balanced, yet perfectly self-controlled neurasthenic. Another paradoxical thing, which I had encountered before, rarely, among the Arabs, was that while he was gentle, kindly, a sweet-natured man, for there is no other word for it, there was an almost mystical smell of violence and death about him. Old Prince Nuri Shalan, Lord of the Roualla, had it. He had gray eyes, too. He was intelligent and a lamb for gentleness. He had killed more than a hundred men in personal combat, mostly with knives, including two of his own brothers who had plotted to split the Tribe.

Well, Malraux upset and interested me so much that I bought, read *Les Conquérants, La Voie Royale,* and then began talking about him with every Frenchman I could find who knew him or had read him.

I learned that he had been born in Paris in 1901, son of a French bourgeois colonial functionary who had been in the Far East. Attaining young manhood, he went to Indo-China, Cambodia, Siam, himself. It is an open secret that he became an adventurer in the highest and most

dangerous sense of the word. I would doubt that he has ever done a dis-
honorable thing, but he gambled on hair-breadth margins with imprisonment, torture, robbery, violent death, not as a reporter, nor as a
literary man seeking copy, but as a participant.

The whole world now recognizes that Malraux is a great writer. How
great, of course, will only be determinable a generation or so after he is
dead. But a thing I assert in the meantime is that, in the International
Tribe of Authors, he is by far the greatest adventurer now alive. He is a
true adventurer in the sense the late William Bolitho used the word in
his *Twelve Against the Gods.* Of such, there are not many. Bolitho
pointed out that Lindbergh, Byrd, the Everest climbers, were not precisely adventurers. He called them "soldiers of civilization." It would be
absurd to assert, without limiting the field to authors, that Malraux is
the world's greatest living adventurer. I suppose Mussolini and Hitler
are — as Napoleon once was. But among adventurers who can write —
though his less personal reputation is simply that of great novelist —
Malraux stands supreme.

DOROTHY CANFIELD, *a member of the Editorial Board, a novelist, essayist, critic, moralist, takes her stand on John O'Hara.*

Appointment in Samarra by John O'Hara

IF YOU are one of those people who feel uneasy unless you "keep up"
with what is going on in the world, you will appreciate being told that
such a book as this has been written. It will be widely read and widely
discussed. Those who like it greatly (there will be many of them) will
affirm that it is a "swell job of writing." It will make a good many other
people physically sick. The point is, I think, that it is one of those books
with no great inherent importance which sum up a literary tendency.
Ever since the war, one school of fiction has been pushing farther and
farther toward what they call honesty. "Honesty" for them is a denial of
any important springs of human action except alcohol and sex, and the
use of a bald outspoken vocabulary (partly eighteenth-century English,
partly contemporary gangster argot) in calling attention to the usually
not-mentioned functions and organs of the human body. Mr. O'Hara
has, with great verve and considerable skill, carried the use of this sort of

honesty about as far as it can go. The setting is any American city of
about twenty-five thousand. The characters are the local Country Club
gang, with a background of a gang of bootleggers, roadhouse hangers-on
and garage men. The description is well done in the sketchy manner of
Burnett or Hemingway. The characters (treated in the same manner)
are drawn clearly enough for temporary reality. The plot moves from
the moment when Julian, the hero, throws his fateful highball, to the
time when (drunker still, if that is possible) he sets his car to making
carbon monoxide in his locked garage. On the first reading it gives an
impression of capable workmanship, and to some extent that impression
endures. Having set himself to write objectively, Mr. O'Hara resolutely
refrains from sentimentalizing his tragedy. He keeps clear of any philosophic generalizations or any ideas, whatever. One cannot even be sure
whether he realizes his hero for the rotter he is. Other elements do not
stand up so well on re-reading. What seemed at first, life-like, almost
witty conversation, proves to consist mostly of drunken foul-mouthed
insults, and of intimate talk between husband and wife on the level of
what may possibly be the tone of a low-class brothel. Well, why go on?
This is enough to tell you what the tone of the book is. It will be called a
picture of life, and so it is, a jazzed-up picture of a singularly dull and
unimportant section of life. As I said at the start, its real importance is
that it seems to sum up all that is possible in the direction of this sort of
"honesty." Perhaps it will be the end of the movement, and may start a
landslide back toward Victorianism.

DOROTHY CANFIELD

LIFE WITH FATHER *was a bestselling book in 1935 and 1936, before it
became a hit Broadway play. E. B. White introduced* Clarence Day *to
the Book-of-the-Month Club audience.*

Clarence Day

by E. B. White

A PERSON reading Clarence Day would never guess that his life has
been a high-spirited, hot-tempered struggle against illness. It was
thirty-six years ago that he awoke one morning aboard a Naval training
ship in New York harbor, paralyzed in the shoulder, unable to get out of
his hammock. Everything he has achieved since has been determined

largely by this rheumatic condition, which is now so acute that he can't leave his bed. Latterly he has lost the use of most of his muscles, and can't even scratch his ear save with the aid of a little wooden wand that he waves stiffly about as an infant does a rattle. He is not touchy about his invalidism — he simply never mentions it. One dines at his bedside, under the terrible gaze of his big frog eyes, and departs at the end of the evening without having exchanged a single clinical remark.

There was a taint of printer's ink in the Day family quite far back. Clarence's grandfather, Benjamin Henry Day, left a job on the *Springfield Republican* to come to New York and start a print shop. Business was so bad he had to found the *New York Sun* to keep the print shop going. Clarence's father, the hero of the "Father stories," was the third son of this Benjamin Henry Day; and Clarence's uncle, his father's brother, was the Ben Day who originated the engraving process which now bears that name. So it is not surprising that Clarence should be steeped in letters.

He wasn't brought up to be a writer, however. He was born on Murray Hill and spent a conventional New York childhood in a house on Madison Avenue between 48th and 49th Streets, a well-to-do little fellow, summering in New London, graduating eventually from Yale. Mr. Day, senior, was a broker in Wall Street, member of the firm of Gwynne & Day, a thoroughly sound citizen who wore a wing collar and always locked up the house at night before he went to bed. When Clarence got out of Yale, in 1896, Mr. Day celebrated the happy event by giving him a job as office boy in the brokerage house at four dollars a week, and a few months later presented him with a seat on the Stock Exchange and a debit of $19,000, the price of the seat. Clarence, scared stiff, reacted by joining the Naval Militia. His father countered by making him a partner. Clarence, sticking to his guns, joined the Navy, and his only appearances in the financial district at this period were on two or three brisk occasions when he showed up, cutlass in hand, at the sub-treasury with two or three other militiamen to collect the payroll for the unit. Mr. Day, senior, was devastated, and said "Damn" a great deal.

In 1899, while still on the training ship, Clarence was stricken with arthritis. The next dozen years were spent on crutches and in wheelchairs. He bought a ranch in the west, and although he couldn't walk without crutches he propped himself up on a pony every day and rode stiffly around Colorado. Through a considerate gesture on somebody's part, he was made secretary of his class at Yale, and began compiling the records of his classmates, startling everyone by setting down actual facts about alumni instead of the usual nonsense. He wrote and sold a few short verses, rather casually, and was surprised to note that they were widely reprinted. Unable physically to follow up his Wall Street destiny, he fooled around with one thing and another — did a book department for the *Metropolitan Magazine*, wrote financial articles. At last he sat down and wrote *This Simian World*, an odd little book testing man's ancestry to the bone. He got a job on the *New Republic*, was discharged, tried free lancing unsuccessfully, and dabbled at long range with stocks and bonds, buying during panics, selling during booms. Revolting from parental authority, he moved out of his father's house, took an apartment on Riverside Drive, grew a long red beard, and became manager of a glove business — receiving his uneasy subordinates in his bedroom, wearing vile, striped dressing-gowns. His father, finding himself with a son on Riverside, a region he regarded as the home of retired police captains, was completely unnerved and considered it the worst thing that had ever happened to the family.

In the gorgeous 1920's, Clarence, still maintaining a desultory connection with Wall Street, made, between quatrains, a great deal of money — on paper. Although loath to leave Riverside, he felt that he should give his mother some companionship, so he bought an apartment on Fifth Avenue and installed a ventilating system of fabulous intricacy at a cost of $15,000. The project was a fiasco. The intake, it turned out, had been installed in an areaway in which were concentrated the cooking smells from all the kitchens in the building, so that Clarence, completely dependent on pure air for comfort, found that he had paid $15,000 to have great blasts of fish and onion smells blown into his chamber. He finally had to summon his father's old coachman to dismantle the thing.

The next thing that happened was that he lost the two million dollars (what was left of it), and acquired a wife. He had met, in 1921, a titian-haired lady from New England, had fought with her steadily through seven sad passionate years, all through the Peaches Browning era in American history. Clarence, studying the tabloids with somber attention, drew fearful parallels between himself and Daddy Browning and pronounced himself unfit to espouse an innocent beauty many years his junior. The lady demurred, Browning subsided from the news, and the marriage took place. They now live — Clarence, his wife, their small daughter Wendy Day, and their underdeveloped Cairn terrier — in an apartment overlooking Central Park from the south. Clarence goes to sleep at 5 in the morning, wakes at 3 in the afternoon, breakfasts at 4, roars and bellows at people for an hour, and settles down to work sometime during the evening. His world is a bed world. At his side are prodigious files — all sorts of scraps and reminders, elaborately indexed. In bed one has time to remember; and Clarence remembers, and writes, steadily. It is an inspiring sight to see him, his pencil held stiffly between thumb and third finger, writing by flexing the muscles of his shoulder blades, which he still can wiggle, his forefinger, useless for gripping the pencil, sympathetically waving about in the air like the feeler of a cricket.

ROBERT FROST'S A Further Range *was a Selection in 1936. The Irish critic and poet Padraic Colum, a close friend of Frost's, strove "to set down some lineaments" of the American poet.*

Robert Frost
by Padraic Colum

I HAVE known Robert Frost for twenty years, and have been with him in various places from Dublin, Ireland, to Ann Arbor, Michigan, and from Pittsfield to Miami, and now as I strive to set down some lineaments of him, what comes to me first is his voice.... He is on a platform, giving a reading of his poetry, and his words sound as if they were flung out from crags — they come to me like the barking of an eagle.

It is a craggy and uplifted world that this poet lives in, but not a bleak nor a lonely world. Robert Frost is one of the most companionable of men. He is the sort who will not go to bed as long as he has anyone to talk to, anyone to talk to him. He is as good a listener as he is a talker. In his talk everything that is pretentious and solemn is disregarded. Humorous reminiscence, shrewd comment comes from him. He makes just appraisal of the worth and work of sincere and able men and women, and he can make the self-seeker ludicrous. He lets such people go some of the way with him, but he knows what they're after; he is glad when they get what they've been after, but they do not know that he has had fun watching them go after it. And he can be inimical. It was a man who could hold anger in his heart who wrote:

> *Some say the world will end in fire,*
> *Some say in ice.*
> *From what I've tasted of desire*
> *I hold with those who favor fire.*

But, if it had to perish twice.
I think I know enough of hate,
To say that for destruction ice
Is also great.
And would suffice.

His scholarship is kept in the background, but his poetry is supported by scholarship more than most readers realize. For instance, there is his familiarity with Latin poetry. It seems a long way from *Mending Wall* or *The Death of the Hired Man* to Virgil. Yet Frost's love of the Georgics and the Eclogues is reflected in his New England narratives and dramatic monologues. Like Virgil, Robert Frost gets the landscape into his poetry. Very few modern poets have been able to do this.

The sojourn that he made in England just twenty-five years ago has been one of the great influences on his career. That sojourn did not help him towards any self-discovery or towards any form of expression. He had discovered his own material, his own form, by the time he went across. But England gave him a sustaining spectacle, a spectacle that America does not offer, that of young men striving to shape their intuitions and experiences into an art or a philosophy without feeling they were wasting time that should be devoted to business. He saw such people as a real society — quarrels went on amongst them, to be sure, but they formed a society, a kind of brotherhood. Amongst them were personalities that have never faded out of his mind — Edward Thomas, T. E. Hulme, that young squire who had a metaphysical system as well as a poetic scheme, Wilfred Wilson Gibson, and that inventive and disturbing American, Ezra Pound. It was the last freely-functioning group that London had.

He was fortunate in his homecoming. In America people had become eager about poetry. Suddeny there were poetry-societies and poetry-magazines and interesting poets. Into an atmosphere of expectancy he came with an audience ready for him and even prepared for him. As he came off the boat he bought an issue of the newly founded *New Republic* with one of his long poems displayed in it. He became a kind of laureate: his was poetry that Americans were on the lookout for, poetry that had in it native scenes and native character, and had, startlingly, the vibration of the voice.

And now the chances are that Robert Frost will become a national figure, a sage, a Yankee sage. He has personal thought; he has wisdom; he has a basic conception from which he can speak; he likes the nation, every nation, and he dislikes the state, every state; he has a dislike of secularism and yet he does not want to belong to any religious community; he is a puritan, but he goes by the dictates of the heart. I remember him on a platform, seated this time, making comments on American life and literature, a blue-eyed man, with thick grey hair, a full and beautifully modeled mouth. As he went on delivering himself of opinions that were at once whimsical and shrewd, a lady next to me said, "Puck in a sack-suit!"

And now I will relate an incident which sounds too good to be true, but which, on my word, happened. We were in Dublin, Robert Frost and I. As the car swung into a courtyard, "Where are we now?" he asked. "In Dublin Castle." "What does one do in Dublin Castle?" "If one is an American," I said, "one goes into that office and asks for a genealogy." It was the office of the Ulster King-at-Arms. "I'll do it," Robert said. "What name, sir?" asked the genealogical expert. "Frost." "Lincolnshire Frosts or Somersetshire Frosts?" Robert did not know. "What Christian name is usual in the family?" "Robert." "Lincolnshire Frosts. There are tombstones. . . ." He named the places. "Then I want the genealogy of the Lincolnshire Frosts. . . . Will you tell me what arms I get?" "A grey squirrel and a pine tree, sir."

Margaret Mitchell *began writing* Gone with the Wind *in 1926. Ten years later, in June of 1936, it was* The *Book of the Month. At first it did not do well for the Club. "Many subscribers, as they had a right to, chose another book," wrote Henry Seidel Canby in his memoirs. But then it caught on. Late in 1936 a public opinion poll asked Americans, "What is the most interesting book you have ever read?" Twenty percent said the Bible; twelve percent said* Gone with the Wind. *Margaret Mitchell never wrote another book. Her publisher, H. S. Latham, told* Book-of-the-Month Club News *readers how Ms. Mitchell presented him with a huge manuscript in Atlanta, saying, "I hadn't any intention of letting you or any publisher see it. I only wrote it for my own entertainment." Mr. Latham bought a suitcase and carried the manuscript back to New York with him.*

Gone with the Wind by Margaret Mitchell

This book has been waiting to be written for many years. One of the unanswered questions in American literature is why we have done so little with the tensions, the tragedies, the break-up of cultures, and the extraordinary exhibition of human nature at its worst and best, which was our Civil War. Here is a theme of the height, if not the magnitude, of the World War, involving everything that a realist, romanticist, a psychologist or moralist, a writer of tragedies or of tragicomedies, could ask for — and where are the first-rate creative books that have recorded its inner history? Some poems of Whitman, *John Brown's Body* — how many more can be added to the list? I do not mean to imply that Miss Mitchell's is a Greek tragedy, or a novel by Dostoyevsky. It is by no means of that elevation. Indeed, it is a first novel I believe, and is unsure in parts, and wavering sometimes between melodrama and realism. But we are not concerned with questions of greatness. What we have longed for is an adequate novel of the Civil War — as the beaten South knew it — a story that would have an authentic picture of the arrogant, provincial, very attractive life of the pre-War plantation South, and not be merely glamorous or sentimental. A story that would see a devastating war, an invading, ruthless, wrecking war, as the women at home saw it. A story that would pass in sharp contrast into the disastrous, dramatic, and confusing era of Reconstruction, when a ruined but plucky civilization presents a picture as sensational and as significant as anything that happened in Germany, Austria, Poland, or Serbia after the Great War. Only Russia in her Reconstruction offers a more dramatic theme than our South in the late '60's and '70's.

Miss Mitchell has written of it all. Her novel has the rise and dip and rise again of a story that unhesitatingly moves through the glamorous, the picturesque, the terrible, the sordid, the mean, the courageous, and the mistaken. And her characters and her scenes are not unworthy of her subject. A woman is her hero and martyr combined. Scarlett is the newcomer among the plantation aristocracy. She is beautiful, intelligent, vain, selfish, and predatory. She ruins the lives of two men, but by her own strength of character keeps her place in the story through intrigue, war hysteria, the burning of plantations, defeat, and the domination of Negroes and carpetbaggers. Her personality will satisfy the realist; her life was romantic. Rhett Butler, the outcast Charlestonian, who was one of her lovers and her last husband, is not so satisfactory, though women will, I think, differ with me. He has a Byronic cast, true to the period, but difficult for the modern reader. He is wrecked upon Scarlett's essential selfishness, although adroitly successful everywhere else. Underlying the pageant of the ruinous decade from '60 to '70, the story of these two carries on with Ashley, the husband of Scarlett's best friend, whom Scarlett also loves, but not enough, not as much as herself, and a group of minor characters that give this novel the breadth and authenticity of a social history.

The title sums up the story. It is all gone with the wind — Tara, the wrecked up-country plantation and its high-spirited life, the young men shot or broken on the Virginia line, the dominance of a class, the culture of an agrarian civilization, Scarlett's vain hopes of having her own way with life — everything has gone down the wind but courage, shrewdness, character, and the will to go on. But the wind is not the wind of a lyric poem, it is an epic wind, a hurricane too strong to stand against, a tempest both physical and spiritual.

I do not wish, however, to leave the impression of a strained and tense novel. Miss Mitchell has neither the mellow philosophy nor the style of Galsworthy, but her book in its leisurely build-up of a civilization in which a group of characters finally become typical, belongs to the school of the *Forsyte Saga;* you see and feel how people, all kinds of people — black as well as white — lived in the plantation era; when Sherman marched through Georgia; when the black Republicans exploited a shattered country. There is business in this book, and farming, and politics, and society, and finance, as well as love and tragedy. The novel, as they say of a history, is well documented, and the documentation seems to be authentic, and what is equally important, is not merely background but (again as with Galsworthy) an inseparable element of the story itself. Minds change here as rapidly as circumstance. Insensibly, not in fade-outs and renewals, all upper Georgia changes under the shock of defeat, and friends, relatives, husbands, lovers, heroes, and villains change with it. Events move fast, but with that suspension of the time sense which comes to us all in critical eras. Thus the feeling of reality is not lost in action — and this is as it should be in a historical novel.

I am describing rather than criticizing *Gone with the Wind.* Readers will make their own criticisms, some of which certainly will be justified, and yet I believe that very few American readers will be more critical of than interested in this rich story. It needed to be done, and if Miss Mitchell is not Tolstoy, she has certainly proved herself to be a very satisfying novelist, at a time when so much of our most skillful fiction is more brilliant than readable. And she has written a novel that may be said to describe not a phase — poor-white, Negro, aristocratic — but all aspects of the South in one of its typical areas, at the crisis of its history.

HENRY SEIDEL CANBY

Margaret Mitchell

by H. S. Latham

THE old adage that "a prophet is not without honor save in his own country" certainly does not apply in the case of Margaret Mitchell. The enthusiasm of her friends, the confidence which they have in her ability, is a marked characteristic of the Atlanta literary group.

Just about a year ago I went to Atlanta looking for possible new authors. One of the first things that was said to me on the occasion of this visit was to the effect that probably the most important novel being written at that time in that locality was Peggy Mitchell's. No one seemed to know what the book was about, but a great many people knew apparently that "Peggy" was at work on something and that was enough to bring cordial, even insistent, recommendation to their lips.

Finally it was my good fortune to meet Peggy Mitchell. She proved to be a diminutive little body with a very lively sense of humor and a proficiency in the art of conversation rarely encountered these days. We talked about a good many things at this first meeting, and more particularly about Southern literature, about which I found she had, as indeed about many things, positive ideas. Finally after my circumlocutions I swung the conversation around to her own work. Imagine my surprise and disappointment when she informed me, very pleasantly but with firmness, that while she might have been playing around with the idea of doing a novel some time or other, she had nothing to show me.

Later on in the day out in the Druid Hills where we had driven to see the dogwood, then at its height of bloom, she said much the same thing. We had to leave it that if ever she did write a novel, she would let me see it.

My interest in Miss Mitchell had been greatly stimulated by my meeting with her, and I made many inquiries of my Atlanta friends about her. I learned that she had been a newspaper woman; that she had many friends in the profession throughout the State, in fact throughout the South; that she had lived all of her life in Atlanta, a matter of perhaps some thirty odd years; and that she was the wife of John R. Marsh, Manager of the Advertising Department of the Georgia Power Company. She was known to have a critical mind, an impatience with shams, an eager curiosity and a striking ability to get at the root of things. A librarian of Atlanta told me that when Peggy got started on the trail of something, the solution was as good as found. She is an indefatigable research worker.

All of these reports made me the more regretful that no manuscript was forthcoming.

A few hours before I left Atlanta, the telephone in my hotel room rang and Miss Mitchell's voice came to me over it informing me that she was downstairs in the lobby and would like to see me. I went down, and I shall never forget the picture I have of Margaret Mitchell as I then saw her — a tiny woman sitting on a divan, and beside her the biggest manuscript I have ever seen, towering in two stacks almost up to her shoulders.

"If you really want it, you may take it, but it's incomplete, unrevised, there are several versions of some of the chapters, there is no first chapter." Miss Mitchell went on hurriedly, as though there were danger of changing her mind if she stopped to think. "I hadn't any intention of letting you or any publisher see it. I only wrote it for my own entertainment. However, your ideas about Southern authors and Southern books have aroused my interest, and I am curious to know what you think of this one. You can't possibly be as surprised at being given it as I am at letting you take it."

You may be sure I lost no time in taking physical possession of the manuscript, and once having secured it I plied Miss Mitchell with all sorts of questions about how she came to write it. She had been working on it off and on for seven years, I learned. The theme of the novel had come to her from something her mother had said. When Peggy was a young girl she had shown little interest in acquiring an education, and her mother, to impress upon her the necessity of a proper education, took her out for a ride one afternoon to the rural sections surrounding Atlanta and showed her the lands that had been laid waste by the War. Even after many years the scars of war were still visible both in the land and in the life of the section. Her mother pointed out to her the homes of some families who had had the ability and the will power to rise above the wreckage of war and reconstruction and also other homes where the families had sunk down because they had no resources within themselves to aid them in surviving the catastrophe. Miss Mitchell explained that this experience stimulated her interest in people who fought things through to success, as well as in those who went down valiantly in the struggle, or who managed just to exist — "Georgians who did come through, and Georgians who didn't," in other words — and this interest finally resulted in the novel over which she worked so long.

My luggage accommodations were limited, and try as I would I could not make room for the manuscript of *Gone with the Wind* in my bag. But I had no intention of letting it get out of my hands, so before I left Atlanta I purchased a suitcase in which to carry it. The next day I began reading it, and I read it all across the continent with increasing admiration, convinced that here indeed was a very significant novel of the South.

On my return to New York I found very shortly that my associates shared my enthusiasm for this book. The problem that we then had was to convince Miss Mitchell that she had written not merely a publishable novel, which she really seemed to doubt, but a more than ordinarily significant one.

I saw Miss Mitchell in Atlanta a few weeks ago. She is unquestionably pleased by all the excitement surrounding the publication of *Gone with the Wind* and the unusual commendation which it is receiving from those who have read proofs or advance copies — and she is genuinely puzzled and bewildered by it too. But the colored maid, who presides over her kitchen and watches over her welfare in every intimate detail, isn't a bit nonplussed. " 'Course I know Miss Peggy's book is good," she said to me from the center of her immaculate kitchen. "Didn't I help make it good by feedin' Miss Peggy right an' keepin' folks away an' tellin' 'em she weren't home, or were sick a-bed when she was writin' it? 'Course I know it's good."

DECADE TWO

1937–1946

CHRISTOPHER MORLEY *writes about* Of Mice and Men: *"Very simply, this story goes deep into the roots where American writing is at its best."* Of Mice and Men *was named a Selection in 1937 but not Steinbeck's later novel,* The Grapes of Wrath. *In his memoirs, Henry Seidel Canby said, "I remember only one instance of a member [of the Editorial Board] obstinately standing out for a book in a minority of one, and unable to make the majority concur with his desires.... I am proud to say that the recalcitrant member was myself and the book John Steinbeck's* The Grapes of Wrath." *But down through the years other Steinbeck novels became Selections of the Club. Harvey Breit, assistant editor of the* New York Times Book Review, *summed up the man and the writer in an article accompanying the 1947 Selection, Steinbeck's* The Wayward Bus.

Of Mice and Men by John Steinbeck

THIS is a love story and a tragedy, but both the love and the grief are quite different from what the reader might expect. And the reception of this little book will be different from what the author may have anticipated. Its publisher has told me that Mr. Steinbeck wrote it "as an experiment"; that he did not even insist on its publication. "Don't publish it if you don't like it," he wrote, and didn't even wish to see proofs of it. I can understand that: a writer who has put on paper something so deeply moving wishes for a while not to think of it again.

In just such casual ways, in this our world of obliquity and squint, do masterpieces happen.

The love story is the love (passing, oh, a long way, "that of women") of two wandering ranch-hands in California; the protecting love and charity of George, a little quick-veined shrewd tough egg, for big Lennie who is a mountain of size and strength, but a half-wit. Lennie, helpless without guidance and control and doomed by his moron qualities to get into trouble, is the pathos of this inevitable tragedy. And the perfection of the tale is its appeasing quality: horror that is inescapable, simplicity that blunders onto death, and the love of the comrade that does not shrink from the last fatal service. There is comedy too, but comedy far too intrinsic for mere laughter. In Conrad's durable words, here we have something that moves "the sigh that is not a sob, the smile that is not a grin."

It is not easy, without imparting more of the story than I care to do, to suggest the tenderness, the charm, the subtle pace of this little triumph. It has in it some ugly and uncomfortable words and you will scarcely notice them because they are the exact and necessary speech of those who use them. It deals with simple and childlike men and one shallow lustful trollop. You will remember her standing in the doorway of the bunkhouse with the sun shining through her flimsy stuff. In the same way the sunshine of a great human charity illustrates this pitiful and sorry tale. The stark language of the bunkhouse becomes more perfect than any dulcet phrasing to dignify the coming-on of Fate. As surely as the sunlight slides and softens round the ranch-houses that Sunday afternoon, comes horor with its even tread. From the first you divined it. It is necessary and complete, it leaves us purified.

Mr. Steinbeck wavers a little in the first two or three pages. He hadn't then quite struck his tune, his tempo. But from the moment the two wandering harvesters, on their way to "buck barley" (load heavy sacks of grain) come to the riverside and sit down to talk, his touch is past faltering. Again and again the reader's breath comes quick: one false note would do such dreadful harm. But he never goes literary on us (after those first tentative paragraphs). So he has the fascinated reader collaborating with him — doing joyfully what is every reader's unconscious delight, seeing more than is told. Steinbeck has learned — and once it is learned *anything* may happen — that the essential things are what are not said; that the best of a story is what the reader writes for you in his own brain. Of the most wildly touted writers of our day, how few have ever guessed that.

So this little idyll — a queer word for it, some will think — is the fable of a love that nothing could smear; a love incongruous, laughable, and magnificent. A love that tries to shield from the loved one the brutality of the world. Oh yes, to put it in such solemn words wrongs it: you will *feel* this story rather than read it. Deliciously puzzled at first, you soon grasp the gist of the situation: the pathetic dream of decency nourished by two casuals of the highway. They've been run off one ranch, they're on their way to another. They're going to earn a stake and get a little home of their own. And the smart one, in spite of the drag of his helpless giant buddy, shields and guards him beyond the end of ends. Don't let me spoil it for you: but I must just say that the recurring incantation about the rabbits — the big idiot dreams of keeping rabbits as life's dearest consummation — becomes as thrilling, as desperate, as lovely, as anything our time has seen in prose. Yes, the two poor devils, one watching over and guiding the other, are going to "live off the fatta the lan'."

And, of course, you know it won't happen. You know it by many subtle twinges of mood. The old "swamper" who has lost a hand; the old stinking sheep-dog who must be shot; the jail-bait tart who has the eye; the boss' son spoiling for a fight — even somehow the flies that dart like sparks through a stripe of sunshine — everything, in a hundred easy hitches, tightens up the foreboding.

Very simply, this story goes deep into the roots where American writing is at its best. It echoes nothing, imitates nothing, extenuates nothing. Those who can see beyond words into the nerve and brain and anguish that beget them will find it written in purest compassion and truth.

CHRISTOPHER MORLEY

The Grapes of Wrath by John Steinbeck

JOHN STEINBECK is on his way to becoming a major novelist. The power of mingled sentiment and anger, the vivid reality of *Of Mice and Men*, are both present in this full-length novel, which is the story of a tragic pilgrimage of men and women seeking a home. There are faults in this book of which the prospective reader should be warned. The language, even for this free age, is frank, unnecessarily frank, and while appropriate to scene and character, will often shock the tender-minded. Furthermore, the economic sermons — rhapsodies would be a better word — with which Steinbeck often opens his chapters, not only break away from the style of the novel into a rhetorical jargon, but are of doubtful logic and penetration. He is much too inclined to attribute all disaster to wicked powers behind the scenes, and to expect salvation from a Christian socialist state. When this has been said, the rest must be praise, and high praise. The story deals with one of the thousands of families dislodged from their home in the Dust Bowl by drought, and seeking a new life in a California of which all that they know is illusion. While the Diesel-drawn tractors of the new large-scale proprietors cut through the door-yard of their house and tumble it into the dust they are preparing to migrate: children, dogs, furniture, grandpa and grandma, once pioneers, quarreling on top of the load, daughter with her unborn child, sons and father; and mother, determined to hold the family together at all costs. On a second-hand car cut down into a truck, leaving a neighborhood forever with just a little money, they begin the 2000-mile migration, and the book is the story of what happens to them in this new nomad life in a depressed America. It is a powerful story of character, with much humor, some deep pathos, and an underlying indignation against the circumstances which break down the morale of good coarse common people. At home they are self-respecting farmers, drinking too much, killing sometimes in self defense, a little shiftless, yet good stuff for a democracy. Now they are "Okies," fugitives from Oklahoma and the rest of the Dust Bowl, vagabonds to be chased from tin-can camp to camp by corrupt constables; and potential cheap labor, to be worked at starvation wages, and then kicked out to drown in the floods, or starve on the hills. The family, thanks to the mother, holds together, though death takes the old ones and the unborn, there are interludes of decency in their hardships; and, at the end, that will to go on, which is the essential quality of the human species, is still strong. But it is a dramatic and terrifying story, the story of the nomads of the machine age, still docile, still asking only for work and a home, but beginning to realize that no one can save them but themselves. Some of the episodes in this novel are not exceeded anywhere in contemporary writing in beauty, power, and concentrated emotion.

HENRY SEIDEL CANBY

John Steinbeck

by Harvey Breit

THE mere presence of John Steinbeck in a room is an experience — even when he is silent, just sitting, and looking, and listening. Maybe it is a little like being with a bear, a not-altogether-domesticated bear. He is built like a bear (monumental chest and all), and his growling bass sounds the way a bear would talk if it could. I have always experienced mixed feelings with Mr. Steinbeck; there is a promise of enveloping warmth, friendliness and comfortableness, but it is in check, contained, withheld, as if by some esthetic or ethical principle that searches another human being out. It is my guess that if the human being in question strikes Mr. Steinbeck as genuinely human, the warmth and friendship and comfort become accessible; if not, the great bear may jolly well pounce. I, for one, would not like to be pounced upon by Mr. Steinbeck, who stands about 6 feet tall and weighs well over a solid 200 — even at the age of 55, a birthday he has just celebrated.

Originally a Salinas and Monterey (California) man, Mr. Steinbeck has become a New Yorker by choice. He has spent more than a little time abroad, notably in Mexico and in France — *The Short Reign of Pippin IV* is an indirect result of a recent sojourn in France — but for him New York contains all the blemishes and beauties of civilization, all the privacy he wants (most of the time) and all the friendship he wants (some of the time). He is a private man, truly; he doesn't like to see his name in newspaper gossip columns; trespassing and ferreting around Mr. Steinbeck are taboo. He is a good friend and comrade, but not too many people know this. The knowable Mr. Steinbeck is a man of profound reticence, of shy, heavy speech, many of whose words are lost because of his barrel-chested basso. But the shy man, among friends and comrades, can laugh and roar, banter and brawl.

Mr. Steinbeck is, both as writer and as man, several men, or one man who complements and completes himself in several ways. He is the bitter novelist of *The Grapes of Wrath*, and he is the bawdy novelist of *Tortilla Flat*. He is the moralist who wrote with such sober social insight in *The Pearl* or *Burning Bright*, the poetic memoirist of *The Red Pony*, and the humorist and sentimentalist storyteller of *East of Eden* or *The Wayward Bus*. He is private and remote; he is social and lusty.

One would have to be a psychologist in order to know how this duality works, and if it works. What I think I know about Mr. Steinbeck and what I think underlies his behavior is struggle — a kind of tense, silent struggle to be one's self, to be steadfastly honest and honorable at each moment. It is not only an underrated struggle; it is a heroic struggle that most of us relax away from. One gets this sense from meeting Mr. Steinbeck in his tangible, granite shape. It is surely one of the first and major reasons why people like to be near him: he is a man of honor and justice, though I suspect he would never want to be a judge.

IGNAZIO SILONE, *the author of the 1937 Selection,* Bread and Wine, *smiles seldom, wrote Martha Foley, but when he does, "the sun breaks through." Miss Foley, noted for her compilations of short stories, tells more about the celebrated Italian author.*

Ignazio Silone
by Martha Foley

A SLIM, dark man, taller than most Italians with a mass of heavy, black hair above a fine, high forehead and deep, quiet eyes. Ignazio Silone stands out against the snows and icy mountains of his retreat in Switzerland, far from the warmer and sunnier Italy of which he is a native, for what he is — an exile. There is a reserve about him, however, that is strangely un-Latin. His sensitive, long-fingered hands remain passive when he speaks, and he does not often smile. When he does smile, the sun breaks through.

Silone is thirty-seven years old. And looks older. His life has not been an easy one. He has loved his people too fiercely and hated Fascism too intensely ever to have known peace. Talking to him one is aware of fires, stoked for the moment, perhaps, but ready to burst forth.

Silone is reticent about much of his past. Significant gaps of certain years in his career permit one to guess of underground work, but nothing is known definitely. What is known is dramatic enough.

Ignazio Silone was born May 1, 1900, in Pescina del Marsi, Province of Aquila, in Abruzzi. This mountainous region is to the east of Rome and a little to the north of it. His father was the landed proprietor of a large estate. Silone was sent for a while to a Jesuit school, but learned mainly farming, sowing and reaping — the education of a peasant.

While he was still a boy, his mother and five brothers were killed in an earthquake. With a remaining brother he went to Trieste, where he became interested in the Socialist Youth movement and was one of its chief organizers. Later he joined the Communist party but was soon at loggerheads with many of its leaders, who accused him of sympathizing too much with the peasantry and forgetting the industrial poor.

In Trieste he worked as an editor of the labor paper *Lavoratore* for several years. Then came the march on Rome, and the offices of the paper were burned to the ground, while the Fascists took over the publication of the paper itself. Warrants were issued for the arrest of the paper's officials, including Silone and his brother.

His brother was captured and sentenced to nine years in prison, but Silone escaped. At the end of three years in prison, Silone's brother died from the results of a beating. For three years, while Black Shirts scoured all Italy for him, Silone remained in hiding, sheltered by the peasants of his native region in the Abruzzi. Finally in 1931 he was smuggled out of the country to Switzerland where he began writing in earnest.

Silone's first work to reach a large audience in America was *Journey to Paris*, a short story printed in the magazine *Story*. His first novel, *Fontamara*, was published in 1934 and from this a play, *Bitter Stream*, literal translation of the title, was adapted by the Theatre Union and ran in New York for sixty-three performances. A collection of his short stories was published under the title of *Mr. Aristotle*. Silone has also written a history of Italian Fascism which is considered in Europe to be the definitive work to date on the subject.

All of Silone's fiction has been about the Abruzzi region in which he was born. The history of that part of Italy alone would have made of a sensitive boy growing up, listening to the distress of its people, a foe of oppression.

"Pescina," he says, "is situated on the reclaimed land of the drained lake Fucino. Gregorovius writes in his *Wander Years in Italy*, 'Laughing shores that recede far back, with luxuriant gardens and vineyards rising above an excellent highway.' But that was written in 1871. Then the beautiful lake was drained, through what was hailed as the generosity of Prince Torlonia. Suddenly it became apparent what the draining meant. The old free peasants of Pescina were turned into beggars. Not only did the fish vanish with the lake water, but the drainage of their soil occurred as well.

"And since the temperaure sank from two to three degrees, the shores of the lake lost their former fertility, the olive and fruit culture disappeared. Unsuited for agricultural purposes, the worthless soil now produces nothing but a meager crop of vegetables. Giving in to the pressure exerted by the outraged population, Prince Torlonia abandoned his plan of settling the country with foreign peasants and graciously permitted the inhabitans of the eleven little towns situated on the shores of the now non-existent lake, to work 'his' farm, the drained bed of the lake. The Prince's 'generous' deed proved to be a piece of unexcelled highway robbery. And Torlonia became notorious as the great Seccatore or Drainer."

It is easy to imagine the stories the boy Silone must have grown up on, in the kitchens and parlors and vineyards of the little towns that had been despoiled: stories of the good days when olives and oranges could be grown where now only cabbages and onions barely survived, tales of vanished prosperity barely evident in shabby furniture that once must have had a grandeur, and bitter mutterings against the Prince Drainer.

Perhaps that was why when Mussolini, also a former Socialist, marched on Rome, Silone, then twenty years old, did not follow him. He saw another Drainer, another and greater despoiler.

Although writing fiction for only a few years, Silone already has received tremendous critical acclaim. In Europe, writers such as Jacob Wasserman and Andreas Latzko have called him the most important new figure on the international literary horizon, while in America John Chamberlain, writing in the *New York Times*, said contemporary Italian literature "is limited to Silone." His most recent book has been given ecstatic reviews in London where one reviewer called it a "shred of the eternal spirit" and another "the deepest, most truly religious book written in our times."

Silone also has been compared to Balzac and Zola. Probably in his skillful balancing of humor and tragedy in the lives of the poor peasants he comes closest to Zola, as well as in his social indignation.

This acclaim has not spoiled Silone. He continues to live simply in a small *pension* in Zurich, writing on, heartbreakingly and beautifully, about the laughter and tears of his own poor, obscure people in the Italy from which he is an outcast.

THOMAS WOLFE *was one of those writers Alfred Kazin referred to, not unkindly, as "a modern prima donna of the American novel." Henry Seidel Canby, who reviewed three Wolfe novels in the* BOMC News *over a five-year period, felt a little different. He called Wolfe "one of the most remarkable talents of our time." Writing about* You Can't Go Home Again, *Canby said, "Like Whitman, like Melville, both true predecessors, Wolfe seems to break, and sometimes does break, all the rules of literature. Yet he remains a tide-mark in American literature — and is unique."*

Of Time and the River by Thomas Wolfe

A VAST autobiographical novel, continuing the story of youth which began in Mr. Wolfe's celebrated *Look Homeward, Angel*. From North

Carolina to Harvard, from Harvard and Boston through Oxford and residence in France, the narrative extends, with no plot but what happened
next to the young hero, but a succession of brilliant portraits and poignant events, set in a frame of prose poetry describing the lovely, impo-
tent continent to which the nervous American is trying to adjust
himself. Read as a novel the book is disappointing, for the reader is diz-
zied by his dips from an imagined world of fiction into what he feels to
be straight autobiography. But read for its scenes, its poetry, and its
character studies, *Of Time and the River* is impressive. It is tremen-
dously vital, powerfully conceived, and written with passion and
beauty: not a great novel, but certainly an important American book. If
Anthony Adverse contained the material for three romances, *Of Time
and the River* has the stuff of an epic, two realistic novels, and a couple
of satires thrown in for good measure.

                                                    HENRY SEIDEL CANBY

The Web and the Rock by Thomas Wolfe

THIS posthumous novel is the first half of a continuous story which will,
unfortunately, conclude the versatile self-analysis and brilliant impres-
sionism of one of the most remarkable talents of our time. As a story, it
goes back to the early years from which *Look Homeward, Angel* was
drawn; but it is a different story, differently told. In a series of episodes — passages from youth they might be called — Wolfe gives us
North Carolina, his extraordinary family, the death of a bad Negro,
small-boy drama — all in a web of experiences. It is hard to exaggerate
the force, the beauty, and the intense interest of these episodes. No man
writing now has excelled them. I am describing the first and by far the
better half of this long novel. This part seems to have been written sepa-
rately, and is an artistic whole, which escapes from the formless excesses
of Wolfe's earlier novels, and carries a youth from the country to his
first maturity in New York with mounting interest and a restrained
emotion which surely mark Wolfe as one of the really important novelists in the American tradition. The last half of the book deals with an
actual affair with a brilliantly artistic married woman, who introduces
the young hero to intellectual and artistic New York, as well as to love.
This affair doubles and turns upon itself, rises to climaxes of great emotional intensity, and sinks to squabbles which come close to the absurd.
It has much of the repetitiveness and unrestrained confession of Wolfe's
earlier novels, faults entirely absent from the first part of this novel. And

the scenes and characters of the New York literary world, many of them easily recognizable, have the same quality of too literal description which fascinated many of Wolfe's readers but which, to others, seemed to escape from imagination into mere reporting. Yet this part of the novel is brilliant too, and suffers only by comparison with the more excellent and more self-contained story of his first youth. It is to be hoped that when all this posthumous writing is printed, the publishers will make new divisions which will reveal, not obscure, the organism of Thomas Wolfe's achievement.

HENRY SEIDEL CANBY

You Can't Go Home Again by Thomas Wolfe

THIS is the most shapely of all Tom Wolfe's sections of the one long novel which was his lifework. And, in spite of many repetitions of idea and personality from earlier portions, it contains, I think, some of his very best work. The hero now, who is, of course, Tom Wolfe himself, is a successful author, learning that a little fame gets one only to the beginning of wisdom. Alas, he has described, in his novel, his home town only too truly, although he thinks he has not copied his friends and acquaintances, but rather interpreted and expanded them. Yet all they see is scandal and exposure. He had gone home before to find them boiling in the perverted and materialistic passion of a great boom. When that bursts, the truth of his studies of the failure of his fellow Americans to live any real and valuable life of their own is only too manifest. He can't go home again, not because he is threatened by those who accuse him of exposing them, but because he sees that you never can go back in life — you must grow out of yourself before that self decays. And so this novel about a novelist takes its hero to Germany, where he is completely happy until the subtle poison of futility and defeat produces the less subtle but more dangerous romantic poison of Nazism, the poison of hate and self-inflation, which destroys the individualist's soul. From then on the story is more and more a psychoanalysis of American life, to find *its* poisons and its hopes. There is a fire in a great apartment house which provides one of Wolfe's most dramatic scenes. There is an English episode in which an obvious Sinclair Lewis is involved in a study, that should become classic, of eccentric genius committed to fame. The best mimic in America, next to Lewis himself, is Wolfe. And there is always Tom Wolfe, a seeker like the Americans of the 40's, a visionary with an intense feeling for absolute realism, a poet in prose. "I believe that we are lost here in America, but I believe we shall be found." That is his theme, and no one will finish this extraordinary flow of incident and personality — all of it the biography of a restless man with an insatiable curiosity exhausting itself upon human nature — without a new insight into his own country. And without, let me add, having the sense of a full and completed story. Like Whitman, like Melville, both true predecessors, Wolfe seems to break, and sometimes does break, all the rules of literature. Yet he remains a tide-mark in American literature — and is unique.

HENRY SEIDEL CANBY

"A NEW AUTHOR," *Dorothy Canfield proclaimed about Carson McCullers. Her novel was* The Heart Is a Lonely Hunter, *in which "bitterness, and pain, foreknowledge of defeat and strange, uncomprehended love are its very texture."*

The Heart Is a Lonely Hunter
by Carson McCullers

A SENSITIVE, very original, and touching story about ordinary people in a Southern town. It is written by a new author, a young Southern woman who has had, we are told, almost no wider experience of life than in a hard-working, grubby, small city like the one which is the background of her story. Perhaps she knew there the original of the pathetic little adolescent heroine — not sentimentalized, speaking at times with startling mill-hand coarseness, yet nevertheless always lovable, always transfigured by her potential gift for the loveliest of the arts, from which poverty shuts her off forever. It is good fortune for American fiction that the young author was able somehow, as the poor child in the book was not, to surmount whatever difficulties lay between her and the practice of her art. For there is real beauty, poetry, and power, as well as heartbreak in this strange, authentic story about people who work grimly for their living, uncomplaining, each one shut up with his own secret trouble and pain, each one longing for more serenity, more peace, more harmony. The book seems to be made up of the most commonplace material — not a trace of the ferocity, horror or savage humor which

colors so many realistic novels of Southern life — with no external
beauty, no material success chronicled in its pages. Bitterness and pain,
foreknowledge of defeat and strange, uncomprehended love are its very
texture. Yet it is radiant with the truest poetry. There is a wild Shel-
leyan beauty in the nightly walks abroad of the little music-adoring
high-school girl, whose only chance to hear it is by listening under the
windows to the radios of the well-to-do — when they chance to leave
their windows open. There is a sweet, quiet Wordsworthian poetry in
the stillness and orderly calm of the plain boarding-house room of the
deaf-mute clerk, which is as near to the realization of an ideal as any of
the characters ever encounter. With his death even this vanishes like a
burst bubble, so utterly that in an hour, in a day, they can scarcely believe that so much good was ever part of their lives. But even in their
loss, their bewildered, inarticulate sorrow, even in the sentence to artistic death of the heroine, there is that inimitable singing vibration which
makes the voice of the true writer of fiction rich with overtones of
deeper meanings and greater values than are in the words set down.

                                                    DOROTHY CANFIELD

SIX MONTHS *before the United States entered World War II*, Darkness
at Noon *was picked as a Selection. The journalist Louis Fischer profiled Arthur Koestler as "the novelist in journalism and the journalist
who writes novels."*

Darkness at Noon by Arthur Koestler

THIS is a superb achievement; if I write about it with careful reserve, do
not think I underrate it. In describing the story I shall begin with poor
tactics. I shall say that it might be considered an essay on political psychology based on a famous quotation from Machiavelli which is reprinted as a motto. I shall say that it is required reading for anyone who
may have wondered about the notorious Moscow trials, and gives us the
first intelligible comment on the pragmatic reasons behind them. And
then, lest this discourage anyone, I hasten to say that it is brilliant reading and anyone who has an adequate chair and a good lamp will not rise
until he finishes it. I know I didn't, and other members of our committee
said the same. Even the good lamp will become an offense in the scenes
toward the end where the hero, Rubashov, gradually disintegrates

under the constant glare of voltage-lighting and confesses to crimes he never committed simply because he no longer cares. In the back of his mind is the inscription he saw over the grave of another political conspirator, DORMIR — to sleep.

This is the kind of novel we have learned to expect from, let us say, Chekhov or Gorki or Dostoyevsky. It is the story of N. S. Rubashov, ex-commissar of the Soviet Republics, who was one of the founders of the Communist régime, served his red Republic abroad, unhesitatingly "liquidated" other secret agents when that seemed advisable, and is now himself to be tried for treason — or in the Soviet euphemism, "political divergencies." We spend several weeks with him in his cell, and in his mind. We get to know the one as vividly as the other. One will scarcely forget the cruel lighting of those iron galleries, the judas (peep-hole) in the door. We know his toothache, the holes in his socks, the carefully preserved cigarette stub when he sleeps on his straw mattress, his unconscious gesture of polishing his pince-nez on his sleeve. What pathos at the end, when he is hustled down that sinister spiral stair, and his glasses, last relic of his days of scholarship, fall on the iron tread and are ground to pieces.

This does not sound like humor, I hear you say. Wait for the astonishing conversations tapped out on the wall in code-alphabet between Rubashov and his neighbor, whom we never see, in cell 406. Perhaps the most extraordinary achievement of this narrative is the clear imagination we get of the Czarist officer in that adjoining cell — his clean-shaved face, his probable monocle, his love of horses, and his erotic nostalgia, all conveyed in a few tapped-out messages. You see, our Czarist equestrian has already been in solitary a good many years. The intellectual Rubashov tries conscientiously to satisfy (by tapped-out messages) his neighbor's desire for sentimental recollections, but he is the Trotsky intellectual type and does not do very well.

The author tells us in a warning note that the characters are fictitious; Rubashov is "a synthesis of a number of men who were victims of the Moscow Trials." In a series of luminously effective flashbacks we are aware of Rubashov's memories; his meetings (in Swiss picture-galleries or Antwerp longshoremen's saloons) with other conspirators of Communism. There is a charming but cool-blooded interlude of his love for Ilova, his secretary who puzzled him by wearing high heels with her peasant garb, but whose white nape as he dictated to her was irresistible. Her also, when necessity arose, he did not hesitate to jettison to the liquidators. So, in a sense, our sympathy with poor Rubashov is intellectual rather than emotional. That is the inward power of the book: however it will horrify or dismay, it gives an extraordinarily lucid picture of "a generation without umbilical cords," the Communist doctrinaires "born without either frivolity or melancholy" and who attempted to fit human life to their rigid gridiron.

CHRISTOPHER MORLEY

Arthur Koestler

by Louis Fischer

ARTHUR KOESTLER has courage. He loves adventure. He first made a big reputation for himself in 1931 when, as special correspondent for the Ullstein newspaper trust of Germany, he flew to the Arctic in the *Graf Zeppelin*. He likes the exotic. He has worked and played in Egypt, Palestine, Syria, Bokhara, Turkestan, and the Caucasus.

Koestler is courageous to the point of recklessness. In February, 1937, as correspondent of the London *News Chronicle*, he covered the Italian fascist attack on the Loyalist city Malaga. The Spanish republicans had no means of defending themselves. Those who could, cleared out. Koestler was with a girl friend and chauffeur. They urged him to leave. He urged them to stay. They stayed to the last minute of safety. Then they left. He stayed. The Italians captured him and put him in a Seville prison. A loud outcry went up in England and the British government obtained his release.

Koestler is probably in his mid-thirties. He looks younger. He has a pleasing face and youngish medium-sized body. Born in Budapest, son of a Hungarian father and an Austrian mother, his education was German, but all of Europe contributed to his mental make-up. He is primarily Viennese, and Freud supplies the pattern of his thinking. He writes psychoanalytical novels. But like many other members of a European generation which felt that its statesmen would soon send it into the trenches again, he saw in Moscow a symbol of protest. The Soviet influence tempered Freud with Marx. To offset this potentially forbidding combination, a touch of French temperament lends him that lightness and cynicism which keep analysis from becoming morbid.

Death in company has less terror. Before even the Panzer divisions and dive bombers moved, Europe was a battlefield on which ideals, hopes, and cultural values were the casualties. Koestler has spent his life on that battlefield. The battle made some people opportunists because they didn't care enough about anything. It made Koestler brave because he didn't care enough about himself. When a world is crumbling and one's friends are dying either physically under bombs or spiritually under Communist compulsion, the value of life is marked down.

The pain of the defeat of decency in Spain, the shock of the Moscow trials and purges, and the ugliness of Anglo-French cowardice in the face of fascist encroachment, did not kill Koestler. He could still fight. In 1938, he was editing the Paris anti-Moscow, anti-Hitler, German-language weekly, *Zukunft* (*Future*), published by Willi Muenzenberg, dynamic champion of human rights. When war came in September, 1939, he joined the French army which was expected to fight Hitler. After the French debacle, he fled to England. The British clamped him into a concentration camp as an "enemy alien." But an enemy of fascism cannot today be an enemy of England. And he is not an alien, except on the dead page of a passport, because he is kin to anyone resisting Hitler. The British have released him.

Koestler is the novelist in journalism and the journalist who writes novels. When the reality of this era taxes the imagination, the chronicler escapes into the sobriety of fiction. These days, a personal history may sound like invention, and the novelist is glad when he achieves the excitement of a newspaper despatch. The public is no longer afraid of or tired of politics.

A rich generation of European men was lost in the First World War; millions were killed and maimed. The next generation, the one to which Arthur Koestler belongs, was lost in the peace; its soul was torn and crippled. Koestler's generation is trying to find itself in the Second World War. If it fails, Europe is lost. Success will consist not only of an anti-fascist military victory but of a clean world after the victory.

THROUGHOUT WORLD WAR II *firsthand accounts of the fighting men were avidly consumed by American readers. Among these books were Ernie Pyle's* Brave Men *and Richard Tregaskis's* Guadalcanal Diary, *both Club Selections and both bestsellers. Ernie Pyle was the GIs' Boswell, and his books are alive today. A fellow war correspondent, Gordon Gammack of the* Des Moines Register and Tribune, *wrote the* News *profile on Pyle. In it he told about Pyle's apprehensions. Riding in a London cab one afternoon, Pyle said to Gammack, "I don't think I'm going to live through this one." Pyle survived the European war*

*but, in 1945, was killed on Okinawa. Richard Tregaskis was luckier.
He was a survivor. His publisher, the raconteur and man about Manhattan, Bennett Cerf, enlightened BOMC members about Tregaskis.*

Ernie Pyle
by Gordon Gammack

ERNIE PYLE won't mind if I say that as a journalist he was considered
before the war as "good in his rather special way, but no great shakes."
That was, on the whole, appropriate for a man who entered journalism
out of no overwhelming urge. Born on a farm in the small town of Dana,
Indiana, he majored in journalism at Indiana University chiefly because
journalism was a snap course. Travel was, perhaps, a sharper desire;
anyway, he went to Japan with the university ball team as bellhop,
which, if you must go to Japan, is a good way to go. His practical journalism he learned while going through the university, and on the *La
Porte, Indiana, Herald*, rounding it out on the *Washington News*. On
the *News* he gave a hint of what he might do. Given the chore of listing
airplane arrivals and departures he made it a good air-travel column. Always travel was in his mind. When, after filling in a few times for
Heywood Broun, he was given an assignment by the Scripps-Howard
chain, it was as a traveling observer of the United States. He and his
wife, Geraldine Siebolds, visited every state in the Union, at least three
times. It was the "small time" stuff that is really the "big time" matter of
a national life that he reported; from soap and dogs, to the leper colony
at Molokai and hard frosts in Alaska. He was published in about forty
papers, which is not much more than obscurity.

Then came the war. Not surprisingly to those who had figured out
what was the pull in those apparently unimportant articles about the
United States, he did a superb job on the London blitz of 1940.

Why has he become the war's best correspondent? Not, as so many
have said, because he is a "little man" writing about the "little man," but
because the quiet, unobtrusive seriousness of the man got to work on the
quiet bigness of the G.I. And there is more than seriousness in Ernie.

He not only knows intimately the "brave men" of the United States
Army — probably better than any man — he is himself a brave man.
But that is not to say that he is a fearless man, for no one is fearless amid
the awful dangers of modern war. The bravery of this frail, lovable man
stems from the fact that he has a terrible, unashamed fear of war.

Last winter he went to the hell of the Anzio beachhead, meaning to stay five days and then go to England. But there, among the uproar of artillery bombardment and air raids, he found the stories of brave men he needed. So he stayed on. Then a big German bomb fell only a few feet from the press villa, and Ernie narrowly escaped death. It was a shaking experience. His revised plans called for him to leave the following day, but once again he stayed on. Later he explained his staying as "self-discipline," but what was probably in the back of his mind was the idea it would help the morale of the others in the villa if he did not leave.

It was not really Ernie's plan or wish to cross the English Channel with the assault doughboys on the day after D-Day of the French invasion last June. But an officer of very high rank invited him to go and, referring to it among his friends as a "command performance," he resolved to go. I am, perhaps, betraying what was meant to be a secret when I say that Ernie thought he would not survive D-Day. For some time before he had had an abiding premonition that his luck had run out. Riding in a London cab one afternoon, he said to me: "I don't think I'm going to live through this one. I can't sleep at night." But he went, though all the time he was in France he believed he would be killed.

Richard Tregaskis

by Bennett Cerf

RICHARD TREGASKIS is a typical American war correspondent, 1943 model. When the first boatload of fighting Marines landed on the Guadalcanal beachhead, Tregaskis was right with them, taking his chances with the rest, reporting this war as he saw it with his own eyes. He wore a "C" band on his arm, and he carried no gun, but he had the same chance of being picked off by a Jap as the Marines on either side of him.

Do you remember when our foreign correspondents were glamour boys, who decorated the bars and deluxe restaurants hundreds of miles behind the lines, and cabled back stale hand-outs from government censorship headquarters? Then they came strutting home with lurid stories of front-line warfare. Only a few of that ilk are still doing business at the old stand, and reporters like Dick Tregaskis are smoking out the ones that are left. It's back to the City Hall beat for the Rover Boys, and a good thing for the American public. We want our war news straight today!

Tregaskis was born on November 28, 1916, at Elizabeth, New Jersey.

By the time he had graduated from Harvard, he stood six feet, seven inches in his stocking feet. His collegiate career was a distinguished one. He was awarded five separate scholarships, and in his senior year won the coveted Harvard Club of New Jersey award. He also won his letter on the swimming team. His idea of a morning dip was a ten to fifteen mile swim up and down the Massachusetts surf. All of his spare time at college, he worked to help pay his tuition. During two summer vacations he went from door to door selling Singer Sewing Machines.

During his senior year, his work on the Harvard *Crimson* and *Advocate* attracted the attention of Jack Malloy, the managing editor of the *Boston American;* when he graduated, Malloy gave him a job as reporter and feature writer for that paper.

Tregaskis grew impatient after a few years in Boston, however. He wanted a wider scope. He approached *International News Service* with a unique qualification: a full working knowledge of the Portuguese language. *INS* was grooming him for a post on the cable desk in either Lisbon or Rio, when Pearl Harbor caused the greatest staff shakeups in the history of American journalism. He was assigned to the United States Navy at Hawaii, and the fact that he was picked for the Solomon Islands job is evidence of the name he made for himself there. When he left, his mates warned him that if the undersized Japs ever captured him, they'd use him for an observation post. Tregaskis put an extra pair of size 14 sneakers in his kit, grinned, and was on his way.

Lieut. Commander John S. Thack, U.S.N., who was with Tregaskis in the Solomons, characterized him as "one of the fightingest, eatingest men I've ever seen in my life." A Marine Major at Guadalcanal wrote to his parents, "Read Tregaskis' stuff on this clambake for the real picture of it. He was right there with us and his stories are absolutely accurate."

Tregaskis started assembling his diary while stranded for ten days on an unnamed Pacific island, awaiting return to Pearl Harbor. He finished it aboard a Liberator bomber. His only distraction, he wrote, was a low circle which the pilot described over a certain Polynesian islet. They were interested in seeing dusky maidens swimming in a lagoon, with or without Lamouresque sarongs. If you had spent eight weeks straight looking only at Marines, Japs, and betel-chewing Melanesian men, you would have had similar ideas. Tregaskis evidently forgot all about the dusky maidens when he landed in Honolulu, however. He descended upon the Pacific Club and ordered three porterhouse steaks. Then he sent on his book.

Guadalcanal Diary was received by Ward Greene of *INS* on November 9, accepted by Random House for publication on November 11, and chosen by the Book-of-the-Month Club judges on November 16. That's a record even in these days.

RICHARD WRIGHT'S Native Son *was selected in 1940,* Black Boy *in 1945. Mr. Canby's report on* Native Son *("certainly the finest novel as yet written by an American Negro") was complemented by a sensitive portrait of Richard Wright, written by Edwin Seaver, a member of the Book-of-the-Month Club editorial staff.*

Native Son by Richard Wright

THIS powerful and sensational novel is very difficult to describe so as to convey its real purpose and its real strength. But it is important to describe it accurately, because it is certainly the finest novel as yet written by an American Negro — not that it was chosen by the Book-of-the-Month Club just because it was written by a Negro. It would have been chosen for its deep excitement and intense interest whether written by white, yellow, or black. Yet, nevertheless, this is a novel which only a Negro could have written; whose theme is the mind of the Negro we see every day; whose emotion is the emotion of that native born American under the stress of a social situation difficult in the extreme; whose point and purpose are not race war or propaganda of any kind, but to show how a "bad nigger" is made from human material that might have become something very different.

Superficially, *Native Son* is a crime story, adventurous, exciting, often terrible — with two murders, a chase and a gun fight over the roofs of Chicago, a trial, and what might have been, but was not, a rape. It is the old story of a man hunted down by society. But the reader will get through only a few chapters before he realizes that there is something different in this story. Bigger — and we all know Bigger — is no persecuted black saint. His family is a good family, as tenement families go; but he is a bad actor from the first. He is mean; he is a coward; he is on occasion liar, thief, and bully. There is no sentimentalism in the writer who created Bigger, and made him chauffeur in the family of a wealthy philanthropist who spent some of the money wrung from Negro tenements on benefits for the race. Bigger is headed toward jail from the first chapter. When Mary Dalton, the flighty daughter of the philanthropist, askes Bigger to help along her intrigue with her Communist lover (also a negrophile), he has no compunctions. But he did not mean to kill her, he did not want to kill her, though he hated patronizing whites. Had her blind mother not come in at the fatal moment, the girl would have slept off her drunkenness, and Bigger would never have got beyond petty crime. With a skill which any master of the detective story might envy, Mr. Wright builds his book on the inevitable and terrifying results of an unpremeditated killing; the burning of the body; the false accusations; the murder of Bigger's Negro girl friend, lest she implicate him; the capture; the trial in which Mr. Max, the defending lawyer, pleads unsuccessfully the cause of a race driven toward crime, against a district attorney needing notoriety for his next election. And finally comes Bigger's confession — not of the murder which was not a murder, and of the rape which was not a rape, but of the obscure inarticulate causes which made him hate, and made him try to make up for his sense of inferiority by aggressive acts against the society in which he lived.

All this highly complicated story is handled with competence by Mr. Wright in a swift narrative style proceeding by staccato dialogue and with rapidly mounting suspense. The characters, too, are fully realized. There is a deadly satire in the portraits of the young radicals — Mary who is killed, and Jan, the Communist, who chooses Bigger to work on, not realizing that this kind of political pity is more offensive to a Negro than color prejudice. And the mob itself is a character, stirred up by sensational newspapers, getting bloodthirsty, wanting to lynch — the mob whose threatening roar is always in the background of the book and of the Negro's mind. Yet even in its characters this is not a vindictive book. Bigger dies without hate for anything, except the obscure circumstances which compelled him to be what he was. Max, his lawyer, with the ancient wisdom of the Jews, pleads for him on the broad basis of an America in grave danger from a conflict of races which only a deeper-going justice can ameliorate. Even the Negro evangelist who tries to bring back Bigger to the emotional religion which has helped so many men and women of his race, is presented with sympathy and pathos.

Indeed, two statements may be made with safety by the most conservative critic about this remarkable novel. No reader, however harrowed by its frank brutalities, will be able to stop in its engrossing story, which coils and mounts until a tale of crude violence broadens into a human tragedy. And no white man — and, I suspect, few Negroes — will finish this narrative without an enlargement of imagination toward the psychological problems of the Negroes in our society — and an appreciable extension of sympathy. This will hold, I prophesy, for South as well as North. Indeed, I suspect that this book and its probings will be less of a surprise to, and more readily understood by, Southerners than by Northerners. Mr. Wright himself was born and educated in Mississippi, and has lived his later life in the North. It is not the ex-slave of the South, or the almost-like-a-white-man Negro of the North, but the essential Negro-in-America of both, that he gets into Bigger and his book.

Let me repeat, this novel is no tract or defense plea. Like *Grapes of Wrath*, it is a fully realized story of unfortunates, uncompromisingly realistic, and quite as human as it is Negro. To the growing list of artistic achievements of a high quality, by a race which is, perhaps, singularly gifted in art, *Native Son* must surely be added, with a star for notable success.

HENRY SEIDEL CANBY

Richard Wright

by Edwin Seaver

IT IS early evening in a town in the deep South, and a Negro lad of about fifteen stands cap in hand before the desk in the public library, while the librarian scans the message he has just handed her. "Please let this nigger boy have the following books," the note says. "Dreiser's *Jennie Gerhardt*, Dostoyevsky's *Poor People*, Tolstoy's *War and Peace*."

As the librarian turns away to get the books, the boy's eyes roam hungrily through the peaceful, inviting room, past the tables where people sit reading, past the magazine racks with all the latest issues, over the shelves along the walls crammed with what to the youth seem an endless store of riches. "What joy," he thinks, "to be free to browse among all these books at one's leisure, to dig now in this volume, now in that, as one has a mind to."

The librarian returns, and after stamping books and card, shoves them across the desk toward the waiting boy, who tries not to betray any sign of eagerness or self-consciousness as he picks them up and makes for the door. But he is really scared. What if the librarian suspects that the "nigger boy" forged the note (as, indeed, he did) so he could use an obliging white friend's card, and that he is taking these books home for himself?

But she doesn't suspect. She has no way of knowing that this gawky lad is Richard Wright, who in hardly more than a decade will be one of the foremost writers of his generation, a Guggenheim fellow, a winner of several literary prize awards.

I questioned Wright how he had known what books to ask for. After all, he had never been to high school, and I knew that in his grammar school days he had been a past master at the art of playing hookey. "How come you were reading Dreiser and Tolstoy," I said, "before you were hardly out of knee britches?"

"I suppose I'll have to blame it on H. L. Mencken," he said. "One day when I was working as an errand boy in Memphis, I read an editorial in the leading paper lambasting Mr. Mencken. He must be good, I thought. Soon after, I accidentally came across his *Book of Prefaces*. That book served as a literary bible for me for years."

Richard Wright was born in 1908 on a plantation twenty-five miles from Natchez, Mississippi, the son of a mill worker and a country school teacher. At the age of five he found himself living in a tenement in Memphis. "Doubtless that town proved too much of an attraction for my father," he recalls, "for he began to drift off for long intervals without leaving coal or food at home."

There are dim pictures in his consciousness of sitting all day long in courtrooms "eating dry sandwiches" and listening to his mother tell the judge about her difficulties, with two children to provide for. He recalls going to live at Helena, Arkansas, with his mother's sister, earning a few pennies by picking up coal on the railroad tracks, selling papers on the streets after school, growing up naturally as a weed while his mother worked.

At the age of fifteen Wright packed his cardboard suitcase and left home. After working in Memphis for two years, he moved to Chicago, where he finally managed to get a night job as a post office clerk. During the day he read omnivorously — he had just discovered Proust, T. S. Eliot, James Joyce, and other "moderns." He read, and tried to write. "I had a notion I wanted to write," he says, "but did not know exactly how to go about it."

The publication of a long short story, titled *Big Boy Leaves Home*, in the *New Caravan* of 1936, first drew the attention of the critics to a new young writer of marked ability. This was the genesis of the book of related stories that was later, under the title *Uncle Tom's Children*, to win first prize in the Story Magazine Prize Contest for W.P.A. Writers.

I asked Wright where he got the material for his new book, *Native Son*. "Mostly from living nine years in Chicago," he said. "But particularly from working in a south side boys' club, where I came up against the type of boy I have pictured in my book."

"Incidentally," he added, "I was about half way though the novel when a big case broke in Chicago that almost duplicated the story I was writing. I modeled the newspaper releases in the book on the actual news stories of this case." It is interesting to note, in passing, that the lawyer's plea for the accused, which is one of the high points in *Native Son*, was modeled on Clarence Darrow's famous defense in the Leopold-Loeb case.

FIRST PUBLISHED *in 1945,* The Thurber Carnival *was revived in a facsimile edition for Club Members in 1986. The enthusiastic response seemed to indicate that Thurber's audience lives on. In his review of the 1945 Selection, Clifton Fadiman noted, "Recommending* The Thurber Carnival *is like recommending love or fine food or any other naturally good thing. Thurber and what he calls his 'amazing stories' and 'beautiful drawings' are now part of us."*

The Thurber Carnival by James Thurber

THE THURBER CARNIVAL marks the dwindling of James Thurber as a modern cult and the emergence of James Thurber as a modern classic. (At least that's what the Book-of-the-Month Club judges hope.) Here, in this fine, fat volume of the best of Thurber (words and pictures) is gathered not merely a great deal of oddity but a great deal of wisdom. Mr. Thurber is that quite serious and even weighty thing — a true humorist. This will become clear to any reflective reader who goes through — and he will find it the pleasantest of journeys — *The Thurber Carnival.*

There is a notion current that because Mr. Thurber has done most of his work for Mr. Harold Ross's amazing family magazine, he can be "appreciated" only by the readers of *The New Yorker.* The fact is that anybody moderately sensitive to fine English and to the tragic ridiculousness of human beings is, whether he reads *The New Yorker* or not, equipped to be a Thurberite. James Thurber, like Ring Lardner and Mark Twain and Mr. Dooley, is, or should be, the property of all of us.

"This book," as the forty-eight-year-old author tells you in his preface entitled *My Fifty Years with James Thurber,* "contains a selection of the stories and drawings the old boy did in his prime, a period which extended roughly from the year Lindbergh flew the Atlantic to the day coffee was rationed." The selection includes six stories hitherto unpub-

lished in book form; six stories from *My World and Welcome to It*; eight
pieces from *Let Your Mind Alone*; thirteen pieces from *The Middle-
Aged Man on the Flying Trapeze*; the complete *My Life and Hard
Times* (probably his masterpiece to date); thirteen of the wry *Fables for
Our Time*; five *Illustrated Poems* (the only Thurber opus that makes no
appeal to me, and so what?); a selection from *The Owl in the Attic*; and
what I believe is known as oodles (a vague but gigantic number) of the
drawings, including the entire sanguinary epic of *The War Between
Men and Women*.

Of these drawings the artist remarks that they "sometimes seemed to
have reached completion by some other route than the common one of
intent." Which, of course, is true. These baffled little men and smug or
ferocious little women, these deeply introspective dogs, these casually
appearing seals and penguins, these libidinous doctors and nightmarish
wives and wistful drunks and odd animals that never were on sea or
land — they are not only drawn *from* the Thurber unconscious, but
seem to be drawn *by* it. If they were not so funny, they would scare us
into conniption fits, for they are freehand, totally uninhibited render-
ings, it seems to me, of the more dubious and dismaying aspects of our
dream-life. Some of them haunt you like a half-remembered strain of lu-
natic melody from another world. In my office there hangs on the wall
the original of a drawing reproduced in *The Thurber Carnival*. It
shows a doctor's office. The doctor is asking a question of a worried
Thurber female who is in the consulting room. The caption reads: "*You
said a moment ago that everybody you look at seems to be a rabbit. Now
just what do you mean by that, Mrs. Sprague?*" The only disquieting
fact about the drawing is that the doctor himself has the head of a rabbit.
Whenever I look at this cartoon it reaffirms my conviction that the
human mind is less a bright, clicking machine than a mysterious dark
cavern.

A few years ago I wrote a few pages about Mr. Thurber in which I
tried, not very successfully, to describe his humor. Perhaps I will be
pardoned for quoting from myself. There are, I said, two Thurber temperaments, or, rather, two sides of the same temperament. "The
Thurber of *Let Your Mind Alone* and the *Fables for Our Time* shows
one side. The Thurber of *My Life and Hard Times* and *The Male Animal* shows another. The first Thurber is the Sane Innocent; the second
is the Confused Innocent. Actually, Mr. Thurber is never confused and
never innocent. His confusion and his innocence, though, are not just
poses, but positions which he assumes in order to allow his humor to

play more readily. The Sane Innocent is the Thurber who makes you laugh because he sees through imposture (such as that of the self-improvement school) from an angle that the rest of us would never think of. He is to comedy what Dostoyevsky's wise idiots are to tragedy. The pleasure you get from this Thurber is the pleasure of sudden illumination. The Confused Innocent is the Thurber who makes you laugh not because he sees through things but, on the contrary, because he is bewildered by them. (Actually, this bewilderment is merely a slyer form of understanding.) The pleasure you get from this Thurber is that wry and rueful satisfaction that comes of watching somebody make a fool of himself in a maze. Don Quixote and a drunk, Caspar Milquetoast and Mr. Pickwick, Mr. Disney's Dopey, all are examples, on varying levels, of the comedy of befuddlement."

But there is still a third Thurber, the Thurber of certain stories which, entertaining as they may be, can only with considerable latitude be termed comic. Written in the most corrosive acid, they establish Thurber firmly as an important and exceedingly uncompromising satirist. Such a tale as *The Secret Life of Walter Mitty* is the final word on the furtive, heart-breaking, imaginary lives that so many of us outwardly adjusted Americans are forced to lead. *The Catbird Seat*, despite its seeming extravagance, is brutal to the point of the grisly. *The Breaking Up of the Winships* is an icy commentary, worthy of Lardner at his best, on a particular variety of American marriage. *The Greatest Man in the World* tears the disguises off a half-dozen elements of our national life — our hero-worship, our frenzy for the machine, our publicity-mania, to name only three. *One Is a Wanderer* tells me more about the nature of our American solitariness than do all the novels of Thomas Wolfe.

The Thurber of these stories is the dispassionate chronicler of our big-city neurotics; of the over-talkative, over-facile, rather under-educated semi-intellectuals who lent their pronounced color to the twenties; of the wilful eccentrics whose whimsey is so near to madness; of our more elegant alcoholics; of the practical jokers whose jokes are a form of half-hysterical aggression. This Thurber combines humor with horror. Were it not that his prose is always lucid and the form of his narratives always perfection, he might be put down — in this mood only — as a surrealist.

I do not wish to overemphasize this quality in Mr. Thurber. Most of the stories are just plain funny; some of them just plain uproariously funny. The laughter in others is tender almost to sweetness. But the fun and the laughter are never unreflective. They are always the expression of a temperament of depth and solidity. Even his parodies have three dimensions, being first-rate literary criticism as well as evokers of the most pleasant mirth.

There is one more quality in Thurber that is tantalizingly hard to isolate: the nature of his wit. It consists, I suppose, of the deadpan statement of an odd or even outrageous idea. A mad fancy is couched in the gravest, even the most business-like of prose. Here is a typical Thurber sentence (I think it one of the funniest and also one of the most imaginative sentences in English). He is talking about his birthplace in Ohio. "In the early years of the nineteenth century, Columbus won out, as State capital, by only one vote over Lancaster, and ever since then has had the hallucination that it is being followed, a curious municipal state of mind which affects, in some way or other, all those who live there." That is Thurber at his wittiest, and I know of no contemporary, unless it be E. B. White, who can match him. Recommending *The Thurber Carnival* is like recommending love or fine food or any other naturally good thing. Thurber and what he calls his "amazing stories" and "beautiful drawings" are now part of us. They express us to ourselves. They live a life in our minds. They are, to put it simply, part of American literature.

CLIFTON FADIMAN

No F. SCOTT FITZGERALD WORK *ever became a Book of the Month. Of course* The Great Gatsby *was published in 1925, a year before the Club came into existence. Fitzgerald led a tormented life, possibly because of his obsessive ambition. He once confided to Edmund Wilson: "I want to be one of the greatest writers who ever lived, don't you?" In her 1945 review of* The Crack-Up, *Bernardine Kielty wrote, "We can place him as definitely as Trollope."*

Tender Is the Night by F. Scott Fitzgerald

THIS novel, the first for a number of years by Scott Fitzgerald, has a brilliant opening, and is interesting throughout. It is loose, inconclusive, and occasioinally careless and irrelevant; nevertheless it shows power and extraordinary ability. Fitzgerald has introduced what seems to be the perfect product of sophisticated, cosmopolitan life, a couple who charm everyone and seem to lead a charmed life. But there is something wrong, which the story reveals to be a tragic split in the personality of Nicole, the wife, due to an incestuous experience of her youth. Her husband has reconstructed her personality, holds it together by his love and his intelligence, and has made his own character in the process. When a fresh and charming girl, a baby star of the movies, enters this orbit, trouble begins. And when Nicole feels at last that she can take care of herself and begins to resent her dependence upon her husband, the tragedy is outlined and develops. This seems to be the theme of the novel, but it is overlaid by so many scenes and there are so many currents and cross-currents in the book, so many incidental characters very interesting in themselves, that it is hard to be sure just what Fitzgerald meant. No one can read this book without disappointment, or without interest and frequent admiration.

HENRY SEIDEL CANBY

The Crack-Up by F. Scott Fitzgerald
(Edited by Edmund Wilson)

FLAMING youth, the Riviera, low-slung fast cars, windblown bobs, house parties, drinking to keep up the pace — the Jazz Age seems as remote as the Restoration, and something like it, while F. Scott Fitzgerald, its spokesman and its conscience, who died only such a short time ago as 1941, is a figure already in a niche. His work has already jelled, and we can place him as definitely as Trollope. Perhaps it is because that brief day of heightened emotions and desperate living was so securely bounded — by a war on the one hand and a depression on the other — that we can see it so completely rounded and finished, an era quite apart from the natural course of history. Perhaps, too, that is why we have so quickly forgotten it. Now, in this book of essays and letters which Edmund Wilson has edited so skillfully around the figure of Fitzgerald, we are tossed back twenty years, and the effect, caught as one is bound to be by Fitzgerald's own dangerous excitement, is strangely disturbing. He left no autobiography. We need none because every novel and story he wrote was himself. But this artful collection is quite as truly a revelation of personality. It includes the essays which he wrote for *Esquire* after he had passed the peak of his popularity and begun his struggle against ill health; several letters to friends, far better than autobiography, because they are so natural and spontaneous; touching letters to his daughter designed as good fatherly advice, but ending too often in scarcely suppressed nagging; his notebooks; and three pieces about him by his contemporaries. None of his actual creative work (except the few articles) is included, but the fragments from his notebooks are an artist's ruminations. These are literary: a plot in a sentence; bits of brilliant phrasing; descriptions of girls — and who has ever described them better? — conversations; anecdotes, observations; lists of songs from other years; bits of vernacular; ideas; nonsense. They are the most appealing notes in this sad jazz ballad. They look back always to youth — not to innocent childhood like every other childhood — but to the days when, very young, Fitzgerald was on top of the world and the world itself was at boiling point. It is a book that you will pick up, put down, and pick up again. It's a whiff of perfume almost forgotten, a quick heart-beat. It will surely lead straight to a rereading of *The Great Gatsby* and *The Last Tycoon.*

BERNARDINE KIELTY

EVELYN WAUGH'S Brideshead Revisited, *a bestselling Main Selection in January 1946, was a repeat bestseller for the Club in 1984, when the novel received a new life through a popular television dramatization. Randolph Churchill (Winston's son), in his summation of Waugh as a person, wrote, "You are bound to love him or to hate him."*

Brideshead Revisited by Evelyn Waugh

THE story of a noble old Catholic family that fell from Grace. Phosphorescent, witty, tenderly erotic and tenderly sad; playing always with fire — but only St. Elmo's fire; just graciously decadent and always (as one of its characters says) "that creamy English charm, playing tigers" — I have to be careful in telling you how hugely I enjoy this sort of thing, for fear you would think I take it too seriously. It is always done, and done beautifully every ten years or so by some English novelist who is no longer quite young. I don't know why, it pains English novelists to approach middle age even more than it hurts anyone else. Perhaps it's because they are so impudently frolicsome in youth? Maybe it all comes from driving on the left hand side of the road.

Mr. Waugh's seductive sardonic novel is peculiarly awkward to estimate for a vast audience. How well I can imagine those who will be puzzled, those who will be shocked. Maybe the fairest suggestion is to say that it revives what was once called the Post-War generation, the hysterically humorous young of 1923 or so, and tells what happened to them afterward. But these are a very special race of young; the young Arlens and Huxleys and Scott Fitzgeralds. Ten years earlier they'd have been reading *Sinister Street*. No historian will ever do a better job of Oxford-mongering than Mr. Waugh does in his chapters on the esthetic set of undergraduates, the Oscar Wilde animals we have known. I was very sorry only that he labeled it with the most worn and ancient of tags, *Et in Arcadia ego*. His detail and decor are absolutely cruelly exact. Cocteau and Cointreau; *Antic Hay* and Alexander cocktails; Firbank and Gide; *The Waste Land* and *The Green Hat* and *Lady into Fox*. Equally absolute is his meticulous taste in choosing the books that Lady Marchmain would read aloud in the great baroque mansion of Brideshead round which such tragic and broken memories are clouded. They are *The Wisdom of Father Brown* and *The Diary of a Nobody*.

A reviewer does not often allow himself (in his dour life) the delight of mentioning the trivial and enormous minutiae that gave him his hard-earned recompense. Mr. Waugh, as a good social historian, is lavish with them; for many readers they really need a gloss. I wish I could have time to expound the local color of such allusions as these: claret cup, cucumber sandwiches, basket chair, Leander tie, anchovy toast, the Gridiron Club (Oxford, not Washington, D.C.), Germer's (a hairdresser), the Golden Cross, the Turf Tavern, Roger Fry, the Bullingdon, Blackwell's, Mercury (a fountain), the Botanical Gardens, battels and why the four Indians in turbans at the Balliol gate are funny. These are all private cues for a limited audience. They are mostly Oxford small talk, and nothing is smaller. But they won't bother you, because they are carried along in fluent and purposeful narrative. And I know nothing more comic in modern American publishing than that one of Mr. Waugh's Oscar Wilde esthetes, a little drunk after lunch of plovers' eggs and champagne (or whatever), cannot recite from a balcony of Christ Church (Oxford) three lines of Eliot's *The Waste Land*, in mockery of the athletes on their way to the river, without the legalistic footnote (completely rupturing the spell) that it is "by permission of Harcourt Brace and Co."

"My theme is memory," says Mr. Waugh's imaginary narrator Charles Ryder. Ryder is a painter of the old stately homes of England, who has won great renown in his volumes of architectural record, both in Britain and Latin America. He knows that noble houses, and their associations, are greater than any individuals. Now, about 1944, he is a captain in the British Army, and his company is moved after long tedious journey to a new billet somewhere in Southern England (Wiltshire, in fact). He finds himself unexpectedly at Brideshead, the beautiful old estate he had known so well more than twenty years before; the seat of an ancient Catholic family. It was the home of his loved Oxford friend, Lord Sebastian Flyte, a younger son of the Marquis of Marchmain. But not really the home; Sebastian, the Oxford esthete, always called it "Where my family live." Not home. No one in this story really has a Home. And, speaking for serious theme, Mr. Waugh's deftly suggested motif is the decline and fall of the Stately Homes, and the arrival of the Age of Hooper. The latter, a crude young brummagem subaltern (lieutenant) in Captain Ryder's company, is cheaply annoying in background and manners. He is the symbol of the new lower-middle dispensation. He is Impossible. But the Age of Hooper is here; and the Age of Brideshead is gone. The marvelous old eighteenth-century statuary fountain is now full of lorry drivers' cigarette butts. The idealisms and idiocies of the Marchmains are gone forever. Sebastian, the beautiful boy of Oxford days, is dying of drink in Morocco. Cordelia, the sturdy baby sister, is a nurse in Palestine. The old Marquis, who vanished after the Other War to live with his respectable mistress, Cara, in Venice, is suffocating of angina and doesn't even care if he sees a priest. It is the collapse of an interbred and ghoul-haunted family. And Julia, the older sister, about whom there hovered the mysterious "bat-squeak of passion," is about to marry a potent hard-faced Colonial. About the ancient house of Brideshead, as the narrator summons his happy and tragic memories, hover these tender and frustrated emotioins. They are electrified, or osmosed, by the dim wraith of the abominable Hooper; who never had a stately home. But the Age of Hooper is here. He is precisely the kind of fellow who would invent an atomic bomb. And no one is left at Brideshead but old Nanny Hawkins, the ancient nurse, and Mr. Wilcox, the butler.

Mr. Waugh's plot is cooked and calculated, and his manner is deliberately soufflé, if you need to put social and serious feeling into it you've got to put it there mostly for yourself. His bravura chaff, his delicate double-talk, is so neatly done that when you come to a passage in which he bares his bosom you scarcely believe it. That is an English habit as old as Chaucer. It goes hard with a puritan reader; it is not his language. Where Mr. Waugh is bitterest you are likely to think he's kidding: for instance the gorgeous description of the loathsome interior decoration of modern ships — "huge without splendor, as though they had been designed for a railway coach and preposterously magnified. . . . Carpets the color of blotting paper; kindergarten work in flat, drab colors; yards and yards of biscuit-colored wood which no carpenter's tool had ever touched; tables designed by a sanitary engineer." And in that abominable mechanized vessel, humming with ventilators and vibrations, wallowed in genuine gale, is one of the most touching impulsive scenes of human love. We suspected it was coming, but we are no less pleased.

I perceive that I have told you nothing of the actual story; of the lost love of Captain Ryder and the spidery-limbed Julia, debutante of the era 1923. It is grim comedy, for sure, and comedy of excessive mannerisms. There's more arsenic than old lace. But I can't help remembering the story Hilaire Belloc used to tell of Henry James. Mr. James in Sussex was appalled to be visited without warning by a group of American lady-schoolteachers who had heard he was a writer. Belloc, always the romantic, asked were they pretty? James brooded a while. "Well," he replied at last, "There was one of them who had a certain cadaverous charm."

Mr. Waugh's novel has the horror and sweetness and delicate contagion of sophisticated memories. If you have none such of your own, you'll perhaps resent it. But some people, and I confess myself one, can be enchanted and transfixed, even corrupted — and still be grateful.

CHRISTOPHER MORLEY

Captain Evelyn Waugh
by Randolph Churchill

THE character and writings of Evelyn Waugh have combined to make him one of the most controversial figures in England today. Even his severest critics admit him to be one of the three or four finest living writers of English prose; yet his recent writings have provoked an astonishing exhibition of irritation and even anger in leading intellectual circles in London.

What is the reason? The other day I asked Mr. Desmond McCarthy, the most eminent of British literary critics, if he could explain this. He is a great admirer of Waugh's work. His explanation of the highbrows' current disdain for Waugh is that the majority of British literary critics are suffering at the moment from an intellectual snobbism about France,

and are reluctant to take creative work seriously unless it is inspired by
the school of Aragon, Sartre and Eluard. "If Waugh wrote in French,"
McCarthy told me, "all our highbrows would acclaim him as a second
Giraudoux."

But there is more to it than this. The highbrows of Bloomsbury suffer
from another form of intellectual snobbism — a proletarian snobbism.
As Waugh put it to me himself: "What they can't stand about *Brideshead Revisited* is that the hero has two love affairs both with women of
his own class. One they might forgive, but two is a sure indication to
Left-wing intellectuals of reactionary crypto-fascist ideology."

I think there is a good deal of truth in this view. The Hemingway
school of writers have cast a mantle of glamor around proletarian adultery, and this trend is so strong in the post-Potsdam world that adultery
among the well-to-do classes is currently anathema to the Bloomsbury
boys.

Waugh, of course, does all he can to irritate and provoke Left-wing
intellectuals like Cyril Connolly, Peter Quennell and Brian Howard.
While they have steadily drifted to the Left in their political views,
Waugh, largely under the influence of the Catholic faith to which he was
converted some fifteen years ago, has moved consciously and deliberately to the Right.

Nonetheless, riper intellects on the politically pink *New Statesman*,
such as Raymond Mortimer and Edward Sackville-West, regard *Brideshead Revisited* as a great English classic. The cleavage about Waugh
does not follow normal party lines. It is said that Sir Osbert Sitwell, one
of our rare reactionary intellectuals, when asked what he thought of
Brideshead Revisited paused for some twenty seconds and then replied:
"I adore Evelyn. Do you?"

Waugh is not one of those who find the modern world attractive. He
seeks to live in an oasis of his own and has adopted a formalism in his
social life which borders on the ridiculous. His aversion to all forms of
mechanical contrivance extends to the telephone: and he is always much
vexed if any of his friends presume to make use of it. A letter, or, at the
worst, a telegram are, in his view, the proper methods of communication
between civilized people.

Waugh is a man about whom it is impossible to be neutral. You are
bound to love him or to hate him. For he is not content to confine his
satirical genius to his writings, it is part of his every-day life; and friend
and foe alike must be prepared to suffer under the thrusts of his poisoned rapier.

Waugh possesses both physical and moral courage in a very high degree. He has seen quite a lot of action in this war. His courage, coupled with his intellect, might have won him a distinguished military career. But he was usually more interested in driving his immediate superiors mad than in bringing about the defeat of the enemy.

One of his superiors, an officer of high standing, had a nervous breakdown after only two months of having Waugh under his command. I had the doubtful privilege of having Waugh serve under me for some months when I was commanding the British Military Mission in Croatia. Early one morning the Germans strafed and dive-bombed the village in which we had our headquarters. Waugh not only refused to get into a slit trench, but felt that honor required that he should stand on a conspicuous hill in a white coat. I felt that this bravado was needless and shouted at him to take the coat off. With an angry gesture he did so and threw it on the ground beside him. For the rest of the day he sulked and was at his most stuffy. Eventually, rather weak-mindedly, I said to him: "I am sorry if you thought I addressed you rudely this morning." "It was not your rudeness I minded," he replied, "it was your cowardice that surprised me."

Behind his spikiness, Waugh conceals a generous heart and he has scores of devoted friends. But to be a friend of Waugh you must be very tough and never take him too seriously.

A connoisseur of food, of wine and of cigars, he finds life in England today extremely unattractive since these tastes are almost impossible to satisfy. He would have been a far happier man if he had been born in the nineteenth century.

His favorite novelist is Trollope. He has never read *Gone with the Wind* and never will. He cannot drive a motorcar. He would much prefer to receive a knighthood than to have his book selected as the book-of-the-month. He has a wife whom he loves and four children whom he affects to dislike. He makes an exception for one of his daughters who, at the age of four, when asked the whereabouts of the other children, replied: "They're hither and thither gathering bilberries as best they may."

He wears a bowler hat and carries an old-fashioned walking-stick. He becomes more old-fashioned and pedantic every day, but his satirical pen will probably grow the sharper as he more and more detaches himself from the modern world.

FOR MANY YEARS *Bernardine Kielty Scherman wrote a column in the*
News. She once called it, "What Are Your Special Curiosities?" The
column covered anything that struck her curiosity, including, here, the
first novel of "a young soldier," Gore Vidal, and a collection of short
stories by another soldier, Irwin Shaw. Shaw's Act of Faith and Other
Stories *was later reviewed by Miss Kielty.*

FIRST NOVEL BY A YOUNG SOLDIER. . . . Gore Vidal was
the youngest warrant officer in the army, and his first novel, *Williwaw*
($2.50), is based on his own experiences while commanding a small
army craft in the Aleutians. The story takes place aboard a similar vessel, and in the ports she visits; there is a storm aboard and storm without, bitter rivalry between two of the men, and the boat is struck by a
"williwaw," a local wind, a sort of hurricane-snow-squall. This is a first
novel of unusual promise; a readable, accurate, and exciting yarn.

IRWIN SHAW, who can't go wrong on a short story, is working
now on his first novel. It is to be a novel about war, enormous in scope.
Shaw was in the Army, and the stories in his current collection, *Act of*
Faith, are all war stories. Shaw is big, strong and twenty-nine, and besides writing plays and stories has worked in a cosmetics factory, an in-
stallment furniture house, tutored children, played professional football
and written radio serials — "Dick Tracy" and "The Gumps."

Act of Faith and Other Stories by Irwin Shaw

YOUR faith in human beings is warmed and strengthened as you read
these twelve excellent war stories by one of the very best short-story
writers. They are stories of boys become men overnight; of soldiers
whose emotions are keyed far beyond normal limits — by fear or heroism or lonesomeness; of "tough guys" and the deeply sensitive; officers
whose relations with the men — believe it or not! — are of the best;
stories of Scots, English, French, Italians and Americans. Mr. Shaw
writes not so much of what they do as of what goes on in the minds of
fighting men. They are stories that have been told before, but the men
are as real as your grocery boy or college chum or garage mechanic.
There is the Navy lieutenant who, entirely unskilled, has to perform an

appendectomy at sea; the Jew in Paris who finally gets a chance to tell a German what he thinks of him; the French collaborationist ashamed before his friends; the father in New York saying goodbye to the soldier son who, up to now, has been a schoolboy; the American soldier who has been through the stiffest of the fighting with two buddies, and is suddenly smitten with the fear that they — like the world all of them are about to re-enter — may also be anti-Semitic. This last is "An Act of Faith," unforgettable for its final resurgence of faith in unquestioning friendship. There is no quarter for cynicism here. You feel a great surge of gratefulness to these boys for what they have done in the course of their soldier's day's work, and you want to see to it that the future does not let them down.

BERNARDINE KIELTY

MRS. FREDERICK C. LITTLE'S SECOND SON, *Stuart, came into the world in 1946. Charlotte, the commonsense spider, made her literary debut in 1952, but E. B. White never stopped writing. Wolcott Gibbs, the drama critic of* The New Yorker, *explains all of this in his love story about Mr. White, which was printed alongside the January 1950 White Selection,* Here Is New York.

Stuart Little by E. B. White

HE was only about two inches high, and he had a mouse's sharp nose, a mouse's tail, a mouse's whiskers and the pleasant shy manner of a mouse. That is a description of Mrs. Frederick C. Little's second son, Stuart. (George, her elder son, was normal size.) It is the third sentence in this book, and by the time the reader gets there he will know whether he is going to like *Stuart Little* very much or not at all. There is no middle ground in fantasy. The age of the reader won't matter here any more than it does with *Alice in Wonderland,* some of Milne, or to come back to mice, the work of Walt Disney. What E. B. White sets out to do here looks easy, but is very difficult. Like a good soufflé, fantasy is wonderful when it is successful and just the reverse when it falls flat. *Stuart Little* is exactly right, done with a light, expert hand. There is a matter-of-fact tone about all Stuart's adventures that gives body to this fantasy-fiction. Some of the details will enchant the younger readers. Thumbelina's bed was a walnut shell, but Stuart being more modern has one made out of four clothes pins and a cigarette box. He has skates made of paper clips. For the rest Stuart leads an urban existence in New York, sails on the pond in Central Park, until he sets out on a quest North. Snowbell, the house cat, is not his friend. The picture of her by Garth Williams shows us why, for he makes her as sinister a character as Stuart is appealing. This is E. B. White's first book in this field. It is no use saying children's book, for age, like size in Stuart's case, is unimportant in this connection. *Stuart Little* should go on that special shelf — to be enjoyed by the whole family.

ROSEMARY C. BENÉT

Charlotte's Web by E. B. White

MR. WHITE, the premier personal essayist (in my opinion) of our time, is also an occasional writer of delightful and distinguished children's stories. He is not only skilful, he is courageous; for his heroes and heroines are as unexpected as those of folk-lore. Last time it was a midget; now it is a spider who devotes her life to making a pig, named Wilbur, famous. Spiders have always, except in the case of Robert Bruce (or was it Wallace?), been the villains of their pieces. Charlotte, who in her habits is pure spider, is a sad, cynical, utterly realistic character, who knows that she is to die in order to give birth to a multitude of little spiders, but in spite of her (to me) revolting ugliness (I hate spiders in general) determines to do the one great deed which has often made heroes out of very objectionable people. You cannot love her; neither can you read of her web without forever respecting the possibilities of life even in a spider. Wilbur is a somewhat stupid but lovable pig, who will certainly be turned into sausages by cold-weather time, unless someone — someone with genius — saves him by a miracle. Charlotte is the genius; her web is the miracle, on which she weaves a broadcast to the family and finally the local world. That does it — that and the assistance of the good-hearted gangster Templeton, a rat. But this is only the plot. There is much more, both wise and funny, to the story. Recommended to children (and grown-ups) who do not appreciate spiders or rats.

HENRY SEIDEL CANBY

E. B. White

by Wolcott Gibbs

NOWADAYS the editorial offices of *The New Yorker,* while still small compared with those of a national magazine, are too extensive and thickly settled for a casual visitor to comprehend at once. By the latest census, there were 149 employes, many with functions that are mysterious even to their closest fellows; there are two full floors of offices and a considerable overflow down onto a couple more; and the precise geography of this warren and the organization of its authority is known only to a handful of technical experts, equipped with blueprints.

Things weren't that way at all when I went to *The New Yorker* early in 1927. The place was a mining camp then, pure and simple, rough and noisy. There were only a few workers, and almost no women and children; and there was no mystery about anybody's function. All the inhabitants, of necessity, worked long and hard, but inevitably there was a little group — five or six at most — whose capabilities and energies were largely responsible for getting a fifteen-cent magazine to its subscribers.

It would be reasonable to suppose that all these leaders would be instantly identified by any newcomer to the staff, and I was indeed familiar with the appearance of all but one of them before I had been in the office a week. The exception was Andy White (Elwyn Brooks White to his sponsors in baptism), and it was, I think, almost two months before I was really sure which of the people who dropped into the make-up room, where I was stationed, was the author of the copy which, even then, I admired so deeply.

The reason for this delay was a certain wild and unmanageable discrepancy between the manner and substance of what Mr. White wrote and the way he looked and spoke. Being rather a young man then and still subject to some literary illusions, I must have expected a conspicuously fiery personality, at least six and a half feet high, dressed with the utmost elegance, and employing a diction that would have been considered formidable at Harvard. I was in no way prepared for a man no larger, no more knowingly attired, and on the whole no handsomer than myself, wearing an intelligent but markedly anxious expression, and speaking, when he infrequently did, in a rather low and hurried voice.

The fact that Mr. White was almost a miracle of protective coloration was, I'm afraid, a sad disappointment to me at the time, and even now, for the purposes of these notes, it remains something of an irritation.

There should be words and phrases in a writer's vocabulary to call up some recognizable image of his subject, especially when it is one he considers peculiarly interesting and important, but in Mr. White's case none come to mind at all. The other day at lunch in the Algonquin, I saw him alone at a table across the room, busy with a dish of cold cuts and a copy of the *New York Times*. With this composition already in mind, I observed him sharply, but nothing useful came of it. All that occurred to me, in fact, was that he was a remarkably modest-appearing man; that, to my astonishment, since I had never thought of him as being any age in particular, he was getting rather grey; and that it was a hell of a chilly day to be eating cold cuts, particularly in conjunction with the *Times*.

Since it seems impossible to do much with Mr. White's appearance or mannerisms, I suppose the next best thing is to deal with him in relation to *The New Yorker*. Insofar as a magazine can be said to have one, then, I think he has always been the literary and political conscience of that versatile weekly. In the beginning, and up to about 1935, this influence was mainly literary, since neither the moral climate of the times nor the tone of his publication was especially well adapted to crusades.

Mr. White campaigned vigorously against the maniacal streamlining of automobiles, claiming that a man ought to be able to get in and out of his car without scalping himself; against the custom of spraying fruit with arsenate of lead, for he has always had a morbid suspicion that science is out to poison him; against the peculiar coagulation of words in *Time*, asking reasonably enough how the human larynx is supposed to manage compounds like "radiorator" and "cinemaddict"; against the windier claims of the advertising profession, remarking once, I think, that it would be quite impossible for *his* mother to pilot her own plane from White Plains to New York. These were all worthy causes, of course, and I'm sure his heart was in every one of them, but still, during this period, what he was teaching his colleagues principally was how to write.

Mr. White's prose had almost nothing in common with the kind I had been instructed to turn out by the various men who had been in charge of my early education, but I had sense enough to realize that it was superior. Certainly, it was a revelation to me — never the remote and literary image, but always the precise and immediate one; never a sentence obviously distorted and ornamented in the interests of prose poetry, but never a dead one, either; never the studied, fatal rhythms of a man with a reputation for a fine style to cherish, but never on the other hand a line that in any sense disappointed the ear; never a word clearly chosen to startle or impress the reader, but a great many words never seen in just the same happy context before; and, above everything else, always a feeling of absolute confidence in the writer, in his ability to say exactly what he wanted to in the best possible way it could be said.

I am not very well equipped to discuss White's present political influence on his colleagues, because, happily no longer desk-bound, I don't get to the office as much as I used to, and so don't know most of them well enough to vouch for their opinions. Long before the war, when isolation was still actually an issue, I knew it was enormous, and that it might even be said that he not only guided social thought on *The New Yorker* but actually created it, when Notes and Comment in his hands moved on from its preoccupation with cigar-shaped automobiles and poisoned fruit to its first questionings of the philosophy of nationalism. It is proof of the extraordinary confidence everybody had in White that almost no one argued about the wisdom of a step that, essentially, changed *The New Yorker* from a parochial and still primarily humorous weekly into something quite different.

The issues now are different — more complex, if no more controversial. I gather that here and there White is considered a little unrealistic ("Fifty thousand years ahead of his time," one man is in the habit of saying, in, I guess, an admiring spirit), but his ideas are still printed on the Notes and Comment page, and therefore must be taken to represent the official opinion of *The New Yorker*. I am often very proud to be associated with it and with him.

FOR SOME UNFATHOMABLE REASON, All the King's Men *by Robert Penn Warren was not picked as a Selection of the Club. Yet here is Canby calling it "the most remarkable novel to come out of the South this year" (1946), a book that "establishes Mr. Warren as novelist of stature and scope."*

All the King's Men by Robert Penn Warren

THIS book establishes Mr. Warren as a novelist of stature and scope. It accomplishes what was attempted by another writer in the melodramatic *A Lion Is in the Streets*. That is, it tells in the round, and with every implication and realism, the rise to political power in a Southern state of a "Red-Neck," a poor white, who smashes the old oligarchy and invites his own final tragedy by making his will his god. Willie Stark, who becomes Governor, is a remarkable character by any standard of fiction. He begins as a naive innocent; is hooked for their own purposes by the politicians; discovers, when for the first time he gets drunk, that he can make the poor, mean, exploited share-croppers and small farmers articulate by speaking for them. As he grows in power, his moral fibre weakens, but he gives his people their roads and their hospital, and a sense they had almost lost of their dignity as men. Unlike most novelists, Mr. Warren does not merely describe the speeches that stir ten thousand — he prints them, and they also are remarkable. This is the story. Its telling is on the grand scale — too grand, for the early part of the book is clogged and moves too slowly. The book is very rich in characterization. Willie is like a gross magnet forced up out of the red soil, which, as it grows in power, attracts every type — the vixen, Sadie, who loves him, and the squashy politician, Tiny Duffy, who eats from his hand, and Anne, the pure type of intellectual aristocrat. Or if they do not come, like the uncorruptible Judge with a hidden past, he dragoons and smashes them. Jack Burden, the teller of the tale, is a disillusioned intellectual, proud of his skepticism. Indeed, the theme of this powerful book is by no means only the dramatic story of a democratic dictator. It is, inwardly, a study in moral skepticism, which has no moral but rather is a case history of what happens when you dirty your hands in order to get what you and the people want. But it is probable that most readers will overlook the philosophic theme in the drama and the diverse personalities of the novel. *All the King's Men* is surely the most remarkable novel to come out of the South this year.

HENRY SEIDEL CANBY

THE WAR ENDED *and immediately George Orwell broke into people's consciousness with* Animal Farm. *It was an important enough book for Harry Scherman to do something he seldom did: urge members to take the book. Three years later* 1984 *was made a Selection, "an account,"* Henry Seidel Canby stated, *"as realistic as if Daniel Defoe had written it."*

A Statement by Harry Scherman,
President of the Book-of-the-Month Club

FOR THE MONTH OF September the five judges of the Book-of-the-Month Club have again made one of their double selections — *The Sudden Guest*, an especially interesting novel about a New England character by Christopher La Farge, described within by Clifton Fadiman, and *Animal Farm*, by George Orwell, which is reported upon by Christopher Morley.... Not more than three or four times in twenty years, so far as I recall, have we advised members not to make use of their substitution privilege. We do so in this case; we do so because of the extraordinary character of the little book by Mr. Orwell. You will gather why in reading Mr. Morley's account of it. "It has been queer," he says, at the close, "to think of this book ticking away like an unexploded bomb deep in the middle of the crowded Main Street of our life. It caused a sensation when it was published in England.... When it came ... to your committee, we cried with one voice, 'This is It!' " So every reader will react, we are sure. Every now and then through history some inspired individual has spoken out for the people of a troubled era, and clarified their thinking by doing so. Just so does this little gem of an allegory express, perfectly, the inner but inarticulate philosophy of tens of millions of free men in our present anxious world. We strongly advise members not to miss this book, which, unlike Mr. La Farge's fascinating novel, calls for this emphasis because of its worldwide importance. Already it has been translated into six languages, and there is no doubt that very quickly, wherever else in the world men are free to read what they want, this book and its influence will spread.

Animal Farm by George Orwell

IN a narrative so plain that a child will enjoy it, yet with double meanings as cruel and comic as any great cartoon, George Orwell presents a parable that may rank as one of the great political satires of our anxious time. It has the effectiveness of the artist who knows how potent it can be NOT to say overtly what you mean. I doubt whether the more grimly documented record of social history could have the moving energy of this troubled allegory. It is plain enough that the satire is explicitly turned upon Russian communism, yet I also wish that the reader might see in it a parable even larger than that. For the impact goes straight to the forehead of any kind of Goliath, any monstrous totalitarianism. It is a smooth stone indeed, sped by a skilful slinger.

Old Major, the prize boar of the Manor Farm, was in his last days. He felt death coming, and had a dream which he wanted to impart to the other animals. They assemble secretly at night in the barn, pigs, dogs, horses, sheep, hens, pigeons — all the creatures of the farmstead, even those strong individualists the donkey, the goat and the cat. Old Major tells them of his vision in which they will no longer be overworked and underfed, exploited by Mr. Jones, the farmer, who is cruel, inefficient and often drunk. They will create a new civilization of their own, based on the simple test that four legs are good and two legs are bad. This will include even the fowls, since their wings are really a kind of legs, not instruments of tyranny like man's cruel advantage, the Hand. Then Major died and goes to his rest; the beasts of the farm find a chance to rebel. They drive out the Joneses and the hired men, and take over management. Animal Farm they call their Utopia. They fly a green flag with the emblems of hoof and horn; they draw up a simple constitution, which the pigs — the cleverest of the animals — manage to paint on the wall of the barn.

Animal Farm is not a fairy tale, it is a scary tale. Man, poor brute, has progressed only a little beyond his animal cousins; the deepest and simplest reports of man's trouble have always been told in animal analogues. The reader gets an extraordinary thrill as he sees, little by little, the sardonic or tragic parallels the author is working to suggest. One of the most skilled of Mr. Orwell's felicities is his adept characterization of the various creatures. There are the big hardworking carthorses, Boxer and Clover, sincere but slow-witted. There is Mollie, the vain self-indulgent carriage-mare; Benjamin, the cynical donkey whom no social doctrine will alter; and the shrewd evasive cat who always vanishes when there is work to be done. And, of course, the well-meaning silly sheep, who take to bleating in regimented chorus, "Four legs good, two legs bad!" — their comfortable answer to everything. There are the savage dogs, ready and eager to come to heel behind any assertive mastership. . . .

Naturally the pigs, with their quick wits and useful cloven trotters, take charge. There are the two rival boars, Napoleon and Snowball, and the slippery little diplomat, Squealer, who becomes official mouthpiece. With growing anxiety, and some malice of recognition, you see the innocent community of equal creatures transforming itself into (shall we say?) Party Lines. How come that the pigs commandeer the milk and apples and even move into the farmhouse? That the sacred inscriptions on the barn are mysteriously altered, or reinterpreted? How come that Snowball, inventor of the great Windmill Plan, is proved to be an enemy of the State? I mustn't tell too much; but ingenious as you are, you will hardly anticipate the ironic climax.

Perhaps, according to private instinct, the reader may identify himself with any of the various beasts of the story. We feel tears for the liquidation of Boxer, noble and helpless burden-bearer of the ideal state; or we may unhappily suspect ourselves as the cat, or the carriage-mare, or the sheep. Myself I enjoy this barnyard morality as I would Chaucer or Swift or Kipling's *Jungle Book* — with smiles and pity and a little cheery despair. Is it doxology or is it recessional? One experienced reader exclaimed that the little book is "The *Uncle Tom's Cabin* of our time."

One of the painful privileges of your surrogates (all privileges have their pains) is that they have to read books many months before they are published. It has been queer to think of this book ticking away like an unexploded bomb, deep in the middle of the crowded Main Street of our life. It caused a sensation when it was published in England. One of the most distinguished publishing houses in America shied away from it like a frightened mustang. But when it came, long later, to your committee, we cried with one voice, "This is It!" Because it deals, in terms simple and unmistakable, with the heaviest problem of mankind today; a problem that no one yet knows is solvable. It may be that the mass thrust of tribal instincts is too strong to be countered. Yet man is still a reasoning animal; even if he perishes he would like to know, in his agony, what it was that doomed him.

CHRISTOPHER MORLEY

George Orwell
by Henry Seidel Canby

MANY a man or woman, many a parent especially, has said, with a shudder perhaps, "What will our world be like after another generation?" Mr. Orwell's novel describes it as it can be in 1984, and his picture is sometimes breath-taking. It is an account as realistic as if Daniel Defoe had written it, of a society which is like a dreadful machine, where men have no security, where women are taught to hate love, where humor is dead, and the past absolutely wiped out. This is what life *may* be like for our grandchildren, if tendencies luridly visible in the

totalitarian states — and present sometimes alarmingly in the democra-
cies — prevail.

The scene is England, in a London where even the names have been
forgotten of once-famous buildings, now ruined by war. The hero is a
plain little fellow, Winston Smith, in blue overalls, the uniform of his
party. We follow him into his dirty apartment house where his first act
is to turn down — he cannot turn it off — the telescreen, which all day
and all night tells him what to believe, what to do, and how to do it, even
to his morning exercises. And always — except in the dark — what he
does, what he looks like while doing it, and what he says day and night,
come to the eye or ear of the Thought Police watching him through this
screen. Privacy is dead.

But Winston Smith is not an ordinary little man. He is one of the last
alive with some spring of rebellion in him. He still wants love, and the
thread of this story is a love affair crushed by the agents of a dictatorship
that distrusts the love of man and woman. Curiosity fans the spark of
independent thought in him. He goes out to re-see with new eyes this
upside-down Utopia. Food is almost uneatable. Books have been rewrit-
ten to extinguish "dangerous" knowledge. Truth about the past is wiped
out, history constantly is altered under his own eyes. Language has been
reshaped into *Newspeak*, by which you express *doublethink*, which
means to believe two contradictory things at once. Personality is a
cursed thing. There is no morality except obedience. The novel tells of
Smith's adventures, sometimes terrible with torture and treachery. It is
a melodrama of pursuit and detection, yes; but not of the cops-and-
robbers brand. What we are confronted with is the grim pursuit that
hangs over the heads of our children, and it is a chase that makes us ex-
amine our own life and times with a new eye.

Your committee have been deeply interested and powerfully im-
pressed by this book. It is not a prophecy of an inevitable future, but a
vivid story of what it *can* be like. They believe that no reader will forget
it, because there are enough present actualities all over the world, in
more than embryo, to make these dread developments not fantasy, but
real possibilities. The lesson is that, with modern technology as its
handmaid, Absolute Power can now result in a more degrading slavery
than anything all the ages past can show. The novel therefore is a
book — a great book, in this sense — of warning!

DECADE THREE

1947–1956

TWO JUDGES

FOR THE FIRST QUARTER CENTURY *of the Club's history, Dorothy Can-*
field Fisher and Henry Seidel Canby were the most influential members
of the Editorial Board. They were thus most responsible for what
Harry Scherman called "the wide reading over the nation of much of
the finest writing of our time." Dorothy Canfield retired in 1951, and
Canby retired in 1954.

In addition to his responsibilities with the Book-of-the-Month Club,
Canby was also the editor of The Saturday Review of Literature, *which*
he helped found in 1924. He was, said the historian Allan Nevins, "the
most constructive single figure on the literary scene." He died in 1961 at
the age of eighty-two.

Clifton Fadiman, who joined the board in 1944, once described
Dorothy Canfield this way: "She always sat at the table with her feet
perched on a velvet-covered footstool, for she was a tiny woman, con-
structed like a beautiful small bird and moving, even in her old age,
with birdlike grace and quickness. She was our conscience. Her culture
was deep, not by reason of erudition (though she was a good scholar)
but because it lay rooted in a truly moral universe of thought and feel-
ing." Nothing better characterizes the Canfield moral universe than
her letter to a member angered by a BOMC Selection she felt would be
compromising to her teenage daughter. When Miss Canfield died in
1958, Robert Frost expressed for the Club his feelings about "the great
lady of Vermont."

Editor's Note: Every now and then our Editorial Board selects a book which is questioned seriously by some subscribers who have teenage children. Recently Dorothy Canfield discussed this matter in a letter to a mother, who had addressed her about it. The point of view of the Editorial Board is set forth so well in her letter that the correspondence is printed below.

My dear Miss Canfield:

The Hucksters has recently been received by me, and partly read, and I am thoroughly disgusted and very angry. Coming so soon after *Arch of Triumph* is probably what has moved me to protest.

Those members of the Board of Judges who are parents must either be parents of older married children, or parents of very young tots. Certainly we who are parents of high school and undergraduate college students are heartsick about receiving books of this kind in our homes.

We can't ask young people that age not to read certain books, or hide them from them. But when I saw my nice young daughter pick up *The Hucksters* and start to read it, I felt positively ill and ashamed.

If there is a group of people whose entire conversation is made up of talk of sleeping with each other, and such dirty stuff, why should it be recorded and foisted upon us as good literature? What is wonderful and beautiful about a woman, married and the mother of two children, giving in to an infatuation for another man and going to a hotel with him? Are our children to read that and believe it is accepted conduct, or perhaps the smart thing to do?

Yours sincerely,
Mrs. M_____

Dear Mrs. M_____

Your letter of June 20th has just come through to me in my Vermont home, and I have such a fellow-feeling for you (I'm not only a mother like you, but a grandmother) that I am moved to sit down at once and answer as clearly as I can the various points brought up in your letter.

What is in question, of course, is the basis of selection for the Book-of-the-Month Club books. Three of the five members of the Editorial Board, Dr. Canby, Mr. Christopher Morley and I, are of Quaker background. That is, I think you will agree, a guarantee of our sober, careful upbringing in our youth, and of our recognition of moral values during our adult life. We have children and grandchildren, so that the whole gamut of the younger generation is very close to us. Mr. Marquand has young children, and so, I think, has Mr. Fadiman. I really think nobody could be more anxious to do the best thing for the young people of our nation than we five responsible, experienced Americans.

But if all the books written by Americans were arranged and restricted so that they could be read by inexperienced young people without shock or harm to them, we would have a very superficial literature indeed — suitable for the immature, but not for those facing the dark complexities of adult life. There are deep and black and grim parts of human life, about which every grown person has needed to meditate and reflect deeply. It might be said that novels could be divided into two classes, those intended solely to entertain or amuse or please, and those intended as invitations to the reader to deepen his understanding of the meaning of human life.

Fiction which is intended to inspirit, encourage and entertain young people is of a very different quality. There must be plenty of that, of course. But to restrict fiction to subjects and considerations suitable only for people under twenty would be very unfair to older people struggling with the deeper problems of life, who need help in interpreting what they actually find around them in twentieth-century life. It is unfair to people entering upon mature life, or in the midst of it, to make them think that human existence is other than what they find it to be. Reality — in fact — comes as a dangerous shock to those who have been led by the books they read to expect from human life something quite different from what any of us are likely to encounter.

I am an elderly (nearer seventy than sixty) rural Vermonter, and I am repelled as you are by what seems to me the overemphasis laid in modern novels on sex-relations. But I feel that if there is in our American twentieth-century life as it is lived by large numbers of people, in actual reality, such an overemphasis, with its resultant misery and dreariness, it would be ostrich-like for our serious novel writers to ignore it. No good is ever done, I think, by pretending that anything is different from what it really is, either in our explicit statement, or by implication. The prettifying of human relations in conventional old-fashioned, mid-nineteenth-century fiction, was responsible for some ghastly shocks when the readers of those pleasant books came up, in real life, against something which the novels they had read had led them to assume did not exist.

I wholly agree with you that inexperienced people should not be exposed, too young, to ugly aspects of adult life, even though such aspects are part of our nation's life, alas! How to protect them from such contacts, and at the same time not force our American writers to work on the juvenile plane, is a great problem to all those responsible for the welfare of the younger generation, and for the protection of literary standards.

But to ask that every novel written by an experienced, reflective author should provide, for young people, a guide to what is "accepted conduct" as you express it — that would result in very superficial and unreal fiction, not at all worthy of the great traditions of literature, which, we all hope, our great country will carry on.

The theme of *The Hucksters* is this, don't you think: the really horrible power over human beings of the greed for money and the really revolting results when men value money more than self-respect. Those men in *The Hucksters* who trembled so when the rich old tyrant came into the room — they were free, able-bodied Americans. Nothing in the world (save their own eagerness to make a lot of money) held them there to be insulted and humiliated by the rich man, as completely as the people around Hitler were insulted and humiliated. Any one of them could, at any minute, have put on his hat like a self-respecting man (as the hero finally did), could have left that horrible set-up, to earn his living like a decent man. The only reason they did not was because they couldn't resist the temptation to get more money from the disgusting old man than they would in some other work.

All in their personal lives that disgusts you and me and any other sane person, resulted from the nervous tension, panic, fear, and bitter self-contempt which filled their wretched lives. They were driven half crazy by their ignoble relation to that old man. Yet his only power over them was that he had money they wanted.

If there ever was a book which said at the top of the author's voice, "Stand up, straight! Keep your human dignity! Don't value money more than self-respect!" it is *The Hucksters*. What might be called its "message" is one which would be a salutary warning to any young person about to begin earning his living. The horrible coarse details are a part of telling truthfully this story of one corner of American commercial life.

We read in the Epistle to the Romans that "The wages of sin is death." But "moral death" is an abstraction that doesn't mean much to people without wide experience of human life. What the author of *The Hucksters* has done is to show what "moral death" really is, in terrible, frightening detail. We who live ordinary, respectable, self-disciplined lives, devoted to our families, surrounded by quiet, pleasant people, we are far away from such dreadful danger as that which ruins the lives of the employees of that coarse old millionaire. Yet an adored son of ours might inadvertently stumble across some analogous danger as he works for his living. We can hardly imagine them, and so could never warn our children against them. But I can hardly imagine a person reading *The Hucksters* who would not recognize, in real life, even in some quite different outer form, the terrible danger of valuing a high salary more than his self-respect.

The great question, of course, is at what age young people may safely begin to encounter, in soundly written books, some of the various aspects of that actual reality which faces them in their adult life. That question has to be answered differently for every young person, of course. And it is a question for parents and teachers. Fortunate are they whose parents put the best and most courageous thinking they are capable of, into getting the right answer to this vital question — as you are evidently doing.

If you really feel that the Book-of-the-Month Club should send out only books suitable for the reading of young people in their teens, or books which always ignore the dangerous moral failures so often made by men and women in real life, wouldn't it be better to cancel your subscription? For a few years, anyhow, it might be safer, till your own cherished younger generation have grown up to an age where they could with profit, begin to encounter, occasionally, in a book, some of the things from which no parent can wholly protect them in real life. Don't you think that perhaps just to keep out of the house any books you think unsuitable for young people might be the best solution of the problem you describe with so much sincere anxiety in your letter?

With every good greeting,

Faithfully yours,
Dorothy Canfield

From Robert Frost

DOROTHY CANFIELD was the great lady of Vermont just as someone else we all admire might be called the great lady of the United States. But there was more to it than just that. It was as a great storyteller with a book called *Hillsboro People* that I was introduced to her by her publisher, Alfred Harcourt, who was then my publisher too. There was nothing she was happier in then storytelling in prose and speech unless it was doing good to everybody and anybody. She came from all directions from as far West as Kansas and from as far East as France. She was brought up by a nomadic mother who pursued the practice of art in

Paris and New York. I believe she won her doctorate in Old French at Columbia University. But everything that ever happened or occurred to her converged as into a napkin ring and came out wide on the other side of it Vermontly. I don't know whether she realized it or not, but even the Basques she lived with and wrote about read to me like Vermonters. The people of her witchcraft story among the Basques might well be Ethan Allen's Green Mountain Boys. Her benefactions weren't restricted to Vermont (I consider her work with the Book-of-the-Month Club one of them). But of course they were most intimately felt there all up and down the state. She made it a welfare state. I remember her remarking that the Puritan word Commonwealth meant exactly the same thing. Her great good nature kept her from thinking too hard about doctrines, though she was plainly proud of a Vermont ancestry, Episcopalian, among the other sects non-conformist that came up from Connecticut and Rhode Island to settle the state. Alfred Harcourt brought our families together from a notion he had that the White Mountains we lived in were neighborly to the Green Mountains she lived in. Many are our family obligations to her. She is often in our thoughts. Only the other day my granddaughter fresh from college asked me about her young resolution to devote her life to doing good. I used a parable to make it out better to do well. She was unconvinced. Hers was the last word: "Wouldn't it be enough of an ideal to do good well — like Dorothy Canfield?"

In Memoriam

Henry Seidel Canby: Colleague and Friend

THOSE of us who, month after month, worked with Henry Seidel Canby on the Editorial Board of the Book-of-the-Month Club owe him an unrepayable debt of gratitude. His judgment, his balance, his scholarship over many years helped to make the Club not merely a successful enterprise but one whose success served to broaden and deepen the reading experience of millions of Americans. However, we who were his colleagues benefited more subtly as well as more directly from Canby. For at our monthly meetings, though he never knew it, he was our teacher.

No man is too old to learn; and, though some of us were of his own generation, we all learned from him. We saw how refined scholarship can adapt itself to broad public service. We were instructed by watching vivid enthusiasm tempered by a respect for the opinions of others.

With his death there passes a man whose virtues the present literary scene can ill dispense with: a certain sanity and kindliness of mind, a Quaker balance, a quiet morality that, never intrusive, nonetheless infused all his judgments. His roots lay in a century more given to these qualities, perhaps, than is ours.

Allan Nevins quotes Canby as saying of an associate, he "enjoyed his own mind." The remark is deeply true of the man who made it. But those lucky enough to be his co-workers will never forget how that enjoyment was transmitted as a continual gift to others.

JOHN MASON BROWN
BASIL DAVENPORT
CLIFTON FADIMAN
GILBERT HIGHET

HERMAN WOUK'S *most recent novel,* Inside, Outside, *was a 1985 Selection of the Club. His first novel,* Aurora Dawn, *was a 1947 Selection. In between, there came* The Caine Mutiny, Marjorie Morningstar, The Winds of War, *and* War and Remembrance, *among others. But* Aurora Dawn *brought Wouk his first notice, and for the occasion one of the premier radio comedians of the day, Fred Allen, wrote a letter of recommendation for Wouk. Who was Wouk? One of the things he was was gag writer for Fred Allen. ("The cannibal had a sweet tooth. He always ate a Good Humor man for dessert.") Read on.*

gentlemen:

i have just finished reading "aurora dawn."

"aurora dawn" was written by herman wouk.

this book is going to provoke considerable comment.

when "aurora dawn" is placed on sale, thousands of delighted book addicts, after regarding the unique arrangement of nouns, pronouns, verbs, adverbs, adjectives, conjunctions, prepositions, etc. and surveying the clever assortment of periods, commas, colons, semi-colons, hyphens, question and quotation marks, etc. that go to make up "aurora dawn", are going to ask themselves one question, to wit:

who is herman wouk?

readers will ask booksellers.

booksellers will ask publishers.

publishers will ask the man in the street.

as sales mount and the curiosity of readers, and denizens of book circles, gains momentum — asking "who is herman wouk?" may well become the country's leading industry.

this question must be answered.

who will answer it? i will.

february
22nd
1 9 4 7

dear mr. scherman...

herman wouk asked me to send you a few words on his book.

his request came when i was busy trying to write a radio program and attempting to help the tax man find out what had become of the money i made last year.

herman said you had to have something by monday or tuesday.

this did not give me much time to assemble a gem.

i read the book and think it is excellent.

have foaled some words (enclosed). if they suit your purpose — okay. if not — sue me.

sincerely...

Fred Allen

i am probably the only living man who
knows herman wouk.

this is the wouk story.

after herman wouk graduated from
columbia university, he came to me —
his diploma in one hand — a pencil
stub in the other. he wanted to write.
i engaged him and for five years young
master wouk helped me conjure up
humorous matter for my radio programs.
he contrived jokes (the cannibal had
a sweet tooth. he always ate a good
humor man for dessert. a doughnut is a
cookie with an enlarged pore.) he
interviewed people with odd occupations. (the lady blacksmith. the worm
salesman. the gas gentleman who
sniffed around subway stations to
trace leaks. the window washer at the
empire state building.) he wrote
sketches. (the g-string murder or
murder at minsky's. mountain justice
or the judge knew his gavel was broken
so he didn't give a rap. jack and jill
as orson welles might present it.)

wishing to better his financial position herman wouk left my employ and
journeyed to washington to become a
dollar-a-year man. he wrote and produced radio shows for the treasury department. his radio shows sold war bonds.

later, he joined the navy. he sailed six
of the seven seas and saw action in
all of them.

when the war ended herman wouk wrote
a book.

many service men wrote books about the
war. (guns over guam. okinawa osteopath.
mess boy at manilla, etc.)

herman wouk left the war to historians and
the men who returned home with diaries.

he wrote about radio and its weird folk.

"aurora dawn" raises radio's iron curtain.

it plucks the gardenia from the lapel of
the puffed tycoon and permits the reader
to peek through the vacant buttonhole
and observe frustration at its source.

it shows the obstacles cupid has to
overcome in the bewildering world of
commercial and jingle.

it proves that man is a neurotic
marionette who tries to cope with
bedlam as destiny jiggles his strings.

herman wouk has not dipped his pen
in the gutter.

he has written with the spirits of
addison and steele looking over his
shoulder nodding approval as each word
has been set in its place.

i think "aurora dawn" is an excellent
book.

i am sure that when you have finished
reading it, you will smack your eye-
lids and agree with me when i say
"aurora dawn should be the book-of-
the-month every month for the next
year."

— fred allen

WILLA CATHER *died in 1947, and Bernardine Kielty remembered this transplanted New Yorker.*

WILLA CATHER is such a hallowed name, and she herself was such an almost legendary figure within her own time, that it was a shock to learn, with her death, that she had long been living in New York — even as you and I; that she had strolled up Park Avenue in the sun to her apartment in the 60's, and gone perhaps to the same butcher and the same movies. If posterity ever localizes Willa Cather it will be as a Middle Westerner, because of *My Antonia* and *The Lost Lady* and *O Pioneers* and *The Song of the Lark.* She grew up in Nebraska, and as a girl used to visit among the foreign-born farmers who were the Cathers' nearest neighbors. It was their stories of the old country that first set fire to her imagination: "I have never found any intellectual excitement more intense," she said in later days. But she lived in New York for forty years — a quiet life with no fanfare. She loved music and doubtless went to many concerts. But she rarely, if ever, appeared at literary functions, and her name was never bandied about in columns. Her beautiful prose was her glory, and she came by that only by dint of hard work and self-abnegation. Like Flaubert she toiled for clarity and exactness, and like him, achieved timelessness.

HISTORICAL ROMANCES *dominated the bestseller list in 1947 with novels by such writers as Thomas B. Costain* (The Moneyman), *Kenneth Roberts* (Lydia Bailey), *Frank Yerby* (The Vixens), *Ben Ames Williams* (House Divided), *and Samuel Shellabarger* (Prince of Foxes). *Some books never make the lists but become classics after the fact — years after the fact. In 1947 Edwin Seaver, the promotion director of the Club, immediately recognized one such book as a classic. In his first sentence of his review of* Under the Volcano, *Seaver takes his stand. "This is a strange, difficult, agonized and altogether wonderful novel, quite the most beautiful writing (in my opinion) since D. H. Lawrence and James Joyce, whom Mr. Lowry more closely resembles." He goes on from there.*

Under the Volcano by Malcolm Lowry

THIS is a strange, difficult, agonized and altogether wonderful novel, quite the most beautiful writing (in my opinion) since D. H. Lawrence and James Joyce, whom Mr. Lowry more closely resembles. The characters are few, the setting Mexico — the realest Mexico ever intuitively grasped by an outsider, although, as the author says, "It is not Mexico, of course, but in the heart." The protagonists are the Consul, Geoffrey Firmin, his half-brother, Hugh, his wife, Yvonne, the ex-French, ex-Hollywood producer, Laruelle. A year ago Yvonne had had a brief affair with Laruelle, had gone away. It was just one more excuse for the Counsul to be drinking himself to death, one more spur to his atrocious loneliness and longing. Now she has returned, still loving him, still hoping to redeem him. Vain hope, since his will is for death, not redemption. Hugh, the leftist, the wanderer, the lost young man of our time, is there, too, for a brief visit. And that's all there is to the story, really. It's all "agenbite of inwit," played out on the lunar stage of volcanic Mexico, which in turn is the reflected image of the souls of the protagonists. It's what John Bunyan meant when he wrote: "Now I blessed the condition of the dog and toad, yea, gladly would I have been in the condition of the dog or horse, for I knew they had no soul to perish under the ever-lasting weight of Hell or Sin, as mine was like to do. Nay, and though I saw this, and felt this, and was broken to pieces with it, yet that which added to my sorrow was, that I could not find with all my soul that I did desire deliverance." (Good old John Bunyan to have summed up our modern malady so neatly!) The curtain descends on this theater of the soul with the murder of the Consul by some Mexican fascists, and of Yvonne in a ravine under the hooves of a maddened horse. Malcolm Lowry is a writer of genius. We have not seen in our time, and are not likely to see, many novels that can equal the brilliance and profundity of *Under the Volcano.*

EDWIN SEAVER

JOHN GUNTHER *was one of the most prolific BOMC authors. Over the years the Club offered seventeen of his books. In 1947, however, Bernardine Kielty wrote about the death of the Gunthers' son, Johnny, and two years later Amy Loveman reviewed* Death Be Not Proud, *a book based on that tragedy. William L. Shirer profiled Gunther on the occasion of a Gunther triumph, the publication of* Inside U.S.A.

Authors Between Books
by Bernardine Kielty

JOHN AND FRANCES GUNTHER'S son, Johnny, died in his eighteenth year, and was buried on July 2nd. He was a handsome, tall, fair-haired boy. He went to Deerfield Academy where he majored in mathematics and chemistry. For fourteen months he had suffered from a brain tumor for which he had had two operations. But even after the second, and about two weeks before he died, he passed his examinations for Columbia. He was one of the finest, bravest boys we've ever known. After his first operation, the doctors asked John and Frances about the advisability of telling Johnny what was the matter with him. He was so intelligently interested that the doctor thought it wiser to explain, and the older Gunthers agreed. The surgeon went to Johnny alone and told him the full gravity of a brain tumor. The boy listened carefully, then looked the doctor in the eye and asked, "How shall we break it to my parents?"

Death Be Not Proud by John Gunther

This is a touching memorial to the son of John and Frances Gunther who died at the age of seventeen of a brain tumor. Johnny was a boy of remarkable and brilliant intellect, who as a mere youngster was enamored of the wonders of science and mathematics, whose maturity of feeling and power of acute observation were notable, and whose strength of character as manifested through a long and harrowing illness was as striking as it is moving. He was at Deerfield Academy, looking forward to the time when he would be ready for Harvard, when he was stricken with what first appeared a slight illness and proved to be a mortal one. The horrified and devoted parents for a year tried every physician and every course of action which seemed to raise the faintest possibility of upsetting the original doctors' prognosis. The boy went through agonizing treatment, and made several apparently wonderful recoveries, only to die almost without warning at the end. His passionate desire for life, his unselfishness, his brilliance, his devotion to his parents and theirs to him, the range of his interests and the heroic determination which carried him through his studies, all come out in his father's narrative, which is heartbreaking in its implications but written with dignity. It is a tribute which fully realizes its intention of showing Johnny to others as his parents and his doctors knew him, and which fills the reader with admiration for the boy and the profoundest pity both for him and his parents. "He is not dead who lives in hearts he leaves behind."

AMY LOVEMAN

John Gunther

by William L. Shirer

Now that I stop to think about it, John Gunther has been trying all his life to get on the inside of things. It is a disease with him, and a passion. By the time I caught up with him in 1930 in Vienna, where we both represented Chicago newspapers, the disease and the passion had consumed him.

I suppose that was why he was never much interested in covering merely "spot" news, the happening of the moment that gets the big front-page headline. Most of us correspondents used to boast of having obtained a "world scoop" now and then. Gunther always maintained that he was probably the only reporter who had never scored a scoop on spot news — or at least the only one who admitted it. What interested him far more was to delve behind the news and get *inside* the situations, which in Austria or Syria or India or a hundred other places on this sorry earth, confused mankind and especially the readers back home. Getting the news was not enough. Understanding it and trying to make others understand it was more important. For that you had to dig and dig for a thousand facts and then relate them.

So far as I can gather, this trait, which made him one of the outstanding reporters in a generation of pretty good American foreign correspondents, developed at a ridiculously early age. He had turned all of eleven and had reached the fifth grade in a public school in Chicago, the city of his birth, when he decided it was time to write an encyclopedia — no less. He proceeded to do so and, as I recall, got through the first four sections, a matter of a hundred pages, with such fancy titles as "All the Necessary Statistics of the World," "The World's Battleships," "Greek and Roman Mythology with Genealogical Tables of the Gods" and "List of Species of the World's Animals" before he decided that such extracurricular activity, though fascinating and exciting, would have to be dispensed with if he were ever to pass has examinations in more prosaic subjects for the sixth grade.

But the encyclopedic turn of mind stuck and helped to make him the kind of journalist and author he is today.

Like a good many other American foreign correspondents (including the author of these notes) Gunther made his first trip to Europe on a cattle-boat. I don't know what there is about working your way across the Atlantic on a boat full of cows that paves the way to a newspaper career abroad, but there must be something. In Gunther's case, the effect was slightly delayed. He quit his cattle-boat in Liverpool, bicycled to London and promptly applied for a job with the local office of the *Chicago Daily News*. The resident correspondent thought he was too young (he was twenty, and had just graduated from the University of Chicago) and told him to come back in a year or two.

This he did — in 1924 — after a couple of years as a local reporter on the *News* in Chicago. The London office of the *News* rejected him again, this time for lack of experience. So he went to work for the United Press until the *News* finally gave in and took him on as assistant Paris correspondent under the venerable Paul Scott Mowrer.

In those good old days, the *News* was a great newspaper for a beginner in Europe to work on. All the *News* men were brought home regularly for three-month leaves-of-absence so that there was usually an important bureau to be taken over temporarily by the second-stringer from Paris. Thus Gunther found himself covering during the next few years London, Berlin, Rome, Geneva, Moscow, Scandinavia, the Baltic and the Balkans, and thus early acquired a first-hand knowledge of all of Europe that was to serve him in good stead in writing his first "inside" book.

The idea for it, he says, came from reading *Washington Merry-go-round*. Or rather, it came from his wife's reading it. Why not, she said in effect — one day in London where he had ended up in 1935 as correspondent of the *News* — do a "Merry-go-round" of Europe? He thought it over, wrote a few hundred pages of notes, flew back to all the major capitals of Europe to refresh his memory and gather the latest data, and settled down in London to see what kind of book it would make. Writing a book after a hard day's work as a correspondent is a grueling job, but by December he had completed a mountainous manuscript.

What would he call it? He didn't know. He felt a title was important. But he couldn't think of one. His publishers and friends suggested a dozen. He didn't much like them. Finally it was decided to call it "Thunder Over Europe" — or something over Europe, at any rate.

One dismal winter afternoon, sitting in a decrepit diner on a train taking him back to London from Wales, where he had been investigating conditions in the Welsh coal mines, an idea struck at him out of the blue. He sat facing some cold mutton, a glass of lukewarm British beer and the London *Times*. The dispatches in that venerable journal, he reflected, somehow got *inside* a situation. That was what he had tried to do in the book — get *inside* Europe.

On the margin of the august *Times* he scribbled a couple of words: "Inside Europe." That night in London he cabled them to his American publisher.

For the next five years the inspiration of that winter afternoon kept him busy. There was *Inside Asia* in 1939 and *Inside Latin America* in 1941, not to mention several revisions of the first book. And for the last twenty-seven months it has kept his nose to the grindstone in his study of his native land, reviewed in this issue.

I have an idea that Gunther has his life-work cut out for him already, whether he knows it or not. After *Inside U.S.A.* there ought to be an "Inside Washington, D.C." Then there is the great dark continent of Africa to be considered. And the cataclysm of war, which has changed

the face of both Europe and Asia, makes practically new books on those
two continents necessary.

That is not all. I forgot to mention that the man has also written five
or six novels. At least three of them, the ones I've read, were exceptionally good. I want some more of them, too.

THREE FIRST NOVELS *were reviewed by the Club in 1948. Two were*
war novels, the third "polished and elegant . . . precocious and preten-
tious, young and decadent." With these books, three brilliant careers
were launched.

The Naked and the Dead by Norman Mailer

TO AVOID misunderstanding it is best to state at the outset that this
long, ambitious, and, in many of its parts, distinguished novel is not ac-
ceptable literary fare for the conventional gentle reader, whose blood
pressure will rise and who will no longer be gentle if he finishes it. Aside
from many moments of stark horror, *The Naked and the Dead* has a
larger vocabulary of plain and fancy four-letter words than I have ever
seen in print, and is conclusive proof that literature is at last released
from prudery and, some might add, from many limits of common decency. Yet so, too, were most American soldiers whose prototypes
march through Mr. Mailer's pages. Their language here is the correct
language of camp and beachhead, no better and no worse than usual
war-theater talk in the recent conflict, and Mr. Mailer's frank dialogue
gives his enlisted men a startling stamp of authenticity and renders their
desires, sufferings, hates and fears poignant without sentiment or exag-
geration. *The Naked and the Dead* is the story of a division's assault on a
Japanese-occupied island in the Pacific, from the rendezvous of the
transports offshore to the final securing. It is a broad and admirable picture of mass military effort, told in the terms of a large group of diverse
individuals, all of whose motives and pasts are revealed before the book
is finished. There is an unforgettable vividness about many of the
scenes. Among them a tropical storm, a night attack, a drunken soldier
seeking for souvenirs among the Japanese dead, and a reconnaissance
march through the island jungles will remain long in any reader's memory. There is a fine authenticity in all of Mr. Mailer's writing. His realism never conceals his sensitive understanding, and his skillful character

delineation gives his battle scenes a significance that is never reportorial. Parts of the book may be too long, much of it is uneven, but more of it is some of the best war fiction that has been written in a long while.

JOHN P. MARQUAND

The Young Lions by Irwin Shaw

THE action of this enormous narrative begins in 1938 and moves through the war years, the final scenes occurring during the Allied occupaton of Germany. An extraordinary variety of backgrounds is called into play: fashionable New York and Hollywood, the Tyrol, wartime Paris, London, Berlin, Dover, North Africa, Normandy during the invasion, the German concentration camps. The three characters who do their best to weave into a pattern the rather loose threads of the story are Michael Whitacre, who represents, one supposes, the nearest thing to an ironic observer of events; Noah Ackerman, for whom the war is Gethsemane and who, perhaps alone of all the dozens of characters, is ennobled by it; and Christian Diestl, the young Nazi, who degenerates under its stress until at the end he is little more than an animal. Possibly the most memorable character is Christian's tutor in totalitarianism, Lieutenant Hardenburg, the fanatical epitome of the permanent, unchangeable spirit of German militarism. Merely to name these few characters, however, is to give no hint whatsoever of the extraordinary variety of scenes and people conjured up in this ambitious attempt at an up-to-date American translation of *War and Peace*. With it one of our most brilliant short-story writers makes an impressive debut as a novelist. His book, for all its faults, offers remarkable scope and variety, a copious narrative flow, and a precise reflection of hundreds of facets of our experience of the war. Its technique, as one might expect, resembles that of the short story. This gives the novel an episodic quality, but it also enables Mr. Shaw to obtain effects of concentrated power (effects which in a few cases lead him perilously close to theatricalism). That it tries to do too much is perhaps a prime weakness. Another is its frequent garrulity, while some readers may find the romantic episodes a bit too tropical. When all these strictures have been made, and when it is admitted that its parts are finer than the whole, the book remains one of the most notable American novels evoked by the Second German War Against Mankind.

CLIFTON FADIMAN

Other Voices, Other Rooms by Truman Capote

THIS curious and perverse first novel is the work of a talented young author who lives in New York and hails from New Orleans. It has to do with Joel Knox, a thirteen-year-old boy who spends a summer at a place called Skully's Landing in the swamp country of southern Mississippi among people he has never seen before. These people include a paralyzed ghost of a father, a stepmother who stalks bluejays with a poker, a queer, decayed, exquisite Cousin Randolph, an ancient gnome of a Negro by the name of Jesus Fever, his daughter, Missouri Fever, whose giraffe-like neck bears a terrible scar left by a man who tried to slit her throat, and so forth. Joel himself is a trifle morbid, as who wouldn't be in such company. Even the house is definitely depressed; it's sinking into the earth at the rate of four inches a year. The nearby abandoned Cloud Hotel looks as if Death has long been the sole guest. Mr. Capote has genuine showmanship; his eerie stage has a phosphorescent glow, and the characters who flit across it and talk to themselves are as elusive as any people you ever met in a nightmare. Brilliant in its surface descriptions and in its creation of moods, grotesque and inhuman but also polished and elegant, at once precocious and pretentious, young and decadent, the book is at least original.

EDWIN SEAVER

A MAJOR *and influential editor for almost fifty years writes about a major author.*

W. Somerset Maugham
by Ken McCormick

THE MASTER of English prose was born in France, spoke French before he spoke English and likes Spain better than any other country in the world although he makes his home in France. This set of paradoxes is not at all out of line with a man who has lived his own life, as he wished to live it.

William Somerset Maugham, "Willie" to his close friends, was born January 25, 1874 in Paris. Both his parents were dead by the time he was ten. He was sent to his clergyman uncle in Whitstable, England, to live in a religious background while he went to public school. This agonizing period of Maugham's life is recorded in the early pages of his autobiographical novel, *Of Human Bondage*. His brothers were going into the law and his uncle preferred that William should go into the ministry. Since his stammer seemed to handicap him for either law or the cloth, medicine was selected as a happy compromise. He went, uninterested in medicine, but fascinated by the thought of leaving his uncle's home to live alone in London. He began his study of medicine in St. Thomas' Hospital across the Thames from the Parliament Buildings in one of London's slums, Lambeth. For the first two years he was bored and studied only enough to pass his examinations. He used his spare time and much that he created as spare time, for reading and writing. With his third year as an interne he began to come in contact with the suffering public and at last was interested because here was the human nature he so wanted to study in order that he might write about it more honestly. Out of the experiences of these years came his first novel, *Liza of Lambeth*.

Once he had completed his study of medicine and was qualified as a Member of the Royal College of Surgeons and a Licentiate of the Royal College of Physicians in 1898 he lost all interest in that profession and set out to be a writer. From London he went to Spain and from Spain to Paris where he wrote and starved for ten years during which he met striving fellow authors, poets and artists, among them Arnold Bennett. During this struggle his plays went unproduced, his novels and short stories unappreciated even though published. But in 1907 his play *Lady Frederick* suddenly became a smash hit in London and from then on he never had a slump in his tremendous success as a writer. The next year four of his plays were running simultaneously on London's Strand.

For several years his time was completely occupied with the theater but in 1912 he rewrote an unpublished novel completed in 1898 for which the publisher refused at the time to give 100 pounds advance royalty. It was called *The Artistic Temperament of Stephen Carey*. When it was published in 1915 it bore the title *Of Human Bondage*.

At the outbreak of World War I he enlisted with a Red Cross Ambulance unit to put his medical experience to practice but was soon changed to the Intelligence Department and sent to Switzerland. Out of his secret service experiences he later wrote *Ashenden; or, The British Agent*.

During this time he married and became the father of a daughter who

herself has had two children. Mr. Maugham, the grandfather, is not as
familiar a figure to the public as Mr. Maugham the writer but he does
not take the responsibility lightly. He finds in his grandchildren a rather
active new study in human nature. Mr. Maugham was divorced in 1927
and has not remarried.

With the end of World War I, with his continuing success as a playwright, novelist and short story writer, the world lay open to him for
exploration. He has always been a traveler by instinct and could never
pass a boat without a desire to get aboard. He has never stayed long in
any country and has traveled over the world many times. Even his
World War I intelligence work gave him opportunity to travel and sent
him to Russia by way of the United States and the South Seas.

Mr. Maugham has been asked which of his twenty-two novels,
twenty-four plays, ten books of short stories, six volumes of essays and
travel impressions, and one autobiographical reminiscence will live to be
read after his death. He answers that a writer's works enjoy a very precarious and unpredictable life after the writer's death. In his own case, if
anything survives, he feels that it will be one or two plays and three or
four short stories.

In 1928 he found the one place he considers home, Villa Mauresque,
on Cap Ferrat in southern France near Nice. It is a villa with a patio and
terraced gardens rising to a swimming pool which overlooks the Mediterranean. Here he lives, entertains, and writes. World War II interrupted this happy life and sent him to America where he did some war
work for the British government. But, although the Italians sacked Villa
Mauresque, the Germans occupied it, the French looted it, and the
Americans used it as a convalescent home, he repaired its bomb damage
and lives there again in splendor.

Although he has never made his home there Mr. Maugham has spent
a great deal of time in Spain, from the time when he was twenty-three
and wrote *The Land of the Blessed Virgin*, to his numerous trips which
led to the writing of *Don Fernando*, to the more recent writing of his
novel *Catalina*. During a trip to Spain this year he discovered that not
only was he the best selling foreign novelist in Spain, he was the best
selling novelist in Spain.

Mr. Maugham is a man of tremendous self-discipline who has earned
his artistic position through, among other things, never deviating from
his work habits which are to write three hours a day, usually in the
morning after breakfast and before lunch. He reads a great deal, swims,
walks, and plays cards. He has a stammer and finds conversation stren-

uous but does not shun it. He is seventy-four and plans to retire as a professional writer next year with the publication of his notebooks which he is at present editing. Even at seventy-four he demands the most of himself and when he found that one window of his study on the roof of Villa Mauresque afforded too distracting a view of the Mediterranean, he had it bricked up.

NEVER *let it be said that BOMC members were ever culturally deprived. Fun and games also figured in the mix. (A book on baseball even became a Selection in 1972,* The Boys of Summer *by Roger Kahn.) The author of this review is the long-standing* New Yorker *sports authority Herbert Warren Wind.*

The Babe Ruth Story by Babe Ruth

As Told to Bob Considine

WITH the assistance of Bob Considine, Babe Ruth has produced an autobiography that lacks the charm of candid confession, is less witty than several objective studies of the Babe, and has the ready morality of a Hollywood scenario. And yet, for all these filterings of the Babe's personality, Ruth's story of his career should have more general appeal than any other baseball book of the past few seasons (with the possible exception of Jackie Robinson's autobiography) because it is fundamentally such a very good story, and Ruth tells it warmly and unhurriedly — the bleak days at the "reform school" in Baltimore run by the Xavierans, the youngster's escape from that world because he could play ball, his first days of glory as the rookie pitching sensation of the Boston Red Sox, his sudden emergence as the greatest long-distance hitter the game has ever known, who made his boasts good and his managers gray, his tragic departure from the big-time, and his gradual resurrection. Throughout the narrative, Ruth never takes his eyes off the Kids of America who three generations ago "made" him, and to whom today he must still report like every good living legend.

HERBERT WARREN WIND

BERNARDINE KIELTY *describes Greenwich Village then and now,*
"now" being circa 1948.

Authors Between Books
by Bernardine Kielty

GREENWICH VILLAGE before World War I was the Latin Quarter, the
Left Bank, Bohemia, its twisted short streets lined with old three-story
brick houses, its inhabitants old-time Irish Ward-ers. Washington
Square lay on its east, the most beautiful square in all New York, and
the Hudson River docks beyond Greenwich Street, dangerous and dark
under the 9th Ave. El, on the west. This out-of-the-way corner of New
York was a find for struggling artists and writers. MacDougal Alley,
Milligan Place and Patchin Place, Grove and Christopher Streets,
weren't "quaint" in those days, they were cheap. Garrets and abandoned stables were easy to get. In many of the bare-floored studios, the
girl — or wife — was the wage-earner, while her man worked long
hours at his easel or bent over his typewriter. This was Radical. This
was not 1913 of Uptown and Accepted Society. But the girls were
happy, and the men they protected and comforted and supported in
time became famous. The men's names are now known to the world, the
girls mostly forgotten — lost, no doubt, in middle-aged married anonymity in Dubuque or Florida or Park Avenue. Intellectuals and Fabian
Socialists and Anarchists, workers for Woman's Suffrage, mingled with
the artists. They ate at Gallup's when they were poor, and at the Bre-
voort when they were flush. Rich hangers-on hadn't yet begun to come
down to the Village, as they did later, to pay the bills in exchange for the
thrill of Bohemia. But just as the *Dome* and the *Cupola* and tourists
have changed Paris's Left Bank, so Nut Clubs and Swing Bands and
Shoppes and apartment houses with high rents have buried forever the
old Greenwich Village. . . . It was the death of Susan Glaspell that
started people remembering — Susan Glaspell who was not only well
known as a writer, but was also one of the founders of the Provincetown
Players, along with her husband, George Cram Cook, and other old-
time Greenwich Villagers — John Reed, Eugene O'Neill, Mary Heaton
Vorse. . . . Two books of reminiscences, which came out this past
spring, describe this long-ago romantic scene — Max Eastman's *Enjoyment of Life* and Alyse Gregory's *The Day Is Done*. Both books express
the frankness about life and casualness about convention, which marked
that "age of reason," that kept the air charged with excitement and

uncertainty and plus-values in happiness, even though that happiness might be short-lived. . . . Joe Tinker's death was on the same page with Susan Glaspell's — Tinker-to-Evers-to-Chance. There may be just as good shortstops coming up, and 2nd basemen and 1st basemen, but there never will be another real Greenwich Village.

WINSTON CHURCHILL *is the champ of the Book-of-the-Month Club — members have bought more than six million copies of his books and sets of books. The record begins with* Blood, Sweat, and Tears *in 1941, continues through the six-volume* The Second World War, *and concludes with the four-volume* A History of the English-Speaking Peoples. *Harry Scherman introduced the first of the war volumes,* The Gathering Storm.

The Gathering Storm by Winston S. Churchill

NO GREAT BOOK has ever begun more modestly than this one. "I do not describe it as history," says Mr. Churchill, "for that belongs to another generation. But I claim with confidence that it is a contribution to history which will be of service to the future." Yet it is not unlikely that this work will be placed, by later appraisers, in the company of Thucydides and Gibbon. For like them it deals with one of the momentous eras of human history; and like them, it makes Olympians of its readers. "So long as the English language is understood," said the *New York Times*, in introducing the book, "these and other words of this versatile and controversial world figure, to whom so many owe so much, will probably be read." Such is the dominant reaction of all who have read *The Gathering Storm* in its entirety.

This beginning volume — the first of five, all now well laid out and well launched by Mr. Churchill — is itself divided into two parts. The great predominant theme of the first half is stated by Mr. Churchill himself: "How the English-speaking peoples of the world by their unwisdom, carelessness and good nature, allowed the wicked to rearm." It can be set forth even more pithily, also by Mr. Churchill. At one time President Roosevelt asked him what he thought the war should be called for historical purposes. "The Unnecessary War," was his instant reply. In a majestic marshaling of fact the first half of the book is devoted to demonstrating the tragic truth of that judgment.

In the second half, "the gathering storm" breaks, the war begins and goes through its first fateful year, until — in one of the most appalling moments of history — the Nazis burst forth and engulf Western Europe. Then his own dismayed people and the whole world turn to this sole man, to save them from one of the greatest catastrophes that have ever threatened the sons of men. This, of course, is unsaid by the author. But there it is, in the record. He is unanimously nominated to be Atlas, with a wobbling world put on his shoulders. And he does not blench. After being called to this great duty, he writes: "Although impatient for the morning, I slept soundly and had no need for cheering dreams. Facts are better than dreams." These are the last words of the book.

"This is a unique man," said one of our judges, "like one of Shakespeare's characters." But he is unique not alone as a natural leader of all men and women of good will, during a great crisis of humanity. He is unique today as a writer; he is a master of that rolling sonorous style which has always been characteristic of the tradition of English at its best. And among men of action he is also unique, this book demonstrates, in possessing the sweeping vision of a great historian. He knows and has pondered history, and can place our times, confused as they have been, within it.

We who live today have had the destiny and privilege of being participants in one of the crucial eras of human history. Yet it can be said straight, no one of us can hope to understand fully the momentous happenings we have lived through, without reading this book. The Book-of-the-Month Club is deeply proud to present it to members, and to be instrumental, as they too will be, in spreading its illumination wide among the American people.

HARRY SCHERMAN

DEATH OF A SALESMAN *was the first play to become a Selection of the Club. A biographical sketch of Arthur Miller accompanied the Selection report. It was written in 1949 by Katharine S. Rosin, the daughter of Harry and Bernardine Kielty Scherman, and a gifted author in her own right.*

Arthur Miller
by Katharine S. Rosin

ONE SPRING VACATION, at the University of Michigan, Arthur Miller decided to write a play. It was an unremarkable decision, one no doubt made by hundreds of stage-struck and ambitious college boys. But in Arthur Miller's case the impulse was mysterious. He himself does not know what led to his decision. At the time he was neither stage-struck nor uncontrollably ambitious. He had only seen one play in his life, an item called *Fog* at a now defunct theatre on 86th Street and Broadway, about which he remembers nothing. He had read only three plays, the titles of which he cannot recall, and which did not specially impress him. He had had the usual Shakespeare course, which inspired him with nothing more than the usual literary admiration. Out of his head, mysterious and full-blown, came the compulsion to write a play. It was a crude play, nothing more than dialogue, really, but the impulse was genuine, for it won him the Avery Hopwood award and was produced by the WPA.

His background, up to that time, had not been conducive to literary ambition. Born in what is now Harlem and brought up in the Midwood section of Brooklyn on a street of small one-family houses, his childhood was typical of that in any American suburb. His father, one of the biggest coat manufacturers in the country, had lost everything in the 1929 crash, and young Arthur had to work at odd jobs every vacation. At the age of twelve he built a porch on the family house entirely by himself, paying twelve dollars for the lumber. While still in high school he took a job in the garment district, at that time still largely non-unionized, and in the turmoil of strikes and depression. His experiences on this job provided him with the material for the ten-day playwriting spree at Michigan which won him his first award. Between jobs and school he played football and went to the movies.

Out of this unspectacular pattern of childhood, so similar to that of millions of depression children, has come the pattern of his writing. The very ordinariness of the people he knew, the sad and small events of lives constantly on the verge of destitution, the unremitting drudgery of ill-paid workers, the half-desperate, half-optimistic spirit of the people who are the backbone of America's tremendous production — these were materials that he did not have to find in books, because they were part of his own life. He has remained happily free of the inverted, class-conscious snobbery of the educated proletarian. Longshoremen and shipfitters are still his friends, but in a perfectly natural way, because they have worked together.

His personal life, too, has stayed largely within the pattern. He has lately made enough money to buy a pleasant old house in Brooklyn Heights, within sight of the harbor. He is a real New York City boy, and feels he would not be quite happy anywhere else. But although he

loves Brooklyn he lacks the traditional fanaticism about it; his interest in
the Dodgers is purely academic. His lovely, dark-haired wife, whom he
met at college, runs the house and two very small children with pleasant
efficiency, with the help of one maid. They spend summers and weekends in an ancient Connecticut house which has been remodeled till
only the old beams remain. Last summer he built himself, single-
handed, a one-room studio on the four-acre grounds. He also spent part
of the summer working in a nearby fruit orchard. Although he has been
making an adequate living since 1942, when he got a radio job writing
plays, he continues to take odd jobs on the waterfront or in local fac-
tories when he has time. He likes the life and feels that it keeps him in
touch with a reality that is lost in New York City's insular, ingrown intellectual life — the reality of actual physical production. He is a genius
with his hands and gets a real joy out of building and fixing things and
in mastering the technique of a new job. During the war he spent two
years as a shipfitter in the Brooklyn Navy Yard. His most recent job was
a phenomenally short one in 1947 — three days in a box factory.
Though rejected in the draft he was assigned to do an Army story for
Hollywood and did full stints in five U.S. training camps, keeping a
diary which resulted in the movie *The Story of G.I. Joe* (which he
walked out on after the producers assigned another writer to work with
him; his dose of Hollywood lasted him the rest of his life).

When at work on a play or a novel he does nothing else, but gives
writing his full energy. *Focus*, that remarkable, hard-hitting novel about
suburban anti-Semitism, was written in six weeks at white heat. Hardly
a word had to be revised. The same was true of *Death of a Salesman*. In
all his wide job experience, by the way, he has never been either a salesman or an office worker, his chief characters in the play and the novel.
Office work, he feels, is a slow death, and his shy, slow-speaking reticence would, he thinks, make him completely unfit to sell anything.

In playwriting he might be called a natural genius. He owes few debts
to his predecessors and none to his contemporaries. After his Michigan
success he settled down to study plays, reading everything from Greek
drama to Ibsen. He feels that he learned something, largely a philosophic approach to drama, from the Greeks, and something of natural
human tragedy from Chekhov and Ibsen. Among modern playwrights
he admires most Sean O'Casey and Synge. His technique in *Death of a
Salesman* is his own; a three-dimensional, almost stream-of-conscious-
ness approach which gives the play the below-the-surface thickness of a
novel. This tall, thin, pale young man with the gentle, bony face, the

rough voice, the Brooklyn accent and the slightly forbidding reserve, has a remarkable sureness within himself. It is not the aggressive cocksureness of a successfully clever intellectual, but a sympathetic, philosophic, humanistic sureness that comes from an understanding knowledge of himself and the people he chooses to write about.

THE CLUB *offered two books by A. B. Guthrie,* The Big Sky *and* The Way West. *In his appreciation of Guthrie as historian, Bernard De Voto says, "What we know now is that with Bud Guthrie, the pioneer West has found its novelist at last."*

A. B. Guthrie, Jr.
by Bernard De Voto

BUD GUTHRIE couldn't talk yet — this is no time for laughter, men — when his parents moved from Indiana to Choteau, the metropolis of Teton County, Montana. But there is a tone in his voice as unmistakably Hoosier as Middletown, Elmer Davis, or a Monon express four hours late. Choteau made a Westerner out of him and added Standard American to his speech, slowing the tempo a little because in Montana everything is so far from everything else that there's no sense in hurrying. When he grew up he went to Kentucky, which gentled it and added overtones of mint and bourbon. It's a voice that has sat round a lot, on the banks of the Wabash, on the gates of corrals, in the court-house square, telling stories. It comes from and observes a threefold tradition of storytelling. Indiana, Montana, and Kentucky add up to lots of stories, as you realize shortly after meeting him. Presently you realize that they add up to quite a novelist too, a born novelist.

They add up to Bud, or shall we say Mr. A. B. Guthrie. He must have been in a hurry sometimes — after all he was a newspaperman for twenty years — but there has always been time for another yarn. They're good ones, too, even when he is usurping my turn. Well, there's his voice, and then you notice his eyes, which are very much a city editor's. He's been scalped a little but the years did it, which is too bad, for if Bud could have played it his way it would have been the Blackfeet, Teal Eye's People.

He knew the Blackfeet on and off the reservation from early boyhood;

he went to school with some of them, rode horses with them, picked up a lot of lore from them and a lot of stories. His boyhood was in the midst of contemporary archeology, for Teton County is pretty young and the Old West was only a minute ago. There were cow ranches and wheat ranches at the end of the street and everywhere there were the variegated remnants and holdovers from the frontier, so that Bud came to know the realities and the mythology of the gold rushes, Indian fighting, bullwhacking, railroad building, and the emigration as naturally as boys at P.S. No. 20 come to learn about Joe DiMaggio and Captain Marvel.

Teton County is the biggest country in the world. It's where the plains break against the Rockies. It can be the loneliest country as well, and the cruelest, as it sometimes is in Mr. Guthrie's books, a country where the casual violence of both men and nature has to be taken for granted. For a lot of people, and Bud turned out to be one of them, it is the most beautiful country too. He must have been pretty young when its loneliness and loveliness and ruthlessness began to shape in him a desire to get hold of all of it even before it was Montana. For the disease of ferreting out Western Americana and when possible buying them is so far advanced in him now that it must have had a long start. You cannot say that history has been a lifelong study for such a man, for what it obviously has been is a lifelong love. What he was after was the Western past but he was after it not as history but as life. We know why now.

He headed east eventually and not long afterward hit Lexington, Kentucky. He and the town liked each other and he stayed there, reporting the local news, copy-editing, running the city desk, adding politics to his inquiries, gathering up anecdotes, and mastering a local art that is based on a glassful of crushed ice. Here was another society with a great pioneering tradition, the first place that the American with the sunset in his eyes headed for, as Montana was just about the last. There were more frontier legends to collect, more old-timers to listen to, and a whole race of pioneers to think about, for the Kentuckians beat even the Missourians to the Rockies. There were also plenty of rare-book dealers who might have that item about John Bozeman, Father Revalli, or the Missouri Company, only six copies known, and if the kid can't wear those shoes to school he can go barefoot, can't he? The yeasts were working now; the need to get the pain and beauty of the Old West into words was growing on him. He was one of the newspapermen who were going to write a novel.

The Nieman Foundation was established to improve the standards of American journalism. Eventually it got round to Bud Guthrie and brought him to Harvard for a year and improved American journalism

by lifting him right out of it. For that was the year he wrote a novel —
and it turned out to be *The Big Sky.* The next thing you or Bud knew he
wa a Big Name and a Professor at the University of Kentucky. Now he's
got a ranch out from Choteau a way, where he spends his summers and
where the local talent are going to take the dude from Lexington and
Harvard for a fine ride. A Western proverb says that it takes a gold mine
to run a silver mine, and the professor who tries ranching on the side is
headed for the cleaner's.

With *The Big Sky* an imagination finer, more subtle, and more powerful than had ever before worked in fiction of the early West came mature
in a single book. It had a rightness, an inevitability that you recognized
at sight and had to marvel at. It was the experiece of men passed through
a mind disciplined by love and learning, and it was also one of our greatest national themes interfused with tragedy. It was distilled from a deep
and true feeling for the wilderness and for the nation which the wilderness begot and which in turn destroyed it. It was also distilled from
those years of mapping with a man's heart the biggest, cruelest, and
most beautiful country.

It was only the first act, for now there is *The Way West.* It is the only
novel about the Old West of which one can say that it is better than *The
Big Sky.* What we know now is that with Bud Guthrie, the pioneer West
has found its novelist at last.

Why mail *doesn't get delivered. Bernardine Kielty explains.*

IF A CERTAIN SUBSCRIBER does not get her mail from the
Book-of-the-Month Club, here's why: the Post Office, when it returns
undeliverable mail to the sender, checks one item on a form list of reasons — "Unclaimed," "Refused," "Unknown," "For better address,"
"No such office in state." Recently, however, a Yankee postman was
stuck. A letter was returned from Charlestown, Massachusetts, with the
indignant message written by hand on the envelope: "Undeliverable,
dangerous dog."

JOHN HERSEY'S *first novel,* A Bell for Adano, *won a Pulitzer Prize in
1945. The next year, as a journalist, he visited Hiroshima. (The book
that resulted from that trip was presented to BOMC members as a Pro*

Bono, a gift from the Club.) And in 1950 came The Wall. *Accompanying the Selection Report was a piece by Norman Cousins, who was then editor of The* Saturday Review of Literature. *Cousins talked about* The Wall, *but also about a visit he had made to Hiroshima and the impact Hersey's* Hiroshima *had on that tragic city.*

John Hersey: Journalist into Novelist
by Norman Cousins

A VISITOR to Hiroshima these days is asked many questions about America. But there's one question that's close to the top of the list. It doesn't matter whether you're talking to the Mayor or the local "Bar-Bar," as one of the local haircutters advertises himself — the leading question is about a person. Not about the President or the Secretary of State or famous generals or even famous movie stars. The person they want to know about is John Hersey.

The first night I arrived in Hiroshima, I had dinner with the Mayor and about a dozen community leaders. The conversation was only a few minutes old when the name of John Hersey came up. Did I happen to know the man who had done so much for the city? Was there any chance that he might revisit Hiroshima, so that the people might tell him directly how highly they regard him as an author and as a person? How was he? What was he doing now? How old was he? Did he have a family? What was his reputation in America?

I told them such facts about John Hersey as I happened to know — that his parents were missionaries and that he was born in China; that he came to America as a young boy and went to school and college here, graduating from Yale about twelve or thirteen years ago; that he became a secretary and assistant to one of the most important of American writers, Sinclair Lewis; that he became affiliated with *Time* and *Life* magazines, for which he was a war correspondent on both fronts; that prior to *Hiroshima* he had written an account of war in the Pacific, *Into the Valley,* and a novel about the American army coming into Italy, the now-famous *A Bell for Adano.*

I told them that I was proud to know Mr. Hersey, that few authors in America enjoyed greater esteem among the American people and, indeed, among their fellow-writers. I told them that the same qualities the people of Hiroshima had admired in Hersey's book about their city — compassion without sticky sentimentality, an almost monumental integrity, an eloquent simplicity, a basic respect for his craft — were the qualities that had brought him to the fore among American writers while still a young man of 35. I told them that he was happily married, lived in Connecticut with his attractive wife and three small children (was wrong about this; there are four), that he was active in the life of his community, especially with respect to schools, and that he was far removed from the cocktail-party world of plush, glamour, and tinsel which is associated with successful authors in the moving pictures that come from America.

At this point, Dr. Fujii, who had been sitting at the far end of the table, spoke up. I was especially interested in what he had to say because he was one of the central characters in Hersey's *Hiroshima.*

"I am glad to hear this," Dr. Fujii said. "You know, when he was here speaking to me, and when I looked at him, I said to myself, 'This young man is the type of American the great President Lincoln must have been. He even looks like the pictures of Lincoln I have seen in the history books. He is slender and tall — one of the tallest men I have ever seen anywhere. And he is so understanding and sympathetic.' "

The next day I visited Dr. Fujii at his rebuilt hospital to find out more about his recollections of John Hersey. Business was slow at the moment and Dr. Fujii was listening to a play-by-play broadcast of a Japanese big-league baseball game. (Baseball broadcasts excite even more interest in Japan than they do in the United States. In the large cities, public loudspeakers on the streets enable the populace to go about their business or to walk from one section to another without losing any of the continuity.) Because of the use of American baseball terms, it was possible for me, with a little translation by Dr. Fujii, to follow the game, then in its late innings.

"Mr. Hersey, he is a remarkable man," said Dr. Fujii over a glass of Japanese beer, after the game had ended. "Everything in his book was just as he said it was. It was remarkable to see how accurate and careful he was with the facts. When he came to visit me, I didn't know that he was a journalist. You see, many Americans had come in to interview me in the ten months since the bombing — some of them were doctors, others were investigators for the American or Japanese government, and I thought Mr. Hersey was one of them. He had sent in his calling card. It had some Chinese characters on it and some American writing. I have kept the card. If you would like to see it, I have it here in my wallet. It's become one of my prized possessions."

Dr. Fujii carefully handed me the calling card. It was easy to see that it had been exhibited in this fashion many times, for it showed signs of wear despite the obvious care given it by Dr. Fujii. In addition to the Chinese characters and Hersey's name, the card listed *The New Yorker* and *Life* magazines, for which Hersey was correspondent, and his New York City address which was his home at the time.

"I did not know at the time," said Dr. Fujii, "that these were the names of magazines, and that Mr. Hersey was a famous correspondent, so I gave him brief answers. When you see him and give him my best wishes, please remember to apologize for my brevity. It was very interesting to see that he remembered every word of our three-hour conversation."

Two days later, I visited one of the other central characters in *Hiroshima* — Mrs. Nakamura, the dressmaker. She still lived in the one-room shack in which John Hersey had interviewed her. Slits and holes in the sodden walls were stuffed with paper and cardboard, and everywhere there were signs of severe privation and poverty. But there was nothing depressed about Mrs. Nakamura. Her manner was cheerful and she was full of optimism for the months ahead. After the initial exchange of pleasantries, she said:

"And do you know Mr. Hersey? He is such a wonderful man. I so enjoyed meeting him. Every time I think of him, I have to smile, because he is so big and this room is so small. He sat on the floor as you are doing now, with his feet propped up in front of him, and it seemed as though his legs filled the entire room. He was so friendly and kind, and many nice things have happened to me since he wrote about me in the book. I have made friends through the mails with many Americans."

As did Dr. Fujii, Mrs. Nakamura paid tribute to John Hersey's accuracy, and expressed admiration at his ability to remember all the tiny details.

I mention these conversations because they highlight, it seems to me, two things about John Hersey that contribute the most to his stature as an important American writer. The first is his conviction that human values, human feelings, and human experiences are the basic building blocks of writing — no matter how sweeping or seemingly abstract the event written about may be. This holds for non-fiction and fiction both. The second is a deep sense of purpose in his writing — the feeling that history-in-the-making calls for the most painstaking care and research, the ability to devote oneself to the task at hand, however time-and-energy-consuming that may be.

These are the ingredients of integrity in a writer, and nowhere are they more in evidence than in *The Wall* — to which John Hersey had devoted much of his time since early in 1945 when, as a correspondent in Russia, he was taken on a tour that included Estonia and Poland. What he saw in the concentration camps, then being liberated, and in what had once been the Ghettos, convinced him that Americans must be told exactly what had happened, so far as it was within his ability as a writer to ascertain the facts and to present them. At first, he thought he would write about it in a series of articles, but when he consulted all the notes and research materials, he decided that a book would be required.

But the biggest part of the research was yet to come. A year went into further digging here in the United States — talking to survivors, examining material sent to this country, going through translations of thousands of letters and newspapers. After many months of actual writing, he decided he would have to scrap everything he had done, despite the fact that the book was almost four-fifths complete. He felt that his book needed a central character around whom the story could develop. It was not enough to tell what had happened in the Ghetto in terms of actual experience; he wanted to get inside one person and make *his* story. He started from scratch again. The result is a novel that will do as much for the reputation of contemporary American literature as for Hersey himself.

THE NORMALLY *acidulous Evelyn Waugh gives us a delicious portrait of Nancy Mitford. Here he is on his best behavior.*

Nancy Mitford
by Evelyn Waugh

IN a world where almost everything becomes daily more uniform and more drab, it is a joy to contemplate the recent metamorphosis of Miss Nancy Mitford. Visit her today. You cross the Seine and penetrate into the very heart of the fashionable quarter of Paris, the Faubourg St. Germain. You go to a quiet side street, so exclusively aristocratic that few taxi-drivers know its name, and ring at a great, white, shabby door which in due time opens, revealing a courtyard surrounded on three sides by low buildings of the period of the restored Bourbon monarchy. Straight in front, on the ground floor, with its glass doors opening into a garden behind, lie the apartments of Miss Mitford. She greets you in a Dior dress, her waist so small that one fears it may snap at any moment. This is the only waspish thing about her; all else is sweetness, happiness and inexpressible levity. She leads you to her salon, full of the exquisite *bibelots* she has amassed, and talks, prattles, giggles — of what? Gossip, outrageous, incredible, entirely funny; of the art of the three great Louis, scholarly, precise, discriminating; of France, with schoolgirlish enthusiasm. Miss Mitford has a crush on France and everything French. You may not even remark in her presence that the matches are bad. She is expecting friends. Whom? Either formidable dowagers of the very *gratin* of French society, or the most discredited bohemians from across the Channel. On each she showers an equal, loving regard, but she does not mix them. She is too wise a bird for that. She will talk of everything — of politics idiotically, of all except her beloved *grand siècle* barbarously — but she speaks little of her own works. You would not know that she has a comedy, adapted by herself from the French, running to enthusiastic audiences in London and New York and that her works are daily reaching a wider and more appreciative public.

How did this delicious creature come into being? Cast back to her home. She is the first of the long line of daughters of Lord Redesdale, a retiring but violent nobleman who is still happily with us. Suffice to say that the portrait of "Uncle Matthew" in *The Pursuit of Love* is thought, by those who know the family best, to resemble him. All the Mitford daughters are beautiful and wildly individual. They include a member of an American left-wing party, an English duchess, and a lady who spent most of the war in prison on unspecified charges of Nazi sympathies. The upbringing of these enchanting objects might be expected to have produced eccentric results. Their mother imposed the Mosaic diet upon them under the belief that Jews never suffered from cancer. It was a common spectacle for guests at the Mitford breakfast table to observe the fair, blue-eyed, long-legged future duchess tucking pork sausages up her knickers to consume in secret. Their father forbade them paint, powder and publicity. Awful storms shook the house when he detected scent on their persons or found their photographs in the *Tatler*. Nancy received no education at all except in horsemanship and French. Liverish critics may sometimes detect traces of this defect in her work. But she wrote and read continually and has in the end achieved a patchy but bright culture and a way of writing so light and personal that it can almost be called a "style."

She married the Hon. Peter Rodd, the second son of Lord Rennell, an ambassador best known for his early friendship with Oscar Wilde. Peter is a man of conspicuous versatility, an explorer, linguist, seaman, boon-companion and heaven knows what else, of startling good looks. With not much money between them Peter and Nancy settled in London in the criminal quarter behind Paddington Station, where their house was much frequented by homeless drunks and socialists. The Rennells had one or two houses in Italy and when the London slums became op-pressive the young couple would slip away to the sun. Nancy at inter-vals wrote her early works, full of private, evanescent jokes, which never enjoyed much success outside the circle of her own friends.

Then came 1939. Peter, of course, went off immediately with the army. Nancy remained in London reveling in the comic incidents of the blitz. Entirely fearless, entirely frivolous, she giggled among the falling bombs, working at the same time tirelessly as Air Raid Warden for her *louche* district. When the dust cleared from the first heavy bombard-ments, she found herself penniless and took work in a Mayfair book-shop, which she quickly made a center for all that was left of fashionable and intellectual London. When we came on leave, we always made straight for Nancy's shop, confident of finding a circle of old friends who had become dependent on their daily dose of Nancy's gaiety. There is at least one American sergeant who will remember those long, laughing sessions among the buzz-bombs.

Then came peace and welfare. Most of us settled down glumly to the drab world about us. Not so Nancy, who, having voted socialist and so done her best to make England uninhabitable, broke from her chrysalis, took wing and settled lightly in the heart of Paris where we find her today. Her present, glittering book (*The Blessing*) gives a picture of what she finds there.

*J. D. Salinger's Catcher in the Rye did not make the annual fiction bestseller list in 1951. (*Franny and Zooey *did ten years later.) Never-theless, it was a sensation and a bold and powerful choice by the Edito-rial Board of the Club. William Maxwell, a friend of Salinger's and his editor on* The New Yorker, *describes how the young author "works like Flaubert."*

The Catcher in the Rye by J. D. Salinger

THE PLEASANTEST task your Editorial Board can undertake is the spon-soring of a brilliant, new, young American novelist, such as Mr.

Salinger. Perhaps, come to think of it, "brilliant" is an unsatisfactory adjective, for one may be brilliant and have little to say. Brilliance is born merely of a smooth reflecting surface. Mr. Salinger, however, reflects in both senses: he has polish *and* depth. His book arouses our admiration — but, more to the point, it starts flowing in us the clear springs of pity, understanding and affectionate laughter.

The hero of *The Catcher in the Rye,* sixteen-year-old Holden Caulfield, tells his story in his own way. When we first meet him he has just been dismissed from his school, fashionable Pencey Prep. He decides to leave for his New York home at once, before the Christmas vacation starts. The story is simply an account of the ensuing forty-eight hours, crazy, desperate, pathetic hours, and, to the reader, often hilariously funny. We seem to eavesdrop upon poor Holden's very soul as he pours out his story, unconsciously revealing his every confusion, his idealism and vulgarity, his fascination by and fear of sex, his hatreds and aggressions, his loneliness, his desire to love and be loved.

We see Holden saying good-bye to the school to whose standardized code of behavior he cannot adjust. We overhear him on the train to New York as he engages in a fantastic conversation with the mother of one of his fellow-students. In new York, unwilling as yet to face his parents, he goes to a cheap hotel. From this point on his adventures comprise a kind of Walpurgis Night of adolescence, involving a mad attempt at elopement, incredible talks with taxi-drivers, an unconsummated encounter with a lady of easy virtue, too much drinking, much mental suffering, and much sharp, critical insight into the nature of his own maladjustment.

Through all the unwisdom and tawdriness of his wild conduct he is somehow sustained by certain symbols of goodness — the two nuns he meets in the course of his errant pilgrimage, the recollection of his dead brother, and, above all, his sister Phoebe, one of the most entrancing small girls to be met with in fiction — or real life. Holden's relationship with Phoebe is the tender heart of a story that is only superficially hardboiled. It is a relationship quite without sentimentality; it is completely unself-regarding; and it is poignant and funny at the same time.

Beneath Holden's fears and guilts and wildness and lies is a profound talent, one feels, for love. What he admires most (he would call this sentence "corny") is the one thing his modish, horrible prep school cannot give him, the one thing his gilded-youth associates cannot give him, the one thing his un-understanding parents cannot give him — the experience of purity of soul. Holden wants to be good; he despises the cheap, the phony, the insincere; but his world is such that few virtuous alternatives are offered him. He does ugly things and despises himself for it. He is in dire need of a code nobler than that adhered to by the young barbarians about him. In fact, he seems to be suffering from an unsatisfied thirst for goodness; and, insofar as that would seem to be the whole world's trouble nowadays, *The Catcher in the Rye* contains implications of general import.

One reads it, hardly knowing whether to chuckle or cry, for Holden, unaware that he is either, is both ludicrous and pathetic. His is the age of uncertainty: he does not yet know whether he is boy or man. He uses his generation's silly slang, soiled by an occasional obscenity. That is his idea of being "male" and grown-up. His fetishistic affection for his hunting-cap, however, is that of a twelve-year-old.

He is a whole civil war in himself, divided between the natural instinct of herd-imitation and the fierce, confused passion to be an individual. He alternates between premature cynicism and the most charming generosity. He hates the world, he fears it, he conforms to it, he wishes to transmute it by love. At times he seems the misfit his parents, teachers and friends think him. At other times his integrity shines forth so lucidly that by contrast it is society that appears the misfit. His friend Stradlater tells him, "You don't do *one damn thing* the way you're supposed to"; but we wonder whether Holden, for all his eccentricities, isn't really superior to most of the sensible people he meets.

In Mr. Salinger we have a fresh voice. One can actually hear it speaking, and what it has to say is uncannily true, perceptive and compassionate. *The Catcher in the Rye* is a short novel; but its power over the reader is in indirect proportion to its length. Read five pages; you are inside Holden's mind, almost as incapable of escaping from it as Holden is himself. The portrait is complete and convincing. That rare miracle of fiction has again come to pass: a human being has been created out of ink, paper and the imagination.

CLIFTON FADIMAN

CONCURRENCE: This book will recall to many the comedies and tragedies of Booth Tarkington's *Seventeen*, but *The Catcher in the Rye* reaches far deeper into reality. To anyone who has ever brought up a son, every page of Mr. Salinger's novel will be a source of wonder and delight — and concern.

HENRY SEIDEL CANBY
AMY LOVEMAN
JOHN P. MARQUAND
CHRISTOPHER MORLEY

J. D. Salinger

by *William Maxwell*

JEROME DAVID SALINGER was born in New York City on January 1, 1919. So far as the present population is concerned, there is a cleavage between those who have come to the city as adults and those who were born and raised there, for a New York childhood is a special experience. For one thing, the landmarks have a very different connotation. As a boy Jerry Salinger played on the steps of public buildings that a non-native would recognize immediately and that he never knew the names of. He rode his bicycle in Central Park. He fell into the Lagoon. Those almost apotheosized department stores, Macy's and Gimbel's, still mean to him the toy department at Christmas. Park Avenue means taking a cab to Grand Central at the beginning of vacation.

Since there is no positive evidence to the contrary, it is reasonable to assume that people who have any kind of artistic talent are born with it. Something is nevertheless required to set talent in operation. With a writer I think what is required is a situation, something, that is more than he can hope to handle. At the age of fifteen, Salinger was sent to military school, which he not very surprisingly detested. At night in bed, under the covers, with the aid of a flashlight, he began writing stories. He has been writing ever since, writing constantly, and often in places as inconvenient as a totally dark, cold, school dormitory.

He was graduated from military school and went to college, in a manner of speaking — to several colleges; but he didn't let the curriculum interfere with his self-imposed study of professional writers. Sometimes the curriculum and his plans coincided, and he was able to take a course in writing. The other students went straight for the large themes: life and death. Salinger's choice of subject matter was always unambitious, his approach to it that of a craftsman.

In the midst of his college period, his father sent him to Europe for a year to learn German and to write ads for a firm that exported Polish hams. It was a happy year. He lived in Vienna, with an Austrian family, and learned some German and a good deal about people, if not about the exporting business. Eventually he got to Poland and for a brief while went out with a man at four o'clock in the morning and bought and sold pigs. Though he hated it, there is no experience, agreeable or otherwise, that isn't valuable to a writer of fiction. He wrote and sent what he wrote to magazines in America — and learned, as well as this ever can be learned, how not to mind when the manuscripts came back to him.

During the first part of his army service he corrected papers in a ground school for aviation cadets, by day; and at night, every night, he wrote. Later he wrote publicity releases for Air Service Command in Dayton, Ohio, and used his three-day passes to go to a hotel and write stories. At the end of 1943 he was transferred to the Counter-Intelligence Corps. He landed in France on D-Day with the 4th Division, and remained with it, as one of two special agents responsible for the security of the 12th Regiment, for the rest of the war, through five campaigns.

He is now living in a rented house in Westport, Connecticut, with, for company and distraction, a Schnauzer named Benny, who, he says, is terribly anxious to please and always has been. Salinger has published, all told, about thirty stories. How completely unlike anybody else's stories they are, and also something of their essential quality, three of the titles convey: *A Perfect Day for Bananafish, Just Before the War with the Eskimos,* and *For Esmé — With Love and Squalor.*

The Catcher in the Rye was originally a novelette ninety pages long. This version was finished in 1946, and a publisher was willing to publish it, but the author, dissatisfied, decided to do it over again. The result is a full-length book, much richer, deeper, more subjective and more searching. It means little or nothing to say that a novelist writes like Flaubert, since Flaubert invented the modern novel with *Madame Bovary,* and it is probably impossible not to write like him in one way or another, but it means a great deal to say that a novelist *works* like Flaubert (which Salinger does), with infinite labor, infinite patience and infinite thought for the technical aspects of what he is writing, none of which must show in the final draft. Such writers go straight to heaven when they die, and their books are not forgotten.

"A year or so ago," he says, "I was asked to speak to a short-story class at Sarah Lawrence College. I went, and I enjoyed the day, but it isn't something I'd ever want to do again. I got very oracular and literary. I found myself labeling all the writers I respect. (Thomas Mann, in an introduction he wrote for *The Castle,* called Kafka a 'religious humorist.' I'll never forgive him for it.) A writer, when he's asked to discuss his craft, ought to get up and call out in a loud voice just the *names* of the writers he *loves.* I love Kafka, Flaubert, Tolstoy, Chekhov,

Dostoyevsky, Proust, O'Casey, Rilke, Lorca, Keats, Rimbaud, Burns, E. Brontë, Jane Austen, Henry James, Blake, Coleridge. I won't name any living writers. I don't think it's right. I think writing is a hard life. But it's brought me enough happiness that I don't think I'd ever deliberately dissuade anybody (if he had talent) from taking it up. The compensations are few, but when they come, if they come, they're very beautiful."

WILLIAM SOSKIN, *an executive of the Club, catches* the *potency of* Invisible Man, *a novel Soskin sensed would become a classic.*

Invisible Man by Ralph Ellison

A BITTER, terrifying story, this novel about the American Negro makes books like Lillian Smith's *Strange Fruit* seem sedate. Sociologically it represents the disillusion of Negroes who have lost faith in the benevolent education movements, the Northern humanitarians, the "Uncle Toms," the nationalist fanatics, the Communist exploiters. As a literary work it is related to those early Faulkner pieces in which the sadistic and horrifying details leave an indelible impression of reality. The story takes a young Negro from Southern boyhood scenes of obscene torture and violence through his college days, during which he comes to understand the futility of education — if it is governed by politicans and opportunists, black as well as white. Eventually he reaches New York City and Harlem, where he meets every evil of the city's Negro proletarian life head on. Slapped around by employers and workers — especially white union labor — he is driven through various purgatories to arrive finally in the hands of the Communists, for whom he becomes something of a district leader. A considerable part of the story is a nightmarish account of the sinister men at the top of this Brotherhood — men who seem entirely monstrous as they pursue the Party line with no regard for human agonies or even death. The chaotic, desperate tone of the novel, written with no restraint or regard for formal patterns, reflects its subject matter accurately. This is reality unexpurgated, the reality of the bottom dogs of our civilization.

WILLIAM SOSKIN

A STILLNESS AT APPOMATTOX *by Bruce Catton was reviewed in the* News *in 1954, and two years later* This Hallowed Ground *was a Selection. Allan Nevins tells how Catton became interested in the Civil War and became one of our major interpreters of that epic period in American history.*

A Stillness at Appomattox by Bruce Catton

THE CIVIL WAR, disastrous and terrible as it was, provides our greatest source of material for national literature. Just when the well seems to have been pumped dry, some new vein fills it up again. Bruce Catton has, by combining old material with a fresh approach and new emphasis, writen a memorable book — memorable for the general reader at least if it does not provide anything of importance for the historian. He has taken the last twelve months of the war, the most desperate, the bloodiest, cruelest and most regrettable point in our national history, and has told of the events leading up to Lee's surrender in almost narrative fashion, creating a picture which is at once true, vivid and horrible. Catton presents battle and the problems and realities of command from the point of view of the common soldier as well as from his own critical point of view, and his overall picture of the strategy, through failure and success, of the Wilderness engagements and subsequent Virginia campaigns is excellent. We are approaching a time in which we may see the struggle between North and South in its true perspective, in which foreground things occupy the foreground and background things the background. Mr. Catton does not trifle with this arrangement. He allows waste, ignorance and error to occupy the foreground and in doing so takes nothing from the awesome spectacle of the background, the incredible durability and fitness of our Federal Union.

RAYMOND HOLDEN

Bruce Catton
by Allan Nevins

IN A cramped office high over Fifth Avenue sits Bruce Catton, busily editing that unique magazine *American Heritage*. On his desk lie manuscripts, pictures and letters; the window ledge back of him shelters a row of new books; a table crowding the single door holds more books and papers. He keeps his typewriter at his elbow to pound at any moment. "Too many contributions deal with the Civil War," he grumbles. With his quizzical smile he adds: "But I guess I'm as much to blame as anybody for *that* vogue."

It is true that Bruce Catton has not only contributed some of the finest books to our stock of true literature on the Civil War, but inspired a great deal of writing, good and bad, by others. His pen communicates a zest for the mighty drama that few can resist. Readers might think he had felt a passion for it from boyhood. The fact is that he grew up in a beautiful resort town on the eastern shore of Lake Michigan, Petoskey, without more than casual interest in the annual G.A.R. parade. When he spent three years at Oberlin College, it was to prepare for journalism, and when he took his first job in 1920 as cub reporter on the *Cleveland News,* his interests were strictly in the era of President Woodrow Wilson and Governor James M. Cox.

The Civil War, speaking in literary terms, has its regulars and its volunteers. We might call Douglas Freeman and Carl Sandburg, biographers of Lee and Lincoln, regulars, for they were hard at work from the early 1920s. Bruce Catton was a late volunteer who went through a roundabout course of training. Reporting successively for the *Boston American* and *Cleveland Plain Dealer,* he learned to observe, judge character and write. When in 1926, having recently married Hazel M. Cherry, he went to the Cleveland office of what is now the Scripps-Howard chain of papers, he broadened his range. For its feature syndicate, the Newspaper Enterprise Association, he wrote book reviews, Sunday supplement articles, editorials, interviews and what not, as ready as any graduate of Dana's *Sun* to turn his typewriter to human-interest material. But still he showed no bent toward history.

However, in these years he did make a great discovery — the regimental histories. In an old bookstore in the mid-1930s he chanced upon three or four of these first-hand war narratives and paid a dollar and a half for them. They enchained him. Students know that between 1865 and 1910 hundreds of these regimental stories, very predominantly Northern, were published. They are highly uneven, some being poor, many stodgy, and a select number minor classics. Catton had chanced upon some of the better titles. Here were jagged, fascinating bits of truth: the rough jokes, the sweat, the agonies of toil and mutilation, the delights of campfire ease, the beauty of mountain defiles, the soldiers' honest opinion of incompetent officers; above all, battle pictures which if crude were etched with unforgettable vigor.

When journalism took Bruce Catton east in 1939 to write a daily Washington columnn for the NEA syndicate, these regimental histories were fermenting in his mind. Now and then he bought another. But he was soon leading a hectically busy life. The country went to war, and he joined Donald Nelson's War Production Board as associate director and then director of information. "At the time, I thought Nelson did a remarkably fine job," he says; "later I had some reservations." In the last two years of the struggle he directed information for the Department of Commerce. He was learning much about war, its difficulties, surprises and intrigues, from the side of government.

Then came the hour of fruition. He was discontented with journalism, unhappy about his career. In 1947 he resolved to retire from daily stints and attempt larger literary tasks. Out of that determination came his first book, *The War Lords of Washington*, an account of WPB trials. Out of it, much more importantly, also came his first Civil War volume. He decided — those regimental histories in mind — to ascertain the truth about the often-betrayed, long-defeated and always glorious Army of the Potomac. He would tell its tale in the whole gamut from McClellan's delays, Pope's blunders and the mean jealousies among generals that cost the North repeated battles, to the glories won under Meade and Grant. Above all, he would tell it as the common foot soldier saw it.

But what should be the form? If fellow-historians envy Bruce Catton one quality more than another, it is his imagination. Like Motley and Parkman before him, he had enough imagination to want to write a novel. Contriving a plot, he turned off one hundred typed pages. Then he stopped, read his MS over and flung it down in disgust. His historical characters and scenes were splendidly real, but his fictional personages were hollowly unconvincing. The novel disappeared, but the history went on — the history that became *Mr. Lincoln's Army.*

Seldom indeed has a piece of military history gained such fervent and general applause as *Mr. Lincoln's Army.* The core of it was Antietam. Two and a half years of heavy fighting remained to be narrated, and Catton rose superbly to the challenge. His *Glory Road,* which carried the theme from Fredericksburg to Gettysburg, was admirable, and *A Stillness at Appomattox* finer still. In fact, we can say that Catton has climbed from height to height. Not able long to give himself wholly to a literary desk, he took a variety of jobs while he wrote books. He assisted Oscar Chapman in the Interior Department; he was Washington correspondent of *The Nation* in 1953–54. Then the historians claimed him, and right proud and happy they were to call him to the editorship of the new *American Heritage.*

Bruce Catton drives forward with an energy that amazes his friends. His editorial work, though he has devoted associates, seems a full-time task. He finds time to talk to the endless stream of writers who come up to his corner office, to answer his ponderous mail, and to read the books for his own bimonthly article, one of the best plums in the whole cake. Not able to decide whether his home is Washington or New York, he oscillates between the cities. He writes for magazines. Ahead of him lies a biography of U. S. Grant on the grand scale, for he will complete the structure for which the late Lloyd Lewis laid a solid foundation in *Captain Sam Grant.* Yet to sit down with him, to hear his rich slow voice in a genial appraisal of men or situations, to catch the shrewd twinkle in his eye, and to share his infectious chuckle, one would think he had not a care in the world.

IN MAY 1955 *a violent novel of Africa,* Something of Value, *was made a Selection. What was notable about this Selection was the dissent of a member of the Editorial Board, Amy Loveman. It was published alongside Clifton Fadiman's report.*

Something of Value
by Robert Ruark

IN THE long history of the Club, your judges have never recommended to members a book even remotely like Robert Ruark's *Something of Value.* It is an astonishing novel, and almost certain to become a record-breaking bestseller. Months before it was published Hollywood paid for it the sum of approximately $300,000 — unexampled, I believe. It will be condemned by many, hated by many. But it is impossible to take it lightly — provided one can take it at all. We bring it to the attention of our members because we ourselves could not lay it down. That is the basic and essential fact. It imposes itself upon the imagination not like a work of art, but like some monstrous event, like a great conflagration. In the circumstances, a few words of explanation, even of warning, are in order. Here they are.

Something of Value deals generally with whites and blacks in the

British East African colony of Kenya. It deals specifically with the recent outrages committed by members of the secret African terrorist organization known as Mau Mau. It deals equally specifically with the reprisals a scattered handful of white men have been forced to undertake, in order to protect their wives, their children and themselves from torture, rape, mutilation and murder.

The book is one of the outcomes of Mr. Ruark's repeated visits to East Africa during the past four years. It is clearly — perhaps, from the novelistic point of view, too clearly — based on facts. Your judges are not experts on Africa, and there is no way of checking completely on the appalling incidents that make up much of this book. Three things, however, must be said. The first is that Mr. Ruark's reputation as a responsible writer who tells the truth has never been called in question. The second is that what records do exist of the outrages of the Mau Mau (though not perhaps of the reprisals) confirm Mr. Ruark's picture. The third is more subtle: the book rings true. It carries so clear and dreadful an impression of genuineness that one accepts without question Mr. Ruark's statement: "The most unbelievable portions are actually a euphemized version of the truth. The actual detail is so utterly revolting and such an unlikely negation of human behavior that it does not suffer print."

Your judges have not chosen this book because it is shocking, though it is. On the other hand, all but one of them feel that they have no right to refuse it just *because* it is shocking. All they can do is be fair with the reader. This is not a book for children or for the squeamish.

The cast of characters runs to a whole population of black men and white men — savages, semi-civilized Africans, Americans, Englishmen, Indians and even a Russian or two. The scene is the mountains, plains and towns of Kenya. The events extend virtually to the present and go back perhaps fifteen years.

The main characters are Peter McKenzie and his Kikuyu companion, Kimani, whom we meet first when both are fifteen. We continue to follow their patently symbolical careers until their early middle age, by which time they have become deadly enemies. Into the ramifications of this story it is impossible to go. Mr. Ruark gives us an exhaustive description of the life of the hard-drinking, hard-loving, hard-talking British settlers. These are men (and women) who are as suited for the ultra-masculine life of the Kenya back country as they would have been unsuited to the more effete life of their English and Scottish forebears. Mr. Ruark admires many of them greatly; some readers may admire them less; but courage, endurance and a superb adaptability to the environment — all these qualities they possess, as did our own pioneers.

Into the story is also woven a fascinating account of the business (almost a profession) of being a white hunter, which is what the hero Peter becomes. I know of no book, fiction or non-fiction, as exact and detailed as is this one in its description of the slaughter of animals, the techniques of camping and trailing, the proper use of the proper machines for killing. Beside Mr. Ruark, Ernest Hemingway sounds like a tenderfoot. Whatever one may think of the author's characterization of human beings, he is superb with animals.

But what will come with even greater freshness to American readers is the picture drawn by the author, mostly in blood color, of the Kikuyu of Kenya and their tribal brothers. It is hard to understand how Mr. Ruark could have learned as much as he apparently has of their ritual ceremonies, their witchcraft-religion, their manifold cults of death and torture, and particularly of their weird manner of thought, which appears to go back to a culture of thousands of years ago. That, as a people, they are being victimized is clear. They are being victimized by an unhappy colonial tradition of exploitation. They are being victimized by their own devilish leaders who, with cold calculation, are releasing in them torrential forces of atavistic savagery. And, if report be true, they are being victimized by the agents of a foreign totalitarian power.

Through the implacable descriptions of torture and bloodshed run several love stories and a great deal of candid description of sexual scenes. Mr. Ruark does not deal in gutter language, thank Heaven, but again I must warn some readers that not all this will be to their taste. Life runs raw and hot in Kenya, among the whites as well as the blacks; and Mr. Ruark is no man for leaving anything out.

I have not mentioned the single great and simple quality that recommended the book to three out of our four judges. *Something of Value*, whatever its faults — and they are many — is obsessively interesting. It is interesting because the subject is grievously timely, touching as it does on the whole inflamed world problem of racial relations. It is interesting because Mr. Ruark is full of his subject, cramming his story with ten thousand exact and astonishing details. It is interesting — let us admit it — because it is shocking. And it is interesting because of its extraordinary energy, so ruthless and driving that one forgets Mr. Ruark's lapses of taste, his odd enthusiasm for people who to others will seem merely vulgar or snobbish, his inability to cut a scene short.

As a journalist-novelist's account of the appalling extremities of conduct to which our desperate century is being driven, *Something of Value* has a value no objective judgment can deny.

CLIFTON FADIMAN

A Dissent

by Amy Loveman

THIS IS an absorbing book, but many readers will find it a shocking one, as I did, and that is the reason I did not approve of its selection. It is not shocking in the ordinary sense of the word, for it contains no obscenity and no deliberate attempt at sensationalism, but shocking by sheer weight of its facts. Mr. Ruark is a journalist, with the journalist's flair for detail and the journalist's zeal for information, and his descriptions of the rites of primitive peoples and the horrors of the Mau Mau rebellion spare the reader nothing. This truly, it seems to me, is a case for the old admonition: *Caveat emptor.*

Robert Ruark

ROBERT CHESTER RUARK, for many years a widely syndicated — and widely traveled — newspaper columnist, was born in North Carolina and graduated from the University of North Carolina in 1935. His particular interest in Africa dates back to boyhood days, a seafaring grandfather having told him tales of Mombasa and Zanzibar and set him to reading books by Livingstone, Stanley and other travelers and explorers. He himself first visited the East African interior some four years ago, on a hunting trip, and was then so fascinated by Kenya that he planned to build a home for Mrs. Ruark and himself there. But a subsequent visit happened to coincide with the Mau Mau "Christmas Killings" of 1952, and still later visits brought him into further contact with the harrowing realities of present-day Kenya life. "I believe I know Kenya well," Mr. Ruark declares, "and I know I love Kenya and its people"; but he and his wife now make their home in Spain, where most of *Something of Value* was written. Its title is taken from the Basuto proverb: "If a man does away with his traditional way of living and throws away his good customs, he had better first make certain that he has something of value to replace them." It is his second book about Africa — *Horn of the Hunter*, a narrative of experiences on safari, having appeared in 1953.

IN 1956 everyone wanted to read the new novel about a Massachusetts political legend who bore a strong resemblance to a real Massachusetts political legend named James Michael Curley. Indeed, The Last Hurrah *was the number two bestselling novel of the year. But who was this author, Edwin O'Connor? Edward Weeks, a long-time editor of* The Atlantic Monthly, *explains.*

Edwin O'Connor
by Edward Weeks

THE Eddie O'Connor story is a success story in quiet dimensions. Here is a young Rhode Islander who had to start earning immediately on his graduation from Notre Dame in June of 1939; and who got out of business just as soon as he could to devote full time to his writing; who lived frugally in a furnished room; who wrote a first novel which was a *succès d'estime* (total American royalties $720) and a second which fell so short of his own standards that he suppressed it. Then he squared away on a really big book, the first of its kind, and made it good. This was to be *The Last Hurrah;* it won the Atlantic Prize; and it hit the jackpot. A few weeks ago Eddie said farewell to the obliging Boston landlady who had been taking his telephone calls for the last seven years, and moved out of Marlborough Street and up to a Beacon Hill apartment whose west windows have a superb view of the Esplanade. Twelve flights up in a refined, creeping elevator. It couldn't have happened to a nicer guy.

Eddie's intention was to study in the School of Journalism at South Bend, but Professor Frank O'Malley, the teacher who was his mentor in college, soon corrected that. "You can learn all you need to learn about journalism in six months," he said dryly. "English literature takes a little longer." O'Connor shifted his courses and began to read intensively.

He got his first job as a radio announcer with the Yankee Network, and Providence, Palm Beach, Buffalo and Hartford liked the sound of his voice. He wrote and produced radio shows, and in the process learned to write with his ears. He has an absolutely true ear for any dialogue in any lingo and is as accurate and devastating a mimic as I have ever listened to. Naturally enough, it is the lilt and cadence of Irish speech which appeals to him most, and it is this which adds such zest and versatility to *The Last Hurrah.*

Eddie's years in broadcasting gave him an abiding interest in radio and television and an equally strong determination to avoid that kind of

employment when he came back to civilian life after wartime service as
an Information Officer in the Coast Guard. His beginning as a free-lance
writer in 1946 was a modest one, financed partly by savings, partly by
his stint as a TV columnist for a Boston daily. He sold his first magazine
piece, a satire on radio, to the *Atlantic* in that year and his first short
story to it a year later. We soon learned that he is a fastidious worker
who goes over and over his manuscripts before submitting them, with
the result that there is very little editing left to do.

Eddie's first book, *The Oracle*, published in the spring of 1951, was
the story of a radio commentator who was, to put it mildly, a heel. It
earned him praise and — since the English edition did better than the
American — enough pounds to permit a visit to Dublin, which next to
Boston is his favorite town. While in Ireland he bought himself the
woolliest tweed coat which has ever been seen on a big man in Boston.
Then, royalties exhausted, he came back to do his television column and
his new writing. It took four years to finish *The Last Hurrah*, and at the
end of that ordeal Eddie was good and tired. Three different juries
passed upon the book, and when at last the news came through that Ed's
novel had won the Atlantic Prize, and after that had been selected by the
Book-of-the-Month Club and by the *Reader's Digest* — with royalties
reaching up to the stars — the wife of one of my associates threw up her
hands in despair. "How terrible!" she said. "He has no wife." Edwin
Greene O'Connor, to give him his full name, is a bachelor.

DECADE FOUR

1957–1966

EVEN THAT PROPER BOSTONIAN *of a Book-of-the-Month Club judge, John P. Marquand, claimed he was proud to be among the authors parodied in Peter De Vries's 1959 novel,* The Tents of Wickedness. *Marquand, in fact, called that novel "a work of art." Comic authors are generally elusive as people, as the nature of comedy is equally elusive. "Talking about theories of comedy," De Vries explained to David Willis McCullough in a 1976 interview, "is like a woman squeezing into a girdle that's too small. There are so many things to laugh at, nothing fits. There's always an overflow." There's more, too, by De Vries on humor, and on himself.*

The Tents of Wickedness by Peter De Vries

CRITICS who have followed the work of Peter De Vries have recognized his steady growth in skill and stature. The unevenness and surfeits so difficult to avoid in any long work of humor have become less apparent with every book he writes, until he is now known as one of the leading satirical humorists of our time. In *The Tents of Wickedness* he seems, to me at least, to have moved much further forward, beyond the topical and perishable Artemus Wards toward the level of Mark Twain. It is all too easy to become over-enthusiastic, in this era of confused and mediocre writing, when one encounters something of unusual brilliance. Yet even after rereading *The Tents of Wickedness* and after discounting its flaws — and of course it is sheer fantasy — I still harbor a suspicion that it is a closer approach to what may be termed satiric literature than anything I have read since I have been on the Board of Judges of the Book-of-the-Month Club.

To carry this brash statement a step further, I am willing to submit that one must go back to Laurence Sterne and *Tristram Shandy* and close to Cervantes to find the same quality of wisdom combined with slapstick drollery that Peter De Vries exhibits in these pages. I do not mean that these three writers are more than vaguely comparable, but they would have understood each other. I can only add that if anyone is skeptical let him read the book himself, but slowly. Nothing need be skipped. It abounds in both barbed and kindly humor, understanding and superb parody.

The Tents of Wickedness, like most of Mr. De Vries's other works, begins in the vicinity of Westport, Connecticut, the stamping ground in these days of so many literary frustrations. Here we find our hero, Charles Swallow, seated in his bathtub, swimming against a stream of consciousness, from which he is rescued by his wife, who asks him to get in the car and call for the new baby sitter, who turns out to be a girl named Sweetie Appleyard and also an old high-school flame of Mr. Swallow's. From here on we find ourselves off the ground, moved by the power of the De Vries levitation into a Never-Never Land nearly as strange as any ever faced by Lewis Carroll's Alice. It is not long before we discover that Mr. De Vries is using his device of plot and structure strictly as a vehicle to take his readers on a modern literary pilgrimage. Actually the whole fantasy may seriously be termed an excellent survey of recent and contemporary literature, providing, in the form of a sequence of brilliant parodies, a more accurate and vivid picture of current intellectual vagaries and fashions than dozens of textbooks recently published. By following the adventures of Charles Swallow and Sweetie Appleyard we find ourselves conducted through worlds of thought beautifully illustrated by parodies of verse and fiction. All our old literary friends are here — among others, Faulkner, Scott Fitzgerald, Elinor Wylie, Dylan Thomas and James Joyce, with the famous Joycean washerwomen speaking their dialogue in a laundromat.

It seems to me that Mr. De Vries's gift of parody lies in the area of genius. Always sharp, always hilarious, he never is malicious and never makes his point by taking advantage of obvious weakness. Instead, every one of his long list of poets and writers is illumined and explained, not degraded.

The pace of *The Tents of Wickedness* never lags. It may be that this air of high-strung, almost breathless farce is the book's main fault, but it is hard to be overcritical when such hilarity and comedy are combined with an artist's perceptiveness. From any standpoint the book is a work of art — one that should, and perhaps will, eventually be read in college courses on comparative literature, and for this reason, among others, I am proud to be among the authors parodied in its pages. Almost anyone who begins this book is certain to respond to its high quality of entertainment and to continue to read with increasing delight. If that is the purpose of good writing, there is no doubt that Mr. De Vries has achieved it.

JOHN P. MARQUAND

Peter De Vries
by David Willis McCullough

PETER DE VRIES, who over the past thirty-six years has written some of the funniest novels published in the United States, said recently that he wondered "why people seem to want permission to laugh." Critics, he says, delight in pointing out the darker shadows in his novels, as if to justify the humor. "Ministers keep asking me to give sermons on the crises of our times. Maybe it's because everything is going to hell in a handbasket, just as I've been saying for years."

Princeton Theological Seminary once offered him its annual L. P. Stone Lectureship. The lectureship was established in 1883 to "provide a lecturer, chosen by the faculty, to speak on a topic related to theological studies." De Vries says, "I assumed it was a clerical error and declined."

"Everyone seems to have a theory about humor. Analysts talk about what we laugh at, but not why we laugh. I don't think you can separate laughter from grief. It's like talking about H_2O and not talking about H or O. Faulkner was our greatest comedian. No one has been funnier, and no one has been more bitter than Thurber or Twain. Talking about theories of comedy is like a woman squeezing into a girdle that's too small. There are so many things to laugh at, nothing fits. There's always an overflow."

De Vries claims to be especially fond of mimicry and impersonation. "It's a bewitching art, and it isn't simply the joy of seeing genius deflated. The parodies you most enjoy are of people you like the most." His new novel, *I Hear America Swinging*, a jaunty yarn dealing with what happens when the greening of America hits the tall corn of Iowa, begins with a parody of Walt Whitman: "I hear America swinging, / The carpenter with his wife or the mason's wife, or even the mason, / The mason's daughter in love with the boy next door, who is in love with the boy next door to him, / Everyone free, comrades in arms to-gether, freely swinging. . . ."

I asked which came first, the novel or the parody. "I can't ever re-member the original idea for a novel once it's finished," he said. "I think it is like blotting out the pain of childbirth." What really came first, dat-ing back more than a decade, was the debut of Clem Clammidge, the novel's "primitive art critic," formerly a hired man. Clem made his first appearance — wearing a plaid hunting jacket and a cap with earflaps — in a brief item De Vries planted in a column in the *Saturday Review.* It told of this strange bumpkin who was causing quite a flap in local New England art galleries by turning up at openings and making homespun comments on what he saw.

"I thought it was time for a primitive critic," De Vries recalls. "It seems that the simpler the artistic endeavor — say, pop art — the more arcane the criticism of it seems to become. I was just trying to cut things back to size."

With seventeen books to his credit, De Vries looks fit and hardy, al-though he says he has to watch what he does and what he eats because of a mild heart condition ("fibrillation rhymes with tribulation") and an inflammation called thrush in his throat ("Thrush is no lark even though it makes you swallow"). He commutes to his office at *The New Yorker,* where he has worked since 1944, from his home in Connecticut.

"There are some critics who keep telling me that I should cut out the jokes and get serious, *really* serious. Granville Hicks on the old *Saturday Review* would almost have a heart attack each time one of my new books came out. 'No more jokes. No more jokes,' he'd say, and I'd solemnly vow never to write another joke. Then I'd sit down and write the first sentence of the next novel and I'd be in trouble. Take *I Hear America Swinging.* I sat down and the first thing I knew I'd written: 'I had just been through hell and must have looked like death warmed over walking into the saloon, because when I asked the bartender whether they served zombies he said, "Sure, what'll you have?" ' and I was off again. It's like an alcoholic's first drink."

RALPH THOMPSON *was the reigning editor of the Book-of-the-Month Club from 1951 until his death in 1979. He was an admirable editor, a patient teacher, and a flag-bearer for the most exacting literary stan-dards. He was also a fine writer and reviewer, his calling (with the*

York Times) *before he came to the Club. This review, written in 1958, is a good sample of Ralph Thompson's style.*

A Death in the Family by James Agee

THE late James Agee, of Tennessee, Harvard, *Time* magazine and Hollywood, is known to a small circle of admirers for an angry, eloquent and extravagant politico-literary tract called *Let Us Now Praise Famous Men.* But among his other books is a childhood novel called *The Morning Watch*, and now it develops that he left behind material for a second novel dealing with other aspects of the same general theme. Whether, had he lived, he would have brought out *A Death in the Family* in its present patchwork form is open to question; but his heirs and editors have done their best to integrate a series of episodes involving a little boy named Rufus; and that Agee was once upon a time Rufus there is no room for doubt. Nor is there much doubt that parts of *A Death in the Family* are superbly realized. Agee was a reporter of great range and lucidity and, for all his aggressive exterior maleness, of almost Proustian-feminine tenderness, sensitivity and patience. Rufus is growing up in Knoxville, Tennessee, about 1915. His mother is a good Catholic. His father isn't, and on other scores as well is a trial to the family. But to Rufus he represents the whole world, and Rufus savors, with small-boy delight or astonishment, every grain and flavor of the paternal relationship. Certain of these savoring episodes are little masterpieces — for example, one where Rufus goes with his father to see a Charlie Chaplin movie. Then the father dies in an accident. The mother gets the news over the telephone. The priest comes to give comfort; the agnostic relatives raise eyebrows; the body lies in the coffin; young Rufus and his still younger sister are lifted up for long, half-comprehending stares at the waxen face and hands. The raw material of a fairly ordinary American boyhood refined and reshaped by an intense adult sensibility. *A Death in the Family* indicates what Agee might have gone on to write had he not himself died, while still in his 40s.

RALPH THOMPSON

HERE IS AN EARLY REVIEW *of the classic* The Elements of Style *by William Strunk, Jr., that had only one byline in 1959. Today it's simply called Strunk and White. And everyone knows what it is.*

The Elements of Style by William Strunk, Jr.

THIS is a curious little book by two authors: a dry, limited, authoritative Cornell professor, William Strunk, and a warm-hearted, modest, brilliant Cornell graduate, E. B. White. Strunk taught English composition, and apparently taught it well. The first version of *The Elements of Style* was a handbook less than fifty pages long which he published in 1918, mainly for the use of his pupils. Mr. White remembered it so well that, when a friend sent him a copy in 1957, he praised it in *The New Yorker;* his readers expressed a wish to read it; and now, over forty years after it first appeared, it is reissued with the addition of an extra chapter contributed by Mr. White himself. The result seems clear, because it is boldly and lucidly set forth; but in fact it is disjointed, heterogeneous and incomplete. Some of Strunk's advice is obsolescent. (Who nowadays is in danger of writing *he don't*, confuses *allude* with *elude*, or says *most everybody?*) Some appears to be addressed to inexperienced typists. ("It is usually best to leave plenty of space at the top of Page 1 of a manuscript.") The chapter which ought to have been the most important, on "elementary principles of composition," gets as far as paragraph structure and then stops — thus omitting any useful advice on the larger design of anything from an essay to a novel. However, there are a few straight and simple counsels which everyone should heed: in particular, "Use the active voice" and "Put statements in positive form"; and some of the book will be valuable to any beginner who does not want to write crude like an adman should. Mr. White's own contribution, the fifth chapter, is written in the same hortatory manner, but on a higher intellectual level. He says, for instance, "The young writer will be drawn at every turn toward eccentricities in language." We might comment that, if the young writer is, then he will not need Strunk's advice to avoid *can't hardly* and *leave it stand;* but we should probably be wrong. This book is a useful corrective for a certain group of new authors who believe that language is merely a barrier to expression, and are trying to smash through it.

GILBERT HIGHET

PUBLISHED IN *1960*, The Rise and Fall of the Third Reich *by William L. Shirer stands by itself as the Club's all-time single bestselling book. Into 1986 over 1,500,000 copies had been distributed to the BOMC family.*

Harry Scherman knew what he had early on, and he exhorted members
to take "one of the great books of our time." None of the BOMC judges
felt they could do full justice to the book since they had no personal ex-
perience with the Third Reich. So John Gunther, who had, wrote the
report. The Editorial Board chose Shirer's The Collapse of the Third
Republic *as the January 1970 selection, and Barbara Tuchman wrote*
about the transformation of Shirer the journalist into a "writer and
scholar."

The Rise and Fall of the Third Reich
by William Shirer

THIS IS ONE of the most spectacular stories ever told. Mr. Shirer, the author of *Berlin Diary*, has returned to the theme he knows best, and in
this book gives us a readable, percipient and closely documented history
of the Third Reich, that is, of Adolf Hitler, who was both a criminal lu-
natic and a man of genius — one of the most appalling, atrocious varieties of madmen ever to deface the earth.

For Nazi Germany and Hitler were one. Seldom has any nation, during a given period of history, been so indissolubly personified by a single individual. Hitler and the monstrous Reich he created rose and fell
together — dying at last together in the flaming Götterdämmerung of
the Chancellor's bunker in Berlin. (One of the startling minor revelations in Mr. Shirer's long book is that the surviving men and women of
Hitler's staff and bodyguard *danced* together, a kind of crazy dance of
the furies, or death dance, as the Russians remorselessly closed in above
them.)

Only for twelve years did the Führer rule Germany. In that brief time
he made the greatest, most destructive war in history, and extended the
frontiers of his grisly domain from the Arctic tip of Norway to Stalin-
grad on the Volga, from the Pyrenees to the gates of Cairo. Not even
Caesar, not even Napoleon, conquered more. Luckily, the Nazi con-
quests were short-lived.

Also, Hitler bears the ultimate and highly personal responsibility for
what is probably the most shocking crime in history — the wanton, deliberate murder of some 6,000,000 Jews. They were burnt alive, gassed,
shot, starved, beaten to death or killed with inconceivable brutality in
"medical experiments." Sometimes, before they went to the gas chambers, their teeth, if they contained gold, were ripped out while they were
still alive. In the last moments of his life, Hitler was still ranting hys-

terically about the Jews. No man has ever been more permanently, fanatically obsessed.

Hitler died in 1945, which means that hundreds of thousands of young people, here in America and elsewhere, have no direct memory of his odious life and works. Even their elders, who should know better, are sometimes accustomed these days to shrug the Führer off or even to give excuses for his murderous behavior. All such should read Mr. Shirer's Chapter 27, which sketches some elements of the new Hitler "order." It is the most appalling record of pure evil I have ever read.

Mr. Shirer tells the Hitler story from its beginnings; everything is here, in the most copious and telling detail, from the early days in Vienna to the Beer Hall *Putsch* in Munich and, some years later, in 1933, the seizure of power from the senile Hindenburg. From this time on war was foredestined; and everybody should have known it, although some fatuous British, French and American diplomats and men of affairs were taken in. The cynicism — and sheer unmitigated duplicity — with which Hitler manipulated opinion are not neglected in Mr. Shirer's pages.

People may think that all this is a familiar story. But it is not. And here I come to what makes this book so important, quite aside from its surpassing interest as a narrative. From 1933 on, the story is based in large part on documents which have never been published before or, at best, are buried in various records which are inaccessible to the average reader. These documents — hundreds of tons of them captured by the Allies after the war — are a unique treasure, and Mr. Shirer has used them well. Here are scores of excerpts from the diary (still unpublished) of General Halder, the Army Chief of Staff; top secret directives of the German High Command; the Jodl and Goebbels diaries; Foreign Office archives; Hitler's own orders to his generals; his letters to Mussolini and Stalin; and other political material and personalia of the utmost interest, much of it heretofore unknown.

Mr. Shirer spent more than five years on this book; and his documentation is so thorough that historians are going to be grateful to him, although he is not a professional historian himself, for a long time to come. One particular item covered fully is the remarkable sequence of abortive plots against Hitler made by his own generals. It seems that conspiracy against the Führer, though feckless, was incessant.

Other revelations major and minor stud these calm, crowded pages. I never knew before that the six children of Dr. Goebbels, whom he ordered to be poisoned to keep them from falling into Russian hands, were named Hela, Hilda, Helmut, Holde, Hedda and Heide; that General Manstein's real name was Lewinski; that General Falkenhorst (born Jastrzembski), the conqueror of Norway, began his staff work for the Norwegian campaign by reading the Baedeker guide to Norway; that the battleship *Deutschland* had its name changed to *Lützow* because Hitler would not risk losing a ship named "Deutschland"; that the Führer thought that the United States sought an *Anschluss* with Canada; that Ribbentrop was prepared to offer fifty million Swiss francs to the Duke of Windsor if he would defect to the Nazis; that Hitler never dreamed that Britain would go to war for Poland; that Goering ejaculated, "If we lose this war, then God have mercy on us!" when the war began; and that the precious Adolf (before 1933) had a lot of trouble with his income tax.

Documents unearthed by the author from secret archives contain countless nuggets. During the Munich crisis Hitler's chief worry was that the Czechs might *submit* to his designs, because he actively wanted a military operation. Hitler had determined to doublecross Stalin and attack Russia at least a year before the attack took place; meantime, he kept up an amicable — and wonderfully hypocritical — correspondence with the Kremlin. If he won the Russian war it was his intention to raze Leningrad to the ground, literally, and present the ruin to the Finns. He personally ordered the army plotters who sought to assassinate him on July 20, 1944, to be "hanged like cattle" — strung up by piano wire from meat hooks. One of his last orders was to destroy Paris by heavy artillery and V-1 flying bombs; luckily his generals refused to obey. *Und so weiter.*

Perhaps *The Rise and Fall of the Third Reich* is too long (it must run to 500,000 words or more); there are sequences — for instance, in the material dealing with the outbreak of the war — where Mr. Shirer has so much to say that he entangles himself in a thicket of footnotes; and if he had had time, after five mortal years, for a last editorial pruning he might have removed a few verbal infelicities. These items do not, however, detract from the worth of the book as a whole. The organization is firm and the structure solid; it reads like a murder mystery (which, in a sense, it indeed is), and I found it gripping on almost every page.

Nobody, on finishing this book, will be able to refrain from asking himself whether the Germany of today has learned its lesson, whether any possibility exists at all that some new Hitler may be born some day to tilt evil lances at the world. All I can say is that this is unlikely if enough Germans read Mr. Shirer's book, and I would like to see it made obligatory reading for every citizen of Chancellor Adenauer's republic. This is a story of such frightfulness that it should frighten — and make ashamed — even the most obdurate of Germans.

Another thought must come inevitably to the mind of any politically interested reader. Khrushchev, for all his ugliness, bad manners and dangerous will to power, is not a madman like Hitler, and it is not probable that he will make a war if only because Einstein and the physicists have irremediably changed the nature of war; even so, he rules by means of a totalitarian system even as the Führer did, and this book is a testament of what colossal damage a totalitarian system can do to the world if it is led by an unscrupulous dictator.

Mr. Shirer's book is a study in frightfulness, yes — but it is something more than that as well. Its story has nobility, even grandeur, in that it proves (in the instance of Nazi Germany at least) that the guilty meet ignominious punishment for the most part and that, on balance, good triumphs over evil in the end. One has a sense that Mr. Shirer feels this, and the reader has the exhilarating perception of the writer being pulled out of himself, lifted to a commanding height, in response to the superb challenge of his theme.

JOHN GUNTHER

William L. Shirer
by Barbara Tuchman

BILL SHIRER represents in his person the evolution of journalist into historian. Having observed and reported the rise of the Nazis, the fall of France and the triumph of the Blitzkrieg, he "brooded over these events," as he recently told me, and thought he must "try to get to the bottom of these two big stories I had covered." To "get to the bottom" — to find out how and why France became ripe for its fall — is the instinct and the task of the historian. *Berlin Diary*, the book "from the center of the whirlwind," as a critic called it, which made him famous in 1941, was the work of a journalist. *The Rise and Fall of the Third Reich* and the present book, supplementing the eyewitness record by extensive and painstaking research and documentation and the assembling of facts not personally experienced, are the works of a historian. How extraordinary has been the nature of the change can perhaps only be appreciated by a fellow writer. Bill has had to transform himself from a journalist working on a daily schedule, accustomed to seeing himself in print within a day or reaching his radio audience and telling his story within a matter of hours, to a writer and scholar willing to work eight years before the act of communication is completed by publication.

Altogether he has spent fifteen years turning his two "big stories" into history, which in itself tells us something about Shirer as a person. He is not content with the slapdash or second-rate — an attitude rare in a period that so easily recompenses both. He is patient, persistent, thorough, uncompromising in pursuit of his goal, not a man in a hurry; and these qualities are reflected outwardly in his appearance and manner and tastes. He is slow of speech, reflective, unexcitable, the opposite of our stereotype of the strenuous, peripatetic foreign correspondent. Last summer he spent his first summer of release from his book soaking up music seven days a week listening to rehearsals and concerts at Tanglewood.

Although, as a result of his two best-known books, he is associated with Germany in the mind of the public, Shirer has known France longer and, as might be expected considering the history of our times, more sympathetically. It is the country where his career began; he learned its language, was caught up in its problems and personalities, liked the people and came to feel that Paris "was my second home." He saw Paris first in 1925, the year of his graduation from Coe College in Cedar Rapids, Iowa. Even though his life work has been centered on Europe, Shirer is a born and bred product of the Middle West. Chicago was his birthplace in 1904 and Iowa his boyhood home. After sowing the seeds of a writer's career as sports editor of the *Cedar Rapids Republican* while working his way through college, he began the next stage by working his passage to Europe pitching hay on a cattle boat. On the last day before his funds for seeing Europe ran out, he landed a job with the Paris office of the *Chicago Tribune*, owned by the formidable Colonel Robert McCormick, who, despite — or perhaps because of — his notorious distrust of foreign countries, maintained an active corps of correspondents abroad.

For the next fifteen years Shirer served as a foreign correspondent, with his base in Paris for the first four years and subsequently in Vienna, where he was chief of the *Tribune's* Central European Bureau. An interlude of two years (1930–31) was spent in India on assignment to cover the civil disobedience movement under Gandhi's leadership. Accompanying Gandhi on his travels, he came to consider him the "greatest man of our times." The advent of Hitler carried him to Berlin, where from 1934 to 1937 he covered the alarming rise of the Third

Reich for Universal News Service, having been fired by the erratic McCormick. When Universal folded in 1937 he moved over, on the offer of a job from Edward Murrow of CBS, to the new field of radio news, just in time to join the remarkable live-voice coverage that kept Americans on the edge of their chairs as they listened to the unfolding of the Munich Crisis.

Thereafter Shirer's voice from Vienna was part of the record as Europe slid toward war. At the time of the Anschluss, when attempting to enter the broadcasting station, he found his way blocked by a cordon of armed Nazis. Not being a man to "argue with bayonets," as he puts it, he turned back — to hasten to London and make the broadcast from there. Reassigned to Berlin in 1939 at the start of the war, he was one of twelve foreign correspondents accredited to the German army in the field, and followed the Sixth Army of Von Reichenau to the unbelievable moment of the collapse and conquest of France. Shirer was with the Germans when they entered Paris, his "second home," in June, 1940, and he scored a scoop on the signing of the armistice at Compiègne when he overhead the proceedings from a German sound truck.

At the end of the year, when German censorship had made further reporting impossible, he returned to the United States to continue as wartime commentator and as columnist for the *New York Herald-Tribune*, and after the war went back to Europe to cover the Nuremberg Trials.

As an observer abroad Shirer had recorded some of the worst years of our time, but it was in his own country that he was to experience personally, as a victim, the effects of fear and evil. During that spasm of peculiar funk when the United States succumbed to the spirit of Senator Joseph McCarthy, the news division of CBS, headed by Edward Murrow, terminated Shirer's services, leaving him virtually cut off from employment by others equally fainthearted. Necessity turned him to the writing of books. The German documentation and evidence for a solid history of the Third Reich having been made available at the Nuremberg Trials, Shirer set to work. The rest was history — in a double sense — and a historian.

IN REVIEWING *a book that lives today, Gilbert Highet called it "the saddest novel I have ever read: almost as sad as history."*

The Last of the Just by André Schwarz-Bart

ACCORDING to a somber Jewish legend, there are at all times thirty-six perfectly good men in the world, and upon these men rests the continued existence of humanity. Were it not for them, God would long ago have permitted mankind to drown itself in its own ocean of suffering and sin. They suffer terribly, these good men. Their existence is a long torment, their death often a martyrdom. Sometimes they do not even know their own nature and destiny, but merely agonize throughout a lifetime of loneliness; sometimes they know dimly who they are, but suffer still more because they feel themselves dedicated but unworthy. Upon that legend is woven this gloomy and powerful novel. Written in French by an Ashkenazic Jew whose family was murdered in a German concentration camp, it was highly successful in France, and has been well translated by Stephen Becker. Its central theme is, to me at least, unconvincing: the idea that one of the thirty-six just men should always belong to the same family, and that sainthood should, as it were, be hereditary. Still, this fiction gives a vivid continuity to the centuries-old tale of Jewish persecution by showing us how, one by one in almost every generation, descendants of Rabbi Yom Tov Levy arose to bear his heavy burden and to be martyred, until "the last of the just," Ernie Levy, weeping tears of blood, died in the gas chamber of Auschwitz. Most of the novel is devoted to Ernie Levy's birth, youth, self-realization, suffering and death; but we, as we read, are always aware that he is one of a long line of dedicated sufferers; and at last he himself comes to understand this fact, and to accept it. This is the saddest novel I have ever read: almost as sad as history.

GILBERT HIGHET

ISAK DINESEN'S Seven Gothic Tales *was a Selection of the Club in 1934. So was* Out of Africa *in 1938,* Winter's Tales *in 1943, and* Shadows on the Grass *in 1961. The Editorial Board liked Dinesen somewhat more than did the American reading public. But Hollywood has caught up to the Baroness, which means that the American public has also. In his portrait of Dinesen that accompanied the 1961 selection, Robert K. Haas, her long-time publisher (also one of the founders of the Book-of-the-Month Club), reported that Isak Dinesen "is three thousand years old and has dined with Socrates."*

Isak Dinesen *by Robert K. Haas*

OVER a quarter of a century ago I had the privilege, as a publisher, of presenting to American readers Isak Dinesen's first book, *Seven Gothic Tales*. Its strange and wild beauty arched meteorlike across our literary skies. Thousands of us kept eager watch for more wonders and were not disappointed. In its trail flashed *Out of Africa, Winter's Tales, Last Tales, Anecdotes of Destiny* and now *Shadows on the Grass*. All blaze with the same clarity and brilliance.

In those first days it was news that "Isak Dinesen" was the pseudonym of Baroness Karen Blixen of Rungstedlund. Today, so wide is her audience, most readers know this as well as many other facts about her. That she comes from an old Jutland family, for example, that she studied painting in Paris, that in 1914 she married her cousin Baron Bror Blixen and went out to Kenya with him and managed her coffee plantation for twenty years, years during which she learned to understand, and became fast friends with, the natives. She then returned to her native Denmark and settled on a spacious seventeenth-century estate near the Castle of Elsinore. Formerly the home of Denmark's greatest lyric poet, Johannes Ewald, it will eventually become a bird sanctuary.

The Baroness visited the United States for the first time only two years ago, at the invitation of the Fund for the Advancement of Education established by the Ford Foundation. Avid to create a closer rapport with her public, she traveled extensively and recited a number of her tales before rapt audiences — and before television cameras in order that tapes might be made available to schools and colleges.

A tiny, frail woman, she had set herself a demanding task, and her health suffered. A tale that would take fifteen minutes to tell sometimes took hours to film. Eventually her chronic undernourishment took its toll (she lives virtually on oysters and sips of champagne) and she had to enter a hospital. She emerged with unflagging spirits and worked harder than ever.

Earlier still, the day after she arrived in New York from Europe, utterly fatigued by the journey, she had greeted a hundred guests at a reception in her honor. A rose brocade wing chair the perfect foil for the black gown she wore, her black eyes smoldering, she held a kind of personal court. No one then present will soon forget her spell.

In one of her stories there is a lady who says, very simply, that a hostess wants only to be thanked. Well, Isak Dinesen has set before us feast after feast. So we should, I think, from deep down in our hearts, thank her for her elegant and sumptuous hospitality. She is a magical person; by her own admission, she is three thousand years old and has dined with Socrates. Our message, therefore, would surely reach her.

*"*HE LOVED *the feel of words," said a eulogist at the memorial service for Theodore H. White, who died in May 1986. That was apparent from his* Thunder Out of China, *which was White's first book and his first of six Book-of-the-Month Club Selections. He was twenty-nine at the time, and he had a lifetime of books ahead of him.*

In 1960 White began his parade of presidential election books; that opener, The Making of the President 1960, *won a Pulitzer Prize. Clifton Fadiman explains why in his Selection report. And John Hersey talks to White about his decision to try to "find out how a man sets out to become a leader of the American people."*

The Making of the President 1960 by Theodore H. White

"HAVING WON a personal victory, John F. Kennedy must personally draw the rules for the next round of American politics — and for the human race." This is one of the pregnant statements in Mr. White's remarkable book. The gravity of tone has not been imposed arbitrarily by the author. On the contrary, it seems even clearer now than it was immediately after the election that the 1960 campaign was of almost unique importance in our history, and that to match it one must go back exactly one hundred years. How valuable, how fascinating would be a book similar to Mr. White's written directly following the election of Abraham Lincoln!

This engrossing account of the 1960 campaign has a triune value. First, quite apart from its specifically political subject matter, it is a superb narrative — first-hand, loaded with concrete detail and animated by extraordinary human beings, projected with a skill that brings home to us the fact that Mr. White is not only a first-rate journalist but a highly successful novelist. Second, it is a brilliant, and I believe it will become a classic, study of American domestic politics *in action.* Third, it places under a powerful lens a moment in time crucial to America and to the world.

These are some of the considerations that moved the Board of Judges (who, quite like our membership, are divided in their political allegiance) to choose Mr. White's book unanimously, following a minimum of discussion that came down in effect to the expression of enthusiasm.

Mr. White's subject is "the most awesome transfer of power in the world." In this case the transfer involved a number of unusually dramatic factors. On the Republican side less drama was produced than with the Democrats (as has often been the case), but even here, where the nomination of Mr. Nixon now appears in hindsight a foregone conclusion, the picture was complicated by the presence and pressure of Mr. Rockefeller. Among the Democrats, Mr. Kennedy controlled far and away the best apparatus, but exciting prenomination competition was provided by four able men of the most varied character and temperament: Humphrey, Symington, Johnson and Stevenson. To these seven men, their hopes and strategies, their advisers and entourages, their speeches and campaign styles Mr. White devotes four colorful preconvention chapters. Particularly telling is his analysis of the minds of Humphrey, Stevenson, Nixon and of course Kennedy, with whom he enjoyed several long and searching conversations. Where Nixon was weak, Kennedy was strong. That is to say, Nixon trusted "only himself and his wife" — an attitude that has something admirable about it but which in the end may have been in part responsible for his narrow defeat. Kennedy, on the other hand, emerges as a firm believer in brains wherever they may be found — and he contrived to collect around him a group of shrewd intellects that ably supplemented his own qualities.

The two major divisions of the book (preconventions and postconventions) are separated by a lengthy chapter called "Retrospect on Yesterday's Future." It gives extra solidity to an account that might otherwise have been merely skillful, thoughtful journalism. In it the author considers the national background of this "most awesome transfer of power." Using the 1960 census as his base, he tries to determine just what the emergent America was for whose leadership Mr. Nixon and Mr. Kennedy were contending. All the patterns of growth, all the new balances of power, are brought into clear focus, whether they are concerned with population shifts or with ethnic and color conflicts and religious differences. In every case Mr. White makes clear the connection with the election itself.

Then comes the account of the two campaigns. Mr. White is fuller and far more telling in dealing with Mr. Kennedy than with Mr. Nixon. In a quiet footnote he gives the reader the reason: of all the candidates in both parties Mr. Nixon was the only one to refuse to receive him. He was forced, as he says, to follow Mr. Nixon's campaign "from fifty feet away." Yet this is not a slanted book, even though it is perfectly apparent that Mr. White admires Mr. Kennedy more than he does Mr. Nixon. He pays sincere tribute time and again to Mr. Nixon's courage, pugnacity, energy and ability and to the sheer guts with which he met so many heart-breaking misfortunes during the campaign.

He makes the most of the sharp differences between the two men. Kennedy he sees as a man of the world, attracted to elegance of mind and manner, a self-confident and unified character. Nixon he depicts as a solitary leader, somewhat suspicious of advice, essentially more at home among small-town people than among city dwellers. From this book Nixon emerges not as the unscrupulous and bellicose fighter his enemies have made him out to be, but rather "a friend seeker, almost pathetic in his eagerness to be liked." Kennedy, on the contrary, never seemed to worry about whether he was being liked or not, and as a consequence projected an aura of greater confidence. The contrast between the two is most neatly drawn in Mr. White's analysis of the television debates, in which it is generally conceded that Kennedy scored over his rival. The superiority may have been intellectual; if so, these debates (in which an astounding paucity of ideas was evident on both sides) did not demonstrate it. What they did demonstrate was that Kennedy was able to project an "image" (whether genuine or not) more effective than Nixon's. He gave us, says Mr. White, "a sense of confidence in a future that darkened." Mr. Nixon, on the other hand, emerged as a well-intentioned, able man but one on the defensive, somewhat overfascinated by his opponent, trying to be too many things to too many men.

In the final chapter Mr. White tries to determine the purely political meaning of the election. He concludes, after careful analysis, that the Republicans not only held their own, but actually gained in certain respects. Thus Mr. Kennedy's victory was a personal one, for which his party can claim only partial credit.

This reviewer is not by nature greatly interested in books about politics. But this one I found fascinating. Because some of our members, too, may think that a book about the 1960 campaign is apt to be dry or technical, I would like to stress again the fact that *The Making of the President* is essentially a dramatic narrative, not a political treatise. It is a record of a highly meaningful national experience, one in which we all recently participated, whether intimately or remotely. That participation one feels again in these fast-paced yet reflective pages.

CLIFTON FADIMAN

Theodore H. White

by John Hersey

"I'm dog tired," Teddy White has more than once been heard to say at the dying down of a fury of work. "That job really drained me." This sort of announcement is White's customary prelude to a one-sitting discharge of intellectual and physical energy that leaves whoever is with him spent — and astonished, and better informed — but only seems to regenerate his private daemon, which drives him to know, if he can, and write, if he knows, the truth. He plunges at once into a new quest.

So it was in mid-October, 1959, when having finished work on a novel, *The View from the Fortieth Floor*, and having announced to his friends his utter exhaustion, he learned that Hollywood had bought his novel. He would have an unaccustomed packet of money. He could voyage; drench himself in books and the sun; loaf for a year. White and his wife, Nancy, drove for an autumn weekend at Fair Harbor, on Fire Island, to discuss these pleasant possibilities.

White surveyed the spot on which he stood. Born forty-four years before, in Boston, into what he has characterized as "that common American family type — very poor, but very honest," he had emerged from high school into the Depression; upon his father's death, he had sold newspapers by day to help support his family, had studied at night and had won a newsboy's scholarship to Harvard; in 1938, graduating *summa cum laude*, he had been granted a Sheldon Fellowship for a year's travel aboard. The year had borne a career. In Asia for seven years, in Europe for five, he had worked as a witness of hardship, desperation, death and politics; and the fruits of his work had been *Thunder Out of China* and *Fire in the Ashes* — both Book-of-the-Month Club choices. Two novels, both bestsellers, had followed; now the second had earned him some leisure. But White's restless thoughts, as he remembers them now, went something like this:

"To be an American is to accept a definition of something that hasn't happened yet. The word 'American' is one that leans forward into the future. If Americans don't choose great leadership this country will dissolve. Other peoples can afford to dissolve; they have their histories. We're new. If America doesn't do great things — then what are we? Then all of us, whose forefathers came here, become nothing but the spawn of Europe's offcasts and refugees. America has to have a purpose. To make a purpose clear, leaders have to come forward who can express it. We have an election year coming up. I'd like to find out how a man sets out to become a leader of the American people. I've always loved politics. I've had European and Asian politics — 1938 to 1953. I like our form of politics best, and I'd like to write this one. The trouble is that the kind of political writing any reporter must do in American politics is cramped by the clichés of publishing — you have to meet deadlines, you mustn't cut deep, you mustn't speculate, you must take a snip of the whole and make it sound like the whole. I've done all that, for all sorts of newspapers and magazines. I don't want to do that again. . . ."

In the two-day conversation at Fair Harbor, White said these things to his wife, and Nancy White, sensing the wind direction, threw that dream year on beaches and boats out the window, and said that with all that Hollywood money he'd better just write the election, for nobody else who would cramp him, but only for himself — do it on his own time, in response to his own needs.

And that is what he did. On October 27, a first tentative scribble went into a notebook: "Nothing yet appears on the front pages about the election. Soviet pictures of the far side of the moon, juvenile delin-quency, the steel strike, Dillon calls for end of trade restrictions. . . ." In December, he went to Paris to see the Western summit conference. Next, he went to Washington to find out how the various aspirants were planning to take the Presidency. Then he was in Wisconsin, and the world was snow-banked and chilly, and the first primary was under way. Then: Washington, the Virgin Islands, New York, West Virginia, Washington, New York, Chicago, Hyannisport, Iowa, Montana, New York, Los Angeles (convention!), Chicago (convention!), Michigan, Idaho, Washington, Oregon, California, North Dakota, Illinois, Mis-souri, New Jersey, Virginia, Alabama, Georgia, Iowa, Ohio, Florida — on and on, for 40,000 miles, at his own expense, with but a fortnight at home with his wife and their two children — until, at last, election day in Hyannisport, with Kennedy, whom he had picked to win.

And now he has written the book he promised his wife and himself that weekend at Fair Harbor. The Hollywood money is gone. White is worn out. "To write a book about a Presidential campaign," he wrote in a letter when it was all over, "you have to be there when it happens. It kills you; drains the vitality; drains the imagination; and utterly exhausts the purse." This was a splendid bulletin. White is pooped. Another beautiful book is definitely gestating.

IN THE EARLY SIXTIES *it was James Baldwin who, as these reviews attest, lit a fire under the complacency of white America. The fire burns on today.*

Nobody Knows My Name by James Baldwin

THE temper of the novelist does not necessarily produce reasonable argument, able reporting, coherent pronouncement on great issues. But James Baldwin has managed these things most of the time in this collection of essays, memoirs and sketches. He talks about Harlem, the South, the expatriate Negro, Richard Wright — and about such un-Negro subjects as Ingmar Bergman and André Gide. He can be searingly intimate, movingly eloquent — as in his dialogue with and obit for Richard Wright, or his essay on the Southern Negro. But he can also be fragmentary, elusive, even vague — as in his piece on Norman Mailer. Mr. Baldwin calls William Faulkner to account for some of his comments on the racial problem; the Nobel Prize winner, quite clearly, may be said to have said some foolish things. Mr. Baldwin is never foolish. In many ways, and for many reasons, one would like a world in which such arguments as his were unnecessary. But this being the world it is, he speaks with a passion that is admirable, and that may even, let us hope, do some good.

D. R. SLAVITT

The Fire Next Time by James Baldwin

THIS small but explosive book appeared on the 100th anniversary of the Emancipation Proclamation. It is already familiar to a fair-sized audience, for "Down at the Cross," the longer of the two "letters" it contains, created a furor when published in *The New Yorker* of November 17, 1962. Mr. Baldwin, a novelist and essayist of remarkable if somewhat unrestrained gifts, has here written a Negro Manifesto. Like its Marxian prototype (though Mr. Baldwin is no Marxist), it is powerful, rhetorically brilliant, sweepingly dogmatic — and will probably stimulate revisionist qualifications. On his indictment of white America Mr. Baldwin brings to bear all the resources of his technical skill, all the force of his passionate indignation. The crime of the whites, he thinks, lies less in their cruelty than in their bland assumption of innocence, their refusal to admit that by a completely irrational fiat based on an accident of pigmentation, they condemn millions of their countrymen to lives not worth living. At heart Mr. Baldwin is a man of good will. He pleads

with the whites to end "the racial nightmare" now, not by gradual legis-
lation, but by a religious act of will. If they refuse, he believes, a fiery
blood bath may be brought upon our country by such militant (and
clearly Fascist) extremists as the followers of the Nation of Islam movement. While it is difficult for any decent white not to feel shame under
Mr. Baldwin's excoriation, it is also natural to ask whether other and
equally responsible Negro leaders share his all-or-nothing emotional-
ism. One also wonders whether the ferocity of his attack may not hinder
the efforts of those whites (and there are many) who not only feel
deeply the plight of the Negro but are also trying to do something about
it. In any case, *The Fire Next Time* cannot and should not be ignored.
Like its naïver predecessors, *Uncle Tom's Cabin* and *Up from Slavery*,
it may well prove a landmark in American Negro history.

CLIFTON FADIMAN

IN *1961 Mark Schorer wrote the definitive biography of Sinclair Lewis.
Schorer was born in Sauk City, Wisconsin, surely a spiritual brother
hamlet to Lewis's Sauk Centre, Minnesota.*

Mark Schorer
by Alfred Kazin

WHEN I heard some years ago that Mark Schorer, scholar and novelist,
was doing a big and assuredly definitive biography of Sinclair Lewis,
my instinctive reaction was one of surprise. Although I had not even
met Schorer at the time I heard of the Lewis project, I had the definite
impression from his work, and from what various friends had told me
about his long-term literary interests, that Sinclair Lewis might not be
to his taste. I had once, at Lewis Gannett's house in the 1930s, heard
Lewis berate every literary intellectual in the room with the bitterness
and scorn of an honest Midwestern Populist denouncing J. Pierpont
Morgan. And Mark Schorer, so far as I knew, was certainly a literary
intellectual. I had read his acute and highly sophisticated book on William Blake, *The Politics of Vision* (*there's* a Sinclair Lewis title for
you!), and I had read enough of his fiction and critical essays to wonder
just how much grist the rustically rebellious figure of "Red" Lewis
could furnish the mill of so intense an admirer of Jane Austen, Ford
Madox Ford and D. H. Lawrence.

Yet Mark Schorer is a Midwesterner, as Lewis was. He was born, in 1908, in Sauk City, Wisconsin — which even sounds something like Lewis' native town of Sauk Centre, Minnesota. To some people this might seem to be credentials enough for writing about Lewis. But I have never believed that all Midwesterners are, out of regional sympathy, akin to one another. Scott Fitzgerald came from the same Minnesota that Lewis did. Willa Cather, from Nebraska, has never reminded me of William Jennings Bryan. My own glimpses of Schorer convinced me, rather, that he is in fact the kind of man who combines to a very remarkable degree the intense interest in personality of the novelist and the steadfast interest in novels of the critical intellect whose first love obviously is the novel as a literary form. I would guess, too, that the intense pathos of Sinclair Lewis' last years would have an immediate creative appeal to Schorer as a literary biographer and as an American sensitive to our American literary tradition of sudden success and heart-breaking decline.

After all, he has the instrumentalities, the fundamental skills, that one associates with good novels of American society and business. He has gone through the whole gamut of American higher education at a big Midwestern university (Wisconsin) from the B.A. to the Ph.D.; he has taught at Dartmouth and at Harvard; and he is now, in Berkeley, California, chairman of what must be one of the largest and most diversified Departments of English in this land. Yet Mark Schorer has managed, while teaching steadily, to publish three novels, a large book of stories, critical anthologies and many critical introductions, essays and reviews. He has managed brilliantly, in short, to do very different jobs and in the best sense of the word to be a professional man of letters without ceasing to be an accredited and conscientious scholar. To manage so well on what are (and indeed should be) very different levels suggests to me a man as disciplined and various as he is sensitive — and above all, perhaps, a man with the born writer's obstinate curiosity and devotion to the professional task.

CATCH-22 *caught on slowly. It was reviewed timidly when it was published in 1961, some critics not knowing quite what to make of it. But catch on it did. By 1975 it had sold more than six million copies in hardcover, and it sells steadily today.*

Catch-22 by Joseph Heller

DURING World War II, at a U.S. air base on the Mediterranean island of Pianosa, the one way of being grounded was to be declared insane. An airman himself had to ask to be grounded. But the catch (Catch-22) was, as someone said when Capt. Yossarian tried to get out of combat duty, "That crazy bastard may be the only sane one left," and so Yossarian couldn't be grounded. According to Catch-22, "They have a right to do anything we can't stop them from doing." Catch-22 is the final law of this cynical and bitterly amusing war novel, and Pianosa is a microcosm of a nightmarish war-governed universe. Yossarian is a frankly cowardly bombardier. An Army psychiatrist who has analyzed him observes, "You have a morbid aversion to dying. You probably resent the fact that you're at war and might get your head blown off any second. . . . You don't like bigots, bullies, snobs or hypocrites. Subconsciously, there are many people you hate." "Consciously, sir," says Yossarian. As the number of missions the men must fly before being sent home grows higher, Yossarian misses by a few each time. The links in the chain of the novel are his attempts to be grounded or sent home. Among the other characters are a hypochondriacal flight surgeon (*"You're* sick? How do you think I feel?"), a black-marketeering mess officer and an administrative colonel who courageously volunteers his men for dangerous duty. Among the scenes are a farcical Kafkaesque court martial, frantic rest leaves in Rome, bombing runs full of horror and hysteria, and a wild and weird Glorious Loyalty Oath Crusade. Mr. Heller's book would be even more pointed were it shorter, but just as it stands it is an effective and savagely funny diatribe against man's inhumanity to man.

LUCY JOHNSON

AS IN THE CASE OF The Rise and Fall of the Third Reich, *a specialist was called in to report on Rachel Carson's monumental work,* Silent Spring. *The specialist was Supreme Court Justice William O. Douglas, a passionate defender of the environment. Said Justice Douglas of Si-*lent Spring, *"This book is the most important chronicle of this century for the human race."*

Silent Spring by Rachel Carson

RACHEL CARSON, the author-biologist who wrote *The Sea Around Us* and *The Edge of the Sea*, now adds another illustrious book to her list. The title sets the mood of the text: man's power of destruction is now so great that, some coming spring, the birds and the bees may be extinct and there may be no fish to cause a swirl on the smooth waters of our lakes. Poisons are in all the menus; the insolubles that make up many insecticides are eventually stored in human tissues. Disease mysteriously appears in man. The alarming story is calmly told, with no theatrics and in a sober, factual way. This book is the most important chronicle of this century for the human race.

The menace of insecticides is a present peril of vast proportions. Up to now the environment of the earth has altered and modified all its children, from flowers to insects to man. The scientific revolution has given man the power to alter the nature of the world. Man's lethal inventions have contaminated the air, the earth and the waters. Strontium 90 that is released through nuclear explosions eventually finds its ways into the bones of the human body. Chemicals used as sprays are like devils that create chains of poison and death.

The ingredients of "efficient" chemicals, so pleasing to the housewife, enter even underground percolating waters and work unknown harm. There are five hundred new chemicals a year; and they contain elements whose immediate and long-range effects are wholly outside the limits of biologic experience. If the kinds produced in one year were used for a millennium and no more were added, life might adjust to them. But the yearly output is so vast that there seems no prospect for the biologist to catch up with their real impact on life.

The poisons that man uses to bombard the earth are really "biocides," not "insecticides." They enter the tissues of plants and animals and even penetrate the germ cells to alter the structure of heredity. They destroy the enzymes that protect the body from harm; they block the oxidation process; and they start malignancies. Darwin would be filled with excitement at the contemporary scene. The unwanted insect or bacillus dies by the millions; but a new one of the same species develops an immunity and the chemical laboratories must go to work again.

Miss Carson brings insecticide after insecticide up for review; and as the story unfolds the horror mounts. One of the chlorinated hydrocarbons is so powerful that even after floors sprayed against cockroaches are washed, the house is so contaminated as permanently to destroy the functioning of a healthy child. Persons have died merely from handling the bag in which the insecticide was shipped or from the drifting spray used in a potato patch. It is startling to learn that the amount of one insecticide that is today used in only one of our farming states is enough to kill more than five times the total world population.

Herbicides or weed killers are supposed by many to be toxic only to plants and to pose no threat to animal life. This is shown to be untrue; they even strike at the genetic material of the race.

Sprays kill vast quantities of birds. The robin dies because it eats the earthworm that has stored the insecticide in its body. The bald eagle eats fish that have accumulated the poisons of sprays. Other birds die — some by the thousands — when they eat chemically treated seeds.

When forests are sprayed against the spruce budworm, the streams become rivers of death; the insects on which fish feed, as well as the fish, die. The same is true when river areas are sprayed against the fire ant or the boll weevil or the mosquito. These rivers of death then infect the estuaries and the coastal marshes; and the fish, crab, shrimp, oysters and clams that live there suffer great losses.

The glass of water on the dining room table, even though it is taken from artesian wells, can be contaminated. Waters that drain sprayed fields find their way into underground streams or into lakes. Modern detergents are commonly insoluble, pass through sewage disposal plants, and soon find their way into our artesian waters. The chemists who analyze the waters have no way of removing the insecticides or detergents. People drink them. They are also absorbed by fish and by the birds that eat the fish. The infected plankton in the water is the start of a long food chain, each link of which is poisoned.

What of the soil and its hosts of toiling creatures? We are taken on a tour of the unseen world under our feet and shown how insecticides prevent root nodules from forming on legumes, how the killing of one organism in the soil may cause an explosion of another and thus do long-range ecological harm. Some soils become permanently poisoned, as evidenced by the 300% increase in the arsenic content of cigarettes between 1932 and 1952. Peanuts, hops, beans, carrots absorb the poisons and often pass them on to man.

The range lands of the West are sprayed, four million acres each year. The spray kills the sage to the delight of stockmen and to the agony of the sage grouse; it also kills willow, so the beaver depart and a wonderland of small fishing ponds disappears. The lawns of suburbanites are saturated with lethal poisons aimed at crab grass. Ragweed, an annual, though sprayed, increases year after year. For the spray kills the other vegetation which in truth would be the ragweed's real enemy if no spray were used.

The way to control noxious plants is often the introduction of the enemies of those plants. Indeed the introduction of marigolds into rose beds infected with nematode worms is a better way of controlling nematodes than the use of man-made poisons. The introduction of beetles has kept the Klamath weed under control in the West; a moth brought to Australia put cactus under control; a parasitic wasp introduced from Korea has been more effective against the Japanese beetle than all the spraying. The examples are multiplied to show Nature's way of keeping her societies in balance — a way far safer than man's chemical sprays. As the book shows, when man uses sprays he uses a shotgun that kills a host of animals. Suddenly a new pest appears, riding toward its Golden Age because its predators have been killed off.

There is a sadness in Miss Carson's book that comes through almost every page. The insecticide "expert" has had his way. This "expert" is the man who may know about insects but be wholly ignorant about ecology. State and Federal men, honest but ignorant, launch massive programs without ever having operated a pilot plant to learn what harm may be done. There is now hardly a meal that is free of residues of insecticides.

What is the effect of our poisoned foods on us? The book gives a brief but ominous account. It also gives a biochemist's analysis of the way matter is transformed into energy and transmitted to each cell and of the way in which insecticides interfere with that process. The evidence is impressive that these insecticides may have a relation to cancer. In spite of the alarms, the consumer has no effective guardian against these poisons. State laws are inadequate; Federal laws lack enforcement staffs; the poisoning of food on so vast a scale is nevertheless officially recognized in that we are placed on "tolerance" schedules. One who learns how these levels are fixed will be ready to march on Washington.

The alternatives to insecticides are not crop destruction or the ravishing of forests by insects. With a minimum of help from man and a maximum of noninterference by man, Nature can use her system of checks and balances. She did it throughout eons of time, long before the insecticides arrived. The search for her ways should be our task.

This is the ringing challenge of the book:

"If the Bill of Rights contains no guarantee that a citizen shall be secure against lethal poisons distributed either by private individuals or by public officials, it is surely only because our forefathers, despite their considerable wisdom and foresight, could conceive of no such problem."

We need a Bill of Rights against the twentieth-century poisoners of the human race. The book is a call for immediate action and for effective control of all merchants of poison.

William O. Douglas

The actor and playwright *Emlyn Williams got a start on his autobiography with* George, *published in 1962. The playwright, director, and novelist Garson Kanin provided the BOMC audience with "the shapes and colors of this strangely structured personality."*

Emlyn Williams
by Garson Kanin

It was during an intermission at Wyndham's Theatre in London. I was giving my visiting friend a run-down on the British theater community.

"Now Emlyn Williams," I said, "is different."

"Different from whom?" asked my friend.

"From Emlyn Williams," I heard myself say.

My friend gave me an "Oh" and a worried look.

Before I could elaborate, the house lights dimmed, and our exchange joined that monumental slag heap of unfinished conversations.

I am grateful for the opportunity to explain now.

Consider two plays in the standard repertoire of drama in the English language — *The Corn Is Green* and *Night Must Fall.* The first: a profound, moving and poetic exploration of a noble theme — human potential. The second: a classic model of a thriller. Is it possible that both these plays could have been written by the same playwright? It is not only possible but true.

Consider next the performances of the leading male roles in these plays. In *The Corn Is Green*, Morgan Evans, the Welsh mine boy, is taken from beneath the earth — "where the corn is green" — remolded, and realized in the crucible of love and determination. It is a performance which remains in the memory of all who saw it. In *Night Must*

Fall it is a psychopath, Dan, who possesses not only the charm of the devil but also his intent. What have these two performances in common? Nothing, except that Emlyn Williams created them both. Here, then, are four contributions to the history of the modern British theater, any one of which would earn a place in that record. All four were made by Emlyn Williams.

Does it begin to be clear what I meant by "different"?

The shapes and colors of this strangely structured personality do not end here. There have been other plays — comical, tragical, historical, inspired, indifferent, artistic and commercial. In each of them another aspect of an ever-flowing cornucopia of creativity is revealed.

One stands out: a play called *Pen Don*. On an evening in 1954 I saw it performed by a group of amateurs in Swansea, Wales, upon a raised platform in the reading room of the Swansea Museum of Natural History. The director of the production, Tyrone Guthrie, preoccupied with the job of mounting the play (which, in this case, involved painting some of the scenery and sewing a wig or two), had invited me to the wrong night. Thus, instead of attending the gala opening I had expected, I attended the somewhat less than gala first dress rehearsal. In the musty, book-lined, creaky old room, the play began. The players had neither the experience nor the confidence to play the play. No matter. The play played them. The result was a soaring performance of a transcendent, inspired play. The fact that *Pen Don* has never been performed commercially in either London or New York is nothing against it, but only another sign of the theater's trouble.

Emlyn Williams' film *Dolwyn*, which he wrote and directed and in which he played the leading role opposite the incomparable Edith Evans, is clear evidence that should he ever choose to become a film maker, the film world will be greatly enriched.

His re-creation of the Charles Dickens readings might be the work of a lifetime for an artist less favored; and as for his Dylan Thomas one-man show, I, for one, think of it as the single most impressive theatrical achievement I have ever witnessed. (Strange that the outstanding Welsh poet and the outstanding Welsh man of the theater, although contemporaneous, never met.)

There is more. As an actor he has played not only in numerous plays of his own but in those of Terence Rattigan, Shakespeare, Ibsen and others. He has adapted plays, directed them, and written for films and television.

He is half responsible for two vital sons. Instead of the usual snap-

shots, he is apt to carry about with him a poster announcing the appearance in Worthing Rep of Brook Williams as Morgan Evans in *The Corn
Is Green*, by Emlyn Williams; and the dust jacket of a soon-to-be-
published novel entitled *Long Run South*, by Alan Williams. ("Children can be trained," said Dr. Schweitzer, "in only three ways: Example, example and example.")

Mrs. Williams, the smiling Molly, deals with all the Emlyn Williamses, a feat more impressive than any of those which he performs.

And even if he had not created this remarkable world of his own, he
would have added to the gaiety of nations and been the delight of his
friends by being an outrageously witty and wicked commentator on his
times.

He once opened in an inferior play which seemed doomed to failure.
Inexplicably, in the mysterious ways of the theater fates, it received an
overwhelmingly enthusiastic press. The astonished company stood
about reading the reviews. "Well," said Emlyn, "all we need to do now
is fight the word of mouth!"

Now he has chosen to write an early autobiography, *George*. Listen
to him as he sings the haunting song of his youth. The music is lovely,
the words are wise, the theme is lofty — the tempering of an artist and
the making of a man.

THE INTRODUCTION *to the Club's presentation of Katherine Anne Porter's* Ship of Fools *partly explains why it took Miss Porter twenty-five
years to write the number one fiction bestseller of 1962. Novelist, poet,
and critic Glenway Wescott explains Miss Porter herself.*

Ship of Fools by Katherine Anne Porter

TWENTY-FIVE YEARS AGO the Book-of-the-Month Club — "partly in
respect for a certain book and partly in the expectation of the author's
work to come" — bestowed a $2500 fellowship upon Katherine Anne
Porter for a volume of short stories called *Flowering Judas*. The award
was one of four, based upon recommendations from thirty literary critics over the nation. Miss Porter's subsequent work, although limited in
quantity, bore out this early judgment, particularly *Pale Horse, Pale
Rider*, a collection of three short novels, which was roundly acclaimed

when it appeared in 1939. "Few writers have built so solid a reputation on so small a published output," wrote a contemporary reviewer, adding somewhat ruefully that Miss Porter was "an extremely slow writer and perfectly contented to be." . . . As Clifton Fadiman noted in his report, for twenty years there had been insistent rumors that she was at work on a full-length novel and that soon — very soon — it would be finished. "Here at last is Miss Porter's *magnum opus* . . . a major achievement by an American writer in whom we may all take pride."

Katherine Anne Porter
by Glenway Wescott

HAVING had the pleasure of lifelong friendship with Miss Porter, I find it irksome to call her "Miss Porter." It has been mainly a comradeship of the literary life, and on that account perhaps, in conversation and in correspondence, I often address her as "Porter." A host of her fellow writers and others speak of her and to her as "Katherine Anne," with or without a basis of intimacy. Somewhat like Jane Austen or like Colette, she has an unassuming sort of celebrity that invites or at least inspires friendliness. Let me now also take the fond and informal tone to celebrate the publication of her novel, twenty years in the making.

First, a few facts: Texas-born, on May 15, 1890, she spent a part of her girlhood in New Orleans, and afterward lived in New York City and in Mexico City and in Paris and in Baton Rouge, Louisiana, and, in more recent years, in upper New York State and in Connecticut and in Washington, D.C. Prior to *Ship of Fools* she had published five short novels or *nouvelles*, approximately twenty short stories (my count), and several dozen essays and criticisms and historical studies. She is a famous conversationalist and an incomparable letter writer, sparkling, poignant and abundant.

"Even when I was a small child," she has said, "I knew that youth was not for me." An important saying, as it strikes me, with reference to the fact that she devoted a third of her lifetime to just one masterpiece of fiction. It expresses her peculiar lifelong uneasiness and knowledge of the fate ahead of her, and her great patience from start to finish. So many writers of our generation brought forth novels in our 20s, immaturely. Often they were novels in name only, enlarged tales, family chronicles, disguised self-portraits. Some of us then hit upon a formula or worked out a method, so as to produce narrative reading matter wholesale; and some of us, on the other hand, simply tired of the great form, or despaired of it. With lesser fish to fry, we let the white whale go. Not Katherine Anne! And when, twenty years ago, as a famed short-story writer, she let it be known that she had begun a novel, she meant precisely that: a large, lifelike portrayal of a numerous and representative society, with contrasts of the classes and the masses and the generations and the ethnic groups, with causes and effects in the private psychology of one and all, and their various influences on one another — every man to some extent a part of every other man's fate — and all of this made manifest in behavior, action, plot! And for twenty years she kept at it, despite passionate life and a good many vicissitudes, despite personal weaknesses of hers and disadvantages in the day and age and in our heterodox present American culture. As the time passed, there arose in literary circles a murmur of skepticism or pessimism to which (I hope) she herself was deaf.

Let me confess that, at one point, when she had confided difficulties and despondencies to me, I began to write her a deplorable though well-meaning letter, advising her to give the novel up, as such; to salvage stories and sketches out of the incomplete manuscript; and to go on to whatever she had next on her agenda. Fortunately I consigned this melancholy suggestion to the wastebasket, and presently visited her on her wooded hill in Connecticut, where, as she wrote to me, she lived "on guard and secretive and solitary as a woodchuck peeping out of its hidey-hole." She then read aloud several chapters that were new to me, and I suddenly caught sight of what was in her mind: the great novel-structure, the whole so very much more than the sum of the parts. I came away repentant, exalted, and did not lose confidence in it or in her again.

She works in a profound way, not just thoughtfully, rationally, methodically, as probably prose writers ought to be able to work, as indeed in her case the finished product suggests that she may have done. "I spend my life thinking about technique, method, style," she told me long ago. "The only time I do not think of them at all is when I am writing."

The years on the hilltop in Connecticut appear to have been the crucial period. In a letter dated April 26, 1958, she described the way she was living then: "I need to keep submerged in the same mood and state of mind for *weeks* at a time, very hard to explain to people who need a change and recreation every day, and sometimes several times a day. . . . Of course I do a little baking, and I water the plants, and walk in the meadow, and even read a little now and then, mostly poetry, but I have stopped listening to music. . . . I must keep silence." (By the way, the bread she bakes people come miles to eat.)

Let me try to describe her, as to her physical presence and personality. Like many women accustomed to being loved she dreads and disapproves of photographers, although in fact usually she has lent herself well to their techniques, and they have been on her side. I remember one of her diatribes, some years ago, against a photographer and an interviewer sent by one of the news weeklies, who, she said, had caught her unawares and committed a misrepresentation of her. In the photograph in question when it appeared she looked (to me) like Marie Antoinette, young, her hair perfectly coiffed and powdered looking, playing her typewriter as though it were a spinet. And it amazed me to note how skillfully she had been able to simplify the record of her life for the interviewer also.

She has in fact a lovely face, of the utmost distinction in the Southern way: moonflower-pale, never sunburned, perhaps not burnable. She is a small woman, with a fine figure still; sometimes slender, sometimes not. Her eyes are large, dark and lustrous, and they are apt to give one fond glances, or teasing and merry looks, or occasionally great flashes of conviction or indignation. Her voice is unforgettable, and of course in recent years she has familiarized a great number of appreciative fellow Americans with it by means of reading and speaking engagements and recordings.

I remember hearing her read her finest *nouvelle, Noon Wine,* one afternoon long ago, at a time of cruel setbacks in her personal life, in a little auditorium on a college campus planted with oak trees. It was hot and the windows stood open. The oak trees were full of bluejays, and they were trying to shout her down. Were they muses in bird form, I remember humorously asking myself, inspiring her to cease publicly performing old work, and to start writing something new?

She had been ill with bronchitis not long before that, and almost whispered the great tale, breathing a little hollowly, with an almost frayed sound now and then. Certainly there were not as many decibels in her voice as in the outcry of the jays. "Furies! Certainly *not* muses," she said afterward. Nevertheless her every tone was sweet, her every syllable full of meaning, and easy to understand, just as it is in print.

Literary critics and historians have often remarked the mighty contributions of the female sex to literature, far and wide and always. For the most part those who have done the contributing have been spinsters, nuns, courtesans, invalids — a little exempt from the more distracting,

exhausting aspects of womanhood as such. Katherine Anne, throughout
her youth and middle age, led a maximum life concomitantly with her
perfect, even perfectionist story writing. As I have said, she is apt to
simplify all that for any sort of questioner. But, come to think of it, except for naturally secret matters of love and marriage and ill health and
economics, it *was* simple. And therefore I (and other friends), instead of
concentrating on ascertaining all the facts, dates and names and loca-
tions, have always interested ourselves in what might be called story-
material about her, which seems more characteristic and more meaningful than the mere biography.

For example, when she was a girl somewhere in the South, she had to
spend many months in a sanitarium with a grave pulmonary illness
diagnosed as one of the baffling, uncommon forms of tuberculosis. She
was too ill to have visitors. Letters also evidently were overstimulating
and exhausting. Even books seemed not good for her; her reading had to
be rationed, just a few pages at a time. Then it was discovered that the
intense restlessness of her bright eyes gazing at the ceiling, examining
and re-examining the furniture, staring at the solitude, gave her a tem-
perature. Her doctor therefore prescribed that a restful green baize cloth
be placed over her face for an hour or two every morning and every afternoon, as one covers the cage of a canary bird when one doesn't want it
to sing. I feel convinced that if anything of the sort were done to me I
should give up the ghost, on account of the autosuggestion and the discouragement. Not Katherine Anne! That was only the beginning of a
lifetime of delicate health and indomitable strength.

Presumably there are forces warring within her. Is it that her phy-
sique wearies of having to house a spirit so strenuous and emotional, and
now and then tries to expel it or to snuff it out? Or is it instinctive in her
soul to keep punishing her body for not being superhuman, and ideal,
and immortal? Neither has exactly prevailed over the other; both have
been invincible. Nothing has come of the great dichotomy; or to be
exact, literature has come of it.

She lived in Mexico for a long time, and a number of the men who
revolutionized that strange great nation were her friends. She personally
publicized the work of Diego Rivera and Covarrubias in New York, and
brought what must have been, as she remembers it, the first exhibition
of Mexican Indian arts and crafts north of the border. One of the revolutionaries wrote a song about her, *La Pelerina*, which (I am told) has
become a folk song; little companies of boy singers, *mariachis*, like boy
scouts in a dream, sing it in the streets.

Years ago someone used to tell everyone that, at an early age, she had been in the movies as a Mack Sennett bathing girl, along with Gloria Swanson, Mabel Normand, *et al.* I did venture to question her about this. It was a matter of journalism, not show business. Commissioned to write an article of some sort, she pretended briefly to be a comedienne for the sake of realistic detail and local color.

Not so many years ago she had a try at earning her living by script writing in Hollywood. With evanescent Western money she bought a slight segment of mountain top for a building site — always hoping to have a home somewhere — but she soon lost it; and a Western wind in the Mojave Desert tore out a window frame and slightly fractured her skull with it. The furies, once more!

Note that I have referred to all these things as vicissitudes or hardships, not as misfortunes. The perils and disorders and, indeed, wounds of a war scarcely seem deplorable to the homecoming soldier concerned (or to his grateful countrymen), unless his battle has been lost; not even then, if he has shown heroism, if his story has been nobly reported. The fearsomeness of childbearing and the fatigues of parenthood are unhappy only if the children perish or turn out to be good for nothing. Likewise one cannot evaluate the experience of a literary genius unless one has perused all that has resulted from it. Obviously there has been heroism, heartbreak, travail in Katherine Anne's case. No youthful or even middle-aged person could have written *Ship of Fools*. It has required an entire lifetime of unshrinking participation in life and unshirking endeavor, of hardheadedness and heat of heart and almost fanaticism, and now we have the result; and surely it must seem to her, in her weariness and pride, cheap at the price.

ESSAYIST, NOVELIST, INTELLECTUAL, *Mary McCarthy is one of the enduring American literary appraisers of the twentieth century. She also, in 1963, wrote a popular book.* The Group *was the number two fiction bestseller that year. Men apparently had trouble understanding it. So says Gilbert Highet in his review, though he had no trouble.*

The Group by Mary McCarthy

AT FIRST, this novel will strike some people as rather cruel and repellent. I know several sensitive readers who have rejected it with embarrassment and even with pain. There is much in it which is embarrassing and painful; but there is much more. It is the story of a small group of women who were friends at college in the early 1930s, who emerged into the world together full of hope and the potentialities of love, who learned about life and watched one another growing mature and unhappy, and who yet retained, from their formative years, a certain mutual sympathy. There are eight of them. (A mysterious and romantic ninth appears in the first chapter and is offstage until the last.) They have jobs, and love affairs, and marriages; they are involved in many misadventures both amorous and domestic. Although when they left Vassar they nearly all expected that, since they had been intellectually bright, they would find excitement and satisfaction in their careers, they discover instead that the most important thing for them is their relations with the various men who invade their lives. In college they lived mainly for the development of their mind and personality. In the world outside they live mainly by their physiology. It takes charge of them in the most disconcerting way, and compels them to worry endlessly about ignoble things: the impotence of a loftily spiritual husband, the toilet training of an anxiously awaited but somehow unsatisfactory son, the memory of a love affair which poisons a later marriage. Within the seven years which the novel covers, from 1933 to 1940, the members of the group undergo many of the ridiculous and pathetic jokes which nature plays upon women. That is the central theme of the book; it strikes me as a good one, which has not to my knowledge been handled with such a skillful blend of clinical realism and sadly smiling sympathy. Men watch women wrestling with the innumerable annoyances of the feminine condition and usually pity them, without fully understanding how much they have to endure. This book, with humor and compassion, explains their sufferings. I have concentrated upon the theme, because it is important; but I should add that the technical skill of the novel, interweaving a number of different destinies within a complex pattern, is highly distinguished.

GILBERT HIGHET

GWENDA DAVID *works for the Book-of-the-Month Club today, keeping the editors informed about new books coming along in England. She knows everyone in literary England and misses nothing that occurs in the trenches of British publishing houses. In 1983 she lost one of her*

greatest friends in Rebecca West. Her letters often contained reports of
a weekend spent with Dame Rebecca. That always seemed to include an
afternoon of cemetery rubbings. In 1966 Gwenda David wrote this
perceptive profile of West to accompany the West Selection, The Birds
Fall Down.

Rebecca West
by Gwenda David

WHEN Rebecca West was in hospital a couple of years ago I went to see
her. Instead of having a jewel case with her, as most women with jewels
as lovely as Rebecca's would have had, she had a box, a most cherished
box obviously, which she asked me to fetch. In it was a typescript. I was
very excited. And so was Henry Andrews, her husband. We smiled at
each other conspiratorially. Here at last, I thought, was the novel for
which so many of us had waited impatiently for a decade.

Rebecca fingered the typescript while I watched jealously. Then,
screwing up my courage, I asked if I might take it and read it. "Take it
and read it! Certainly not," said Rebecca in her firm and vibrant voice. It
was not yet finished, and she intended to work on it in hospital. But she
was too ill and found herself unable to work.

I fretted. But one doesn't argue with Rebecca. She is always clear as
to what she intends to do, and even illnesses or domestic crises rarely
stop her. When she is worried she writes long longhand letters to her
friends, mentioning her troubles in passing as it were, and then continuing about something else, something exciting or likely to arouse controversy, and sweeping away argument. She is impatient of fools. And
when she enters a restaurant there is a stir. No, she isn't beautiful in the
conventional sense, but it is clear that someone very alive has entered,
and ripples of admiring comment flow quickly around the room.

After her illness she moved into the Ritz in London for a short while
to recuperate, and reported to me that the hotel sheets were wonderful.
This made me chuckle, for the sheets in her own delightful country
house in Buckinghamshire, some thirty miles northwest of London, are
grand enough. I went there for lunch not long after she returned, hoping
to read the new novel. Lunch at Rebecca's house is always very special,
with a fine wine. Henry met me at the station, and we stopped on the
way to see the new Landrace pigs he is rearing on the farm attached to
the house. In the house there was a new picture which Rebecca had
bought, and as always there were new books everywhere and flowers

everywhere. I once counted forty flower vases of every shape and size stored in a small anteroom by the main door; the house is invariably full of flowers from the gardens or the hothouses. But the final chapters of the novel were still unfinished.

Rebecca and Henry Andrews have been married for more than thirty-five years, since 1930. Her career as a writer began long before that, her first book, a study of Henry James, appearing in 1916. She was born Cicily Isabel Fairfield in County Kerry, Ireland, in 1892. As almost everybody knows, the name she signs to her books, "Rebecca West," is a borrowed name, borrowed from that of the strong-willed heroine of Ibsen's *Rosmersholm*, a part she played in a brief stage career. Earlier novels like *The Thinking Reed* (1936) and works of history or reportage like *Black Lamb and Grey Falcon*, which appeared in 1941, or *The New Meaning of Treason*, which was a Book-of-the-Month Club Selection in 1964, have given her a unique place among writers of her generation.

Finally I did, of course, read at my leisure the typescript of the novel I had caught a glimpse of in the hospital room — *The Birds Fall Down*. The life in it swept me away; I was lost and thrilled and utterly absorbed. Sighing with pleasure, I sat down and wrote to Rebecca, thanking her for the book and telling her it was lovely and using other unprofessional words. She and Henry were in Sicily on holiday at the time. When she returned we met and talked, and she said, "Isn't it exciting? Two Book-of-the-Month Club Selections in a space of two years for a woman in her seventies. Isn't it grand?" And I agreed. "Bless you," she ended, as she always does when happy.

A FREELANCE READER AND REVIEWER *for the Club, Edward Kent characterizes* The Autobiography of Malcolm X *as "a classic document and statement of a uniquely American kind."*

The Autobiography of Malcolm X
With the assistance of Alex Haley

MALCOLM LITTLE, who called himself Malcolm X — Black Muslim leader and assassination victim — was a fascinating and not unsympathetic figure to many, white or Negro, who knew him personally. This study, labeled his autobiography though in reality the product of a series of outspoken interviews he gave to Alex Haley, is in some respects as revealing a self-analysis as anything by James Baldwin or the late Richard Wright. Born in Omaha, Malcolm was, as he saw it, in effect orphaned early in life by his father's violent death and his mother's subsequent mental illness. Eventually he joined the "underlife" of the Negro ghettos in Boston and Harlem and was jailed for housebreaking. Later converted by the Black Muslims, he worked for the sect for twelve years. In time he fell out with its leader, Elijah Muhammad, and started his own Muslim "nationalist" movement, in the course of speaking for which he was shot and killed in Harlem early in 1965. This outline merely skims the surface of the present book, which in fact describes in extraordinary detail the career and motives of a man who was by no means merely the "hatemonger" portrayed in the American press. Malcolm was a rough-cut diamond, certainly, but he had many facets, none of them dull, and great strengths as well as great ambitions. His dramatic book, for all its special pleading, should endure as a classic document and statement of a uniquely American kind.

EDWARD ALLEN KENT

In Cold Blood by Truman Capote was the nonfiction sensation of 1966, a landmark book for what came to be called "nonfiction fiction" or "faction." It was the model for a generation of writers. Harper Lee, the author of To Kill a Mockingbird, *helped Capote with his research for* In Cold Blood, *and in her portrait of Capote to accompany the Selection she revealed some of the tantalizing elements of his genius.*

Truman Capote

by Harper Lee

On a chilly fall day in 1959 Truman Capote set out for Kansas armed with a footlocker of comestibles sufficient to support a few weeks of life in that forbidding land, little knowing that he was to devote the next five years to a work infinitely tantalizing and a true challenge to his genius.

At first it was like being on another planet: a vast terrain indifferent to the creatures that walked upon it, an untrusting populace suspicious of anyone alien to it, bone-cracking winters turning to dust-choked springs to parching summers. Nevertheless, in the due course of time Truman became as much a fixture to Finney County, Kansas, as are the roadside signs proclaiming its many virtues.

What he found in Kansas is on the pages of *In Cold Blood.* What did Kansas find in Truman Capote? To begin with, looks that are deceiving. One sees a beautifully modeled head, sensitive hands, a graceful carriage, blue eyes behind thick glasses. One's impression is suddenly modified by the casual strength his handshake conveys, and rightly so, for beneath the elegant lines of his suit are hidden a hard body and the stamina of ten battalions.

When one encounters his tough-mindedness first impressions fade altogether: here is an acute intelligence, a highly trained sense of observation, an intuition that makes accurate assessments with lightning speed. If one is conscious of an impersonal gaze, one is equally aware of total commitment and single-minded sense of purpose — qualities shared, oddly enough, by criminals and geniuses.

Truman was born in New Orleans in 1924, and after an unhappy, nomadic childhood published his first work at the age of 16 — not surprising when one considers that he began writing the moment he began reading. As a child Truman was interested in little else. It was then that he developed the vocation, the disciplines of language and self necessary to his art; he was born with the rest. He produced his first novel (unhappily lost to posterity) at the age of 10.

He never really had a childhood: his astonishing intelligence was mistaken for foolishness; his boredom with formal education was thought to be listlessness; his insatiable interest in human motivations was called unhealthy curiosity. But he kept his own counsel and in his apartness he quietly pursued his craft. Over the years Truman made himself the master of any literary form he chose to employ.

He is a short-story writer of the first rank: "Miriam" is already a classic. He was 23 years old when *Other Voices, Other Rooms* established his reputation as a novelist. Then followed (not necessarily in this order) more short stories, a joyous adventure in screen writing called *Beat the Devil,* the musical play *House of Flowers, The Muses Are Heard* and *Breakfast at Tiffany's,* among other works. All are different, each is stamped with the same sensibility and craftsmanship.

He is a born wanderer. Since adulthood he has lived in various parts of the world — France, Haiti, Italy, Sicily, Africa, Greece, Russia, Switzerland. Always sensitive to his surroundings, Truman first settled down on the western plains with the wryness of General Grant: he proposed to fight it out on that line if it took all summer. It took longer.

In addition to receiving his literary gifts with sometimes maddening innocence, rural Kansas made the pleasant discovery that Truman Capote's personal characteristics are accented by an irrepressible capacity for enjoyment. He is never bored and is never boring. His conversation is astringent; his mordant wit softens into easy laughter. He likes nothing better than to split the landscape in fast sports cars. When given the opportunity he will swim a mile out into the ocean. He plays jazz records loudly and with no encouragement will perform a twist of his own invention called I'm Beside Myself. He seldom goes to films, but when he does he will see three in one day. He likes to be comfortable; he collects antique paperweights; his household includes a fat bulldog and a thin cat, both travelers, both spoiled.

When its inhabitants drew close enough for a less superficial inspection, Kansas found him to be, in spirit, an aristocrat; Truman pursues excellence; he suffers fools only when necessary; he is impatient of bad taste and cannot tolerate mediocrity in writing or in people. By instinct he is a democrat — his friends come from every station in life and speak in a bewildering variety of tongues. People always react sharply to his presence, sometimes with stirrings of envy, most often with the feeling that when he comes into their lives he gives them his best.

For over five years Truman Capote gave Kansas his best — identification complete, involvement total. His task was epic: the material he assembled in the course of his labor is the size of a sand hill (in Kansas, a modest mountain). His sense of estrangement was at first acute, but slowly, with infinite patience, he wove himself into the fabric of the country, becoming at one with the land and looking with his unique gifts into many hearts.

Kansans will spend the rest of their days at the tantalizing game of discovering Truman; what Truman found in Kansas will make people everywhere discover themselves.

DECADE FIVE

1967–1976

THORNTON WILDER'S *first Selection for the Club was* Heaven's My
Destination, *published in 1935. Thirteen years later came* The Ides of
March, *and in 1967 came* The Eighth Day. *With* The Eighth Day *Selection Report, Paul Horgan, novelist, historian, and one-time judge at
the Club, wrote about the seventy-year-old Wilder.*

Thornton Wilder
by Paul Horgan

LATE ONE EVENING last summer the guests at a small party in New
Haven were expecting Thornton Wilder, who had promised to drop in
after dinner.

The late summer twilight was quite gone when rapid, firm footfalls
came along the wooden porch at the front of the house. There came a
fine rattling at the screen door. The hostess went to assist. Offstage —
for this was the effect — she greeted her old friend who came, and in
offstage reply rose a genial response in a voice of resounding strength,
uttering what sounded like the abstract vocables of a giant in a tale.
Then this robust address fell several notes lower as inquiry and answer
established who was waiting within; and then Mr. Wilder, informed,
came to the others, striding rapidly, taking each by the hand, conveying
the impression that in a fleeting glance he penetrated with accuracy and
sympathy into the nature of each presence in the room. He then established himself on the edge of a deep sofa, leaning over his knees in a

youthful posture, and set out to amuse the company by inviting its best efforts with his own.

In tearing spirits, he made all the others play above their form. Speaking in rhetorical cadenzas about a dozen things, he smiled without cease. His great spectacles danced with the light of his eyes. He was ruddy, full-fleshed, his fringe of hair and his clipped mustache were whiter than gray, he was carelessly dressed, he accepted a highball glass and drank deep, and then held what was left with both hands and almost never sipped again. His vitality was so great that even in repose he seemed to distribute motes of life. Listening to someone else speak, he did it so intently that he seemed to be creating what he heard. Now and then someone else would suddenly be aware that Mr. Wilder was regarding him in silence, without expression except in the eyes; but there in the eyes were strong, though mannerly, hints of human concern, calm understanding and springing intelligence.

Mr. Wilder seemed in great good health. He had just finished his new novel — his longest, his first in many years, certain to be of the highest literary significance; he was among people who had known him for decades, it was all first name, and everyone else present gave him, with simplicity and justice, the unspoken deference which people offer to a great man, not so much for the pleasure which this may give to him as for that which it gives to them.

For — the evening's jest — he had recently entered his seventieth year, and behind him rose the stages by which he had reached his eminent position: a record of uninterrupted accomplishment, through seven decades of self-unsparing discovery.

The outline was familiar enough — birth in Wisconsin in 1897, childhood in China, undergraduate years at Yale, teacher at Lawrenceville, resident at the American Academy in Rome, professor of English at Chicago, Norton lecturer at Harvard, recipient of countless honors, awards and gold medals, member of the Institute and the Academy, officer in the Air Force during the Second World War, unofficial laureate of world recognition as a writer. And, as a writer, the innovator who brought new dimensions of intellectual and emotional range to the form of fiction; the playwright who liberated from the picture-frame stage, with its elaborate furniture, those dramatic allusions to common experience which to be seen as meaningful must be recognized in the very air around us; the man of ideas enclosed within the masterly artist of letters.

In his work and in his presence Mr. Wilder was all of a piece. Both his talk and his writing were spellbinding in the same way, reaching to the delights of the intellect through the values of intuitive feeling. A student for all his life, he lived with the wide world's philosophies. His natural climate was that of the formal Mediterranean classics and with these he was always able to align his vision, however colloquial its expression. His sophistication was always so comprehensive that, quite ouside the prevalent imperatives of contemporary style, he was free to come full circle to his own variations on those classic verities of the spirit to which enduring art has always given unself-conscious respect.

He had recently entered his seventieth year? So he said, and the gaiety of his statement promised more comedy to come. His humor — warm, witty, self-teasing — always played a part in even his serious statements. Seventieth — and he recalled that somewhere Goethe (this was paraphrase), Goethe said that each of us is born with some inner resonance that for all our lives tells us what our ideal age is, no matter what our years may say. Mr. Wilder gleamed about the room like a domesticated lighthouse beacon and said, "*I* was an old man when I was twelve; and now I *am* an old man, *and it's splendid!*"

With his abounding vitality, his relieved sense of achievement in completing what is surely his finest novel, his animated plans for the future, it was a declaration he could happily afford to make.

AMERICAN LIFE *in the late 1960s. Nobody was more knowledgeable about this discordant period, according to David Willis McCullough, than Norman Mailer. McCullough called* The Armies of the Night *Mailer's "best-written, most controlled, most insightful book in years."*

The Armies of the Night by Norman Mailer

"YOU KNOW, Norman," said Robert Lowell to Norman Mailer (according to Norman Mailer) on the eve of last October's antiwar march on Washington, "Elizabeth and I really think you're the finest journalist in America." It was not a compliment Mailer appreciated — at least as he tells the story in this remarkable eyewitness report on the march — but many readers will be surprised to find themselves agreeing at least in part with the Lowells' opinion. In *The Armies of the Night*, Norman Mailer has produced an incisive, if downright idiosyncratic, work of journalism that is as knowledgeable an appraisal of aspects of American life in the late 1960s as James Agee and Walker Evans' *Let Us Now Praise Famous Men* was of far different aspects thirty years ago. Mailer is pro–New Left, although hardly uncritical of it; his language is as scatological as ever; but he has created his best-written, most controlled, most insightful book in years. It is also witty, the wit being largely at Mailer's expense and at the expense of other well-known peace activists (such as Paul Goodman, Dwight Macdonald and Robert Lowell) — beginning with Mailer's making a fool of himself while addressing a pre-march meeting in a Washington rock-and-roll palace. His presentation of that meeting is a grotesquely comic tour de force, for he is able to combine a drunk's sense of absolute self-righteousness with a seemingly accurate description of what actually happened. The next day, Mailer — "his English vest and suit, his avoirdupois, his hangover, his endless blending of virtue and corruption," as he describes himself — attends the anti–Vietnam War demonstrations: the turning in of draft cards, the endless speeches at the Lincoln Memorial, the march on the Pentagon. There, a scuffle with Federal marshals leads to Mailer's arrest and brief imprisonment. Several chapters from the end he shifts gears to sketch in events he had not witnessed (the novelist passing the baton to the historian, to use his metaphor), and the book ends on a dry, factual note that is not a little boring — a Brechtian twist that only further underlines the brilliance of the first three-quarters. The value, then, is not in the record of what happened in Washington on an October weekend (there are enough fairly accurate accounts of that), but in the author's sharp observations of the behavior of the participants on both sides of the police barricades, Mailer included.

DAVID WILLIS McCULLOUGH

JOHN K. HUTCHENS *reviewed Mario Puzo's first novel,* Fortunate Pilgrim, *in 1965, calling it a "vibrant and appealing tale of an Italian-American family." Four years later Puzo was writing about a different kind of family, a family that turned out to appeal to a larger reading public and, later, to the family of moviegoers. Puzo's next two novels,* Fools Die *and* The Sicilian, *were Selections of the Club. With* Fools Die *came an appreciation of Mario Puzo by friend and fellow-author Bruce Jay Friedman.*

The Fortunate Pilgrim by Mario Puzo

IT BEGINS in the late 1920s and ends in the 1940s of World War II, this vibrant and appealing tale of an Italian-American family whose universe is New York City's Tenth Avenue, over near the Hudson River waterfront, only a few blocks west of midtown Manhattan but an immeasurable distance from it in time, tradition, culture. On the face of it, Mr. Puzo's novel is in the familiar pattern of the immigrant parents who have followed a dream from overseas to our presumably golden shores, of their stubborn retention of the old folkways in a society they have no wish to enter into, of their children who rebel against the familial customs and disciplines as — for better and worse — they become first-generation Americans. What sets Mr. Puzo's book apart from the general run of the school of fiction that it recalls is the depth and extraordinary variety of individual characterization with which he portrays one such family, headed by a superbly vital matriarch, Lucia Santa Angeluzzi-Corbo, mother of three children by her first marriage and three more by her second. In her middle years, Lucia already has lived a strenuous lifetime and still has before her the drama of passionate joy and passionate tragedy that Mr. Puzo presents with such emotion, skill, and profound sympathy. This is a turbulent and loving chronicle with a vivid figure at its center who turns out to be not only a "pilgrim" but a kind of American pioneer.

JOHN K. HUTCHENS

The Godfather by Mario Puzo

MARIO PUZO's novel about the workings of the Mafia will hardly gladden the hearts of Italian-Americans. It is a tale of violence, brutality and sexual grossness that builds a devastating picture of the Mafia's iron control over impoverished, landlord-ridden Sicily and the thriving, far-reaching empire in the United States. The narrative opens in 1945 with the Long Island wedding of a girl named Constanzia Corleone. The hundreds of guests have come not only to fete the bride but also to pay homage to her father, Don Vito Corleone, a man of substance and dignity, who has nevertheless bribed, swindled, stolen and even murdered and who is now the leader, the "godfather," of a Mafia clan or "family" in and around New York. As Mr. Puzo tells the story, Don Corleone's influence is challenged by leaders of other "families" who need his political connections for their expansion of the illicit drug trade. *The Godfather* traces the events of the next decade as Corleone fights to hold on to his power and trains his sons and heirs, one of whom develops into a smooth New World type with a Dartmouth education and a conviction that the "modern" Mafia should operate legally in areas of legitimate business — though with recourse, when necessary, to traditional underworld tactics. Not a delicate story, and far from pretty in its language or its manners, *The Godfather* is based on the chilling assumption that corruption is universal and that all policemen, all politicians, all judges and all juries can eventually be bought.

HELENE MANDELBAUM

Mario Puzo

by Bruce Jay Friedman

HOW DO you tell an old friend that he has written a great American novel?

After I read Mario Puzo's new book, *Fools Die*, I called him and said: "Hey, I read your book. It's wonderful."

"Is that right?" he said.

"That's right. I loved it."

"No kidding."

"It's quite an achievement." And then, idiotically, "Like a big, delicious dinner, totally satisfying, yet you don't feel full when you've finished."

"I'll be darned," he said.

But I never said anything about it being a great American novel. A very difficult thing to say.

When you start a friend's book, the voice is, of course, familiar, and there is the uneasy sensation that the friend is going to be talking to you for hundreds of pages, whether you're in the mood for this or not. That happened for a few pages of *Fools Die*, but then it dropped away as I got caught in the storytelling grip of the book, always in a hurry to find out what was going to happen next. As an old friend, and an "insider," I thought I recognized people and events, but they got magically transformed into other people and events and I had the fun of being fooled by a master magician — which, incidentally, is a component of the book, the writer as magician, able to control and transform the world. *Fools Die* is populated by the "high and low," as they say, of Vegas and Hol-

lywood and New York. In the narrative, the phrases and concerns —
"soft hookers" — women who "second-card" you ... "change or
die" — seem to go dropping into the language and the culture like peb-
bles. There is at least one magnificent character, a complex and spiritually lush young woman named Janelle. Still, the book didn't get great
on me until a week had passed and I began to realize the sweep of Puzo's
accomplishment.

"If you think it's a great novel, why don't you tell him," said Candida
Donadio, a mutual friend and literary agent.

"He's too rich and famous."

"Don't be ridiculous," she said. "We're talking about Mario."

So I called him up again and we made plans to have dinner. Part of the
fun of telling a friend that he has written a great American novel is that
you get to see that friend. In the last decade Mario and I had only been
successful in seeing each other in Hollywood and Las Vegas, never in
New York where we both live.

He came tumbling out of a limousine and he didn't seem as uncomfortable with it as he had with his first one. He told the limo driver, who
was hired to drive him into the city from Long Island, to come back in a
couple of hours. The driver had apologized for reading the condensed
version of *The Godfather* because he didn't have time to read the whole
book. Mario was not annoyed at this so much as amazed. "How come I
have time to write the whole book, and he doesn't have time to read it?"

Another thing that amazed him was the now-fabled $2.5 million he
had gotten for the paperback sale of his new book, a figure that made
him the Babe Ruth of reprint rights. Puzo is the only one who is allowed
to talk about that kind of money to another writer. The most damning
charge you can make against him is that he is such a nice man that you
don't get to feel envious of him. When he first got all that money, he told
me it wasn't as good as it looked because he'd had to "throw in" the reprint rights to *The Godfather*. Now he was worried because the publisher who had paid him the money had called him aside at a party and
asked him — as a special favor — if he could please explain the last couple of pages. "It's one of those endings you can't explain with precision.
I felt bad about this because for $2.5 million I felt he deserved an expert
analysis."

We both laughed about the old days at Magazine Management Company, where I had hired him as an editor of *Male* and *Men* magazines,
holding out the promise that he could earn as much as $200 a week, a
fabled sum at that time. It's hard to believe, but only a small part of this

nostalgia was about money. It was about craziness and "success" and the upside-down nature of life — the theme of his new book.

At one point, the main character in *Fools Die* talks about a woman he meets (and eventually marries) in a writing class who has a knack for writing but is not willing to "give up her life for writing" in the manner of the hero. The hero of the book is many people, but at that moment he is Puzo who more than anyone else I know of has taken this direction. Puzo is a proud spokesman for the writer and the writer's craft. He has just read a recent book that maligns a favorite of his, Somerset Maugham. The author says Maugham's writing suffered because he was a repressed homosexual. Mario says this is idiotic, and, ironically, "the book only comes alive when Maugham is quoted and speaks for himself."

Another thing that fills him with wonder is that a major magazine is writing a cover story on him and has alerted him that he may as well grant them an interview because otherwise they are going to "write around him." He can't quite get over that. "I'm important enough to be 'written around'!" he said.

I ask what I think is a logical question. Now that he has written a giant, wonderful book, what is he going to do next? He had once suggested to me that when this book was completed, he was going to hang up his gloves. He jokes about getting his weight down to 165 pounds — his next target. I mumble something about his doing a play — as if things have to be thought up for him. A look crosses his face and he says he's found out that he only loves to write novels. Other adventures don't seem to have worked out with as much satisfaction; the black-and-blue look suggests that that includes Hollywood and Las Vegas and many of the other "rewards" of success.

We go back to talking of the old days at Magazine Management and decide that we had come up with a weird and tattered group of elitists. He pulls a cigar out of his pocket the size of a violin and offers it to me. I have written articles about the joys of cigar smoking, but I don't smoke them anymore. He doesn't try to tempt me the way others do. He smokes the violin-size cigar in such a way that magically I don't notice or crave it. It's a fine dinner and not because of the food. At some point it becomes easy and natural to tell him I think he's written a great American novel. I pull back a little, quibble about the prose of his book and complain about a crazy, almost suicidal opening which the book surmounts. But I *do* tell him.

"Is that right?" he says.

"I really mean it."

"No kidding?"
"Honest."
"I'll be darned."

"AN INSPIRED MESS," *wrote David Willis McCullough about Kurt Vonnegut's most personal work*, Slaughterhouse Five.

Slaughterhouse Five: Or, The Children's Crusade by Kurt Vonnegut, Jr.

HERE is the novel that Kurt Vonnegut's fans have been hearing about and waiting for as long as, well, probably for as long as they have been Vonnegut fans. It is the book about the Dresden fire-bombing (135,000 killed as compared to the 80,000 wiped out at Hiroshima) that Vonnegut himself lived through as a prisoner of war in Germany during World War II. It is also the book that for as long as anyone can remember, Vonnegut has been telling interviewers he has been working on. The result is something of an inspired mess, part autobiography, part black comedy and part pulp science fiction straight out of the 1950s. It is even something of a review of other Vonnegut novels when such old favorites as Eliot Rosewater, Howard W. Campbell, Jr., and Kilgore Trout drop in as minor characters. The hero is one Billy Pilgrim, a successful optician from Ilium, New York, who goes to war, is captured by Germans and held in an old slaughterhouse in Dresden at the time of the Allied air raids and who later helps — as did Vonnegut — dig out the ash-filled city. But Billy Pilgrim also believes that he has been taken to the distant planet of Tralfamadore (where the flying saucers come from), where he is exhibited naked in the zoo with the beautiful film actress Montana Wildhack, his mate. Billy is able to fall in and out of time, and, like Merlin in *The Once and Future King*, is often able to know what is going to happen without being able to remember what already has happened. The novel is Billy's story, full of all the lackluster details of life in Ilium juxtaposed with the horror of Dresden and the exotica of Tralfamadore. It is a sad, funny combination that only Vonnegut would think of mixing and the only Vonnegut fans would possibly put up with.

DAVID WILLIS MCCULLOUGH

BEFORE Stilwell and the American Experience in China, *Barbara Tuchman wrote* The Guns of August *and* The Proud Tower, *both Club Selections. After* Stilwell *there was a further procession of distinguished works. Tuchman, as you will see from Elizabeth Janeway's piece (Janeway was a prolific author in her own right), had established her credentials. In 1986 the Club published a special edition of* Stilwell *in its "American Past" series. In the new introduction to this volume John K. Fairbank, Professor of History Emeritus at Harvard, summed up Tuchman's touch. "Barbara Tuchman," he wrote, "has been a vocal, incisive and widely persuasive advocate of history as a readable story."*

Barbara W. Tuchman
by Elizabeth Janeway

SOMEWHERE in his memoir, *Speak, Memory,* Vladimir Nabokov remarks on "the essential spirality of all things in relations to time." Barbara Wertheim Tuchman's affair with the Far East is an elegant example of such turning and returning. Her previous books, notably *The Guns of August,* won her high praise as an analyst of European and American politics and culture from the turn of the century through the First World War. Then suddenly she directed her gaze to the other side of the world. How odd! But no, not odd. One would do better to say, "How spiral!" For Barbara Tuchman did her first job of research in Tokyo and received her first check from a publisher for a manuscript dealing with Russian and Japanese fisheries. It came to $30, and she spent it on a record player (they were cheap in Tokyo in 1935) and a recording of *Madame Butterfly.*

At the time her connection with the Orient seemed casual enough. Fresh out of Radcliffe College, she had been recommended for the job — research on an economic handbook of the Pacific area — by the president of Radcliffe. The scene of her labors was Tokyo, largely because the organization sponsoring her work was eager to offer liberals in Japan a chance to maintain ties with the West in an era of growing militarism. One of the few results of this good intention was to give Miss Wertheim, as she was then, a year in Japan and a view of China, for she came home across Asia. It was an odd journey through semistabilized chaos: a month in China, where the Japanese kept a constant watch on the American Embassy (whose newly arrived military attaché was named Joseph Stilwell), a trip across the puppet state of Manchukuo, and then a seemingly endless trundle west toward Moscow, eleven days on the Trans-Siberian Railway. For Miss Wertheim, that seemed to be the end of her Eastern adventure. Later, her work as a reporter for *The Nation* took her to Spain; her interests centered on European affairs; she reported on America for the English *New Statesman*. In 1940 she married Dr. Lester Tuchman.

Then came Pearl Harbor. Dr. Tuchman was ordered abroad in 1943, and, like many another young wife, Barbara Tuchman went looking for a job. Her European knowledge and connections suggested to officials at the Office of War Information in Washington that she would be an excellent choice to explain to America's Allies a special aspect of America's involvement in the war, that is, its commitment in the Pacific. Since Britain and America were both deeply concerned in the China-Burma-India Theater, Mrs. Tuchman found herself studying the action there with particular attention. The American commander was General Joseph Stilwell, and, until 1945, it was part of Mrs. Tuchman's job to explain what he was doing in Asia to the British public.

The war ended; the Chiang Kai-shek government retreated to Taiwan; China vanished behind the Bamboo Curtain. Little was written about that vast country, and what did appear tended toward partisan polemic. When, during the 1950s, Mrs. Tuchman turned again to her historical studies, they dealt with the day-before-yesterday era in Europe and America which did so much to shape our own times. Her daughters were growing, and, with more time for her career, she was crossing the boundary which separates a housewife who works at writing from a professional author. Like most professionals, she had "her field," and her first great success, *The Guns of August*, which won her a Pulitzer Prize in 1963, confirmed her mastery of "la belle époque" and its shattering end. In *The Proud Tower*, which followed, she examined some of the characteristic attitudes and behavior of the period that died when the guns began in 1914. Both books were Selections of the Book-of-the-Month Club.

Mrs. Tuchman then projected a book which was to have been a further look at this era, a study of the Balkan Wars of 1912 and 1913; but she found herself hesitating. Americans of the 1960s had seen clearly that the war which began in 1914 had ended an age and laid the foundation for another. President Kennedy had even recommended to the Joint Chiefs of Staff that they read *The Guns of August* with special attention to its documentation of how a process of competitive commitment could get out of hand. But the tempest in a teapot of the Balkan Wars, the imperial claims of Czarist Russia, the slackening grip of Turkey — would all these really speak to our times? As she hesitated, Mrs. Tuchman found herself in Washington one day talking with a veteran of the Burma campaign, Colonel Trevor Dupuy. When he learned that she was, in her own way, a veteran of those wars, he urged them on her as material for her next book. Soon after, in San Francisco, she met another "old China hand," Marine General Samuel Griffith, and he gave the same advice. In Pasadena, staying with her daughter and son-in-law, Lucy and David Eisenberg, Mrs. Tuchman mentioned the counsel she had received to spiral back once more toward the Orient. "Ma," said her daughter firmly, "you must do China!" Though it was couched in cavalier terms, the repetition told. Mrs. Tuchman agreed, and settled down to "do" China.

Her research was, she says, the most exciting and rewarding she has ever done, and the book the most difficult to write. She plumbed untouched archives; she traveled to Taiwan and interviewed there men who had been close to Stilwell when he commanded Chiang's troops; she viewed, in India, the start of the Burma Road. For the first time her research could not simply come out of books. She talked with hundreds of people who remembered Stilwell and China in those troubled times. Out of it all, she has written not just a remarkable book but clearly one that will begin a much-needed and long-awaited examination of America's relationship to the Far East.

A BIBLE *as the Main Selection of the* Book-of-the-Month *Club? In 1970 the members of the Club's Editorial Board decided that* The New English Bible, *with a new translation of the Old Testament and the Apocrypha, bound with the New Testament, would make a suitable and eloquent Selection. Gilbert Highet, the board's most erudite judge, a classical scholar, teacher, and linguist, explained the choice.*

The New English Bible

MEN HAVE ALWAYS been of two minds about translating the words of God. All over the world, holy scriptures have been treated in two ways.

One method is to preserve them exactly as they were first written down. Even when their original language ceases to be spoken and grows, for all other purposes, obsolete, they are kept unaltered because they are sacred. Not one jot or one tittle must perish from the hallowed text. Now, since national destinies, and languages within them, are constantly changing, this means that the holy books — once addressed to all the people for their instruction and comfort — in time become unintelligible except to a few experts: priests and scholars. Even these find the ancient writings difficult to comprehend; and so, generation after generation, an increasing body of commentary on the scriptures accumulates. This sometimes makes the texts even more complex and difficult for the ordinary man. Religious services also are affected. Where once the whole assembly of believers could join in every part of the service of worship, now much of the ritual must be conducted in a dead language, spoken or chanted by the priests, a language which the ordinary worshiper cannot speak (apart from a few phrases learned by rote) and in which God cannot communicate with him. The gulf between the Creator and the creature grows wider. Because God's words are now impossible for most people to understand, they find it easier to hold him in awe but more difficult to love him.

The other method of handling sacred books is, when they grow old, to translate them into the new speech of the people. Sometimes this is objected to as profaning the holy language. Occasionally it is condemned as an invasion of the mysteries which God intended to keep secret from all but a few. Often it has a curious and awkward result. The translation itself in time becomes partly or wholly unintelligible — and, at the same time, because of its age, acquires a sanctity comparable to the original. Therefore it is seen as blasphemy to suggest that, after the first translation, a new one should be made. For a thousand years the people of western Christendom read the Bible (when they could read) in the Latin form which St. Jerome gave it about A.D. 385. This was only a translation of the original Hebrew, Aramaic and Greek; yet for many centuries it was canonical, and attempts to supersede it by translations into more modern and more widely used languages were bitterly opposed and severely punished.

This kind of thing has happened in many countries with many religious books. Three things cause it. One is the fact that most people do not fully realize that language lives and changes and that, therefore, when they read a translation written in their own tongue, they may be seriously misunderstanding it if it is several centuries old. The second is that — although (as St. Paul said) the letter kills but the spirit gives life — people cling to the letter, the form of words which they are accustomed to; they will defend it, whether they fully understand it or not. The third is that most of us are in search of authority, particularly in the moral and religious realm; we find authority in stability; we are disquieted when a central idea in religion or law keeps being redefined and rephrased and reinterpreted; and every fresh translation, by rephrasing an established set of concepts, seems to make such concepts questionable and insecure.

Nevertheless, if an important book such as a book of religion is to be fully meaningful and to exercise all the power that it can, it must be translated again and again; and the instinctive resistance which many conservatives feel for such innovations must be overcome. Ideally, every book should be read in its original tongue. Serious students of the Bible must know Hebrew, Aramaic and Greek. But most of us have not sufficient time, energy and talent to master several languages. Therefore in every century, perhaps in every generation, all great works should be translated afresh, so that the latest advances in scholarly interpretation may be incorporated and so that readers may read the books in something suitably close to the language in which they speak and think.

These thoughts came to me as I read the new translation of the Holy Bible published by the University Presses of Oxford and Cambridge. I know Greek, and when the translation of the New Testament was published in 1961, I reviewed it from the standpoint of a man who knows both the original language and that of the translation. I do not know Hebrew; therefore I approached the translation of the Old Testament as an ordinary reader, desiring to get closer to the meaning behind the words. Much of the Old Testament has always puzzled me. I found that hundreds of passages which had appeared obscure to me for many years were at last clarified.

One salient instance first. In the Bible as I have always read it, the sixth of God's commandments is *Thou shalt not kill*. There it stands in Exodus, chapter 20, verse 13, repeated in Deuteronomy 5:17. Now, anyone who can read will soon realize that this does not mean that no human being must kill any other human being. Go on in Exodus to chapter 21, verse 12. God is still giving his commandments. He says clearly that a murderer must be executed. *He that smiteth a man so that he die, shall surely be put to death.* The Lord goes on to say that anyone who strikes or curses his father or mother shall surely be put to death (verses 15 and 17) and that a kidnapper must be executed (verse 16). Death, says the Lord, is the punishment for witchcraft, bestiality and sacrificing to strange divinities (chapter 23, verses 18–20).

Thou shalt not kill therefore does not forbid us to execute criminals. Does it mean that we must not kill rebels in our own country? Not according to the Holy Scripture. Read on to the 32nd chapter of Exodus. When Moses brought the commandments down from the mountain, he found the people dancing from the mountain, he found the people dancing naked around a golden idol. He said to the Levites, *Thus saith the LORD God of Israel, put every man his sword by his side . . . and slay every man his brother . . . and every man his neighbor.* Three thousand men were killed. God approved.

Thou shalt not kill. Perhaps it means that no one must make war on other nations. Not according to the word of God. When Joshua led the children of Israel into the promised land, he and his army killed all the inhabitants of many cities which resisted them — men, women and children. Such was the fate of the city of Ai, *according unto the word of the LORD which he had commanded Joshua;* and in all the country he *utterly destroyed all that breathed, as the LORD God of Israel commanded* (Joshua, chapter 8, verses 21–29; chapter 10, verses 28–43). Therefore God did not mean that killing in war was forbidden. How could he have said *Thou shalt not kill?*

This worried me for years, until I asked a Hebrew scholar about it. He told me that the sixth commandment does not say *Thou shalt not kill.* The word *kill* is not used. The special word in the commandment refers to the unlawful killing of a fellow citizen. The correct translation for today is given by the new version of the Bible: *you shall not commit murder.* *

That is only one example to show the precision of the new translation. The moral injunctions of the Bible are now much more clear and harder to misunderstand.

The visions of the prophets, being mystical experiences, can never be totally clear. But the old translations sometimes made them quite incomprehensible. Thus, Ezekiel sitting in exile had a vision of God's

* The same commandment is quoted by Jesus (Matthew 5:21, Mark 10:19, Luke 18:20) and St. James (2:11); and there too, in the new version of the New Testament Greek, the translators give the crucial word as *murder.*

temple in Jerusalem defiled by idolatry (Ezek. 8). *The spirit*, says the old translation, *brought me . . . to the door of the inner gate that looketh toward the north; where was the seat of the image of jealousy, which provoketh to jealousy.* Incomprehensible. But now the new rendering makes it clear. *A spirit . . . put me down at the entrance to the inner gate facing north, where stands the image of Lust to rouse lustful passion* — evidently the idol of one of the Eastern sex cults.

We have usually seen the Old Testament printed as though it were all prose. This is wrong. Much of it is poetry; and an utterance made in a poem, intensified by rhythm and penetrated by imagery, is not to be read and literally understood as though it were a statement couched in plain prose. The new version makes this clear to eye and mind by setting all the poetic passages as unrhymed verse. They even look more beautiful. And, even at their most exalted, they are clearer. Answering Job's complaints, the Almighty describes the wonders and mysteries of the universe, among which man is but an insignificant creature. In the traditional rendering (Job 38:32-35) God asks, *Canst thou bring forth Mazzaroth in his season? or canst thou guide Arcturus with his sons? Knowest thou the ordinances of heaven? canst thou set the domination thereof in the earth? Canst thou lift up thy voice to the clouds, that abundance of waters may cover thee? Canst thou send lightnings, that they may go, and say unto thee, Here we are?* This sounds grand but vague, and it is not like the language of a disputant, even when that disputant is divine. Most readers will understand this better:

> *Can you bring out the signs of the zodiac in their season*
> *or guide Aldebaran and its train?*
> *Did you proclaim the rules that govern the heavens,*
> *or determine the laws of nature on earth?*
> *Can you command the dense clouds*
> *to cover you with their weight of waters?*
> *If you bid lightning speed on its way,*
> *will it say to you, "I am ready"?*

Indeed, one of the greatest services done by the modern translators is to lay open to the public a treasure of poetic ideas, some of them never realized before, and some long obscured by errors in expression. In the same Book of Job (39:19-25) there is a splendid little paean to the warhorse. Many readers have thought it simply quaint to read that the spirited charger *saith among the trumpets Ha, ha* and have wondered why God declares that *the glory of his nostrils is terrible.* Now we see.

> *Do you make him quiver like a locust's wings,*
> *when his shrill neighing strikes terror? . . .*
> *at the blast of the horn he cries "Aha!"*
> *and from afar he scents the battle.*

For students of the Bible who do not know Hebrew, this translation has a further quality, which some fundamentalists may think a defect. Its prose is so lucid that it shows up some of the discrepancies. Experts have long known of these discrepancies. Some stories are told twice or three times over, and the different versions do not agree in all points. The most obvious example is the four Gospels, which cannot, as they stand, be fully harmonized. Some of the Old Testament narratives offer a similar problem, and somehow it was easier to overlook it in the solemn cathedral-like dimness of the traditional version. For example: how many of each kind of animal did God tell Noah to take into the ark? Everyone will answer, "The animals went in two by two." So God commands in Genesis 6:19–20, and so, in the next chapter (Genesis 7:8–16), the animals enter, one male and one female of all living things. But between God's first command and Noah's obedience comes a second (Genesis 7:2–3): take with you *seven pairs . . . of all beasts that are ritually clean and one pair . . . of all beasts that are not clean; also seven pairs . . . of every bird.* Now, Noah did not do this. Did he disobey the word of the Lord by taking only one pair of each? Surely not. Surely the second command was inserted later into the narrative by some pious man who wished to emphasize the distinction between clean animals and vermin unfit for food — the distinction given as law by God to Moses many centuries later (Leviticus 11) — and who was too reverent to alter the rest of the narrative so as to make it fit.

It is not possible to understand the Bible intelligently if one blinds one's eyes to these discrepancies, most of them due to combination or interpolation done for laudable motives. But the new translation is so plain and straightforward that it brings them out more sharply — that is, it makes a higher demand on the intelligence of the reader and gives him a larger reward.

How does the new Bible sound when read aloud?

The narrative sections and the plain prose speeches are much crisper and more forceful. When Jerusalem was being rebuilt by Nehemiah, the poor Jews complained that they were being oppressed by the rich (Neh. 5:1–5). *Yet now,* they said, *our flesh is as the flesh of our brethren, our children as their children: and lo, we bring into bondage our sons and our daughters to be servants.* The new rendering of their protest is more drastic and more biting: *Our bodily needs are the same as other people's, our children are as good as theirs; yet here we are, forcing our sons and daughters to become slaves.* A little later (Neh. 5:18) Nehemiah says that he provided beef, mutton, poultry and wine every day for the chief citizens, *yet for all this required not I the bread of the governor* — meaning what? That he did not need bread also? No. *In spite of all this, I did not draw the governor's allowance.*

In the poetic passages, the vocabulary of the new version is much less copious but somewhat more vivid and sharply edged, and the syntax more orderly, than that of the old. No longer does the prophet Jeremiah (Jer. 5:28) sing of the wicked *They are waxen fat, they shine: yea, they overpass the deeds of the wicked.* Now we have:

> *They grow rich and grand,*
> *bloated and rancorous;*
> *their thoughts are all of evil.*

No longer does David in his distress (Ps. 77:4–6) cry, *Thou holdest mine eyes waking: I am so troubled that I cannot speak. I have considered the days of old, the years of ancient times. I call to remembrance my song in the night: I commune with mine own heart; and my spirit made diligent search.*

This is passionate but incoherent. Now he sings:

> *My eyelids were tightly closed;*
> *I was dazed and I could not speak.*
> *My thoughts went back to times long past,*
> *I remembered forgotten years;*
> *all night long I was in deep distress,*
> *as I lay thinking, my spirit was sunk in despair.*

Every reader must judge for himself, and only those who know Hebrew and English equally well are able to judge authoritatively. To me it seems that words so direct, in rhythms so straight and simple, will give less of a sense of incommunicable mystery and more genuine sympathetic understanding.

Yet one question remains. Does the new version contain immortal phrases, things of independent beauty which stay in the memory like the best of Shakespeare, as lustrous as diamonds and as fragrant as roses? The King James translation was full of such charms and treasures. As the new translation is read and used and meditated upon, it may be that many passages — particularly in the poetic sections, where the meaning is now much clearer and the language more direct and forceful — will likewise work their way into our collective mind and imagination.

Of one thing I am certain. Our culture has notably changed in the last fifty years and will continue to change very rapidly. If the Bible is to maintain its powerful and beneficial influence upon us, it must be (in the quaint phrase of the Book of Common Prayer) "understanded of the people"; and in that, the new translation is remarkably successful. It is the first time I have ever read the Bible for hours at a time, without pausing every few minutes to ponder over an obscure locution or a vague and cloudy sentence, and puzzle vainly, and move on in discouragement. This translation is what all translations must be first, and most essentially: a triumph of clarity.

THE SELDOM-HEARD *Indian's voice in American history is raised in* Bury My Heart at Wounded Knee *by Dee Brown, a far-reaching chronicle that became a major 1971 bestseller.*

Bury My Heart at Wounded Knee
by Dee Brown

TO PUT IT quickly and plainly, this is nothing less than a thirty-year crime story, a blow-by-blow account of the destruction, between 1860 and 1890, of the culture and civilization of the Indian of the American West. It opens with the butchery of the Navahos in the Southwest and closes with the massacre of the Sioux at Wounded Knee in South Dakota. Between the first act and the final curtain are such outrages as General Custer's attack on the Southern Cheyennes' village at Washita Creek, the even more savage destruction of the Cheyennes at Sand Creek by Colonel John M. Chivington's Colorado Volunteers, the betrayal of Chief Joseph and his Nez Percés who surrendered to General Nelson A. Miles and then were sent away to malarial swamps, many of them to die there. Even when the Indians fought back successfully, as when the Sioux and Cheyennes whipped General George Crook on the Rosebud River and General Custer at the Little Big Horn, the victories tended to be Pyrrhic ones; the hosts of the Great White Father simply redoubled their efforts as Manifest Destiny went along on its treaty-breaking way. To be sure, much has been written about this terrible record, but seldom from the Indian point of view. What distinguishes Mr. Brown's excellent work is that the Indian's voice, seldom heard in American history, enters these pages through excerpts from the records of treaty councils and other meetings. Or, as Mr. Brown states it: "Americans who have always looked westward when reading about this period should read this book facing eastward."

JOHN K. HUTCHENS

CLIFTON FADIMAN *made a wise bet in the opening paragraph of his report on Frederick Forsyth's* The Day of the Jackal. *He bet BOMC members "that even readers who do not usually rush to read police novels" would find themselves hooked by the book. And the author himself explained how he came to write about the attempted assassination of Charles de Gaulle.*

The Day of the Jackal by Frederick Forsyth

LET'S not equivocate: this is grand, high-grade escape reading, which in its genre may rank as high as the Sherlock Holmes stories do in the field of the straight detective novel. Its genre is not exactly straight-detective but rather what the French call the *roman policier*, the police novel. In any case your Board of Judges is willing to make a modest bet that even readers who do not usually rush to read police novels will soon find themselves hooked by *The Day of the Jackal*.

Frederick Forsyth's whole (and satisfactorily long) book turns on two factors: a brilliant central premise and an ingenious narrative device that is at least as old as the 18th century but which has, to our best knowledge, hardly been used in suspense fiction. The central premise is this: one day in Paris in 1963 — on Sunday, August 25, 1963, to be precise — there occurred in the Place du Juin 1940, at the southern end of the Rue de Rennes, a fiendishly well-planned but unsuccessful attempt to assassinate De Gaulle.

The narrative device? Well, let's begin at the beginning. Mr. Forsyth starts with an actual fact: with the execution, on March 11, 1963, of a certain Lieut. Col. Bastien-Thiry, OAS leader of a gang of Army officers who had set up a roadblock and attempted to shoot De Gaulle, believing he had betrayed France in Algeria. (The OAS, or *Organisation Armée Secrète*, was the extremist organization which hoped to block Algerian independence. De Gaulle's verdict on the attempt was characteristic: "They can't shoot straight.")

Now, this incident is, as we have noted, historical. The news of the execution was broadcast. Then, according to Mr. Forsyth's novel, "In a small hotel room in Austria the broadcast was to set off a train of thoughts and actions that brought General de Gaulle nearer to death than at any time in his career. The room was that of Col. Marc Rodin, new operations Chief of the OAS."

With this sentence we pass from fact to fiction. But the transition is so cleverly handled, and the following narrative is so realistically detailed, that we are almost deceived. That is, we get the feeling of reading an account of an actual happening, made all the more sensational by the eminence of the central figure. Col. Rodin is, of course, an invention, and so is the man known as the Jackal, whom Rodin selects as the assassin; but De Gaulle is real enough, and so are other characters in the story. Thus the reader, though he *knows* he is being fooled, nevertheless cheerfully surrenders to that willing suspension of disbelief that accomplished novelists know so well how to evoke — Defoe, for example, in *Robinson Crusoe.*

The plot against De Gaulle can succeed only if the killing is done, as Rodin mutters, by "a man who is not known" to the French police. A process of elimination leads to the choice of a tall, blond Englishman, the Jackal, a gentlemanly professional killer who is absolutely unknown to *any* police force. As with at least a dozen other characters in this remarkable book, the figure of the Jackal has been carefully studied by the author. The Jackal is not, as in a James Bond novel, a mere counter on the game-board of intrigue but supremely shrewd and knowledgeable — on the order of Balzac's famous master criminal, Vautrin. He does not merely *claim* to be "the best and therefore the most expensive" living criminal; every one of his hundreds of actions and decisions marks him as a convincing superman of crime. To assassinate De Gaulle, needless to say, will be no small problem. As Mr. Forsyth explains it, it involves a series of disguises, a series of fake passports and identities, and the construction of a fantastic one-of-a-kind rifle loaded with specially prepared bullets.

Against the Jackal and his OAC employers are mobilized, as the tense story develops, almost the entire anticriminal forces of France, the security agencies of seven other countries (especially England) and, last but not least, the quiet, methodical Claude Lebel, Deputy Chief of the Criminal Division of the Paris police. Lebel has soft brown eyes, a toothbrush mustache — and a brain: "the best detective in France," as his superior calls him. Lebel is so well-realized that one hardly thinks of him as an imaginary person. He deserves a place with Javert, Maigret and a few other truly memorable police detectives in the annals of fiction.

For some time Lebel has almost nothing to work with. He knows nothing about the wanted man except that he is a foreigner. He is further handicapped by the fact that De Gaulle himself refuses to take the necessary precautions or to change his schedule of public appearances. Then an OAS guard, Kowalski, is trapped, tortured, and in his delirium gasps out . . . but it is best to reveal no further details.

We may hint, though, that there is a first-rate erotic interlude in which the Jackal seduces a willing baroness, also a chase from Milan to Paris in which the Jackal outwits Lebel. And there are such remarkably intimate descriptions of Paris streets, cafés, houses and small-time citizens that one wonders how Mr. Forsyth knows as much as he seems to about a city to which he is of course not native.

Indeed, apart from the ingenious basic idea and the mature tone (this is no ordinary cops-and-robbers hackwork), what makes *The Day of the Jackal* outstanding is its general believability. Mr. Forsyth seems to have had the entrée to a hundred interiors, from the workshop of a criminal gunmaker to the reception room of Britain's Prime Minister at 10 Downing Street, London. One feels that one is in the hands of a man generally knowledgeable — and especially so in the world of criminal psychology, detection and contemporary undercover violence.

The Day of the Jackal is a book to enjoy.

CLIFTON FADIMAN

Frederick Forsyth
An Author's Note

THERE is little or nothing of the contemporary fashionable mold about my background. No upbringing in seamy backstreets bordered by rat-infested tenements, no struggle to survive in a hostile society calculated to turn any infant into a crazy mixed-up kid. If I achieved that status, it was through sheer effort.

I was born in Ashford, Kent, in August, 1938. My parents were and still are solid middle-class business people; they jointly ran a gown and fur shop in Ashford until they retired five years ago. Ashford is a small market town midway between London and the Channel coast.

Our house was large and roomy. I had a governess and a housekeeper to look after me while Mother was at work and Father in the Army. I spent long hours in an air-raid shelter during the first six years of life, emerging briefly to collect fragments of shrapnel with which Mr. Hitler's bombers were dosing the countryside around Ashford on their way to London. I regretted the end of the war in 1945, since it had enabled me to meet a variety of interesting people like the sergeant from Texas who parked his Patton tank on our rosebed and offered to let me come with him on D-Day if I could get my mother's permission. Rather unsportingly she refused.

After attending a kindergarten school in a village outside town, I was sent in 1948 to a boarding school from which in 1951 I won a major scholarship to Tonbridge School, one of Britain's top public schools. My parents had made friends with a French family through Rotary, and I spent summer vacations with them in France, so by the age of 13 I spoke French.

Tonbridge I hated; it was full of rules and regulations that made no sense and contributed to the development of a strong streak of rebel in me, so that to this day I dislike authority and establishments. Determined to get out as soon as possible, I took to heart my father's promise to take me away if I passed the necessary examinations. I began vacationing during summers in Germany, learned German, then started on Russian.

By my mid-teens I had three ambitions: bullfighting (I was intoxicated by Hemingway's *Death in the Afternoon*), airplanes and getting out of school. At 16 I won a Royal Air Force flying scholarship, through which I could learn to fly at a private club with the RAF paying the bills. I used to keep a small motorcycle in a shed in the town, slip away on sports afternoons, ride the twenty miles to the flying club, have my lesson in a beautiful old open-cockpit biplane called a Tiger Moth, and be back in time for prayers. After passing my flying test I flew back over the school and beat the hell out of the headmaster's house. On my return he beat the hell out of me. I did not like Tonbridge precisely for this unsporting attitude, so I left next semester, having passed every exam available to me. I refused to go on to college.

* * *

Just turned 17, I went down to Granada, in Spain, and spent the next four months practicing capework in the arena with other aspirant matadors, but to no avail. No one would take my aspirations seriously, so I quit and went over to Tangier, then a center of international smuggling. My parents came down and took me back home. At 17½ I joined the Air Force as a pilot. A year later, at 18, I was converted to single-seat jets and at 19 got my "wings" — the youngest fighter pilot in the Royal Air Force at that time. Then I decided I wanted to be a foreign correspondent, so I left the service and started work on a provincial daily newspaper as a cub reporter.

After three years I joined Reuters news agency and in 1962 was posted to Paris. At that time, and for a time thereafter, the French OAS (Secret Army Organization) was trying to kill President de Gaulle, and it was from my experiences there that I decided one day to write the story of the Jackal. In September, 1963, at the age of 25, I was appointed Reuters Bureau Chief in East Berlin, covering East Germany and Czechoslovakia, which was a fascinating assignment in those days, as I could by this time almost pass for a German.

Transferred back to Paris in 1964, I covered stories in Bonn, Rome, Madrid, Brussels and Palermo, finally returning to London in April, 1965. In October of that year I joined the BBC, working first as radio reporter. The following February, I got the job of Assistant Diplomatic Correspondent. Sent down to cover the start of the Nigeria-Biafra war in July, 1967, I displeased the British Ambassador in Nigeria, who complained bitterly about my dispatches to the Commmonwealth Office, who in turn passed their displeasure on to BBC. Recalled and rebuked, I quit in February, 1968, and went back to Biafra as a freelance reporter. In all I spent eighteen months inside the enclave, and the sufferings I witnessed there marked me deeply, partly because they were unnecessary, partly because they affected especially the child population, and mostly because the British Government headed by Harold Wilson was solidly behind the Nigerian dictatorship which had brought these sufferings about. So far as I am concerned, Biafra was Britain's Mylai, except that the Wilson Government got black fingers to pull the trigger.

In the spring of 1969 I wrote a book telling the story of what really happened — The Biafra Story — and Penguin published it in June, 1969. It still sells in America. At the end of '69, with Biafra finally being pulverized, I faced the bleak prospect of merely scratching a living as a freelance reporter or turning to something else. Journalism had lost its savor by this time, so, starting on January 1, 1970, I sat down and wrote the long-delayed *Jackal.* De Gaulle was by this time retired. The book was finished in thirty-five days and nights, and I gave it to my agent.

Throughout the spring and summer the manuscript was rejected by four London publishers, and I came to the view it was probably not going to be taken by anyone. My savings were almost exhausted when, in September, a publisher was found. After that, things snowballed. As of now, all the major world rights are sold. The film rights went to Romulus Films of London, who engaged Fred Zinnemann to direct it, and I have been engaged to write the screenplay.

As for the future, I am researching another novel, and I remain incurably convinced there must be something terribly interesting going on over the top of the next hill.

OVER THE YEARS *Samuel Eliot Morison was a favorite author of Book-of-the-Month Club members. Columbus, John Paul Jones, and Samuel Champlain were subjects of biographies by this "Admiral of the Vast Seas of History," as Page Smith called Morison. Then there were the cosmic volumes like* The Concise History of the American Republic *and* The Oxford History of the American People. The European Discovery of America: The Northern Voyages *was a Selection in 1971. In his appreciation of Morison, Smith called him "the greatest historian of our time."*

Samuel Eliot Morison
by Page Smith

WHEN one has summed up all of Samuel Eliot Morison's accomplishments and honors — over forty books, two Pulitzer Prizes, the first Balzan Foundation Award in History (which he received in competition with historians from every country), the Gold Medal of the American Academy of Arts and Letters, and many more — it is clear enough that his credentials as the foremost historian of his day are impeccable. But what kind of man is he?

Almost twenty-five years ago I sat in his lectures at Harvard and pondered that question. He was a delightful lecturer, dryly witty and enormously learned. He wrote a prodigious amount, and I, still only half serious about being an academic historian myself, wondered how he did it. He liked an essay of mine on Samuel Adams or Sir Francis Drake, perhaps both, and invited me to tea in his stately old house on Brimmer Street. He was so remote and austere that I felt a little as though God had summoned me to the throne of grace; indeed, in a real sense Morison's sympathy and encouragement were the salvation of an uncertain veteran with a wife and two small children to think of.

Later, as assistant in his course in Colonial history, I was able to give more thought to the question of what made at least *this* eminent historian tick. He was, after all, rather conventional in his thinking — he had none of the intellectual brilliance that distinguished some of his Harvard colleagues; he did not, so far as I could see, spend his time buried in some cubicle writing laborious notes on little cards (though he must certainly have accumulated through his life a veritable pyramid of notes, I never saw him surrounded by the papery paraphernalia of scholarship); beyond that (and this was most encouraging to an apprentice) he led a very pleasant and civilized life. From the splendid candlelit feasts in the handsome dining room at Brimmer Street to the brisk horseback rides in the Blue Hills or the leisurely cruises along the Maine coast there was no hint of hurry, of programmed "relaxation," but a direct and simple pleasure in all the good things that the life of a prosperous Bostonian had to offer. He saw, perceived, noticed, touched, observed and enjoyed an infinite number of things, specific tangible things, and, less obviously, experiences. Discriminating, opinionated (or at least of strongly held convictions), with a deep New England reserve that often appeared glacial to those who did not know him, and with more than a touch of the curmudgeon about him, he was (and is) a gentle, loving man. As I came to know him better and to know others who had known him longer and better than I, I heard of many unassuming kindnesses, acts of thoughtfulness and generosity that had been done by this formidable man.

It seemed to me that part of the answer to the Morison riddle which I had set myself so presumptuously to unravel was that he is an aristocrat, quite impregnably situated in the kind of social class that has virtually disappeared from American life. This, I suspect, has given him an easy confidence in his own powers and a disarming lack of self-consciousness, so that he often says things quite naturally and simply that would sound pretentious or absurd in the mouth of another man. More important, his Brahmin background gave him a good-natured disdain for the historical fads and fashions that so preoccupied the academic world, and for its petty feuds and squabbles as well. He took that not-always-particularly-attractive world on his own rather Olympian terms, which was probably good for his disposition and for his history as well.

It was apparent that he had three consuming passions: the sea and all that pertained to it, Harvard College, the Puritans — in roughly that order. Some years after the death of his first wife, he married the beautiful Priscilla Barton, and she at once became his ruling passion, his pride and delight.

The particular form that Morison's passion for the sea, for Harvard, and for the Puritans took was that he wished to give, in the great phrase of Ranke which he loves and quotes so often (and which is so often misquoted by pedantic historians), "a true picture of the events which have occurred." With his unique feeling for the specific details and textures that give flesh and blood to the dry bones of history (and thereby give that history power over our own lives), he picked up the great tradition of narrative history from the man he is pleased to call his master, Francis Parkman, and spun it out in literally dozens of absorbing volumes which can be read with pleasure by the ordinary reader as well as by the professional historian.

I am afraid I never solved the riddle of what makes Morison the greatest historian of our time, the legitimate successor to those other New Englanders, George Bancroft, John Lothrop Motley, William Prescott and Francis Parkman, but I got some hints and glimmerings. Beyond the very important fact of his remarkable and apparently inexhaustible energy — he is now well into his 80s — there is the notion contained in another of his favorite quotations: "Dream dreams, then write them — aye, but live them first!" That is to say, he is determined to live life as he understands it should be lived; to relate that experience carefully, explicitly, lovingly, to the lives of other people in other times, to try to penetrate to the core of those lives by the faithful observation of them "as they were" — and to put down the results in lucid prose, of classic simplicity, a combination of the elegant and the earthy, as Morison most indubitably is himself. That is the accomplishment of Samuel Eliot Morison, Admiral of the Vast Seas of History.

DANIEL BOORSTIN'S *most recent book,* The Discoverers, *enthralled readers everywhere. But that's not uncommon with the Librarian of*

Congress. He has a way of making history live, and he explained how he
does it to Walter Goodman in an article that accompanied Boorstin's
1973 Selection, The Americans: The Democratic Experience. *Goodman*
writes on cultural events for the New York Times.

A Conversation with Daniel Boorstin
by Walter Goodman

BORN in Georgia in 1914 and raised in Oklahoma, Daniel Boorstin went
on to win honors in Harvard and Oxford and a doctorate at Yale. In
1944, after teaching assignments and a brief period of practicing law in
Massachusetts, he settled at the University of Chicago's history department, and remained there for the next twenty-five years, retiring in 1969
to become director of the National Museum of History and Technology
of the Smithsonian Institution in Washington, D.C. His journeys as a
visiting professor have taken him to Cambridge University, to the University of Rome and the Sorbonne, to Kyoto University in Japan, and
elsewhere. He and his wife, Ruth, who has been his close collaborator
over the years and to whom this latest of his books is dedicated, now live
in Washington.

The Americans: The Democratic Experience *gives us a picture not of
statesmen and politicians, but of people, ordinary and quite extraordinary, inventing, innovating and investing, producing, packaging and
promoting, borrowing, buying and selling, going to school and going to
the pictures, raising children, moving around, doing all the things that
add up to what is called a "way of life." What prompted Daniel Boorstin
to take this "everyday" approach to the writing of history? The question
was on my mind when I called at the Boorstins' new home, not far from
Washington's National Cathedral. The rooms are big, light and emphat-
ically modern, with an ample supply of the amenities celebrated in* The
Americans, *from air conditioning to an elevator to an intercom system. I
brought up the subject of his "everyday" approach to history at the first
opportunity. His reply told me what I wanted to know.*

A. I'm interested in what it's like to be alive, rather than the kinds of
things most historians write about. Perhaps it's because I didn't come to
this by being trained as a historian — I'm a refugee from the law. Too
much history is written about subjects that professionals think they
ought to write about. Historians write history because they're historians. I started doing history because of my interest in the flavor of life.
I'm more interested, for instance, in packaging than in tariffs. It seems to

me there are too many books today, and the only justification for writing still another one is that you can't help it. A subject grabs you; you're obsessed; you can't help it.

Q. *If everybody followed that rule, there'd be very few books written.*

A. I suppose so. But I don't have any fancy intellectual reasons for doing this kind of history. It's just that I find subjects like air conditioning, glass, the growth of Las Vegas fascinating. The fantasy of everyday life.

Q. *Writing about things that are part of everybody's own experience must make it rather difficult for you to assume the role of expert.*

A. Well, it is harder to be original when you're dealing with our own times. In a sense, everybody is an expert. The real authorities about things like dictionaries, for example, are not the people who usually write about them but the people who use them. That's precisely why I choose to do social rather than, say, political history — because it's more important to more people. The kind of house a person lives in, whether it's hot or cold in his rooms — things like these are more important on the whole than who's elected President or what treaty has been signed. More unprecedented things have happened in America in the past half-century than in any other time or country. Yet they happened so fast that people tend to take them for granted. I try to discover the charm and the mystery of the obvious.

Q. *One thing that separates you from the political historian in this book is the way you use the word "democracy." You speak of the "democracy" of the classroom, of consumption, of comfort, of credit, even of crime.*

A. Yes. I don't use the word "democracy" in its familiar sense, universal suffrage and all that. I use it to mean the tendency to make everything more like everything else — every place, every time, every person, every experience. I'm trying to describe not a type of government but a quality of life.

Q. *How about an example?*

A. Well, take the phonograph record that brings us Franklin Roosevelt's voice. It used to be that when a man was dead, you couldn't hear his voice. It was that simple. Now you can, and of course you can see him in the movies as well. So the distinctions that people used to find most vivid are removed. The distinctions between times and places are blurred. Most people may not think that has anything to do with "democracy" — but that's what I mean by it: a leveling of experience.

Q. *Is that good or bad or both?*

A. You can come away feeling how wonderful man is to be able to control death, life, winter, summer, space and time. It's a fantastic thing. But I hope that I've shown not only the accomplishments but the price we've had to pay for them.

Q. *What sort of price?*

A. Well, take what I call the "repeatable experience." Now we all can hear Beethoven in the elevator — but does it mean more or less to people to hear it than it did when the music wasn't so readily available? I speak of "attenuation," the thinning-out of experience as it spreads. A lot more people can hear opera — but what does it *mean* to hear opera? That's the democratic question.

Q. *And the answer will always be more and less, gain and loss?*

A. Every advance, discovery, invention has its price tag. But we can't see the price tag till it's too late. We've already made the purchase, and there are no returns or exchanges.

Q. *Do you think of your book, then, as an attempt to make an accounting of sorts?*

A. Yes, but I try not to impose the standards of other times and places. I try to let the categories grow out of the civilization itself. I try to tell what is distinctive about us, what holds us together — the clothes we wear, the way we shop. The fact that we don't like to watch TV commercials doesn't mean they aren't a way of holding us together. We're held together by ordinary things — the cash register, the income tax. This is my effort to see what American civilization adds up to.

Q. *You've worked on this book for ten years. Are you ready for a rest?*

A. No. This was an apprentice project. Now I'm going to try to write a history of man.

WHO COULD INTERVIEW *Gore Vidal for a piece to go with the Selection of his* Burr *in 1973? Nobody could but Gore Vidal himself. Read on for his urbane and mildly scatological opinions of Aaron Burr and lesser mortals past and present.*

A Conversation with Myself
by Gore Vidal

Q. *Why a novel about Burr instead of a biography?*

A. Because in the novel one has the right — the duty — to speculate on motives, while the biographer is honor-bound to deal only with facts.

Q. *Then you don't feel yourself honor-bound to respect facts?*

A. None of that! I've spent several years trying to avoid what Jefferson so nicely called "false facts." Two or three times I have rearranged chronology, but I never ascribe to any actual figure views he did not hold.

Q. *Why did you pick Burr as a subject?*

A. When I was 10 years old my mother married a man called Auchincloss whose mother was a descendant of the Burr family. In fact, the ladies on that side of the family were so proud of the connection that Burr was always part of the names they were known by. Annie Burr, Emma Burr. . . . My half sister has now burdened one of her sons with the name Burr Gore Steers. Not only does the lurid light of us Gores and of those Burrs flicker about his innocent head, but his name sounds like the national food. Fortunately he is not yet old enough to hate her for what she has done to him. In any case, I was Burr-conscious at an early age; recall a family portrait of Burr's daughter Theodosia; knew that he had been a great gentleman (a species valued in the years before the Second War but now impossible to describe in less than seven hundred pages).

Q. *How did you research your subject?*

A. Three years ago an Aaron Burr collection came on the market, and I bought several hundred items, the basic texts. On visits to New York I haunted the New-York Historical Society Library. Finally my publisher nicely (nervously?) put two historical researchers onto the book and they triple-checked my true as well as my false facts.

Q. *Is there a lesson for today?*

A. There is always a lesson for today in the past. Whether it's painted on the walls at Lascaux or buried in last week's Congressional Record. If we don't know where we've been, we cannot determine where we are and so cannot chart a future course.

Q. *Doubtless you regard those early days of the republic as more virtuous than the Age of Watergate?*

A. No. I am not romantic. The founders were vain, irritable, tricky, and by no means devoted by the system of government they had contrived. Yet unlike today's politicos, Hamilton and Jefferson were, first, men of extraordinary brilliance and, second, they believed passionately in their own theory of government. I cannot for the life of me determine what Nixon or Humphrey, Agnew or Kennedy believe in except winning elections. The collision between Jefferson and Hamilton struck real sparks. Each was a sort of monster driven by vanity, but each was also

an intellectual philosopher of government, and each thought he was
creating a perfect or perfectable system of government. Our politicians
have not thought about such matters for half a century.

Q. *Why were these men so different from the politicians of today?*

A. Jack Kennedy asked himself the same question in the spring of
1961 at Hyannis Port. "You know," he said, "in this . . . uh, job I get to
meet most of the important people in the country, the best minds, and
I'm struck by how mediocre they are." Modestly he included himself
amongst the reigning mediocrity. He had read so little, had mastered no
foreign language, no art. Then he asked, "How did the original United
States, a colonial society of three million people, produce so much intellectual genius?" More leisure, I proposed. Slow travel. Short sessions of
Congress. Long months at home in the country reading and writing and
thinking thoughts. Kennedy was not convinced. He thought there was
something in the air that was different then. I suppose — now — there
was: the sense of human comity, that a good life makes contribution to a
good society. Now we live entirely in the age of the little foxes, and
what grapes are not spoiled are soured for all.

Q. *Obviously you like Burr, but he certainly cannot be regarded as a
good man or a philosopher of government. In fact he was one of the
first professional politicians, representing only himself.*

A. That is not quite true. Burr's mind was as good as Jefferson's or
Hamilton's but he was not a zealot. Yet, to the extent he was the man on
the make — to that extent — he is interesting to us now. Also, don't
forget that the idol of his generation was not Washington the Dull but
Bonaparte. Every ambitious man of the period saw himself conquering
the earth, like Bonaparte. Both Hamilton and Burr wanted to conquer
Mexico, Cuba, South America — and simply for the fun of conquest
and the delights of a crown.

Q. *In doing your research what most surprised you?*

A. Jefferson's hypocrisy.

Q. *What surprised you most about Burr?*

A. The journal he wrote in Europe for his daughter to read. His described in great detail every sexual encounter.

Q. *What was their relationship?*

A. Perfect, I should think. "Women have souls," Burr used to say, to
the consternation of those whose minds had been shaped by his Calvin-
ist grandfather Jonathan Edwards. Burr had no son, so he brought up
his daughter the way he would have brought up a son. He made her a
prodigy of learning and of charm. Burr was a devoted women's libber

and despite his lechery, he really liked women, preferred their company to that of men. This was as un-American then as it is now.

Q. *What about Jefferson?*

A. Jefferson never forgave Burr for having behaved well when they both tied for President in 1800. Jefferson was also eager to have a Virginian succeed him. To accomplish this Vice President Burr must be railroaded.

Q. *Yet Jefferson was a great man.*

A. Certainly an interesting one. I like him better than Burr does. But in action he was not unlike the late Joe McCarthy. For decades he used to smear his enemies as "monarchists" — the equivalent at the time to yelling "Commie" in the 1950s. He tried on two occasions to break the Supreme Court. With Nixonian zeal, he went after editors who disapproved of him. Kurt Vonnegut to the contrary, he did *not* free his slaves. He allowed some to buy their freedom. He had a penchant for other men's wives.

Q. *But he wrote the Declaration of Independence.*

A. He was a bit like Jack Kennedy. Sooner or later Kennedy said something very wise and luminous on almost every subject, then did nothing about it. After battling Hamilton's ideas of government, Jefferson ended up the sort of President Hamilton would have been, deliberately subverting the Constitution in order to buy Louisiana in order to create what he called with satisfaction "our empire."

Q. *You have been called a cynic.*

A. I have always resented the word! "Realist" is more fitting.

Q. *Whatever. Lately critics have been saying that your dark view of America since the Second War might be justified in the light of Watergate.*

A. Yes. Watergate has been a revelation to a good many inattentive people. To me it is simply a confirmation of what I have known for some time was wrong.

Q. *But when — how — did it go wrong?*

A. When Adam ate the apple. In our case the apple was empire. It is not possible to have a just and democratic society and also be an empire. Pericles knew this, and Jefferson knew this. But Jefferson coldbloodedly launched us upon empire. Jackson (whom I really dislike: Burr loves him) continued the process by the savage removal of the Indians to the West. We've been on the march ever since. As I write, our bombers are destroying Cambodia, even further to the west. But then perhaps empire is a good thing and I am out of step.

Q. *But whom do you like among the early figures?*

A. George Mason, who was responsible for the Bill of Rights. James Madison was a good man, with a first-rate mind — like Jefferson but without Jefferson's vanity and strain of madness. John Adams gives pleasure for his sublime tactlessness. Washington commands awe. He was one of the worst generals we have so far produced, but as a politician he was without equal until Eisenhower. People thought Hamilton used the dimwitted old general to create the Federal Government. Nonsense. Washington the shrewd land speculator and millionaire used the brilliant but unstable Hamilton to put together a government which would protect the rights of property. I found Hamilton, all in all, enchanting, and usually "right." It is interesting for someone like me who has often been identified with the American Left to find most appealing in our history the figures of the Right. I suppose it's because they knew what they wanted and were practical. Certainly the Left as represented by Jefferson and Jackson was simply dizzy — *laissez nous faire.*

Q. *Is your character named Charles Schuyler real?*

A. No. Charlie evolved. One of Burr's wards was called Charlie and turned into a novelist. That was the germ, but I did not mean for Charlie to become a writer. However, his character got stronger and stronger as the story proceeded.

Q. *Was there really such an establishment on Thomas Street as Mrs. Townsend's bordello?*

A. Yes. And Helen Jewett was also real. I got the story from Philip Hone's diaries. Invaluable for a picture of the 1830s. When I say there was a red moon over the Battery on such and such a night, I have taken it from his diaries.

Q. *Do you prefer to live in Europe because you are discouraged with America?*

A. No. I live in Europe because it gives me a better perspective on America. My *ci-devant* cousin Louis Auchincloss observed recently: "You are an exception to the general rule that those who live abroad do so in order to forget their native country. If anything, your interest in America becomes more intense." Incidentally, the writers of the period I deal with all expatriated themselves for long periods of time. Washington Irving was abroad continuously for fifteen years, mostly in Spain. Also, Fenimore Cooper, Hawthorne. For me it is a necessity, since I work with a telescope not a microscope and so need distance to see detail.

Q. *What effect do you think your novel will have?*

A. Do books have effect now? I only know that readers can learn in a few hours just about everything it took me twenty years to discover about the first half-century of the American republic. And I am slightly resentful. They won't have to work (I assume!) as hard as I did. Burr's view of our history is unusual but accurate; and I think the thoughtful reader might be heartened to know that things were always pretty bad but that, from time to time, a few devoted figures were thrown up by history to save us from ourselves.

Q. *It has been said that Americans don't like history.*

A. History is the least popular of fifty subjects listed in a recent national high school poll. But what kid could enjoy the endless Mount Rushmores carved in soft soap our schools present them with?

Q. *Then why do your write about things that most Americans are not interested in?*

A. To try to make these things interesting. To teach myself. After all, to make the past live is a lovely task. Without undue self-congratulation, I wish that at 20 I had had *Burr* to read. Instead I had to write it, and that was the hardest work I have ever done.

IN 1938 CHRISTOPHER MORLEY *reviewed* Brighton Rock, *one of Graham Greene's first "entertainments." In 1948 Clifton Fadiman wrote about a Greene Selection,* The Heart of the Matter. *In 1973 Elizabeth Easton, an editor at the Club, interviewed Greene in connection with another Selection,* The Honorary Cousul. *In between and since then, many of Greene's works have been used in various ways by the Club.*

Brighton Rock by Graham Greene

MR. GREENE gives this brilliantly shocking story the odd subtitle *An Entertainment.* This seems a pity, for perhaps it moves the reader to take it less seriously than its remarkable merits deserve. A gangster story laid in good old bourgeois Brighton — England's pre-Victorian Atlantic City — and named for that resort's staple sugar-candy, is shrewdly concocted to startle the innocent customer. The American equivalent would be Salt Water Taffy. But there's very little taffy in this grim yarn. Mr. Greene has shown us in previous books his talent for macabre narration. He seizes the apprehensions with his first sentence and carries us through a sardonic plot which is an effective study in morbid psychology. The protagonist is Pinky, 18-year-old-leader of a race-track gang, wizened and sadist, with a horror of sex and drink. The cold-hearted rubbing out of Hale, the journalist, is well described, and as the coroner finds it "natural death" all seems serene. But the big achievement of the tale is Ida, the big bosomy friendly trull, who happened to feel sorry for the hunted victim. Ida, with her big voice and kindly sense of fun, believes in fair play. Without quite knowing why, she tracks down all the clues and in the nick of time rescues the pitiable girl who has fallen for Pinky. It is a brutal and sultry tale, written with extreme skill, and a vivid sense of horror that would have pleased the author's distinguished kinsman, R. L. Stevenson. Not to be missed by the hardy.

CHRISTOPHER MORLEY

The Heart of the Matter by Graham Greene

MANY readers know Graham Greene as the author of a number of streamlined, chromium-plated, highly literate super-thrillers. With *The Heart of the Matter*, however, he takes his place, one would say indisputably, among the truly serious novelists of his country and generation. Your judges feel fortunate in being able to recommend to their readers in the same year two such works as Thorton Wilder's *The Ides of March* and now this extraordinary novel by Graham Greene.

The geographical setting of the novel is a run-down British colony somewhere on the northwest African coast. Its real setting is the interior, lighted in chiaroscuro, of a human heart. The external atmosphere is made up of tropical heat and damp, an atmosphere in which the slightest scratch festers and corrupts. Flying ants, rats, cockroaches and jiggers add their petty miseries to the gray boredom in which the colonial bureaucracy is engulfed. But the true atmosphere of this book is spiritual, not physical.

The Heart of the Matter is the rare thing in our time, a religious novel, painfully concerned with the most essential of all relationships — that of a man to his God. Do not be misled: the book is no evangelical tract, and has nothing in common with such confections as *The Robe*. For true analogies one must go to the beautiful novels of Mauriac, or the stormy ones of Dostoyevsky.

The center of the story is Assistant Police Commissioner Scobie, a Catholic convert married to a woman whom he has ceased to love, but not to pity. "He was bound by the pathos of her unattractiveness." It is this pity, truly religious in its intensity and spontaneity, which is Scobie's fatal flaw, if a virtue may be called a flaw. Scobie is that inevitably tragic thing, a truly good man. His goodness takes the Christian form of feeling personally responsible for the weaknesses and griefs of those near to him, beginning with his wife. With him pity is a kind of passion, and this passion leads him to the commission of deeds which, though undertaken from the noblest of motives, lead him further and further into guilt and deception, until at last there is no way out for him except through complete spiritual disaster.

In order to secure the money with which to send his dissatisfied, nagging wife on a vacation to South Africa, he is forced to put himself in the dubious hands of Yusef, a rich Syrian money-lender. In her absence the survivors of a torpedoed ship (this is during the late war) are landed on the coast. With one of them, a nineteen-year-old girl, Helen Rolt, he conceives a friendship which soon has all the appearance of love. In reality it is pity again that moves him, rather than passion; while it is Scobie's self-regardless goodness that moves Helen, even as it moves evil characters, such as Yusef.

Scobie is maneuvered, without his knowing quite how it has come about, into a position where he must partake of Communion in a state of sin. This to him means quite literally eternal damnation. The scene at the altar rail in which this man, hungering for God, torn with guilt and quite unconscious of the heroic beauty of his own character, takes God into himself and condemns himself in his own mind to an eternity of deprivation, is one of the most moving I have encountered in recent novels. Its intensity is exceeded only by the final chapters in which Scobie finds himself forced to commit the final unforgivable sin which puts a human soul outside the mercy of God — self-destruction in a condition of despair.

It should be made clear that this novel could have been written only by a man deeply committed to the Catholic tradition. From this tradition it derives its passion and its power and, if a non-Catholic be permitted to say so, its beauty. Yet there is nothing dogmatic here, nothing exclusive. Their familiarity with the theology back of Scobie's dilemma may give Catholic readers an added sense of that dilemma's terrifying aspect; but the book's appeal is not parochial, any more than that of *The Divine Comedy* is parochial. No one but a village atheist can fail to respond to the torment in Scobie's soul, for that torment may be discovered in the depths of any man who discovers that goodness involves suffering, that the price of being a whole man is to feel responsibility for all mortality, that inner peace is never to be found through merely personal relationships, and that all men, unless they feel that they are the creatures of God, must voyage through this brief life in stark, essential solitude.

It may seen strange to say that this somber story is refreshing; and yet in a way it is. We have had so many novels recently, particularly by young Americans, in which the main characters are stickily immersed in their petty egos, that a novel about a man who dares to live outside himself, as it were, in terms of a belief that rises above the mundane and the quotidian — such a novel has a certain power of invigoration.

Perhaps I have overstressed that somber atmosphere of *The Heart of the Matter*. I have neglected to state that it is beautifully plotted, that its story is taut (and even a trifle theatrical on occasion), and that its minor characters are small triumphs of satirical, yet always pitying, observation. The beginning, I must warn you, is slow, and may put off some readers: but once fairly launched into Scobie's strange story, you will, I think, stay with it to the very end. Even if the dogma upon which Scobie's final adventure turns should be unacceptable to you, you will find yourself suffering with him, you will find your own vision of man's spiritual condition broadened, enlarged and sharpened.

The judges believe this novel to be a work of the gravest intent and import. How high it will rank as literature it is too early to say, but we consider it one of the finest novels we have been privileged to offer our readers in many, many months.

A Conversation with Graham Greene

by Elizabeth Easton

As I SAT in the subdued grandeur of the lobby of London's Ritz Hotel, a variation of an old nursery rhyme kept running through my head:

> *Pussy cat, pussy cat, where have you been?*
> *I've been to London to visit Graham Greene.*

About to meet Mr. Greene, I was apprehensive. He had the reputation of being austere, shy, remote. Would he answer questions? My frame of mind wasn't helped by the problems I had encountered in trying to arrange an interview. Before leaving New York, I learned from Michael Korda, Greene's New York editor, that an interview date might be difficult to fix. "Greene may be in Antibes, or Paris, when you're in London," Mr. Korda said gloomily. But he agreed to inquire.

The day of my departure approached without word from Mr. Greene. I called Mr. Korda. "I absolutely can't telephone him," he said. "Is he so difficult to deal with?" I asked. "No," said Mr. Korda, "he's not difficult at all, but he's a very private person." Finally, a cable came. Yes, Mr. Greene would be glad to see me in London on a given day.

I put the nursery rhyme out of my mind when he came up to me in the Ritz lobby, a tall man with blue eyes and a gray suit that matched his gray hair. We sat in his second-floor quarters, the sun streaming in the windows and Sunday crowds strolling along the edge of Green Park outside. We began to talk about *The Honorary Consul.*

EE: *Do you have trouble beginning a book?*

GG: I can't begin a book until my characters have names. The moment when I was able to begin this book was when I'd got the name of Fortnum, who is the honorary consul, and of Plarr, the doctor. They came in the space of a day, suddenly, like that — when I was doing something else. Then one could begin the book. Names, as you know, have a curious value. In Africa, a boy from a tribe has three names. He has a name if he comes to be a "boy" working for a European — he has a name which the European calls him by. Second, he's got his tribal name. And he's got a name which only his parents have known, which he doesn't tell anybody. And there is a curious, I think mystic, thing about names. If you call your character by the wrong name, he doesn't come alive. You can't get on with it.

EE: *Do any of your characters in* The Honorary Consul *represent you yourself?*

GG: Probably bits of one's self are distributed all the way through.

EE: *Do you see people who sometimes give you ideas?*

GG: Yes, and dreams also give me ideas. Dreams are perhaps too important to me, because sometimes a whole story is based on a dream.

EE: *Was that true of* The Honorary Consul?

GG: *The Honorary Consul* began with a dream. It began with a dream about an American ambassador, in fact. What I dreamed was completely different from what I've written in the story, though.

EE: *Do you have a sense of playing God with your characters?*

GG: No. I have much more of a sense of their playing God with me.

EE: *How's that?*

GG: Because sometimes the story suddenly alters in a way which one had not intended at all. The characters are controlling me rather than I'm controlling the characters. I've had a character run away from me.

EE: *Which one?*

GG: That was Minty, in a book called *England Made Me*, which is now in America called *The Shipwrecked.*

EE: *That was one of your earlier books.*

GG: Yes, and the character called Minty was a minor character and became much too important.

EE: *What did you do about it?*

GG: Nothing, I just let him have his way.

EE: *How does your writing go?*

GG: I used to be able to write 500 words a day, whilst I was working, with intervals of holiday in between. Now I set myself about 300 or 400 words a day. But one rewrites that and rewrites *that*. When I say rewrite, I mean with corrections so extensive that the page becomes unintelligible. I write longhand, and the longhand becomes unreadable even to my secretary. So I have to dictate it.

EE: *Do you find writing fun or is it agony?*

GG: There are moments of pleasure when one feels that something has worked — but mostly it's a pain in the neck.

EE: *What do you do when you finish a book? Take a vacation? Or do you yearn to start another book?*

GG: I don't yearn to start the next one. You know, at my age, which is 69, the thought of beginning a book which may take three years is daunting, and one prefers to try and do little things.

EE: *Where was* The Honorary Consul *written?*

GG: Mainly in Antibes, but I write wherever I am.

EE: *What makes a place a good place for you to write in?*

GG: That's a mystery. There are places which I've never succeeded in writing in. London I always found difficult. I could much easier write in a hotel than in the flat I used to have in London. I can write in Antibes; I wrote most of *The Honorary Consul* there. But I haven't yet been able to write continuously, except just for revisions — small things — in Paris, where I've got a flat. It's a mystery, I don't know . . .

EE: *Do you go off alone or is your family with you when you write?*

GG: Well, I'm separated from my wife. But no, in any case I'm alone. When one writes, one's alone.

EE: *In the introduction to the collection called* The Portable Graham Greene *the editor discusses the importance of political frontiers in a number of your novels, and frontiers play a part in* The Honorary Consul, *too. Do you use this symbolism deliberately?*

GG: I think I'm conscious of it, probably because of my critics.

EE: *What's your favorite European city?*

GG: I think Bath. And Edinburgh, perhaps.

EE: *Why Bath?*

GG: I think it's one of the most beautiful cities in Europe.

EE: *Shades of Jane Austen.*

GG: Curiously enough, I don't like Jane Austen. I've never been able to read her. The humor of Jane Austen has always struck me as being so overplayed and so obvious. I suppose it's one of my blind spots. We all have blind spots — like I can't read Milton. Jane Austen is my blind spot in the novel. I read certain novelists whom I admire and like.

EE: *Who are they?*

GG: Well, one recently died — Evelyn Waugh, whom I liked very much and was very fond of. It's very difficult — whenever one is asked for names, you know, they all disappear out of one's head. But one has one's admirations, and one's admirations in the past — Henry James, Conrad, Ford Madox Ford — sort of, as it were, images in a side chapel.

EE: *I read somewhere that you admire François Mauriac.*

GG: Yes, up to a point. His views of Catholicism and mine differ enormously, like my views of Catholicism and Evelyn Waugh's differed enormously. But one or two of his books I liked enormously.

EE: *I believe Mauriac once said, "Every novelist should invent a style for himself." How would you describe your own?*

GG: I'd say one doesn't consciously invent a style, but one tries to say something as plainly and clearly and in as few words as possible, and out of that perhaps a style becomes detectable. I don't know.

EE: *You have a reputation for being a very private person, and yet you've been a newspaper correspondent. How do you explain that?*

GG: I've only been a newspaper correspondent for a few months at a time, in the space of a few years. I was a newspaper correspondent in Vietnam during the winters for four years. I was a correspondent for *Life* in Malaya, but that was only a question of three months. I've done special newspaper assignments, but they wouldn't amount, in effect, to more than at most two years of my life, it one put them end to end.

EE: *Do you think that* The Honorary Consul *departs from the mainstream of your other novels?*

GG: No, I would have thought it was very much *in* the mainstream; I would have thought it was in the mainstream of *The Power and the Glory* and *The Comedians.*

EE: *Which of your books means the most to you?*

GG: I think probably *The Power and the Glory*. I think *The Honorary Consul* is good, and I'm very fond of *Travels with My Aunt*.

EE: *Why did you put* The Power and the Glory *first?*

GG: Because I think . . . technically perhaps, I think it's my best book.

EE: *A lot of people would agree, but they haven't read* The Honorary Consul *yet. Would you care to say anything about your future plans?*

GG: No. I have no future plans.

EE: *What more would you like to accomplish as a writer?*

GG: I don't know. Just write a good book.

THE NOTABLE Chicago Tribune *columnist Mike Royko deals with Studs Terkel, perhaps the quintessential Chicagoan. Terkel's book is* Working, *and Royko gets Studs talking about how he came to write about such a seemingly unsexy subject.*

Studs Terkel

by Mike Royko

WHEN all the silly arguments about "new journalism" have been exhausted, Studs (Louis) Terkel might be what's new. Born in New York in 1912, a graduate of the University of Chicago and the University of Chicago Law School, he is probably the country's most sensitive, intelligent and energetic interviewer, as he demonstrates each day on his Chicago radio broadcast and with his earlier books.

He takes on no small subjects, social freak shows or fads. His *Division Street* (1966) was about those who live in an American city. *Hard Times* (1970) was an oral history of the Great Depression by those who endured it. Now his subject is work, as discussed by those who do it.

"This one is different than the other two books," Terkel says. *Division Street* was about a city and what happens to people's thoughts. Then came the Depression book, which was about a time. Here, there is neither time nor place. In that way it was the toughest.

"Why work as a subject? How many books have been written about sex? Millions? Sometimes it seems that way. But work? Hardly any. Yet both are key drives of man. I wanted to know how people felt about what they did. When you think about it: eight hours, EIGHT HOURS, out of a day. If it is meaningless, then how can the rest of a man's life be anything but an escape from meaninglessness?

"How can you talk about a person living unless you talk about what he does for his living? How else can a man's life be discussed? The nature of his work can determine what he is."

Terkel roamed around the country with his tape recorder, finding his interviews through the fantastic number of friendships and contacts he has built in his remarkable career as writer, broadcaster, lecturer, jazz authority, actor — and needling conscience of Chicago. His findings, and he sounds depressed when he says it, were that the overwhelming majority are unhappy with what they are doing.

Not liking a job isn't new, of course. The coal miner who saw the sun only on his day off, or the blood-spattered stockyard sledge-swinger, the sweatshop immigrant, the railroad laborer, the cotton picker — these rarely bounce out of bed whistling. For generations they were exploited and overworked. Their working conditions drove men to organize and create machines to share the load.

That's the joker in the deck, the jolt of Terkel's book. Conditions did improve. Work has been lightened and leisure extended. There's less sweat and more money. But people are unhappy still.

Now, Terkel finds, people are asking: "What in the hell am I doing?" In the Depression and before, people didn't ask that question. Man worked to make his living, to bring home his daily bread. Man didn't question his lot. Religion helped to keep him from asking by telling him that work was part of the cross he had to bear. Maybe people didn't like their work, but they never dreamed of questioning it. It would have been sacrilegious. Now people are asking for something besides the income.

"Take the young guys in, oh, say the auto plant at Lordstown, Ohio. Their fathers worked like hell in the early days and they were proud of what they did, mostly because they brought bread home. But these guys figure, 'What the hell am I doing working at the speedup setup when I don't need all that dough?' They say, 'Here I'm doing the same damn job, spot-welding the same spot day after day. It's driving me nuts. I don't see the product I'm making. I'm just a machine. So I'm going to take some time off.' So there's absenteeism, and you never had this much absenteeism in the Depression. Their fathers didn't take time off like this. And it's not only guys on assembly lines. The little girl who is a bank teller says the same thing: 'I'm just a machine.' "

Part of the ache in Terkel's people comes from the need for recognition. A workman tells how he would like to see a skyscraper with a plaque bearing the names of all the workmen who put it up, not of just the architect and builder. "Who built the pyramids?" he asks. "We don't know the names of those guys. All we know is Pharaoh. But who built them?"

A supermarket checker describes herself as "nothing." A garbage-truck driver sees himself as a horse pulling a wagon. A washroom attendant says: "My work is superfluous."

And the machines, which were to be liberators, are now distrusted, even envied for their status. When a worker is hurt, he is hauled away, but when a machine sputters, there is executive concern. The airline reservation girl says the computer is her God. The spot-welder says the conveyor belt is his God.

Conversely, those who like their work know who they are. And they feel needed and useful. Tommy the fireman likes helping people, and not feeling competition with his fellow firemen. The stone mason is proud when he sees the wall he built, flaws and all. The druggist feels close to the people in and out of his store. The inventor threatens to fire any employee who calls him boss.

Terkel's book leaves us pondering this thought: If people find their work to be empty, what do they find their lives to be? The so-called silent majority, he demonstrates, are silent only because nobody has asked them the right questions.

You think *it all began with Richard Nixon and John Mitchell and Haldeman and Ehrlichman? It truly all began with Carl Bernstein and Bob Woodward and their book that got the Watergate Follies started —* All the President's Men. *The Watergate break-in took place in June 1972, and by October of that year Bernstein and Woodward had a book contract.*

A Conversation with Carl Bernstein and Bob Woodward

by Walter Goodman

As I moved toward the departure gate for the flight that would take me to my appointment with Carl Bernstein and Bob Woodward, the young *Washington Post* reporters who have spent the past two years probing the murky mysteries of Watergate, a big man in a rumpled overcoat shambled out of the shadows. He was holding a parcel wrapped in brown paper. His eyes frisked me: "You a friend of Mr. Simon and Mr. Schuster?" I shrugged my Peter Lorre shrug. He slipped the parcel into my arms and returned to the shadows.

What did I have? Incriminating documents, perhaps, to be deep-sixed in the Potomac? Compromising memos for the office burn bag? Dangerous tapes marked for erasure? No. What I had was the first set of galley proofs of *All the President's Men*, for delivery to the authors — whom I located not in the underground garage where Bob Woodward was wont to meet his top-secret, high administration source, Deep Throat, but in the big, bustling newsroom of the *Washington Post*. The merchandise having been handed over, we adjourned to a coffee shop across the street for lunch. My interview of the interviewers began with the nature of the celebrated Bernstein-Woodward collaboration since the June, 1972, Watergate break-in.

WOODWARD: The main advantage to the collaboration was simply that there were two of us — two sets of eyes, two sets of ears. It was a big story. There were lots of avenues to be tracked. Since we're both divorced and couldn't have much family life, we were able to spend evenings and weekends following up leads.

BERNSTEIN: Our skills happened to be complementary. Bob is much better at laying things out quickly than I am. I tend to pore over them, diddle with language. So he would knock something out, with lots of cold facts, and I would try to tailor it.

WOODWARD: At first, there was some mutual distrust, simply because we came from different backgrounds. Carl had been working on newspapers since he was 16; he'd been at the *Post* since 1966. I'd been there only nine months. He was much more experienced than I was and knew a lot more about writing.

BERNSTEIN: For some reason, I was usually able to tell where the story was going to go. I guess it's because after you spend enough time in Washington, you learn to think to a certain extent the way *they* do.

WOODWARD: As we worked together, it turned out we were a lot more alike than we thought. I had the reputation of being much more cautious than Carl — but sometimes I would write something and Carl would be the one to say — "Now, wait a minute, we're going too far."

BERNSTEIN: I tend not to trust other reporters, but Bob and I got to trust each other to a point where either of us could do a story and it would run under our joint byline.

GOODMAN: *When did you start on this book?*

WOODWARD: We signed up for it in October, 1972. We thought then that the story would die after the election and never surface again . . .

BERNSTEIN: . . . and we had all this information that we didn't think we could ever get printed in the newspaper.

WOODWARD: We put together three or four chapters of strictly expository material — Hunt did this, Liddy did that. We didn't put ourselves in it at all. Then the story exploded, and we realized that after all the coverage, people wouldn't be interested in just another rehash.

BERNSTEIN: So we ended up writing the only kind of book that nobody but us could write — telling how we went about working on the story.

WOODWARD: We were hesitant about doing it this way. It might seem like an ego trip. But we decided to give it a try. I sat down and wrote a hundred pages, and we talked about it and realized we could do it. So I wrote the first draft — 700 pages, double-spaced.

BERNSTEIN: Whenever there was a period that I knew more about than Bob, he would leave that blank — like the Segretti story, where I'd done all the legwork for the paper.

WOODWARD: We discussed it continually. It was difficult because all this time the story kept developing.

BERNSTEIN: After Bob finished a draft, I did the rewriting.

GOODMAN: *What next for Bernstein-Woodward? Are you going to switch from being reporters to being authors?*

BERNSTEIN: I like the idea of doing books — the writing freedom it gives you. But I like newspaper reporting, too.

WOODWARD: We want to do both. Neither of us is an advocate of the New Journalism in general, but there's one aspect of it that is good — writing about your own personal experiences, getting close to your own feelings and reactions. That's what we tried to do in our book.

BERNSTEIN: Good reporting has always been very personal, and we want to be good reporters.

WOODWARD: We're going to keep on collaborating.

BERNSTEIN: Definitely.

THEODORE H. WHITE *talks about the bravery of Cornelius Ryan and the artistry of Cornelius Ryan, and of his qualities as a person and a storyteller. He also has a word or two to say about Ryan's 1974 classic,* A Bridge Too Far.

Cornelius Ryan

by Theodore H. White

LET me indulge myself by approaching the matter of Cornelius Ryan as memory carries me. For it is always difficult for one old friend to talk of another without clearing his mind of irrelevancies. And, sometimes, the irrelevancies are as important as substance.

There is, for example, the entirely irrelevant fact that Ryan is a very brave man. Bravery, of course, has nothing to do with good writing. But those of us who shared the comradeship of war correspondents knew Connie Ryan as not only a brave man (a series of volunteer raids over Germany while he was a reporter for the London *Daily Telegraph* for example), but one who savored bravery in others. His writing is thus moved by a marvelously old-fashioned appreciation of bravery in men as style. In an age of cynicism, he still nurses the faith that ordinary men can rise above themselves and offer their lives as sacrifice for others.

The next thing that springs to mind is equally irrelevant — that Connie Ryan, born in Ireland in 1920 (he has been a U.S. citizen since 1950), was schooled as a violinist in the Irish Academy of Music and played with numerous Dublin salon orchestras. Happily, he has never been able to shake off that conditioning. Music has left its mark on not only the rhythm of his speech but the cadence of his writing. Those who cannot appreciate the swing and fall of a great prose sentence, who cannot savor the snap of a staccato phrase, its alternation with a lyric passage of description and the crack of a crisp anecdote, miss half the delight of a Ryan book.

There is next, alas, the fact that Ryan sweats. I mean, literally, sweats. As he comes to the end of one of his books, there is about him the high, heady aroma of a plow horse turning the last furrow of the day. Ryan, a jovial gasconading companion at other times, becomes tart and short-tempered, impossible as his books approach conclusion. For above all, he takes his art seriously and so should all the rest of us — which brings me to what I most want to say about Cornelius Ryan: that he is one of the great living masters of the well-told story. He is one of those who have brought to climax that particular American excellence in the Contemporary Narrative which marks our generation as distinctively as did the dominance of Hemingway, Faulkner, Fitzgerald and Wolfe over the novel in the 1920s and '30s.

I do not at all mean by the phrase "Contemporary Narrative" what is meant by the self-serving gentlemen who have recently offered us "the new journalism," a form of journalism which collects quick facts, then uses them as steppingstones whereby the author leaps from data to quote to description, filling in the gaps with what his imagination fabricates as bridge material. I mean the most difficult, disciplined, painstaking form of the craft of storytelling — where the imagination must deal with facts as they come raw and bleeding and unsorted, with episodes which the master must weave together to tell us of the action the way it really was. In this art form the story is made splendid by the writer's own understanding of men, of how their actions fit together when they were happening.

It is probably a disservice to Ryan for me to describe him thus as an artist. Most people shrink from art. Yet one must place him there in that sequence which began with John Hersey *(Hiroshima)* and continued through Bruce Catton's work on the Civil War, to the best of what is now being published of events-as-they-are by the best of American writers — which makes, as I say, a new American art form.

"Art" is not a word to shrink from. The best of the great artists were the popular artists of their own time. The great Elizabethan dramatists knew that they had to compete for attention with jugglers on one side of the Globe Theater and bear pits on the other. And Kipling, most popular of all writers of his day, is only now beginning to earn attention from learned critics who find that what the people liked to read when they bought Kipling's books was very much worth reading then and now, after all.

It is thus, perhaps, not entirely an irrelevance to talk of Connie Ryan's popularity. Over 10 million hard-bound copies of *The Longest Day*, *The Last Battle* and his other books on World War II have been purchased by readers who knew they had bought themselves five or six hours of solid entertainment. There is a rather amusing measure of his importance — a book-buyers' poll once taken in France. Who were the authors French book buyers liked best, asked the pollsters. And then followed the answers: Victor Hugo, Alexander Dumas, Margaret Mitchell, Cornelius Ryan, Emily Brontë. Of these, Cornelius Ryan was the only one living.

Writers should be read, and authors should be remembered, not because of what the critics said or by pollsters' ratings. They should be remembered for the excitement they give the reader who wants to tuck himself away from the day's problems and indulge in a shameless communication with a storyteller who invites you to share adventure.

So now does Cornelius Ryan's *A Bridge Too Far* sweep you off to adventure. The story begins softly with the sound of horses' hooves, church bells, village clatter in occupied Holland, on the banks of the Rhine. Then the Dublin violinist tunes up. The theme comes in now, hard. It is only sixty-four miles from the Allied bridgehead on the Dutch border to the Rhine crossing at the great bridge of Arnhem. A swoop, a dash, an ultimate act can grab that road, seize that bridge, and once across the Rhine at Arnhem — the Ruhr lies naked, Germany can be gutted, the war closed. The air fills then with the sound of planes as the greatest airborne army in history — three-and-a-half divisions of Americans, Britons, Poles — prepare for the swoop. Then you are in battle: the Irish Guards, pressing the snouts of their single-file tank column into ambuscade as they spearhead the push to reach the paratroops; Major General Jim Gavin's 82nd Division Americans crossing the river in canvas landing craft to seize the bridge at Nijmegan; and the doomed handful of Frost's 2nd Battalion holding the bridgehead of Arnhem, promised relief in forty-eight hours, waiting and dying for seven days, spending their last ammunition as gallant misers. ("Stand still, you sod," yelled signalman James Haysom, shooting off his last few rounds at a German, "these bullet cost money.")

The story of *A Bridge Too Far* is all story — but is also stunning history. His merciless treatment of Field Marshal Sir Bernard Law Montgomery is accompanied by Eisenhower's excoriating personal recollection of Montgomery's personality and generalship; Ryan's treatment of the bewildered Major General Roy Urquhart and the command confusion in the leaderless First British Airborne Division is based on contemporary logs and direct interviews with the participants. His reconstruction of the German response comes not only from the German battle archives but their field commanders, down to brigade level.

I, being burdened with professional obligations, must describe the book to you as both fine art and immaculate history. But that is not the reason for reading *A Bridge Too Far*. It is to be read simply because it delights the heart and intrigues the mind, because it recalls and recreates a world that youth and gallantry would have made you proud to join.

ALEKSANDR SOLZHENITSYN *may be somewhat out of fashion in 1986; his biblical prophecies tend to frighten people. But his works, including* One Day in the Life of Ivan Denisovich, Cancer Ward, The First Circle,

August 1914, *and his volumes on the Gulag Archipelago, burn a hole in the heart as they reveal the indecencies human beings practice on one another and as they exalt the human will to endure and triumph over such horrors. Harrison Salisbury, a* New York Times *correspondent in the Soviet Union for many years, wrote the report on Solzhenitsyn's first Gulag volume.*

The Gulag Archipelago
by Aleksandr Solzhenitsyn

AT NOON on April 9, 1972, fifty friends of Aleksandr Solzhenitsyn's were invited to assemble at the apartment of his wife, Natalya Svetlova, just off Gorky Street in the heart of Moscow. The Secretary of the Swedish Academy, Dr. Karl Ragnar Gierow, was to present to Solzhenitsyn, most belatedly, the Nobel Prize for Literature which he had been awarded in the autumn of 1970, some eighteen months earlier.

The ceremony never took place. At the eleventh hour — after invitations had been issued and every preparation made — the Soviet authorities refused to issue a visa to Dr. Gierow. Solzhenitsyn had prepared the traditional laureate's address for delivery on the occasion, but his voice was silenced. Only with the publication of the Nobel Yearbook for 1971 in August, 1972, did his words become known.

Now, with the publication of *The Gulag Archipelago*, the significance of his Nobel address becomes clear. The address is, in essence, Solzhenitsyn's introduction to *The Gulag Archipelago*. He began the book in his mind in those years when he, too, inhabited the Gulag Archipelago. Thus his newest and possibly greatest work was born in that gray, dank, dangerous prison world which in Stalin's time was populated by 10 or 12 million people and which, even in the Soviet Union of today, harbors from 10,000 to 20,000 intellectuals and possibly 1,000,000 "ordinary" Russians.

This is the world which Solzhenitsyn explores, charts, records and exposes for us — for all of us, non-Russian as well as Russian — in *The Gulag Archipelago*. As a correspondent in the Soviet Union over many long years, I often enough brushed close to this world. I saw the barbed-wire outposts and the wooden watchtowers with their tommy gunners even in the heart of Moscow, and I knew friends who vanished into its depths, never to return.

Yet no one, I think, not even those who have survived years of prison and forced labor, knows this shadow land better than does Solzhenitsyn.

Only by reading *The Gulag Archipelago* can we in the West begin to plumb the depths of degradation to which human beings have been subjected in the name of a regime which came to power with the slogan of banishing human misery from the earth.

From childhood we have trembled at the names of prisons and punishment systems — the Inquisition . . . London's Tower . . . the Bastille . . . the Tombs . . . the Czarist exile system . . . Hitler's extermination camps.

All these are dwarfed by the landmarks of the Gulag Archipelago — the Lubyanka, that old-fashioned office building (it housed the Rossiya Insurance Company in pre-Revolution days) on Dzerzhinsky Square in Moscow, just across the street from the most pleasant of stores, the Children's World; Butyrka, a relic of Russia's "enlightened" empress, Catherine the Great; Lefortovo, a monument to early Moscow architects; Krasnaya Presna, a horrible transit prison set in the most proletarian of Moscow districts; Vladimir, known to the ends of the Archipelago as an "isolator" for political prisoners; Sukhanova, that most terrible of prisons, from which only a handful emerge — and they usually raving mad or physical wrecks.

A long list could be compiled of places like these. And page after page of *The Gulag Archipelago* is filled with stories of men and women, almost all of them decent, intelligent, patriotic, hard-working, devoted, delivered up by fate to the Soviet terror machine — stories painstakingly gathered by Solzhenitsyn, true stories that make the blood run cold.

Solzhenitsyn does not tell these stories simply to chill the blood. He recalls them for the specific purpose of exposing an arch-evil.

"Woe to that nation whose literature is interrupted by force," he said in his Nobel essay. "This is . . . the amputation of its memory. The nation can no longer remember itself, it is deprived of spiritual unity. . . . Silent generations grow old and die without ever talking about themselves, either to each other or to their descendants.

"This is . . . a tragedy for the whole nation, a danger to the whole nation. And in some instances a danger to the whole of mankind when the whole of history ceases to be understood as a result of such a silence."

To Solzhenitsyn, the convenient explanation that the terror and the prisons began with Stalin and ended with him does not wash. The trouble began, he believes, on November 7, 1917, the day of the Bolshevik Revolution. The whole apparatus of terror, of brutality, of surveillance,

blackmail, denunciation, secret police, torture, death camps — all this
dates back to Lenin's time. It was simply perfected by Stalin. And Stalin's heirs, while giving lip service to reform, while turning free hundreds of thousands of survivors and "rehabilitating" more hundreds of
thousands of the dead, have preserved intact the whole apparatus and
still employ it, if on a reduced scale, against dissident writers, freethink-
ers, religious believers, anyone who does not meet the cast-iron Party
code.

Reading *The Gulag Archipelago* is like no other reading experience
of our day. We may, perhaps, have thought that Solzhenitsyn's *One
Day in the Life of Ivan Denisovich* or *The First Circle* carried us into
the depths of the inferno. But *The Gulag Archipelago* explains to us
why Solzhenitsyn called the latter novel, set in a *"sharashka,"* a prison
scientific research institution, *The First Circle.* The novel carried us
only to the threshold of Soviet depravity, only to the first circle of hell.
Even *Ivan Denisovich*, with its simple story of a simple prisoner managing to survive a single day in concentration camp, gives us only a
glimpse of the second circle of hell. *The Gulag Archipelago* thrusts us
into the inner circle. It is the kind of work Thomas Mann could have
written had he been incarcerated in and survived Buchenwald and then
dedicated himself to telling the full story of Hitler's horror. Or Dante,
had he been a victim of the Inquisition.

The Gulag Archipelago is a whole continent of terror. Every railroad
station has a prison cell or two and a detachment of interrogators; every
quarter of Moscow has its own great prison and subsidiary prisons. The
tourist who admires the marvelous 12th- and 13th-century cathedrals at
Vladimir is within shouting distance of a prison Torquemada would
have envied. Russia's great Pacific port of Vladivostok has been closed to
foreigners for nearly thirty years because it is the main transit point for
the shipment of labor convoys to the slave gold mines of Arctic Kolyma.

It is not easy to categorize *The Gulag Archipelago*. It is conceived on
a titanic scale, like a mural covering the wall of Grand Canyon or, as
someone said, like a literary Sistine ceiling. It is not fiction, nor is it
nonfiction in the conventional sense. It is the product of the powerful
creative imagination of probably the world's greatest writer fitting into a
mosaic of heroic dimensions thousands of details.

Comparisons seem inadequate. One might mention Dostoyevsky's
Notebooks from the House of the Dead. But Dostoyevsky's experience
in the Czarist prison system seems almost idyllic when contrasted with

experiences suffered under Soviet power. The elder George Kennan's *Siberia and the Exile System,* a classic of the 1880s, was regarded in its day as a shocking exposé. Compared with *The Gulag Archipelago,* it seems almost a pleasant travelogue. Compared with those who brought about the hundreds of thousands of executions and the millions of deaths in the Soviet terror system, the Czars seem almost benign — having taken only a few thousand lives even in the bloody years that followed the 1905 Revolution. Solzhenitsyn notes bitterly that some 80,000 Nazis have been convicted for concentration-camp atrocities since the end of Word War II. In Russia the number of men executed for their part in the Stalinist terror is less than thirty. As for the brutalized Soviet prison guards, every effort was made to find them good jobs when certain camps were closed down during the Khrushchev era. Many wound up as Moscow cabdrivers.

To some American readers *The Gulag Archipelago* may appear to overstate the case against Soviet terror. Our minds boggle at the thought of a systematized, routine evil, under which three or four or more million men and women were sentenced each year to forced labor and eternal exile — and in a manner so casual that the prisoners often were not even told what their sentences were nor what crimes they were supposed to have committed. Whole armies of human beings were sent to Siberia — all the Russian men and women who survived Hitler's prison camps and managed to get back to their homeland were automatically shipped eastward, by the trainload, to Stalin's terror camps. Entire small nationalities vanished into the maw of the prisons. Shortly before his death Stalin was considering plans to exile all Russia's Jews to Siberia to "save" them from a pogrom which he was about to launch — or so Moscow rumor had it.

Solzhenitsyn did not write *The Gulag Archipelago* merely or even mainly for Americans or other non-Russians. He wrote it for his own countrymen. As he said in the Nobel address, "It was my fate to survive, while others, perhaps more gifted and stronger than I, have perished. I myself met but a few of them in the Gulag Archipelago . . . and virtually no one managed to return. A whole national literature remained there, cast into oblivion not only without a grave but even without underclothes — naked, with a number tagged to its toe."

He writes for his comrades still in the Archipelago and for his fellow Russians everywhere, and he has already suffered the consequences: exile and loss of citizenship. One day, he believes, his people will rise up and bring the Archipelago and the forces which created it to an end. Russia he feels sure will endure. Russia's strength is greater than that of any one ruler or regime.

Still, Solzhenitsyn can be said to write for all mankind — for, as he says, "countries and even whole continents repeat each other's mistakes at a later date."

And so for readers at large *The Gulag Archipelago* is not only a shock but also a warning.

HARRISON SALISBURY

As DAVID WILLIS McCULLOUGH WRITES, *the Club lost a shining "conscience of quality" when Bernardine Kielty Scherman, the widow of Harry Scherman, died in 1973.*

THE NEW YORK TIMES brought news of Mrs. Scherman's death: Bernardine Kielty Scherman, 83, widow of the founder of the Book-of-the-Month Club, Inc.

Harry Scherman was, of course, the founder, and it was altogether fitting that he should propose to Bernardine Kielty from Fitchburg, Massachusetts, in front of the stone lions outside the New York Public Library. She was a woman of great energy and curiosity. A phone call from her might include requests for information on subjects that ranged from the Revolutionary War in New Jersey to the latest reference book on Hollywood. She had, her friends say, a unique way of blending practicality, directness and human sympathy.

She wrote a number of books for both adults and children. She was a regular reviewer — and one-time columnist — for the *Book-of-the-Month Club News*. She had an intriguing way of signing some reviews Bernardine Kielty and some Bernardine Scherman: there must have been a code there somewhere. She was, it seemed to me, a conscience of quality at the Book-of-the-Month Club. To see her in the halls, and she would frequently drop in, would seem to remind us that we were indeed the original book club.

When I first came to work at the Club I was told there was one word I must know how to spell: Bernardine. It was misspelled in the *Times* obituary, the kind of mistake that would have infuriated Mrs. Scherman, and amused her.

RAGTIME, *published in 1975, was the breakthrough book for E. L. Doctorow, establishing him as an important contemporary novelist. Since* Ragtime, *Doctorow has solidified his reputation with other glowing works. But* Ragtime *made it for him, and to honor the occasion properly Doctorow's then editor, James Silberman, now president of Summit Books, interviewed his author in New Rochelle, in a house that greatly resembles the one that dominates the novel.*

E. L. Doctorow

by James H. Silberman

"THE images of history work in all of us all the time," said E. L. Doctorow. He sat in his writing room at the top of his 1906 house, in a suburb of New York City, and talked about *Ragtime*. "I wrote it here — and the first line of the first draft was 'I live in a house that was built in 1906.' With that certain images sprang to mind: Teddy Roosevelt was President, people wore white clothes in the summertime, women carried parasols. That's how history exists in most people's minds — a sets of images. I've used some of those images and constructed a novel from them."

As an author Doctorow has always been drawn to America's past. His first book, *Welcome to Hard Times*, is set in the Old West, and *The Book of Daniel* reaches back into the 1930s. And now *Ragtime*, which is set in America before the First World War.

"The novel has been in retreat before journalism, before sociology and psychology. People today read psychologists for entertainment. In the past thirty years the novelist — that free-roaming savage — has been forced onto a kind of reservation of personal experience — a barren territory of no value to anyone." He laughed and went on. "One of the ways for us to deal with this is to break out, to attack. Reconstruct the world. That, after all, is what historians do, and politicians."

A stunning delight of Doctorow's novel is that he has filled it with the people of the turn of the century — Harry Houdini, the escape artist; the beautiful Evelyn Nesbit; Harry K. Thaw, who committed "The Crime of the Century" for her; Henry Ford and J. P. Morgan; Booker T. Washington; Emma Goldman; and Sigmund Freud. All these people become involved in the lives of the lesser-known characters, and early readers have asked how much is literally "true." Did J. P. Morgan ever spend a night alone inside an Egyptian pyramid? Did Houdini really meet the Archduke Franz Ferdinand?

"A society that deifies facts, as we do in America, tends to see every novel as the true story of thinly disguised people. Why not turn that around — and write about imaginary events in the lives of undisguised people. When you do that you are proposing that history has ended and mythology has begun. That's what *Ragtime* is getting into — an American mythology. So my answer to the questions — Is this really true? Did Morgan really meet Ford? Did Evelyn Nesbit really meet Emma Goldman? — My answer is, they have now, they have all met now."

Doctorow's personal history began in 1931 in New York City. He went to P.S. 70 and to the Bronx High School of Science and spent his summers in a camp in Massachusetts, a few miles from where he has recently built a family cabin. He graduated from Kenyon College, went on to Columbia University and to the U.S. Army in Germany. He came back to New York and got a job as reader for a motion-picture firm and then went on to edit for a paperback house. Subsequently, he became editor in chief of the Dial Press. During these years, he wrote *Welcome to Hard Times* and *Big as Life.* "As an editor, I worked my twelve-hour day, and then I'd go home, sleep till 11:00 or 12:00 and then write until morning. Eventually I quit publishing and found a teaching job in California which allowed me to write mornings — a tremendous luxury. To this day, getting up in the morning and writing dazzles me."

Doctorow's third novel, *The Book of Daniel,* came out in 1971 to a remarkably enthusiastic press. That same year he began to teach at Sarah Lawrence College and to work on the novel that became *Ragtime.* He was awarded a Guggenheim Fellowship in 1972 and a Creative Artists Program Service Fellowship in 1974. He lives now in the 1906 house with his wife, Helen, his nearly grown daughters, Jenny and Caroline, and son, Richard.

As he talked of his new book, Doctorow looked out the window of his workroom to the street where, in the opening pages of *Ragtime,* Houdini is said to have driven his Pope-Toledo. "One of my motives in *Ragtime* was to write a novel that was totally accessible, that could be read by people who usually don't read books, as well as by readers who like the art. I also wanted to use narrative the way it was used before the novel became modern. A lot of novels that have come out over the last few years seem terribly static. But I discovered that certain narrators from an earlier time excited me in a much simpler, more primitive way than anything contemporary — Defoe, for instance, or Kleist, the German writer. That's the strategy I chose in *Ragtime* — to commit myself to the *ongoingness* of the story. I wanted to write a book in which what happens is the paramount question." Doctorow paused and smiled. "And now you know all my secrets."

IN 1976 DAVID WILLIS MCCULLOUGH *interviewed William Zinsser, author of* On Writing Well, *and then Master at Branford College, Yale University. We liked what we read about Zinsser so much that, three years later, we went out and hired him. Zinsser is General Editor of the Club and the doctor everyone calls on to heal stress fractures of the language.*

David Willis McCullough's Eye on Books

FOR thirteen years William Zinsser was a reporter and critic on the old *New York Herald-Tribune.* For five years he wrote a column for *Life.* He has ten books to his credit, and now he's up at Yale University teaching what he calls "pruning."

Actually, he is Master of Branford College, editor of the university alumni magazine and teacher of a course on writing nonfiction. That's where the pruning comes in. "The students' biggest writing problems," he says, "are clutter and a lack of respect for what words mean. I try to heighten their awareness of words, to get them to think before they write and to prune away what's unnecessary."

His new book, *On Writing Well,* is, he says, "an attempt to get the course down on paper." It is a snappy, no-nonsense, often humorous little book that gives advice on avoiding clutter, on style, usage and the meaning of words. It also sets down some practical rules on how to begin an article and how to end one, how to conduct an interview or write a sports or travel piece or how to write about scientific subjects. "The science assignment is the turning point for most students in the course. I just have them describe how something works, and many of them are forced to realize for the first time that B does indeed follow A."

Zinsser says that after ten years of sitting in a Manhattan apartment and turning out free-lance articles he enjoys being Master of Branford. He lives in the college with his family and oversees about 480 students. "It's like living in a C. P. Snow novel. Although my biggest job is simply being available, what I actually do runs from the ceremonial to the janitorial, from marching in academic processions to picking up trash on the quad." He was amazed at the popularity of his nonfiction course. "The students are desperately eager to write about the world they live in, and they have an acute awareness of the fact that they don't know how to write."

Assignments in Zinsser's class don't exceed five pages. "American language is becoming bloated," he says, "and the bloat is contagious. College writing is being killed by assignments of twenty-page papers, more than half of which is excess. The kids are cranking out bloatage, papers that are sheer padding after page five. It is a dangerous habit to pick up."

The phrase "American language" pops up frequently in conversation with Zinsser, and I asked him what he meant by it. "It's more than simply using elevator for lift or truck for lorry. American language is more informal than British language, looser. It has absorbed American Indian words, such as succotash, and words from waves of immigrants. It accepts regionalisms and invented words from industry and advertising. But a danger in this democratic looseness is that sleazy and pretentious words can creep in. The greatest danger to American language right now is pretentiousness. The word bartender is American language at its best. The meaning is obvious. The man tends bar. But the language is at its worst when it is afflicted with a pretentious euphemism, such as 'mixologist.' "

Zinsser claims to feel a special horror for social science jargon, such as "potentialize" or "input." "No one should write what he cannot comfortably say. There are many useful new words. There are, for instance, about thirty excellent counter-culture words, such as up-tight, rip-off and freak. I don't consider them slang words because they have precise meanings. We may not want to use them years from now, but they are useful words for today. One of the strengths of American language is that it accepts such words as hassle and drop-out. The first time you hear them you know what they mean."

He also stresses the value of humor in writing. "A joke," he says, "is no joke. If a writer can sell himself, the subject will exert an appeal of its own — and humor is an excellent lubricant. A writer is, after all, an entertainer at least about 20 percent of the time, and a writer must believe in himself. Writing is an act of ego, and you might as well admit it."

IT IS SOMEWHAT DISCONCERTING *to note that Saul Bellow's first BOMC Selection came late in 1975, with* Humboldt's Gift, *although* Henderson the Rain King *was reviewed in the* News *in 1959 and* Herzog *in 1964. In her interview with Bellow coinciding with publication of* Humboldt's Gift, *Martha Fay, a free-lance journalist, found one possible source for the Bellow magic. "My first loyalty is to my imagination," the Nobel Prize–winner told Fay. "I happen to believe that there is some affinity between that loyalty and the truth."*

Henderson the Rain King by Saul Bellow

Now and then you meet a big, tall, tough, energetic, worried, loud-mouthed man who seems to be quite out of place. He should have been a Viking, or a Janissary, or a Conquistador. He is out of place almost everywhere. He belongs to clubs, but the other members think he is a crazy and rather offensive eccentric. He has one present wife and two or three previous life-partners, with children here and there; but he is not really a husband or a father. He was mercurial and erratic in the war, sometimes crazily courageous, sometimes a blowhard misfit. He has trouble about his drinking. He still wishes he were 20 years old, and he hopes that life once more, for a short season, will become interesting. Such a man is Henderson, the unhappy, garrulous millionaire who is the hero of Saul Bellow's amusing new extravaganza. He goes to Africa because — well, everything in America is used up and full of problems, and only in Africa can anyone still search for the unknown, meet the unpredictable, unscrew the inscrutable. After a long and confused trek into the interior, he meets a charming, well-educated and thoughtful African chief, a man much more intelligent than Henderson himself. Henderson may not be bright, but he is strong. He does several feats of unusual strength, and becomes a sort of grand vizier, the rain priest of the tribe. His life as a voodoo man is a mixture of macabre action episodes and comically angular intellectual conversations; there is one particularly mad sequence in which he learns, for an hour or so every day, how to fraternize with a lion and roar convincingly, while he spends the rest of the time discussing philosophical and political problems with the chief. This is an original and constantly unexpected story. Perhaps it is a parable about modern American man in flight from togetherness, in search of the soul which he does not fully possess. If so, it might be set to music by Gian-Carlo Menotti and produced in the style of *The Emperor Jones*. Perhaps it is a parody of Joseph Conrad: "Mistuh Henderson, he rain king." Perhaps it is a cheerful wheeze: Henderson played by Paul Douglas; Dahfu played by Harry Belafonte; Romilayu played by Louis Armstrong; chorus of Amazons, warriors and witch doctors from any Tarzan picture; the lion, by our old friend from MGM. Blest if I know: I am as puzzled as Henderson; but we both had a good time.

GILBERT HIGHET

Herzog by Saul Bellow

"CONSIDERING his entire life, he realized he had mismanaged everything — everything." Even out of context the sentence contrives simultaneously to sadden and amuse the reader. One senses behind it the pressure of a grotesque personality. And such a personality indeed is Moses Herzog. Herzog, of all the non-heroes produced by the contemporary school of the antiheroic novel, is one of the oddest. Mr. Bellow has done to the life a type one would have imagined done to death: the big-city Jewish intellectual. Son of a Russian-Jewish-Canadian bootlegger, Herzog has become a professor of history; a constant writer of unmailed letters (to himself, to Nietzsche, to Adlai Stevenson, to Eisenhower, to his scholarly colleagues, to his mistresses); a more or less acquiescent cuckold; a twice-divorced husband; a dazed father; an even more bewildered adulterer; a nonstop ponderer on the blind alleys of our epoch; a neurotic with a genuine genius for suffering; a murderer manqué; a free-association wit; and a man who, when we first encounter him as he reviews his life, sums himself up thus: "If I am out of my mind, it's all right with me." Doubtless many readers will be bored by Herzog's endless ruminations, self-recriminations, and the inchoate quality of a mind which judges that the best life can offer is "a favorable balance of disorderly emotions." Many other readers, however, who have, from *Augie March* and *Henderson the Rain King*, got the hang of Mr. Bellow's unanchored, free-flowing, energetic imagination, will follow Moses Herzog with a kind of distressed pleasure. For these latter the wry, dark, tormented comedy in which Mr. Bellow excels seems to connect well enough with our centrifugal time. In few books the reviewer can recall is the intellectual as comic figure developed with greater inventiveness, insight and sheer energy.

CLIFTON FADIMAN

Saul Bellow

by Martha Fay

SAUL BELLOW occupies a peculiar and special place in American literature. Often regarded as the finest novelist writing in the country today, he is widely read, a three-time National Book Award winner (for *Augie March, Herzog* and *Mr. Sammler's Planet*), on everybody's list of home-grown intellectuals, creator of wondrous and memorable characters who have quickly become part of our collective consciousness. Bellow is also something of a terror, an enigma, a reproacher, alive, well and still thumbing his nose eastward in the direction of the literary bureaucrats, refusing to acquiesce, for one thing, in what he views as the entirely premature attempt to categorize and define his work.

"Here I am," Bellow said one morning recently, "still trying to get started, and there they are, treating me as though I were finished." He paused a moment, pleased, and said to his interviewer, "Write that down: Here I am — still trying to get started — and there they are — treating me as though I were finished."

The remark and Bellow's delight in having phrased it so disingenuously reflect a long-running, if necessarily part-time, battle with "them" — the cultural sermonizers and embalmers of art, with whom Bellow has been at odds for a good part of his 60 years. And although he has been a voluntary citizen of Chicago most of that time (between extended stays almost everywhere else), Bellow can't resist explaining his affection for it backwards. "The main thing about Chicago," he says, "is that it's not New York. There are no writers to talk to in New York, only celebrities on exhibit. If you're not prepared to join their gang, as chorus, supernumerary, lickspittle, and if you will not compete with them for attention — in short, if you have a different idea . . ." The thought is completed by a slow lift of the eyebrows above eyes that seem to have just been spooned from a vat of steaming chocolate. Mr. Bellow smiles.

And Chicago? "In Chicago," he says with enthusiasm, "you have a city in which there *is* no literary culture, in which the most-dressed-up people are artistic, in which restaurants and shops and wines and cheeses and parties and sexual delinquencies are all the art life the city boasts." Reminded of the huge and rusting Picasso perched in front of City Hall, Bellow adds, "And a paperweight Picasso which is not heavy enough to hold down all the files of wrongdoing in the building!"

Bellow's curious case for Chicago sounds much like the case made by Charlie Citrine, hero of *Humboldt's Gift,* his latest, and ninth, book. How close are the two, Bellow and Citrine, prize-winning writers both, friends of the dead, especially dead poets? "It is really terribly difficult to identify yourself with a character in a book. If you are not a naturalistic writer and if you stylize your characters, they very quickly leave you. The rule of consistency effectively takes over. You part company by the time you've written the first few paragraphs. It is clearly someone else. If Charlie is going to a beat of 8/16, my normal beat is 3/4. The resemblance is not going to continue very long. We are as unlike as five sharps and two flats."

Bellow pursues the analogy. "I have in mind how the book should be read, how the inflections of voice should be followed. Something recorded at 33 and played at 78 is not going to sound right." Approaching the final stages of a book, Bellow reads it aloud to a typist to make sure that he hasn't got "the rhetoric of the page mixed up with the rhetoric of the voice." The names in *Humboldt* are indeed lovely to read, lovely to pronounce, and Bellow does not collect them from phone books or on the subway. "I listen to my own mind, my mind makes many suggestions. I try to fit the person with a sound."

The name Bellow is of course wonderfully aural, not visual, and is rarely fitted publicly with a face. But face to face, Bellow is a natural charmer, a laugher, amused and playful, no matter how ascetic, how mournful he sometimes appears, as his mind and conversation jump from serious idea to complicated pun or allusion. He gazes steadily and politely at his questioner one moment, out the window at the University of Chicago campus the next. Bellow is a Fellow of the Committee on Social Thought there, teaching literature to a select group of graduate students in the social sciences.

Bellow has always had some kind of job to support himself and his writing, wives and children, and when asked why he never got into commercial writing instead of teaching, he said that he has tried but always gets fired. He told the story of his brief and little-known career with *Time,* the news magazine.

"I was young, inexperienced and tired of knocking about," Bellow began. "I had some friends at *Time.* They said there was a job open as a movie reviewer, why didn't I see about it? I did and I was hired. For one day I was a movie reviewer. Then Whittaker Chambers, who was editing the section, took one look at me and said, 'Well, what do you think of Wordsworth?' And I said, 'What does that have to do with movie reviewing?' And he said, 'I want you to answer the question, what kind of poet was Wordsworth?' So I said, 'He was a Romantic poet.' And Chambers said, 'There's no place for you in this organization.' "

Bellow laughed, "I wasn't surprised, really. They had reviewed my first book — *Dangling Man* — and hadn't much liked it. The title of the review was" — he paused a moment, and then, beaming, said, "Introspective Stinker."

For some people Bellow is indeed an introspective something, and they are intimidated by his characters and ideas. Bellow is sympathetic but says, "I have to deal with people with ideas in my books. Ideas are the only things that will save us. My advice to the reader is: Read confidently and believe in the writer's good will and sense of humor." But in Bellow's own books, the humor is often overlooked by critics in search of cerebral content. "I know," he says, somewhat disappointed, "they tend to think of me as a brain."

"My first loyalty is to my imagination," Bellows says. "I happen to believe that there is some affinity between that loyalty and the truth. I do think it's much better to be truthful than partisan. I don't know why a writer has an obligation to be useful to society. We are not schoolteachers or social workers or toilet trainers, or flag wavers on the barricades. Not to write a boring book is the main thing. I think a writer has an obligation not to bore the reader. What an imposition, you know, the money and the time you ask for a book."

DAVID WILLIS MCCULLOUGH *in search of S. J. Perelman. A match made in heaven.*

David Willis McCullough's Eye on Books

"IF PEOPLE expect me to be funny, they are in for a rude shock. I figure my job ends when I leave the typewriter and get out of the swivel chair. People make a mistake when they confuse a writer with a performer."

The speaker is S. J. Perelman, author of a new book called *Vinegar Puss*. He is sitting in the living room of his sparely furnished apartment overlooking Gramercy Park in Manhattan. On the walls are hung a few Saul Steinberg drawings and several maritime maps of Indonesia. Centered on one of the maps is the island of Ceram, a port in the Banda Sea that Perelman visited twenty years ago and still dreams of as the site of a retirement home. "The only guidebook to the place was published in 1856 by a friend of Darwin," Perelman says, "and it is still up to date."

The room has an air of transience about it, a sense that fully packed suitcases are stacked in the closets. In fact, Perelman is about to leave on a nine-month around-the-world tour which should be considerably more leisurely than his last circumnavigation of the globe. That eighty-day dash is chronicled ("Around the Bend in Eighty Days") in *Vinegar Puss*, a distinctly tart collection of essays that deal, chiefly, with Perelman's recent Babylonian captivity in Britain.

In 1970 he announced that the United States — and New York in particular — was getting too brutal for him and that he was off to England and civilized living. A few years later he was back in town, muttering that it was impossible to find a good corned beef on rye in all of Albion.

Perelman claims that his exile was never intended to be permanent. "I went to investigate the clichés about the gentility of the English. I had done English bits before. But I found when I actually lived there that the place didn't seem so bizarre and eccentric as it did from over here."

As for New York: "It was bad when I left it and it hasn't gotten any better."

The eighty-day trip was an attempt to duplicate the events of Phileas Fogg's famous race with time. In 1956 Perelman had won an Academy Award for his script for Mike Todd's version of *Around the World in Eighty Days*, so it was a subject that interested him. "Also," he says, "like Fogg I am a member of the Reform Club in London."

For his own variation on the Jules Verne story, however, Perelman decided to hire a beautiful young Amazon (from Pass Christian, Mississippi) for the Passepartout role. This wasn't his first experience with female luggage carriers. Years ago while in Africa writing some *New Yorker* pieces, he saw a sign advertising for fifteen women to form the first all-girl safari. He promptly signed up and marched across Uganda with them.

He is not optimistic about the new crop of comic writers: "The prospect is bleak. It's a form that seems doomed, the Ring Lardner–Benchley tradition. Woody Allen is sometimes good. Mel Brooks is good when he is doing the 2000-year-old man. Russell Baker is the most active, but I think you can say that the last couple of generations haven't been much interested in verbal gaiety."

As for Perelman's famous use of unusual words, he says: "I don't go out of my way to search for exotic words, but I think writers should use words that have exact meanings. I do like unfamiliar words and I use a thesaurus. It might even startle a reader into looking up what the words really mean."

A final question: Is S. J. Perelman himself a vinegar puss? He just looks out the window, off towards the Players Club across Gramercy Park, and smiles.

HOW FITTING *that a new multivolume life of the United States should begin in 1976, the country's bicentennial year. And how astonishing that Page Smith, author of a 1962 Selection on John Adams, has been able to write seven volumes of his "people's history" of the Republic, massive works each, in just ten years. (He works faster than the two Durants did.) At the time his first two volumes were published, Smith told West Coast writer Jack Fincher about his narrative approach to history and how it differed from the straight academic approach. "All my work is discovery," he said, "not recording."*

A New Age Now Begins by Page Smith

How many of us have, since our school days, read a significant book about the American Revolution — or reflected more than casually upon an event that so largely determined what we are? Starting Page Smith's history, I aimed the question at my guilt-laden self. Finishing it, I found my guilt replaced by greater knowledge, understanding and pride. In a Bicentennial year polluted by hucksters and political demagogues, I can suggest no better way to celebrate our national birth than by reliving, in this massive but constantly absorbing two-volume work, the splendor of our early history. It seems to me that *A New Age Now Begins* belongs on the shelves of anyone who seeks the source of our heritage. As a reference work alone, it should have an immense value for ourselves and our children and our children's children.

The subtitle reads: "A People's History of the American Revolution." People's, yes. Populist, no. The author of the magisterial *John Adams* (offered Club members in November, 1962) is well aware that in the mid-eighteenth century a happy fortune threw up an array of unexampled leaders. But the Revolution was not won by the character of Washington, the energy of Adams, the brain of Jefferson, the rhetoric of Tom Paine. It was won — here we touch the book's heart — because if a whole people, or most of them, reach a common understanding of freedom and then highly resolve to be free, they will seek out the means to become so. George III, his ward boss Lord North and his able but politically stupid generals could not among them collect the wit to grasp this simple truth; and so the British lost. Thus we gained not only from our own resolution but from Britian's ineptitude. Against the greatest imperial power in the world we employed the ultimate weapon, which is endurance; and so turned what might have been a tedious tale of contending armies into a dramatic story "of ordinary citizens determined to be free."

Thus the subtitle. The title is no less loaded with meaning. Page Smith derives it from the motto, drawn from Virgil, on the Great Seal of the United States: *Novus Ordo Seclorum.* The humble Philadelphia tradesman, the tarry sailor out of Boston Harbor, the small Virginia farmer — these knew little Latin and less philosophy of history. Nonetheless their energies were in part fueled by the vision, unconfined by time or place, of the Founding Fathers. The Revolution's action was circumscribed, its immediate goal practical. But behind both action and goal vibrated an idea, nonparochial and therefore of limitless potential power. Were this not so, those oddly assorted children of our Revolution — the French, Russian and Chinese Revolutions, not to mention many minor ones — might not have seen the light, or might have put on very different forms. The American idea of "a new series of ages" exerted generative force for almost two centuries. Page Smith believes that that force is still unspent. Reflecting on the Revolution's deepest meaning, he writes: "The United States is a kind of interim stage between the old parochialism of the nation-states and a more universal society."

By its very dimensions *A New Age Now Begins* announces itself as a major effort. The canvas is vast, the tempo leisurely, the view expansive. The story does not begin with the Stamp Act, even though, agreeing with the pioneer historian who called it "the hinge of the Revolution," our author goes so far as to say that it decided the outcome: all that remained was to win. It starts rather with a portrait of each of the thirteen colonies, their origin, their growth, their tone and temper. The Revolution began long before the Revolution, long before identifiable resistance. In his ruminative old age John Adams concluded that it began decades before Lexington and Concord, in the hearts and minds of the people. Yet it could not have so begun had not the people been a most peculiar one indeed. For, though prefigured by Cromwell's Roundheads and the Glorious Revolutionaries of 1688–89, they were something new. "What then is the American, this New Man?" asked Crèvecoeur. He published his *Letters from an American Farmer* as late as 1782, but his New Man had been developing since Plymouth Rock.

Page Smith distinguishes four stages of pre-Revolution colonial resistance: theoretical formulation, passionate reaction, political organization, popular education. Then, having with thoughtful brushstrokes limned his background, he proceeds to his central story. He is, the reader will perceive, a battle buff. I know of few more colorful and even suspense-filled accounts of all the major, and dozens of minor, engagements, by land and sea, in the North, the Middle States, the South, in Canada, and on the border. But each confrontation, each campaign, is viewed not only tactically but in a social and cultural light. He makes clear how we "won" or "lost." More to the point, he makes us sense the thick human reality behind the engagement. We suffer or triumph or despair with those who struggled at Golden Hill, at Lexington and Concord, at Ticonderoga and Dorchester Heights, at Valley Forge and Bennington, in the Wyoming Valley and on the high seas. Each battle is important, not because one side retreated and the other advanced, but because all of them fused in a crucible out of which issued a people and at last a great nation.

Quieter, non-bloody battles were fought in London. The story again and again roves back to the center of the Empire, where many Whigs spoke of the American troops as "our army," and where George III, that "decent sort of villain," aided by a not over-bright First Minister, ingeniously constructed his own defeat. Battles of the mind were fought in Philadelphia; in careful detail the day-by-day sessions of the First and Second Continental Congresses are traced for us. Battles were fought — one of history's most extraordinary phenomena — in the state capitals where were hammered out the state constitutions that produced the ideas on which the federal Constitution was to base itself. And there were agonizing battles, too, that went on inside the hearts of American Tories, an underprivileged minority treated in these pages with impressive sympathy.

Only specialists can calculate the exact measure of the fresh or at least unfamiliar material Mr. Smith provides. But to me, a nonspecialist, his book came almost as a revelation. We all know, or think we do, the outlines of the main actions, the life profiles of the main actors. Yet these are no more than silhouettes. Mr. Smith fills every inch of a vast mural. One test, for example, would be his treatment of George Washington. Through the use of anecdote and a hundred small touches he moves Washington off the dollar bill onto the stage of actual life. We see Washington as a passionate nature tempered by stoic reserve. Not a first-rate strategist or tactician (Benedict Arnold was probably a greater general), Washington was beyond doubt a great leader. Mr. Smith makes us feel why this must have been so. "All political unions," he writes, "must begin in a union of hearts." He makes us understand exactly how it came about that Washington and his men loved each other and how in that love were planted the seeds of a new nation.

Giving new life to the supremely great, Mr. Smith gives it also to the common men and women. It was they, not the firebrands or the middle-class intellectuals, who *made* the Revolution. To convey them into our imaginations Mr. Smith has blown the dust off documents known only to lifelong scholars of the period. The masonry of his complex edifice is built of primary sources: "letters, diaries, journals, newspapers, public documents, and memories of the men and women who were involved in the event of which this nation was born." Only by an almost painful adherence to the concrete fact, the thing that actually happened, could he fulfill his purpose: "to take [the Revolution] away from the academic historians, the professors, and return it to you."

He returns it to us two centuries after its start. We live again, he suggests, in times that try men's souls. Therefore this, if ever, is the hour in which to reflect on our beginnings. The Founding Fathers had a vision of freedom and independence. It was a flawed vision (only John Woolman and a few other anti-slavery men had a complete one), yet it had magnificent dynamism because it was held out, if only in theory, to all mankind. That vision is still to be realized, among us as among all nations. But it had to start somewhere. It started with the Founding Fathers; and as the author says, "it is our obligation to create a future in which they will be at home."

CLIFTON FADIMAN

A Conversation with Page Smith
by Jack Fincher

A hulking, hawk-faced figure in fleece-trimmed corduroy coat and cap, Page Smith materializes out of a foggy Santa Cruz, California, morning trailing the gobble of turkeys. Gentleman farmer? Most certainly. Also maverick writer pursuing his own revolution against the academic tradition that says you can't take a scholarly step without leaving a footnote.

He led me into his study, a rustic wood outbuilding choked with books and hung with the paintings, sculptures, tie-dyes and fur-and-feather fetishes of his artist wife, Eloise, and their four grown children. They are the creators in the family, he says. "I think the creative level of the historian is actually very low." He laughs. "When my son was young he brought a friend in, pointed to the shelves and said, 'These are the books my father writes his books from.' "

There is truth in his son's words. Smith says that he has never taken as much as one card of notes. He writes "books, not chapters," from start to finish, typing long quotes directly from the voluminous reading that attracts him, setting down digressions as they occur and later gluing everything together where it seems to belong. His enjoyment of such unbuttoned sentiments as his son's must be all the more galling to academic historians because Smith's scholastic credentials are impeccably eggheaded. He took his undergraduate degree at Dartmouth, got his Ph.D. at Harvard under Samuel Eliot Morison, taught history at UCLA, and was the very first provost at the University of California's visionary Santa Cruz campus. It was a post he later resigned in protest against the publish-or-perish demands of modern academe. Smith himself, happily, has never been plagued with that problem. He has written ten volumes in twice as many years, on everything from the history of history and women to the nature of towns and chickens.

Eloise Smith left us with coffee, English muffins and honey, and our conversation began.

JF: *What's the critical difference between your narrative approach and the academic?*

PS: All my work is discovery, not recording. I don't believe in objectivity. You bring your preconceptions. I believe in sympathy and compassion and understanding, in attachment rather than detachment. To me discipline is passion, caring enough about the thing to discover the order in it.

Most academics are obsessed with the analytical, the interpretive, the expository. They've gone wrong in thinking their mission is to explain things, in believing that if you collect all the data the data will speak to you. Which is obviously ridiculous. It's predicated on the premise that all these little monographic experiments are going to add up to truth some day. They're not. They're going to add up to a lot of little monographs.

JF: *Doesn't the academic concept of historical distance lend, if not enchantment, perspective?*

PS: That's another snobbery. The best history of the American Revolution was written by people who were in it. That's why I like to use the analogy of time as a mountain. When you're up on top — 200 years away — the academic historian says you can look back down the years and see things as they really were. I say the situation is more like an archaeological dig. The past lies buried under the mountain; the accumulation of intervening experience distorts your view. You have to sink a shaft down to the stratum you want to study and reconstruct what happened out of the remnants and shards.

JF: *And once you get to that point, what?*

PS: Contrary to popular misconception, there is an absolutely staggering amount of material from the Revolution. John Adams said if you read a lifetime you couldn't cover it. But I believe it's a fallacy to assume you have to read everything in order to understand something. You could still misunderstand it. Some one thing an obscure person says can outweigh masses of "important" material.

Often the power of the original fact is so great you're awed by it. As Charles Francis Adams said when his grandfather, John Adams, and Thomas Jefferson both died on the same day — the Fourth of July, 1826 — there is nothing so eloquent as fact. Incidentally, my editor called to ask if I knew how many pages my book runs in final form. I whimsically guessed 1776. She said, no, *1976*. I'm a believer in synchronicity, serendipity, chance. History is full of those. They should play as important a role in research as they seem to play in life.

DECADE SIX

1977–1986

THE EDITORIAL BOARD *chose a novel called* Voyage, *subtitled* A Novel *of 1896, for the Club's first Selection of 1977. For Clifton Fadiman it evoked echoes of Richard Henry Dana, Melville, Conrad, Stevenson, Jack London. Sterling Hayden was keeping pretty good company. Hayden's life, as he described it to writer Martha Fay, had been split three ways — actor (he preferred to call himself "male starlet"), seaman, writer. He also told Fay, "Some people don't make sense. I don't make sense."*

Sterling Hayden
by Martha Fay

STERLING HAYDEN sits in a rocking chair facing south in a suite on the twenty-eighth floor of the United Nations Plaza Hotel in New York. The room's small, modern, prefabricated style seems a peculiar wrapping for his huge bearded self. But it has a broad and almost unobstructed view of the East River and something approximating a sea breeze can reach him when the air conditioning has been turned off and the slanted windows opened.

He wears a deep tan and a large towel held up by a belt and he looks exactly like Harwar, the 59-year-old drunken, brave, cowardly, failed, angry, gentle sailor who is a pivotal character in Hayden's first novel, *Voyage.*

Thirteen years ago, a friendly reviewer of Hayden's autobiographical *Wanderer* wrote: "Mr. Hayden has finally realized his boyhood ambi-

tion to write a book. He — and the reading public — may profit if his
future writing is about the sea. These are his best chapters."

Now Hayden has fulfilled an adult ambition — to leave behind an always unhappy career as an actor and call himself a writer permanently.
And he is absolutely delighted, at the age of 60, to be so publicly and
profitably rewarded for doing so. "When the wire came," Hayden said
after hearing that *Voyage* had been made a Book-of-the-Month Club
Selection, "I was thrilled. It meant a great deal to me. I could say, in
spite of everything, 'You old, drunken bastard, you've done something.' "

Most observers would not have put it quite that way: the one thing
that has always been conspicuous about Hayden, besides his size, is his
habit of doing something. He was born Sterling Walter, in Montclair,
New Jersey, in 1916. His father died when he was 9; when his mother
married a man named Hayden, the child took the name. (For years,
news stories referred to "Sterling Hayden, born John Hamilton." In
fact, he adopted the name Hamilton during World War II, when he was
in the OSS and his first wife, Madeleine Carroll, was in the Red Cross in
France. Both were eager for some privacy.)

At an early age Hayden went gratefully to sea. "It's so fortunate when
you're enamored of something," he says of having had the nerve to go,
"and I was enamored of the sea, totally. In the winter of '33, I was 16
and terrified, standing on a dock, trying to decide whether to stay or go.
In my heart I really wanted to go back to school and row on the crew
and have the coach massage my leg and all that stuff. But I was trying to
make myself a man."

The first time out, he was "an ordinary seaman on a schooner from
New London to San Pedro." At 21 he had his master's papers. Then, in
1940, Hayden wound up in Hollywood, a "male starlet" playing, more
or less, against Madeleine Carroll and Fred MacMurray in the movie
Virginia. After that came roles in dozens of pictures, famous or quickly
forgotten, including *The Asphalt Jungle, Prince Valiant, Johnny Guitar, The Eternal Sea* and *Dr. Strangelove.*

Attempting politely to explain what made him trade in the sea for the
screen, Hayden says, "The idea of going from sailing ships to becoming
a male starlet was very intriguing." The bewildered look on his face
suggests that the very idea seems so preposterous that he can hardly
stand it. Finally, he says, "Some people don't make sense. I don't make
sense."

What many people remember best about Hayden is his spectacular

departure from the U.S. in 1959, in defiance of a court order which forbade him to take his four children around the world under sail. His ex-
wife had charged in court that the intended vessel, Hayden's 98-foot
schooner *Wanderer*, was not seaworthy. Hayden, who had had custody
of the children since his divorce in 1955, fled, with a novice crew and
three children besides his own, south-southwest to Tahiti, where the
wanderers found a haven. Ten months later, they returned; Hayden was
fined $500 and received a five-day suspended sentence. He spent the
next three years writing *Wanderer*, which told of that voyage and of the
several selves he had been until then: lonely child, contented sailor, miserable actor, supplier to Yugoslav partisans in World War II, Communist Party member in postwar Hollywood, namer of names before
the House Un-American Activities Committee in 1951, analysand,
drinker — the list is a very long one and one is hard pressed not to add
to it in an effort not to overlook any of the major themes of Hayden's
life.

He was similarly concerned to get it right in *Voyage*, casting back almost a century in search of the appropriate setting. "There's a character
named Harwar," he says rather simply, as though a reader might not
have guessed. "I had Harwar being myself, but aged 30. I had worked
on the book from '64 to '68 and then I put it aside. Then about a year
and a half ago I met John Dodds [his editor at Putnam's, his publisher],
who encouraged me to pick it up again. John was beautiful about it,"
Hayden continued, "and he said, 'I think you should make him your
own age.' You see, I was contemplating myself as I might have been at
30 — we all like to think of our ideal selves. But when John, in his infinite wisdom, suggested I make Harwar my own age, then I really bore
down."

Much of the writing was done on a canal boat, or barge, "what I like
to call a *péniche*," on which Hayden has lived much of the time for
eight years. The barge was until this summer moored in the Seine in the
middle of Paris and has recently been moved to the French countryside.
Hayden's third wife, Kitty, and their two teenage sons live, much of the
time, in a house in Wilton, Connecticut, and a great deal of commuting
is the result.

"I'm incapable of moderation," Hayden says. "I live either here" (he
raises his hand above his head) "or there" (thrusting it below his knee).
"And I'm totally prepared to pay the price. I drink until three or four in
the morning and then I lose the next day. On the third day I start to
work again. This book was written that way.

"I have these vivid memories of crawling around, standing up to write, and suddenly the typewriter would veer off to the right. I said to my wife at one point that rather than continue this chain smoking and chain drinking, I wouldn't write. So I gave it up for six months, and finally I said, 'To hell with it!' I wanted to write."

IN 1977 JACK NEWCOMBE, *Executive Editor of the Club, traveled to a bayou called Bogue Falaya, just above Lake Pontchartrain, to talk with Walker Percy. This mild-mannered Southern gentleman could have practiced medicine but, luckily for us, chose to write. Newcombe and Percy talk about writing, particularly about Percy's latest novel,* Lancelot.

Walker Percy
by Jack Newcombe

IT WAS a day of exceptional November cold in St. Tammany Parish, Louisiana. In Walker Percy's home, set comfortably on the edge of the Bogue Falaya, a bayou just above Lake Pontchartrain, the fireplace glowed with heat, and a silent color TV set flickered with the familiar Saturday afternoon images of college football. "The Bear will bring them back," Percy said, mocking the Southern faith in Coach Bear Bryant, whose Alabama football team trailed at half time against Notre Dame. Saturday is traditionally football and family day in the Percy home, as it is in households all over the South. But there is no TV sound conflicting with conversation with his wife and visitors, including his married daughters, Mary Pratt and Ann. It is a time for pleasant lounging in the sweater, slacks and loafers he favors and for talk about the new book-and-antique shop recently opened by Ann and her husband nearby in the town of Covington. A dependable seller in the store is *The Moviegoer*, which earned Walker Percy the National Book Award in 1962 and, suddenly and uncomfortably for him, focused attention on him as the possible Southern heir to William Faulkner's prominence in the world of letters.

Three novels (*The Last Gentleman, Love in the Ruins, Lancelot*) and fourteen years later, Walker Percy finds comparisons to other authors from the South and/or investigations of his literary quest somewhat disquieting. He still seems mildly surprised that he is a published author and not a practicing doctor of medicine, a career that he chose because he did not want to be a lawyer, as most members of his family had been.

Law and literature were strong waves in the atmosphere in which Walker Percy grew up in Greenville, Mississippi, the adopted son of an uncle, William Alexander Percy, after the death of both parents. Uncle Will was a lawyer, a poet, the reluctant manager of the huge Percy cotton plantation. His autobiographical *Lanterns on the Levee (Recollections of a Planter's Son)* is still in print and was much praised by reviewers at the time (1941) for its literary quality and the candor of "the Southern aristocrat's point of view." At Greenville High, Walker Percy surprised schoolmate Shelby Foote (the Civil War historian) when he showed him the poetry he had been secretly writing. Growing up as a Mississippi Percy in the early 1930s required the choice of a profession. Walker decided on medicine and enrolled at the University of North Carolina. According to the university's placement test, writing was hardly one of his facile areas; he had applied what he considered a fine Faulknerian flow to an essay question in the exam and was placed in the "retarded" section in freshman English. But he did get published for the first time at UNC — "a scholarly study" of movie fan magazines in the campus literary monthly. The one informal picture of him in the yearbook shows Walker, lean and intent as he is today, standing in the waiting line for a matinee at the Carolina Theater.

Moviegoing, with all its hallucinatory splendors, was an enthusiasm he took with him to New York when he started his medical studies at Columbia University's College of Physicians and Surgeons. He recalls getting relief from *Gray's Anatomy* by going to the movies and by dropping water bombs on passersby on the streets below his residence hall room. Walker Percy would surely be looking back today at such student follies from a doctor's office if he had not contracted TB while performing autopsies at Bellevue Hospital. The young intern was sent to Saranac Lake in the Adirondacks for a recuperation that lasted two years.

"It was a strange experience," he said, "not to see anyone for weeks except the person who brought the tray of food three times a day. [He had been placed in a private home because the sanitarium was full.] If I hadn't had that time alone I wouldn't have gotten into writing." Percy used that protracted exile to get acquainted with the humanities that had not been part of his medical education. "I read the Russians, then the

French, and I listened to a great radio station in Montreal." When he was cured of the disease he began a new life — and the slow, painstaking process of becoming a writer.

Through moviegoing Percy found a way for the protagonist of his first novel to view things in a world where people no longer seemed to know what to look for. The displacement of reality which movies offer supplied the framework for *Lancelot*. Walker and his wife, Mary, were taking a long-delayed tour of antebellum mansions on the River Road. "The young guide gave much more emphasis to the movies made on location than to the people who lived there or the famous generals who stayed there. 'Now here is the spot,' the guide would say, 'where Bette Davis pushed over the vase that killed Olivia de Havilland.' To the local people the movie made in the mansion had more reality than what actually happened."

When he started *Lancelot* Percy was determined to tell a story, to provide a novel with suspense. "I've been criticized because my other books didn't have enough action. They didn't go anywhere." It took four years of writing and much revising to get it right, to provide that subtle, not quite definable line which holds Percy's works together.

At his office in Covington — the writing room away from home — Walker Percy spends about three hours each day, making notes and drafting pages in longhand. He is a great admirer of the delicate satire of Swift's *Gulliver's Travels*, which he is rereading. "Maybe I can do something between science fiction and the metaphysical novel," he said, referring to a satirical zone few contemporary American novelists would risk trying to enter. "Remember *The Body Snatchers*?" he asked with the enthusiasm of an old, discriminate moviegoer. "Now I would like to try something light like that."

IN HIS REPORT *on* The Path Between the Seas, *John K. Hutchens called it "an appropriately splendid work, one marked by the most admirable diligence, dramatic sense and style." Diligence and style don't come easy, says David McCullough, who is sometimes confused at the Club with Book-of-the-Month's David Willis McCullough. A project starts for this McCullough with scrupulous research. It ends with* right *pages extracted from the remains of* wrong *pages. "I'm not a writer," McCullough told Jack Newcombe. "I'm a rewriter. I have to make it all perfectly clear."*

David McCullough

by Jack Newcombe

DAVID MCCULLOUGH'S reputation is clearly that of a writer of large books on huge, sprawling subjects. His first book centered on an event which disordered the lives of thousands (the Johnstown, Pennsylvania, flood); his second was on a feat of construction which had vast political-social consequences (the building of the Brooklyn Bridge). Now the forty-four-year international effort to create the Panama Canal.

"People ask me, 'How come you are always writing about water and construction jobs?' " he says. "Well, I think my work *does* have a continuity. The books are derivative. I am writing about self-reliant people who don't give up, people who deal with large things. And I care a lot about the roles personality and courage play for those who get involved. There's a quote in Saint Exupéry's *Wind, Sand and Stars* that helps sum it up for me: '*But there are other ways than war to bring us the warmth of a race, shoulder to shoulder, toward an identical goal.*' "

Despite their titles, McCullough's books don't fit snugly into categories. "The Canal — it's not one subject," he says, "it's so many. It's nineteenth-century medicine, it's international politics, finance, engineering. Think of the repercussions, the currents it released. And it's all those wonderful people!"

McCullough's scrupulous, item-by-item research pays him greatest rewards when he is able to flesh out a figure and provide an insightful characterization that has not been offered before. His research on Ferdinand de Lesseps, which included conversations with his grandson in Paris, enabled him to give "a different picture" of the famous Frenchman. In the archives of the Ecole Polytechnique in Paris, he discovered material revealing the illegitimate birth of Philippe Bunau-Varilla, an unknown fact that helped explain some of the man's behavior. A high point of McCullough's investigation — which hit him like the sudden grasp of an elusive clue by a persevering detective — was the reading of General Goethals' letters to his son. "The letters are a window thrown open upon a sensitive and appealing man" — one who was viewed by critics as being totally devoid of human emotion.

The McCullough pyramid of research for a book is an awesome assembly. For the Canal story he consulted more than 400 books, some 100 technical journals, newspapers, magazines. The study of official documents and correspondence, much of it in the National Archives, occupied him for more than a year. There are 15,000 items in the Goethals collection; 10,000 listed under Bunau-Varilla in the Library of Congress. He is a confirmed user of photographs for research and had hundreds copied so that he could study them. He plunged into fiction of the period in search of mood and atmosphere. Conrad's *Nostromo* and the writings of Jules Verne were particularly useful.

McCullough's need for on-the-site research was minimal. But he and his two oldest sons, David, then 14, and William, 12, spent two weeks in Panama. "I found it even more beautiful than I had imagined," he says. "And, of course, the Canal is excellently run." He carried his impressions (actually, pleasing confirmations of his research) back to his home in West Tisbury, Massachusetts, where he is a year-round resident of Martha's Vineyard. There, in an efficient, eight-by-twelve-foot, cedar-shingled writing studio in the back corner of his acre lot, McCullough goes through the agonizingly labored post-research period — the writing of the book. "I'm not a writer," he likes to say, "I'm a rewriter. I have to make it all perfectly clear." The wastebasket fills during a writing day with what his son Geoffrey calls "wrong pages." There were nearly 200 of them in the early draft of *The Path Between the Seas*, and he had to start all over again after deciding that he must give a detailed account of the French contribution and not use it simply as background to the U.S. involvement.

The McCullough island-home seems a remote distance from sources for (and scenes in) the book. But he found several descendants of Canal people on the Vineyard, including three members of the Goethals family. Through the local library he has access to Library of Congress materials, including microfilm which he reviews at the local school. He has, he believes, the best of worlds in which to work and to raise five children (daughter Dorie, 7, cannot remember a time when her father was not working on the Canal book), two dogs (one docile Samoyed and a lively collie) and a cat. He and his wife, Rosalee, feel privileged to be able to take long walks on a winter beach without encountering anyone except perhaps another strolling islander. Already in the work studio on Music Road the files are beginning to grow on his next project — a portrait of Teddy Roosevelt, the man, before he became President. In time it will be finished and be quite recognizable as another McCullough original.

"THERE HAVE BEEN *other books about the Vietnam war. None measures up to this." So wrote Gilbert Highet in his report on Philip Ca-*

puto's A Rumor of War. *Caputo arrived in Vietnam in 1965 with the first ground combat unit sent to that war. He left a year later with the Vietnam experience "gnawing at my guts." Out of it came this book. Marsh Clark, who covered the war for* Time *magazine, interviewed Caputo in Moscow in 1977, where both were working as correspondents, Clark for* Time, *Caputo for the* Chicago Tribune.

A Rumor of War by Philip Caputo

READING Philip Caputo's extraordinary personal account of his experience in the Vietnam war, I was irresistibly reminded of two European artists who made scenes of warfare into immortal works of art. Jacques Callot in *The Miseries of War* recorded some of the events of the Thirty Years' War with a cool precision that turns deeds of violent cruelty into a ballet of devils and the damned. Francisco de Goya's *Disasters of War*, on Napoleon's invasion of Spain, show close-up pictures that pull the spectator into the action until he almost hears the cries of the suffering victims.

Mr. Caputo is not so great an artist as Goya or Callot, if only because he is younger, less mature. His book is largely built around what happened to him at the beginning of a war everyone refused to call a war, so that it is far less objective than the European war pictures. Other people — his fellow officers, the men of his platoon, the Vietnamese villagers — are lightly sketched in; and one of the unintentioned ironies of his narrative is that some of its characters become fully real only when they are wounded or killed. Then (like Goya's women and men) they leap, agonized, right off the page.

That is Caputo's chief virtue as a writer — and perhaps only a rather self-centered man could have attained it so fully: he sees, he hears, he smells (the jungle, the foul water, the other marines, himself, he smells them all and remembers all); and his descriptions are in strong, vivid prose full of compassion yet scarcely touched with hysteria or rancor.

I spoke of Callot and Goya because, although their techniques were radically different from each other, they shared and translated into art one harsh and dominating conception of war: that it makes ordinary people do and suffer extraordinary things. This is the basic theme of *A Rumor of War*. It portrays young men who in peacetime would have been tending bars or running gas stations, with no excursions into violence and daring except an occasional fistfight or deer hunt. And it

shows them, through comprehensive training and conditioning proce-
dures, through their control of a variety of deadly weapons, through
their inevitable alternation between the pressures of danger and the
boring routines of base camp or recreation area, and through their exposure to myriad trials they would never have faced at home, transformed
into new men, partly heroes and partly madmen. Caputo's own mind
and his moral standards were collapsing toward the end. He found himself and some of his men facing a court-martial for allegedly murdering
civilians. And he conveys to us fully and clearly just how the same acts
might have been committed by anyone so transformed and so pressured,
and how bewildered he was when they were reviewed and condemned
by the cool, rational representatives of the law. His book is more than a
collection of action-pictures and a skein of reminiscences. It is a powerful spiritual drama.

There have been other books about the Vietnam war. None measures
up to this. Not one gives such a close and sympathetic account of the
conflict. But this is written from a special point of view, which might
easily be overlooked. Caputo was in the Marine Corps, which has always had, or claimed, great esprit de corps. His tour of duty ended well
before Vietnam became a scream in everyone's throat. Some recent
books have shown soldiers of the United States behaving badly, in and
out of combat. Nothing of that here. In 1965–66, the marines stuck together. "Two friends of mine," Caputo writes, "died trying to save the
corpses of their men from the battlefield." And he adds a fine positive
note, which has been true of many wars despite their miseries and disasters. "Such devotion, simple and selfless . . . was the one decent thing we
found in a conflict otherwise notable for its monstrosities."

GILBERT HIGHET

Philip Caputo
by Marsh Clark

PHILIP CAPUTO lives only one flight up from me in a dingy Moscow
apartment building set aside for foreigners. Now Moscow correspondent for the *Chicago Tribune*, Caputo is a sturdy man who has witnessed much of life and death in his 36 years. As he sat in my apartment
conversing lightly about his experiences, wearing tan cowboy boots and
blue jeans and drinking beer, I marveled that he was still alive to talk
about them. He was a combat officer in Vietnam, arriving in Danang in

1965 with the first ground combat unit sent to that war. He later returned there as a war correspondent, barely escaping from Saigon during the frantic American evacuation in 1975. He covered the war in Lebanon for the *Tribune* and was captured by Palestinian guerrillas, thrown into a hole and threatened with execution. He rode on camelback with Eritrean insurgents in Ethiopia. He covered the 1973 Yom Kippur War in Israel.

Raised in a working-class suburb of Chicago, Caputo fled from home "much the way young men in the old days would go to sea in sailing ships to see the world." In his case the conveyance was the Marine Corps. After basic training he was assigned to command an infantry platoon near Danang. "At first, in the good old American tradition, I saw myself fighting to make the world — or at least Vietnam — safe for democracy. Later, disillusionment set in, but politics is not what my book is about."

War has been characterized as interminable periods of boredom punctuated by seconds of sheer terror. It was during the long lulls that Caputo started a diary. "I didn't want to lose any of the experience. Going to war when you're young and unprepared for it, you realize how transitory everything is, even your own life. You want to do something permanent, so I started keeping a record." When Caputo left Vietnam in 1966, his footlocker was jammed with combat boots, fatigue uniforms, a camouflage bush hat, some campaign ribbons and his loose-leaf diaries.

"I had a hard time settling down when I got home after I got my discharge, so I took off for Europe with $2,000 in my pocket. After six months, I found myself, nearly broke, walking down the Ramblas, the main drag in Barcelona, taking sausages off the stands. I figured it was time to go home and work." After a brief try at writing advertising, he was hired by the *Chicago Tribune* as a junior reporter. Two years later, he shared a Pulitzer Prize for his reporting of Chicago vote frauds.

"About this time I started the book. I tried it first as a novel, then as a series of sketches. When the *Trib* moved me to Rome, I worked on it some more. Finally, I realized it couldn't be fiction. I had to tell the story straight, but with some techniques of fiction by trying to make the reader feel he was out with us on patrol in Vietnam. The book kept gnawing at my guts. I wanted to write not a traditional military memoir, but something that conveyed a sense of smell and sound and place — a book that would last.

"Here I was writing about one war in Asia and hearing the sounds of the other wars I was covering in the Middle East. I wrote and rewrote. I couldn't have done it without the diaries. I could recall individual incidents but it was difficult to get the sequence right."

Caputo's efforts to work on the book and cover one more war were seriously shattered some twenty months ago. He had just filed a story to the *Tribune* and had stepped out into a deserted Beirut street when two leftist Moslem riflemen opened fire on him. A bullet fragment hit him in the left arm. Caputo fled but ricocheting bullets struck him in the leg and head, knocking him down. He got up and was hobbling for cover when another bullet smashed his right heel. Bleeding profusely, Caputo crawled around a corner and was dragged to safety by a citizen.

Groggy from painkilling injections following three operations to mend his wounds, Caputo started to work in earnest on *A Rumor of War*, composing sometimes only a sentence or a paragraph a day at his parents' home in Westchester, Illinois. But as he gained strength, the writing pace accelerated. Finally, last summer Caputo gathered his wife, Jill, and their two young sons, Geoffrey and Mark Anthony, and went into seclusion in a small bungalow in Key West, Florida. There, rising at 5:30 each morning, he worked in khaki shorts and tennis shoes, the surf murmuring in the background. At night, he took solitary strolls along the shore, remembering the distant sound of the South China Sea at Danang. Caputo wrote the book's final sentence last October 30, just ten hours before he and his family boarded an airplane to fly to his new assignment in Moscow.

Caputo walks with a limp today but he says he feels much stronger. He has even taken up cross-country skiing through the Russian forests, the one athletic activity he can manage. His mind is busy with book plans. "My next will be a novel set with a war backdrop in Ethiopia. Perhaps one day I'll write about Beirut but I'm a little too close to it right now."

THE MEMBERS *of the Editorial Board are generally cool appraisers. They read, they ponder, they decide. They are not exhorters. When Mordecai Richler read* Song of Solomon *by Toni Morrison, he became an exhorter. "If I may inject a personal note," Richler wrotes in his report on the novel, "we on the Book-of-the-Month Club's editorial board do a good deal of reading. We try our utmost to approach each book afresh. With appetite. But sometimes, to come clean, it's difficult. The words fly in, the words fly out.* Song of Solomon *was something else." He goes on to explain what he means; he exhorts.*

Song of Solomon by Toni Morrison

SONG OF SOLOMON is not so much the proper subject for a nicely balanced review as a cause for celebration. My only fear is that once having applauded merely deserving novels (tunes well played if somewhat familiar), there isn't sufficient praise left to hail a novel as magnificent as this one, a novel full of haunting melodies that simply haven't been heard before. *Song of Solomon* is beautiful, funny, enormously moving, enchanting, laden with cunningly wrought mysteries. It is the best novel of the black experience in America since *Invisible Man.*

If I may interject a personal note, we on the Book-of-the-Month Club's editorial board do a good deal of reading. We try our utmost to approach each book afresh. With appetite. But sometimes, to come clean, it's difficult. The words fly in, the words fly out. *Song of Solomon* was something else. From the opening pages, I sat bolt upright, aware that I was in the presence of a major talent. A writer who does more than bring us news of another world, much more: Toni Morrison alters our perception of the black experience. She has composed a novel that is everything *Roots* was supposed to be but wasn't. Let me put it another way. Ostensibly *Song of Solomon* is about grindingly poor blacks trapped in the slums of Detroit, and other seemingly ignorant blacks, even more penurious, vegetating in the backwoods of Virginia, and yet — and yet — one emerges from the other end of this book envying the characters for their way of seeing, the texture of their experience and the beauty of the legend of Milkman's great-grandfather, Solomon. Solomon, torn from Africa; Solomon, who, finding no other escape from slavery possible, mounts a hill in Virginia, flaps his arms, and flies away home.

> *Solomon done fly, Solomon done gone*
> *Solomon cut across the sky, Solomon gone home.*

I'm going to commit a further indiscretion and quote from one of our reader's reports. Martha Fay writes: "Nothing is simple, and nothing for sure is black and white, especially the people in this book. The descriptions are sometimes so sweet they make your chest hurt."

This is a story about characters named Macon Dead and his son Milkman, who was born with an urge, incomprehensible to him, to fly, and who is called Milkman because someone saw him suckling at his mother's breast when he was already 4 years old. It's about Milkman's sisters, Magdalene (called Lena) and First Corinthians, born into com-

parative affluence on Not Doctor Street, a street so known out of respect
for their grandfather, a black doctor who actually got to treat the odd
white patient. It's also about Milkman's avenging friend, the fulminat-
ing, driven Guitar. And, above all, about Pilate, her daughter Reba and
her love-obsessed granddaughter, Hagar. Pilate's an outcast, partially
because she was born from her mother's dead body without a navel.
A teller of spellbinding tales, Pilate, before she became a bootlegger
of sorts in the slums of Detroit, dispensing both booze and magic,
wandered through the South, carrying a geography book in one
hand and claiming a rock from every state she stopped in. A rock and
a story.

Though the novel deals realistically with the conditions of life in the
Detroit ghetto and Virginia, attuned to the most subtle nuances of class,
acutely aware of the differences between urban and rural blacks, it is the
effortless flow of so intricate a story, and its gallery of memorable characters, that makes *Song of Solomon* so arresting a novel. The characters
stop short from time to time and, in a language that soars, tell us their
stories. Such is the impact of these tales that we find our sympathy
leaping from one to another until it includes everybody. If, for instance,
we are, to begin with, convinced of the utter meanness of Macon Dead,
the hustling slumlord, then we are stunned into something more than
acceptance once he tells Milkman his own tale, how he once worked beside his father in the fields and of his difficult courtship of the boy's
mother. Our sympathy shifts yet again once Milkman's mother reveals
the story of her father, her upbringing and marriage. Other characters,
say Magdalene and First Corinthians, who seem shadowy at first, suddenly speak out, emerging with a terrifying clarity.

Song of Solomon abounds with life. It's a remarkable novel. Read it,
please.

MORDECAI RICHLER

JOHN FOWLES *found an audience from the moment his first novel,*
The Collector, *was published in 1963. In a 1969* News *review of* The
French Lieutenant's Woman, *the reviewer referred to it as "a novel in
the great tradition of Hardy and Lawrence."* The Magus *received spectacular reviews, too. And in 1977 came a different kind of novel (actually, all of Fowles's novels are different from one another),* Daniel

Martin. *"It springs from a deeper level of consciousness," wrote Clifton Fadiman in his Selection review. In the biographical sketch that accompanied* Daniel Martin, *Fowles talked about his goals as a writer.*

About the Author: John Fowles

SINCE the publication of his first book, *The Collector*, fourteen years ago, English author John Fowles has been winning new readers, a great many of them young Americans, and putting critics everywhere on the defensive. He was called "a very brave man" for demanding total acceptance of his bizarre theme in *The Collector*. In a review of *The Magus*, Brian Moore said Fowles was himself a magus — "a magician or juggler, the caster of dice and mountebank in the world of vulgar trickery." *Time* said, "Fowles has produced a literary shell game with so many mysterious switches that one can never be quite sure there ever was a pea." (A revised version of the book recently made the bestseller list in England.) Joyce Carol Oates, who admired Fowles's risky dual role as Victorian novelist and 20th-century novelist in *The French Lieutenant's Woman*, decided that the book was "a rewarding excursion into the mind of one John Fowles, half scholar and half magus." *The French Lieutenant's Woman* — "the kind of work that gives success a good name" — helped make an unlikely bestseller of *The Ebony Tower*, a collection of four stories and a translation of a medieval romance.

A relentless experimentalist, Fowles has said that the word "novel" suggests a story not told before, a view of life never before imagined. "It is my ambition to write one book in every imaginable genre." Fowles would of course like to find an audience for the "novels" ahead, but he doesn't require one. "I get much more pleasure from writing than from being published. I like the creation of another world. That is very beautiful and satisfying to me. As soon as a book leaves this room, this house, there's always a diminution of pleasure."

Fowles writes in an 18th-century villa overlooking the English Channel in the resort of Lyme Regis, the town which served as a background for *The French Lieutenant's Woman*. He and his wife, Elizabeth, have lived there for more than a dozen years, tending their lush garden. He considers himself a good enough field naturalist and is a longtime collector — as a child he collected butterflies (like the protagonist in *The Collector*); more recently he has acquired rare books, old china, pottery fragments from the Dorset coast and tropical plants.

Fowles was born in England 51 years ago and attended Bedford School outside London. He had a conformist, middle-class upbringing, was "head boy" at Bedford and a captain of cricket. He was, he himself says, nonintellectual and without writing aspirations. (He maintains an enthusiasm for cricket which he compared favorably with American baseball not long ago: "Though I like the various forms of football in the world, I don't think they begin to compare with these two great Anglo-Saxon ball games for sophisticated elegance and symbolism. Baseball and cricket are beautiful and highly stylized medieval war substitutes, chess made flesh, a mixture of proud chivalry and base — in both senses — greed. With football we are back to the monotonous clashed armor of the brontosaurus.") After Bedford, Fowles attended New College, Oxford, studying French (*Madame Bovary* left a vivid impression: "For me it is still the perfect novel"). He was in his 20s before he decided he should write, that there were books he must bring out. He was in his mid-30s before the success of *The Collector* confirmed that he could grow in the art of the novel which, as he once put it, is "being able to caress people's imaginations."

Malcolm Cowley *nearing eighty, by David Willis McCullough.*

David Willis McCullough's Eye on Books

"It's as though I were a cop killer," Malcolm Cowley said the other day. "They sent me up for life with no chance for parole." Cowley, who will be 80 in August, was talking about his sixty years as a professional writer. It all began when Cowley, then a Harvard dropout, settled in Greenwich Village with his girlfriend Peggy. An old friend of Peggy's was an editor on *The Dial*, and he let Malcolm review novels at a dollar a throw. "I'd pick up a pile of books at the magazine and go over to Union Square, where I could polish off six in an afternoon and then sell them at a secondhand bookstore on Fourth Avenue for thirty-five cents a copy. The dollar a review came only on publication. The thirty-five cents was cash on the barrelhead, and that's what kept us in groceries and coal." Later would come the publication of Cowley's own books of poetry, history and literary criticism, his French translations, his editorship at

The New Republic and his friendships with the likes of Hart Crane, Hemingway, Fitzgerald, Wolfe, Stein and Faulkner on to John Cheever (whose first short story he published) and Ken Kesey (who was his student at Stanford).

To celebrate his sixtieth anniversary as a writer, Cowley has just completed —*And I Worked at the Writer's Trade*, which combines informal autobiography with some serious thought about the vagaries of literary fame. "I now see myself as a literary historian," Cowley said when we talked about his new book, "and I'm especially interested in the waves of new literary generations. They come about every fifteen years and reflect a complete change in style and judgment, but the waves alternate between expansion and contraction, from looking outward to looking inward. I think I've lived through six ages so far." Beginning at the turn of the century, they are the Reform or Muckraking Age (outward looking), the Lost Generation (inward looking), the Jazz Age (outward) followed by the Depression, which Cowley believes lasted until 1945 and is something of an anomaly. After the war came the Silent Generation (inward), then the Rebellious Generation (outward), and we are now in the Me Generation (inward), which is marked by literature Cowley finds "unpeopled and inhuman."

Through all these alternating generations literary reputations are made and broken. "I never cease to be amazed why some of my friends became famous and others, just as talented, didn't. I've come to suspect it's a matter of wanting fame or not, and those who don't want it, don't get it." But fame can be fleeting. "I doubt if Thomas Wolfe will ever be popular again. By always saying in ten words what he could say in three, he put a terrible burden on future readers, while Hemingway would never say in three words what he could say in two. His reputation will be in eclipse for a while but he'll be back. When I read a good Hemingway short story I can smell pine needles, and I can't say that about anyone else."

—*And I Worked at the Writer's Trade* ends with an intriguing sentence: "No complete son of a bitch ever wrote a good sentence." Cowley says, "The key word there is 'complete.' You can point to a lot of SOBs (Hemingway, perhaps), but few complete ones. No writer has total control over his images and rhythm, so if a person is completely false, it will come out somehow in what he writes, and you can see it on the page."

I asked Cowley why he had never written fiction. "My essay style is really very close to fiction. You can easily read *Exile's Return* as a novel.

But I'm not good at observing character. I suspect that so much of my life has been spent reading that I haven't looked around enough." With that, Malcolm Cowley headed back to Connecticut, where he is at work on his next book, his memoirs of the 1930s.

HAIL TO THE REIGNING CHAMPION *of fiction in the Book-of-the-Month Club. James A. Michener made his BOMC debut in the* News *of 1947 with the review of* Tales of the South Pacific. *Since then, nine of Michener's novels were made Selections. No other writer of fiction comes close. In his report on Michener's 1978 novel,* Chesapeake, *John Hutchens talks about what makes Michener what he is: "the skillful narrator and almost incredibly diligent student of those factual details that bring the past to life as vividly as this morning's newspaper brings the present." With the Hutchens review is a piece by Michener himself on how he came to write* Chesapeake *and how a baseball player named Jimmy Foxx contributed to that decision. Writing about the author in 1982 (Michener was then seventy-five and had just finished* Space*), free-lance writer Joseph Barbato covered Michener's past, present, and future, and particularly his generosity to other writers.*

Chesapeake by James A. Michener

HERE IS James A. Michener at his characteristic best, the skillful narrator and almost incredibly diligent student of those factual details that bring the past to life as vividly as this morning's newspaper brings the present. *Chesapeake* is, I think, the most satisfying of his books since the early ones that established his reputation, beginning with the Pulitzer Prize–winning *Tales of the South Pacific* in 1947.

Like other of Michener's more than twenty books, *Chesapeake* is both a panoramic novel and a social history that marches through some four centuries of the life of Chesapeake Bay's Eastern Shore, from the sixteenth century to the present day. It is a tale that calls for its readers' careful attention, involving as it does successive generations of several families, their marriages and intermarriages, their descendants, their relationships with neighbors in the small Maryland town called Patamoke and with sundry true-life figures outside it. A long and complex novel, yes, but one full of rich reward for the reader.

It is 1583, and the first in the stout cast of Mr. Michener's characters is a Susquehannock Indian, Pentaquod, who wearies of his tribe's passion for war and moves south to Chesapeake Bay to join a nation whose leader he becomes. Then it is 1606, and Captain John Smith, small, vain and ill-tempered, is setting out from London to conquer Virginia with a company including an Oxford scholar, Edmund Steed, whose progeny we encounter throughout the novel, together with that of Edward Paxmore, shipbuilder, and his Quaker wife, the latter a bold abolitionist in a slave-ridden area; Tim Turlock, an indentured servant from England who escapes and founds a family of swampland sailors, hunters and fighters; the slave Cudjo and his wife, Eden, who achieve their freedom and become major figures in Patamoke's beleaguered black community.

The years run by, bringing scenes notable for their force and authenticity. The beating and hanging of a Massachusetts Quaker. The capture and sale of African blacks to an American slaver; the pure hell of their life on his ship; a mutiny that fails. The deadly, day-by-day degradation of slaves even at plantations like the Steed family's, where with few exceptions they are not beaten, starved or "sold south." The pirates coming up from the Caribbean and sailing the Chesapeake with impunity, ravaging plantations and murdering their owners. The surrender of Cornwallis at Yorktown, where the Marylanders are excluded from the final ceremonies as being uncouth and less than presentable. The horror accompanying the fugitive slave laws, and how eight escaping slaves are saved in Pennsylvania from their Southern pursuers. The dramatic revenge a wily Chesapeake waterman scores over an English captain who had twice defeated him in battle.

No less memorable are the scenes in which certain famous citizens appear: Benjamin Franklin, representing the Colonies in France, "well past 70, bald, paunchy, squint-eyed and as lively as a chestnut on a griddle," speaking "abominable French with a vigor that made his pronouncements sound fresh and challenging"; Senators Henry Clay, Daniel Webster and John C. Calhoun, in the tense decades before the Civil War, visiting the Steed mansion and discoursing on the issues that will come to a climax in 1861. Their talk, as Mr. Michener imagines it, has the immediacy of dialogue in a first-rate play.

When the author goes afield from Maryland history, it is with a reason. Why, for example, does he dwell at some length on the family life of Canada geese? He does so with admiration for those superb, intelligent birds, and also to emphasize their value to the economy of the South. He writes vivdly of the great movement of the geese, from the Arctic south through Canada to their winter refuge on the Eastern Shore, with huge congregations filling every field and estuary along the Choptank River. He tells of the regional value of the ducks, crabs and oysters and describes the hard life of the watermen who still go out in winter months under sail to work the oyster beds.

There is a sense of both sadness and exhilaration in Mr. Michener's long revealing of the history of Patamoke. The tense relation between blacks and whites in the population, from one decade to another, is at best an armed truce. As the years go by the situation improves and by the 1970s black students are playing football at Patamoke High School and teammates, black and white, celebrate a victory together in a local ice cream parlor.

When at the end "the final storm which overtakes all existence" crashes down along the Chesapeake, taking with it one whole island at the mouth of the Choptank River where the Steeds' plantation hall stood, one mourns for this place where "for a few centuries life had been so pleasant." Mr. Michener has enabled us to share the experience of its hardy inhabitants, their failures and triumphs, their past and present. We close the book with the realization that we have come to know this land, this "place of dignity," very well.

JOHN K. HUTCHENS

BEHIND THE BOOK:
A Search for Jimmy Foxx in Sudlersville
by James A. Michener

WHEN my last book, *Sports in America*, was nearly completed, I still had not made up my mind about what I would write next. Three attractive possibilities were competing for my attention, all of which I had considered and studied for years and about which I was prepared to write: the Muslim world, the Caribbean, the Chesapeake Bay.

What made the Chesapeake appealing was that it formed a neat enclave, a beautiful little world of its own, laden with history and meaning and significance for the future. It was a compelling magnet, offering a universe of problems which will always be of importance to our nation. Again, very little of substance had then been written on this unique little world, and this perplexed me. A lot of sentimental memories of plantation life, and great mansions and important families, but very little about the reality of life along the shores. One might conclude that a book about the bay was a real necessity, and I am always happy when that's the case. I felt the same way when I was about to write about Israel, and Hawaii and the American West.

But I was getting ahead of myself, for there was still one important detail I hadn't yet faced on the sports book. To do justice to Jimmy Foxx, the great baseball player, I knew I ought to go down to his hometown, Sudlersville, Maryland, and check some of his old cronies. I wanted to treat this tragic figure sympathetically, and I needed to walk over his stamping ground and see the little towns in which he played. So, I called my boating friend Bill O'Donnell, and he said that he and his wife, Karen, were free to take off two or three days, spend a day at Sudlersville and then some time exploring the towns to the south.

Big decisions are made so simply! I had a most fruitful day in Sudlersville, meeting the garrulous barber who used to cut Jimmy Foxx's hair, and through him visiting with men who had worked with Jimmy, and through them spending an afternoon with one of his female relatives. It was she who told the really perceptive stories about her famous cousin. She had not liked him, but she did sympathize with the miseries through which he had lived. She judged that he had brought these upon himself by his incompetence. It was a sad, sad story, much of which I did not feel free to repeat. I had known Jimmy when he stood astride the baseball world, champion in every sense of the word, a massive, natural hero. And now I was learning of him in his long years of eclipse. Well, that's what I wanted to insert into my essay on sports.

After Sudlersville we drove south and toward dusk approached the waterfront village of Oxford. To our right appeared a rather large cornfield, its stalks cut. At first I could not discern what was happening on the field, but I thought it was moving. I called to Bill to stop the car, and there, close to us, nibbling at fallen grains of corn, stood some two or three thousand geese, great dark birds that previously I had known only at a distance.

As we watched them feeding, and saw how their sentinels patrolled the area, and how they had learned that danger never came from a parked car, only from men who got out, I felt a sense of identity with those birds so overpowering that I knew I had found the leitmotif for my novel. I knew that for me the Muslim world and the Caribbean had faded. I knew that for a period of years I would commit all my life to the Chesapeake. Everything I did or said or thought would involve this bay, and these birds, and the men and women who lived with them. There would be no after regrets, no turning back. This was the job to be done.

At a small store in Oxford I purchased a schoolboy's notebook, and that evening as we sat in the Robert Morris Inn awaiting a shore dinner, I jotted down a complete outline of the novel and went to bed that night satisfied that I had made a good decision, certainly one with which I could function.

Next morning, when I awakened, I did not once go back to the rejected subjects, for I became excited by the explorations we conducted that day: down to the tips of a dozen peninsulas, across the ferry to the northern shore, down to the marshes south of Cambridge, back and forth across the Choptank, the river that even then I suspected would be the focus of my novel.

That second night I made a few additional notes to my outline and started to draft the maps upon which I would base my novel, and things fell so beautifully into place that I was almost ready to start writing. I felt myself engaged on a great project, and as soon as possible I intended being back on the Eastern Shore, renting a house and getting down to work.

The geese had made up my mind for me.

James A. Michener

by Joseph Barbato

WHEN James Michener was about 10 years old he rewrote the *Iliad* — he didn't want Troy to lose, he recalls. Today, at 75, when he blends fiction with diligent factual research he's very well paid for it. "I marvel at my good luck," he says. "I've always been able to go wherever my curiosity takes me."

Michener was talking about his extraordinary writing career, which began in 1947 with his Pulitzer Prize–winning *Tales of the South Pacific* and has included such epic novels as *Hawaii, The Source, Centennial* and *Chesapeake*. His more than two dozen books — including nonfiction works on art, politics, sociology and sports — have made him one of America's most popular writers.

Now, almost inevitably, the man who has taken so many millions of readers on historical tours explores what he calls "our new frontier in the skies." Though Michener has long been interested in mathematics and astronomy, the science and technology of space exploration have left him "struck dumb with wonder," as he told a Senate subcommittee in 1979. In that same year he became a member of the National Aeronautics and Space Administration Advisory Council. He spent the next three years visiting NASA laboratories and bases.

There's an assumption in publishing that any Michener novel will be a surefire success. But there's no complacency in this genial Quaker, who looks more like a Norman Rockwell grandfather than a major American literary figure. "I have a feeling that I'd be allowed one bad book and that would be it," he says. Over the years he has "junked" three novels.

Michener talks about his craft with deep seriousness and affection. Recently, at the cottage in Maryland where he and his wife Mari Yoriko Sabusawa live much of the year, he reflected on his career with satisfaction. His mail — several hundred letters a week — continues to bring the greatest pleasure. "What move me," he says, "are the letters saying that my books are too short — that the readers projected themselves into this imaginary world and it became very painful to leave it."

Among his contemporaries he feels a special kinship with those writers "who generate ideas like a dynamo." He names Saul Bellow, John Updike, Bernard Malamud, Philip Roth, Joyce Carol Oates, and Joan Didion. "Their minds are so prolific, their antennae are so highly attuned."

Michener won't speculate on how readers 50 years from now will respond to his fiction. But he takes "perhaps the greatest pride" in *The Source*, his book about Israel, and feels confident that his travel book *Iberia* ("any writer would be proud to have done it") and his lesser-known studies of Asian art will survive.

"Great novels elaborate the human soul in the tradition of Jane Austen, Flaubert and Henry James," he says. "What I do falls into a second category, which includes writers of semi-factual narratives like Dickens, Tolstoy, Balzac, Sinclair Lewis and Dreiser."

But it is the careers of younger writers that most concern Michener at 75. (He quietly donates a high percentage of his royalties to support scholarships for young writers and artists.) "The good books that I see now are as good as any that I knew in my youth," he says, describing works that he admires by Thomas Berger, Brian Moore and Anne Rice, among others. "There's a tremendous amount of raw talent in the United States. Some writers simply never get a break."

His own break — the good luck to which he refers over and over — came with World War II and the years that immediately followed it. The war not only gave him the basis for his first fiction; it also provided the immense readership for his later novels about distant places.

"If I had begun writing 50 years earlier," he says, "I would have been small potatoes. America wasn't looking outward then. There was no interest whatever in Asia, for example. But when I came along, 10 million servicemen had been overseas. Corporations had branches in Arabia, Tokyo and Hong Kong. With the great externalization of American interests I could find an audience."

He could also write full-time for that audience after Rodgers and Hammerstein adapted their classic *South Pacific* from his first book. "My income from the musical gave me the freedom that other young writers didn't have."

Many themes occur to Michener for such a writer to explore. "For years people have urged me to write about Alaska," he says. "Obviously I should. I suspect that because of my age and various obligations I'll never do it. It's a great sorrow. The same is true of the Caribbean. And a good football novel. And the Watergate story. So there they sit."

But he will keep the Southwest for himself. "I'm moving there this fall to look around and presumably write a long novel about the Texas experience as a study in power. I have it pretty well organized in my mind. Now I'll have to see whether it will bear fruit."

TALK ABOUT SELECTION CHAMPS *in the Club. If there hadn't been a Winston Churchill, William Manchester would be the leader in nonfiction sales.* Goodbye, Darkness *was Manchester's third Selection, and there have been two more since then —* One Brief Shining Moment *and the first volume of a biography of Manchester's BOMC rival, Winston Churchill. Manchester told Alden Whitman of the* New York Times *how he came to write* Goodbye, Darkness *and why it was the most difficult of all his books to put down on paper.*

Goodbye, Darkness
by William Manchester

HE HAD been there before, as a young marine in the Pacific in World War II. He went there again, more than 30 years later, to recapture, verify and analyze what he had learned in an experience that had continued to haunt his life. He is William Manchester, a first-rate writer, as his biography of Douglas MacArthur (*American Caesar*) and his other books have attested, and this memoir is a masterpiece of its kind.

It's a memoir, he stresses, and not a history. But it has the quality of an epic, covering the full sweep of action in the Pacific as the fighting man saw it and lived it — from the Philippines and New Guinea to Iwo Jima and, finally, Okinawa. Manchester writes with the eye and ear of a skilled military historian, describing the battles in absorbing detail.

But he has also written an intensely personal book. Manchester not only distills his own experiences on the battlefield; like a good novelist, he brings to life a rich gallery of people. What James Jones did so well in fiction, evoking the character of men at war in their strength and in their vulnerability, Manchester has achieved here in the literature of fact.

Manchester was 19 at the time of Pearl Harbor. He enlisted a few months later, partly as a tribute to his father, who had served as a marine in World War I, suffered a wound at the Argonne that ultimately destroyed him, and was a hero to his son. That son was an unlikely soldier-to-be — "a gangling, long-boned youth," not by nature a fighter. In fact as a schoolboy he was so averse to violence that a girl once beat him in a fistfight.

But off he went, an aloof collegian, to the savage boot training at Parris Island — which, "astonishingly, I adored." His goal was to surrender his uneasy, detached individuality, and he succeeded. He learned to cherish the fellowship of men he would not otherwise have known and whom he would regard with warm feeling throughout the war.

As an officer candidate at Quantico, Virginia, he was so offended by the devious rivalry for promotion that, after something like insubordination, he gladly accepted dismissal to "Tent City," at New River, North Carolina. There he became a sergeant in the Sixth Marine Division, the leader of a small intelligence unit composed mostly of Eastern college men like himself who came to be known as the "Raggedy-Ass Marines."

Their first stop was Guadalcanal, where the men of the First Marine Division, all but abandoned by the vessels that had brought them, had been under siege and isolated for four months, reduced to eating roots and weeds along with their moldy rations and suffering from malaria, dysentery and fungus infections. Later, on Okinawa, death was to "become kind of an epidemic" for the Raggedy-Ass Marines, but it was on Guadalcanal that Manchester lost the first of his men to a Japanese sniper.

Is it possible, he seems to wonder today, that we have forgotten so much? Manila, for instance, where the Japanese killed about 100,000 civilians. Or the Bataan death march, when the Japanese guards shot prisoners suffocating from dust and sun and perishing of thirst.

Or Iwo Jima, one of the last steppingstones on the way to Japan, which was supposed to have been only a brief skirmish. But the enemy had dug in so deeply that our naval bombardment hardly disturbed them, and the American forces, unable to dig foxholes in the volcanic ash, eventually suffered almost 30,000 casualties. "It resembled Doré's illustrations of 'The Inferno,' " Manchester writes. "Essential cargo — ammo, rations, water — was piled up in sprawling chaos. And gore, flesh and bones were lying all about."

Or Okinawa, where Manchester's military career came to its climax. It was the bloodiest island fighting of the war, and Manchester was hit twice. Though he insists that he lacked physical courage, he went AWOL from a hospital to rejoin his regiment when he learned that it was scheduled for an amphibious landing on the southern part of the island. Why? It was "an act of love. These men were my family, my home." They fought with a pride and a love of country that would now be regarded as passé, Manchester says. This time he was wounded almost to the point of death, and thus he came home — to his surprise, evidently, for he had been quite certain from the beginning that he would die in the war.

His anger on certain scores remains. He still so resents the Japanese that in 1978, seeing Japanese naval officers in Hawaii, he felt the same strong revulsion. Nor does he spare his own government. He sees no reason for the attack on Peleliu, for instance, because MacArthur's strategy made it possible to bypass Japanese outposts that offered no threat. Nevertheless the attack was made, and the result was 10,000 American casualties. He despises much of what the United States Navy did in the Pacific, and he coldly records Washington's messages early in the war to MacArthur and Manuel Quezon, president of the Philippine Commonwealth, that convoys of men and materiel were on their way to Bataan and Corregidor. They were not.

Before his return journey in 1978 the author was often haunted by nightmares in which young Sergeant Manchester berated the older Manchester for America's failure to achieve what the young sergeant and his generation had fought for. With the return to Okinawa his nightmares ended. The terrors and memories had been exorcised, though not his nostalgia and admiration for those simpler patriotic times. It remained for him to write a superb book.

JOHN K. HUTCHENS

William Manchester

by Alden Whitman

"FOR 30 years I tried to write about World War II in the Pacific, but I was too scarred and the memory of my three years in the Marine Corps was way, way too deep, too repressed," says William Manchester in explanation of the odyssey into his combat past that led to *Goodbye, Darkness*. "Going back to the battle sites of my youth both healed my memory and resolved a long-recurring dream of the war in which my youth and my older self confronted each other."

After the assassination of Robert F. Kennedy in 1968, Manchester recalls, he got out his old Marine Corps pistol and threw it into the Connecticut River near his home in Middletown, Connecticut. Then the nightmares began. After wrestling with them, he says, "I decided that the only way to exorcise the problem was to revisit the islands where I had fought as a marine."

So, in the autumn of 1978, the stocky, 56-year-old, profoundly distressed writer left his Wesleyan University retreat, with its precise array of reference books and its boot-camp-neat desk, for three months of jouncing around Guadalcanal, Tarawa, Saipan, Peleliu, Iwo Jima, Okinawa and other Pacific Islands — and the very battleground on which he had been massively wounded.

"To try to recapture the past that had been withheld from me in the daze of a long recovery from my wound," Manchester continues, "I went back physically to stimulate a psychological remembrance of things past. On Guadalcanal, for instance, I went out to Bloody Ridge, dug a foxhole and spent the night in it." Stirring awake, he would make notes in addition to those he regularly made every evening.

Although during the war he had not expected to see service in the Pacific, Manchester now thinks it eerily fortunate that he did. For there, unlike the situation in Europe, rusting tanks, guns, planes and barbed wire still lie on the battlefields — abandoned as if to evoke a survivor's recollections. "What I remembered most vividly when I saw those silent artifacts of my youth was the mud and terror of fighting," Manchester says. "War is cruel and sordid, not glorious and heroic."

Because *Goodbye, Darkness* is so personal, its author found it the most difficult of all his books to write. "I had to put the pieces of myself together all over again."

If there is any message he wants his book to convey, it is that the romantic view of combat hardly fits the realities. He wants Americans to adopt the values of humanism, to reject the barbarities of war. "I spare the reader nothing," he says — in fact, at readings over the past several months "there is usually a shocked silence when I conclude, particularly among older people in the audience. My book is a strong antiwar statement."

A writer of admirable discipline, which he traces to his newspaper days in Baltimore, Manchester has made his living from books since his late 30s. There were false starts before he mastered his métier, which he now regards as fixed. A somewhat formal person, he has an office in the Olin Library at Wesleyan, where he is a writer-in-residence and an adjunct professor of history. His duties are pleasant and light — they consist mostly of talking to students at a weekly dinner.

His working time is the afternoon. He types steadily from his notes, but when an apt thought doesn't immediately flow, his fingers jiggle the typewriter keys. The next morning he pencil-edits the pages he wrote the previous day.

Once a project is completed Manchester goes on to his next book. In this case, however, the war theme persists: he is focusing on an analytical biography of Churchill. Nightmare-free, he is gearing up to visit, at least in his research, the wars in Europe.

JOHN CHEEVER *first came to the attention of the* BOMC News *in 1957, when Clifton Fadiman, reviewing* The Wapshot Chronicle, *called it "funny, brilliant, unexpected, improbable." In 1973, when David Willis McCullough interviewed Cheever in connection with the publication of* The World of Apples, *a short-story collection, nothing was improbable about John Cheever.* The Wapshot Chronicle *had won the National Book Award for fiction and Cheever had had six collections of stories published. In 1978 came* The Stories of John Cheever, *sixty-one of his stories, and the judges were so enthusiastic that each asked to write the report. A compromise was reached. Each judge was allowed to comment on the Cheever artistry.*

The Wapshot Chronicle by John Cheever

FUNNY, brilliant, unexpected, improbable: these four adjectives (among others) seem suitable to this disjointed fiction by one of our most talented short-story writers. Mr. Cheever's New England is unlike Mr.

Marquand's — indeed, it is unlike any with which books have made us familiar; but, true or fantasticated, it is made real by the author's sureness of touch, wealth of detail and power to characterize. The scene is St. Botolphs, formerly a fairly lively seaport in Massachusetts, now in respectable decline. The Wapshot family, with whose fortunes the chronicle deals, has also in past days been livelier; but even its declining days as observed by Mr. Cheever are far from dull. Whatever slight thread of plot the narrative possesses is provided by Aunt Honora Wapshot, whose money is to go to her two nephews, Moses and Coverly, provided they produce male heirs. The quest for suitable — they turn out quite unsuitable — wives supplies a certain amount of suspense; but the book's qualities depend essentially not on it story, which is on occasion absurd, but on the characterization, particularly of Leander Wapshot, with his wonderful diary composed in the style of Mr. Jingle; Aunt Honora — the eccentric elderly New England lady has never been better done; Justina Scaddon, the half-mad, wholly wealthy cousin whose ward, Melissa, Moses finally marries. The book is full of sly humor, farcical bedroom episodes and accurate satire, directed particularly against the ultrarich. Highly enjoyable stuff, beautifully written — but also highly special. One doubts that many old New England families will take the *Chronicle* to their bosoms.

CLIFTON FADIMAN

The World of Apples: Stories by John Cheever

ONE STORY says he was thrown out of Thayer for smoking; another (Cheever's own) says he was a "lousy student." Whatever the reason, he never went back to school again, but promptly sold his first short story — "Expelled" — to *The New Republic*. Eventually he made his way to New York City, where he paid the rent on a boardinghouse room on Hudson Street by turning out scenarios for M-G-M, at $5 a throw. Since then he has made his living as a writer: 250 stories (by his count), most of which appeared first in *The New Yorker*, and three novels, including *The Wapshot Chronicle*, winner of a 1958 National Book Award and a Book-of-the-Month Club Alternate. *The World of Apples*, his sixth collection of short stories, has just been published by Knopf.

I drove up to Ossining to talk with John Cheever in his handsome 18th-century Dutch stone farmhouse. Set deep into the side of a hill facing away from the Hudson River (and Sing Sing Prison, for that matter), the old Boatman place is the home of Cheever, his wife, Mary, their youngest son, Fredrico, a dowager Labrador retriever named Flora and several cats. The property includes a brook (newly polluted by some mysterious source upstream), several ponds and an apple orchard through which Cheever enjoyed skiing until a recent accident stopped him.

Cheever maintains a rather studied indifference toward *The World of Apples*. He says he never rereads a story once it is written, and his best stories, he adds, are written in three-day spurts and then forgotten. But the book seems to me to be a mellow collection, more mellow than usual for Cheever. Many of the stories deal with people whose lives have come to a moment of pause, giving them time to look back. True, there are the hints of madness and mystery which always lie just under the surface of a Cheever story: the husband who suddenly stuffs a kitten into the blender; the unknown authors who write romantic, Victorian novels on men's room walls, where once they wrote obscene words. All in all, it must be one of the most humane books of the season.

Why has John Cheever stayed with the short story and why do his novels often read like short-story cycles? He says, "All my relationships have been interrupted. I never know where my characters come from or where they are going. The short-story form proved very accommodating." He paused for a more apt word than "accommodating," but let it go.

It is when talking about his early days as a *New Yorker* writer (he can give an excellent imitation of Ernest Hemingway emptying the Rose Room of the Algonquin Hotel with a string of profanity) or his two trips to Russia that Cheever becomes most animated. His most recent novel, *Bullet Park* (a Book-of-the-Month Club Selection in 1969), sold better in Russia than in the United States.

"Literature," he says, "is the most acute and intimate form of communication we have, and perhaps because the Russians have fewer distractions — little or no television, for instance — they can appreciate that more than we do."

What Cheever seems to enjoy most about Russia is his friendship with the poet Yevgeny Yevtushenko ("I can drink him under the table, but only just"), who turned to him one day in a crowded Moscow elevator and in a burst of emotion said, "You have a perfect working-class face."

Then Cheever turned to the fact that he is over 60. "There is so much I've had to give up. I get cross with dogs. I'm a man who talks to dogs."

He is currently at work on a novel, a long novel, the longest thing he has ever written. And when he finishes, he says, he will stop writing. Then he adds that maybe he will write but he won't publish anything. He squints his old schoolboy eyes and looks, as though he didn't believe a word of it.

DAVID WILLIS MCCULLOUGH

The Stories of John Cheever

IF YOU KNOW John Cheever only as one of America's major novelists you are missing a great literary treat. For years now as a writer of short stories, Cheever has carried the impact of such predecessors in the field as F. Scott Fitzgerald and Ernest Hemingway. When this collection of his stories came up for consideration by members of the Editorial Board there was unanimous support for the book as a Main Selection. We asked the members to talk about their enthusiasm — and personal preferences — for Cheever's short stories. Following are some of their comments:

> Reading the sixty-one stories slowly (not too many at a time) convinces one of their permanent interest and value. At first they seem to be tied to a place, a time, a class. But on reflection one sees that, as with the best of Kipling's Indian tales, the limitations are only superficial. Of the earlier ones the famous "The Enormous Radio" still holds up. Cheever touches here one of his recurrent themes — the precariousness of modern "good" marriages. If I were forced to choose only two more. I think I would tick off his undoubted masterpiece "The Swimmer" and that terrifying, heartbreaking tale of a woman's revenge on her seducer, "The Five-Forty-Eight." But one need not pick and choose: Cheever is our best since Hemingway.
>
> CLIFTON FADIMAN

> The very first of the stories you find here comes at you with the impact of certain major predecessors in Cheever's field from the turn of the century down — Crane, Fitzgerald, Hemingway, Parker, O'Hara, Welty. "Goodbye, My Brother," that first one is called, a story of intrafamily hostility that has the compactness of a novella. In "O City of Broken Dreams" there is the pathos of a small-town Indiana family naively bent on Broadway fame and promptly trapped in the New York theater's sleazy underworld; in

"The World of Apples" a widower New England poet, long an expatriate in Italy, still envisions the Nobel Prize he will never win
but the dream of which will sustain him in his old age; in "Just
Tell Me Who It Was" an aging husband is haunted by the cer-
tainty he feels of his wife's deception of him. These, and fifty-
seven others. The short story, it sometimes seems, is a vanishing
form. It is still safe in the hands of such an artist as this.

JOHN K. HUTCHENS

Cheever's collected stories are not only individually distinguished
but they cunningly complement each other, sturdy beams in a
house of fiction built to endure. They are fundamentally about
people we know — people overly concerned with crab grass,
shopping lists, faulty plumbing, baby sitters, yesterday's shining
morning faces, now men and women who drink too much, age too
quickly. They have been written with a lyrical mingling of irony
and regret, a certain tenderness, a rare grace, and composed in a
prose that is at once lean and evocative and incredibly economical.
Cheever can convey in one paragraph what takes a noisier, more
prolix writer a career.

MORDECAI RICHLER

We read these stories as we would a perfectly splendid novel. If I
had to pick a favorite, it might be "Torch Song." Depicted here
with exquisite precision is the sinister import of a victimized
though gallant doer of good deeds, a good Samaritan. Without
skipping a beat Cheever juxtaposes ominousness with benevolence
in his mysterious central character, pulling us into the net steadily
as the story's weave thickens. "Goodbye, My Brother," another favorite, is the story of a torn family. It tells of dark and capricious
withdrawals among the family members, as well as of ardent attempts to capture an intimacy that blood and marital ties do not
automatically confer. At the end Cheever gives the quite contemporary dissection a nearly mythic life: "The sea that morning was
iridescent and dark. My wife and sister were swimming — Diana
and Helen — and I saw their uncovered heads, black and gold in
the dark water. I saw them come out and I saw that they were
naked, unshy, beautiful, and full of grace, and I watched the naked
women walk out of the sea."

LUCY ROSENTHAL

Cheever establishes strangeness instantly on an empty beach or a
commuter platform or just watching a family play backgammon.
The first sentence is like entering a dark wood dappled with sunlight. Terror mingles with joy. The god Pan and the Angel of

Death are in there, and the House of Usher — and we haven't even left the suburbs. Cheever is the last of the great enchanters, a genuine spellbinder. He can achieve the effect of a Grimm's fairy tale out of a spilled martini. All his stage props are ordinary and his characters are like old friends, but it is like meeting them in dreams. One awakes with a smile or a pounding heart. I have, to answer your question, about fifty-eight favorites out of the sixty-one collected here.

WILFRID SHEED

IN A SENSE, *Robert Ludlum was discovered by the Book-of-the-Month Club. His first two novels,* The Scarlatti Inheritance *(1971) and* The Osterman Weekend *(1972), were BOMC Alternates and helped him reach a wide audience. Every year or so Ludlum has a new novel published, and now his audience is ready and waiting. In the spring of 1986* The Bourne Supremacy *was a Selection and the newest member of the Editorial Board, Gloria Norris, wrote: "He [Ludlum] clearly has no rival as a puppeteer of suspense entertainment." Upon the Selection of his 1979 novel,* The Matarese Circle, *Ludlum told free-lance writer Robert G. Deindorfer how he switched from an acting career to that of a writer, a personal upheaval that had only the pleasantest of consequences.*

Robert Ludlum
by Robert G. Deindorfer

"WHY DID I abandon my career as an actor and producer for something I hadn't really tried before?" Robert Ludlum, a witty, outgoing man, paused for a moment. "Well, frankly, I had become bored stiff with the theater. I wanted some control over my life, too."

If Ludlum previously felt trapped by his success in a highly competitive field, he had good reason to. After all, he had managed to support a wife and three children. He had played in more than 200 television shows, not to mention legitimate theater in New York City, and himself had produced dozens of shows in a regional theater in suburban New Jersey. "But I knew it was time, past time, in fact, to shake up my life," he said. "I left with absolutely no regrets — for better or worse, for richer or poorer. I didn't just burn my bridges behind me. I actually blew them up."

What made Ludlum's career change eight years ago so unusually speculative was the fact that he had no book contract, no literary agent, no reputation as an author. Except for some work on the undergraduate magazine at Wesleyan University and a few potluck television scripts, he hadn't done any serious writing. Robert Ludlum looked like many another aspiring novelist whose manuscripts were unlikely to see the light of print.

Yet at the age of 51 Ludlum is one of America's most successful novelists. *The Matarese Circle* is his eighth book; his previous seven all made the bestseller lists. Four of the books have been sold to the movies and his titles are prominent on paperback shelves in the U.S. and overseas.

Dressed in a tweed jacket, sleeveless sweater, open shirt and gray slacks, Ludlum finished a second cup of coffee in his comfortable home on the Connecticut shore of Long Island Sound. Outside the picture windows, a blue-topped tennis court gleamed in the sunshine, a small guest cottage stood near the garage. He admits to enjoying those and other creature comforts without losing his hardscrabble old values.

"I've never taken money all that seriously," Ludlum said. "I like to live well, of course, the same as most people do. But I lived surprisingly well when I was poor. I even remember my unemployment number: one, three, four, four. I've worked as a waiter and barkeep and if things don't work out, I can always go back to that."

His successful conversion from one discipline to another, which has astonished a number of people, surprised Ludlum himself not at all. Even in the beginning he never nourished any twanging doubts. "Look, the theater is a marvelous training ground for a novelist," he said. "It's a quicksilver arena of impressions and flavor, and the theater is built on conflict. Besides, there is a discipline to it."

Ludlum applies a strong discipline to his writing career. He rises long before sunup, seats himself in his study at 4:15 every morning of the week, proceeds to get on with his latest thriller in longhand — #2 Ticonderoga pencils, long yellow legal pads — until around noon. Even with time away from the writing desk for research and extensive travel to fix foreign atmosphere in his mind, he averages a new book every year.

Whatever the specific plot Ludlum first develops in outline form and discusses with his wife, agent and editor, his books are full of suspense, intrigue, violence. Ludlum is convinced that no realistic thriller can do without violence even though he has a distaste for it. "In terms of the story it wouldn't be honest to walk away from violence," he says.

The fact that he seems so expertly tuned-in on the half-lit realm of intelligence and espionage can't help but make an occasional reader wonder whether he ever served professionally in the world of spies.

"I'm a storyteller, that's all I am," Ludlum said with emphasis. "I am not now nor have I ever been in intelligence work. I read a lot about it and have developed some grasp of how it works. But I'm an innocent myself."

As an innocent, Ludlum squeezes authentic background flavor wherever he can find it. He has spoken with several American and British intelligence men by way of research and has a couple of old college friends in the business, but he conjures much of his material out of thin air. He likes to quote World War II spymaster William Stevenson's dictum: "Intelligence is really an extension of the imagination."

Every so often Ludlum wonders how far he can stretch his own imagination. Despite a thick bulge of 3″ x 5″ file cards marked with possible future projects, despite the whisper of other new story ideas when he travels abroad to soak up atmosphere, despite the fact that he's never suffered the writer's block all too common among many successful authors, he wonders if this new second career can go on indefinitely.

Meanwhile, the former actor and producer is enjoying himself immensely, as he sits in the pre-dawn drinking coffee and writing, writing, writing another new thriller he expects to complete by summer.

THE BOMC REVIEWER *of William Styron's first novel,* Lie Down in Darkness, *published in 1951, said that Styron "reveals himself as a writer who may be disliked or disagreed with but is not likely to be ignored." Styron has not been ignored.* The Confessions of Nat Turner *was a Selection in 1967 and Robert Penn Warren wrote about Styron the man and the brooder. Twelve years later Willie Morris, an author and editor, wrote about* Sophie's Choice *and about his friend Bill Styron.*

William Styron
by Robert Penn Warren

THE NAME was originally Styring, and the form Styron, a smootheddown relic of the Danish Conquest, was brought over by a Yorkshireman to North Carolina. The mother's family, Scotch-Irish and Welsh, was from Pennsylvania. The paternal grandfather, a courier in a North Carolina regiment, shared the great moment at Chancellorsville, but the Pennsylvania grandfather, and some granduncles, wore the Yankee blue. Thus the family origins, and loyalties, were mixed.

The Pennsylvania mother, however, died when William Styron was little more than an infant, and his raising was strictly Southern. He was, in fact, born at almost the last moment when it was possible to get, first-hand, a sense of what old-fashioned Southern life had been, or to hear, actually, the word-of-mouth legends about it. Newport News, where Bill was born, was, of course, a naval base and a center of shipbuilding, but the boy grew up knowing the life of village and country in those days when neither had yet accepted the urban psychology and values. The land he knew lay along the James River and in Tidewater North Carolina, a flatland gutted by tobacco a century and a half earlier, now gone to sage and clumps of old field pine, with here and there, back from the road, an abandoned farmhouse falling into a last desuetude, family burying grounds long since lost to briers and love vine, streams torpidly uncoiling seaward, and further east, the slow, silvery reaches of estuary and tideland.

A country high school, and two years in an Episcopal prep school, Christchurch, on the lower Rappahannock, provided a faithful mirror of the current civilization of that region, and long visits with the paternal grandmother, down in North Carolina, provided a mirror of the civilization that had once been there. She was a very old lady, born well before the Civil War in the tobacco and cotton country of the Pamlico River, and she told the boy about the two little slave girls she herself had owned in the old days and how much she had loved them. But Nat, Nat Turner, was there too — the Nathaniel born the property of one Benjamin Turner of Southampton County, Virginia, in October, 1800, the same month and year in which John Brown was born, far north, in Connecticut.

Before the period at Christchurch, Bill Styron had attended a country high school that played baseball and football against the Southampton County high school in Courtland; and Courtland was only the new name for the town of Jerusalem which Nat had set out to capture but where he was to come only to die. The bloody tale was there in the garbled talk of the boys of Nat's home county, something violent and inexplicable, illogical and yet inevitable, a tale denied its true meaning and yet fascinatingly undeniable. And so Bill discovered Nat as a presence in that forlorn and beautiful land which, in many ways, had changed so little since Nat's eyes had last rested upon it.

Bill discovered that presence and, no doubt, quickly forgot it. For the world was beckoning. There was Davidson College, in North Carolina, with a saturation in the Presbyterian Bible, then Duke University, then the war. Bill is reported to have gorged himself on bananas and half foundered on water to make weight for the Marine Corps. "I would have cut off my right arm to a lieutenant of Marines," he once said to me, and it took no great effort of imagination to detect in that man of 40 some shadow of the lieutenant the boy of 18 became. That lieutenant was not, however, to see battle. As he reached Okinawa, the bomb was dropped.

After the war there was Duke University to finish, an unhappy six months in a publishing house, from which he was happily fired for "general inattention," then a brief period at the New School in Manhattan, where the old Bible reading merged with a new social conscience, quite personally defined. Long since, Bill had determined to be a writer, and in 1949 he began *Lie Down in Darkness.* By 1951, when, to a general round of applause, it was published, the author was again in the uniform of a Marine. Camp Lejeune, North Carolina, where Bill did his time in this war, provided the background for his second book, *The Long March*, written just after his discharge, in Paris, in a single six-week spurt.

It was now generally conceded that William Styron was indeed a man to watch. But the watch was long. *Set This House on Fire* did not appear until 1960, and when it did appear it was, in the author's words, "bad news." The difference in intention, method, scale and temper between this and the earlier novels may have had a great deal to do with the fact that most critics ignored the growth in both range and depth and the essential force of the work. But if the news was bad at home, the news abroad was very, very good, especially in France, where, for both critics and readers, the book was a smashing success.

By this time Bill was married and the father of a family. In 1953, in Rome, where he had gone as the winner of the award of the American Academy of Arts and Letters, he met Rose Burgunder, whom, in the spring of that year, in the Campodoglio, he married. The next year they settled in an ex-farmhouse in Roxbury, Connecticut, where, surrounded by four children, assorted livestock and, usually, hordes of guests, they now live.

The Bill Styron who now approaches the age of 42 is about six feet tall, with good carriage, good shoulders, considerably more girth than that of the boy who once gorged bananas to make weight for the Marine Corps, long, rather thin legs, and smallish hands and feet. The head is large, high, well shaped and sometimes carried with an air of authority little short of arrogance. The hair is straight and very dark, almost black, lightly tinged with gray. The face, with unusually pale skin, somewhat slick-looking, is fleshed out but cleanly modeled and dominated by a strong, rather aquiline nose. The eyes are dark, perhaps a trifle smaller than might be expected in the large head, and sometimes seeming even smaller when, unexpectedly, they take on a hard, assessing, detached look, like a hunter squinting out from the cover of brush. But the whole impression is, ordinarily, one of good humor.

Good humor — for Bill, at least the social man, is gregarious, easygoing, outgoing, appreciative of the broad human spectrum, easily admiring the qualities of other people, more apt to be generously amused than censorious when confronted by faults and failings. The social man has a gaiety that ranges from the touch of fantasy to the rambunctious and the obscene, is a spontaneous and accomplished mimic, is a maker of the pungently funny phrase. This man, too, is something of a sybarite, with an educated taste in whiskey and an educated palate for vintages. He is, furthermore, inclined to be a little captious about the cookery set before him. But this sybarite is not infrequently found unshaven and is not universally admired as a model of tidiness.

There is, it must be insisted, another Bill Styron quite different from the social man who shines in easy and self-indulgent gregariousness. To begin with, this other Bill is capable of great sympathy and devotion in friendship, a talent rare among the really gregarious. Furthermore, he admits to a great need for, and joy in, the depth, fullness and order of domestic life. For years a motto from Flaubert has been tacked near his desk: "Be regular and orderly in your life, like a good bourgeois, so that you may be violent and original in your work."

This other Bill is capable of long periods of withdrawal. He is a night worker and a morning sleeper, and very often, after the party in the ex-farmhouse is over and the last quest has fumbled his way upstairs, the host goes off to his study, in another building, and picks up his pad of legal foolscap and begins to write, in pencil, in a peculiarly fastidious, precise and old-fashioned calligraphy; and in a foreign city, when the fit strikes, he can withdraw for hours, or days, with that blue-lined, yellow pad, into the anonymity of a hotel room. Some need to work things out alone, in secret, is there — the need without which we would not know the name of William Styron the novelist.

This need is associated with the fact that Bill is not an "intellectual," a person who lives by an interest in, and a passion for, ideas. He is that rarer thing, a man of extraordinary intelligence, and if he is interested in ideas, it is not for their color and curiousness, or for any pleasure in manipulating them, but for the possibility that they may immediately nourish the full life process. For instance, he rarely talks about ideas as such, and rarely mentions the books that he continually rereads — Dostoyevsky, Conrad, *Moby Dick, Huckleberry Finn* and, strangely, Orwell. And one might know him for years and not know that poetry (the Elizabethans, John Donne, Yeats, Emily Dickinson, Wallace Stevens) is at the very center of his rereading, that he is soaked in the Bible and continues the soaking, and that music (Handel, Beethoven, Bach, Telemann, Mozart) is perhaps even more important than literature as a nourishment for his own work, or rather, for his existence in its inwardness.

Inwardness: there is a smoldering quality here that occasionally may manifest itself in a flash of unaimed irascibility or a streak of sadism that may suddenly appear in mimicry or rollicking humor. But the same inwardness, the same tension and exacerbation of spirit, would seem to be working itself out, less accidentally, in the fiction. A book like *The Confessions of Nat Turner* has come out of a long brooding — not planning or calculation, but brooding, an activity deep, personal and, at any conscious level, aimless, the process of finding a self for the story and a story in the self. In this book Bill withdraws into the scenes of his own childhood, the flat fields, the sage and pines, the slow sad rivers, the far shadow of the Dismal Swamp. The story of Nat belongs to this scene not merely because it was the land Nat knew, but because Nat himself came to Bill Styron as a dim unresolved presence in that boyhood world. The writer has now, it may be guessed, found the right ratio of distance from that world, the right perspective in life experience, and we thus have this splendid release of power into life, a power springing from the past to illuminate the world that is our own present.

A Later Look at William Styron
by Willie Morris

I THINK it fitting that Random House will bring out my friend William Styron's extraordinary novel *Sophie's Choice* on June 11, his 54th birthday. The timing is appropriate not only because this is Styron's most powerful and ambitious book in a succession of distinguished contributions to our literature — *Lie Down in Darkness, The Long March,*

Set This House on Fire, The Confessions of Nat Turner — but also
because, perhaps more than most great novels, it springs in its
profoundest impulse from recognizable autobiographical sources.

His previous book, *The Confessions of Nat Turner*, had been published in 1967; it was number one on the best-seller list for many weeks
and subsequently won the Pulitzer Prize. After this, he began another
novel, *The Way of the Warrior*, set largely in Camp Lejeune, North
Carolina, and in Japan during the Korean War, its protagonist a U.S.
Marine colonel of much complexity and brilliance. After months of hard
work, Styron felt the novel was not going especially well. "Not that I
was ashamed of it," he says. "I wasn't. But I'd been floundering with it
for several weeks." One spring morning in 1974, in his house in Roxbury, Connecticut, he awoke to the awareness of a vivid dream he had
had — "almost as if the dream had given me an urgent message, a man-
date. I don't want this to sound too metaphysical, or dramatic, or
spooky, but the dream was a return in my memory to a girl I had known
in Brooklyn many years before."

The time was the late 1940s. He had moved into a boardinghouse on
Caton Avenue facing Prospect Park to begin writing what would become his first novel, *Lie Down in Darkness*. One day he met a beautiful
blond Polish girl who rented a room on the second floor. Her beauty
stunned him, and then he noticed the tattooed numbers on her arm. She
was a survivor of Auschwitz, and her name was Sophie. Her English
was poor, and at first they communicated in broken French. She served
elaborate delicatessen lunches in her room, as if she were trying to elude
starvation itself. To the fledgling writer from Tidewater Virginia she
seemed desperate for companionship. Yet she had a rather attractive
Jewish boyfriend from Brooklyn, and Stryon grew to know them. The
sounds of their strenuous lovemaking reverberated through the house,
sometimes rattling the chandelier in the reclusive young writer's room
on the first floor.

The morning of his dream, and over the next several days, he sat
down in a high pitch of energy. Calling himself "Stingo," he wrote the
opening section of *Sophie's Choice*, a hilarious autobiographical sequence about his first lonely days as a Southerner in New York City.
When he had finished these introductory pages, he resolved almost immediately to go to Poland; he felt he had to see Auschwitz. On his return, the novel unfolded for him slowly but steadily. He had always
been a deliberate, painstaking writer, and *Sophie's Choice* would take
him more than four years, his imagination moving inexorably from the

real Sophie and those summer days of the 1940s in Flatbush into a narrative of compelling and tragic magnitude, so that the actual choice Sophie had been forced to make at Auschwitz, undisclosed until nearly the end of the tale, becomes the ultimate expression of modern despair, dreadful to the heart, the final anguish of our being human.

Lie Down in Darkness, published in 1951, had touched me strongly in my youth, and when I came up from the South in the early 1960s, as callow and provincial as Stingo, to work for *Harper's* magazine, Bill Styron was one of the people I wanted to know. My Mississippi and his Virginia are different places, having produced quite different strains of the Southern-American personality, but writing is a mutual thing, and so too beneath the surface disparities there is finally a tenacious bedrock bond between our two native states, having to do with many old nuances of the greater American fiber. The best way to get to know Styron, I sensed, was to persuade him to do a magazine piece. The piece would be about his fascination as a young man growing up on the banks of the James River with the black slave Nat Turner, that legendary, heroic presence of Styron's neighborhood of lower Virginia. I drove up to Connecticut to confer with Bill and met him for the first time in C. Vann Woodward's office at Yale.

It was the beginning of a comradeship that over the years would span many miles, literally and figuratively, on the American landscape: an interest in one another's families and work; a common regard for the written word; evenings of conviviality in the house in Roxbury and in the farmhouse my wife and I had across the ridge in New York; the lofty plateaus and dismal swamps of two writers' lives; the growing up of our children; the gradual formalizing of an occasionally boisterous but, one hoped, not unedifying intellectual partnership called by common consent "The Bill and Willie Show" on college campuses from Carolina to Texas; the death of our beloved friend James Jones as he struggled to finish his trilogy of men at war; the rhythms and continuities of getting older.

From these many years of knowing Bill in numerous moods and moments, from the antiseptic lounges of Los Angeles and the oyster bars of the French Quarter to the watering spas of Manhattan and the faculty suites of Ivy League universities, I believe I grew to recognize in him the sources of his genius as one of America's foremost novelists. Writing fiction is a hard and draining calling, and at the core of his talent, both protectively and toward the fruition of high creativity, lay always an abiding human intelligence — that humane intuitiveness which outlasts mere brilliance and cannot be taught in a man — this undergirded by his own especial obsession with the haunted land of the Old Dominion and the dark resonances of its past. This, and more: a passionate belief in the better instincts of our nature against the insufferable odds of existence, if only the best in men might fight unfettered against those odds. "If the crazy side roads beguile you, my son," the father advises the boy in *Lie Down in Darkness,* "take a long backward look at Monticello."

Abetting these impulses of the spirit, two people more than all others contributed to his commitment and accomplishment as an artist. One, his wife, Rose — née Burgunder — a beautiful Jewish girl from Baltimore, whose poetic feel for literature (she herself is a poet), and her talent as an editor and an advocate have supported him beyond measure, and whose boundless giving and buoyancy have provided a milieu for immemorial fellowship, as well as four healthy, intelligent American children.

The other, his father, William Clark Styron, who died in 1978 at age 88. *Sophie's Choice* is dedicated to this splendid man, a Southern gentleman who never spurned his country origins and whose loyalty to Bill never deviated. The expression of joy which washed his features when his son and I came to fetch him from a nursing home in North Carolina to bring him to Connecticut three years before he died will remain with me to my own dying day, and the character of Stingo's father in *Sophie's Choice* is his deserved memorial.

It is all such as this, I think, which has helped give Bill the courage in his work to address himself to the great moral themes of life, to "the old verities and universal truths" toward which one of his heroes encouraged those of us who write. In *Lie Down in Darkness* the theme was the disintegration of family and community in a transient age, in *Nat Turner* it was the institution of slavery, and in *Sophie's Choice* it is the 20th-century madness, the totalitarian bestiality which engulfed all humankind. "The literature that has meant the most to me," Bill said recently, "was written by people who concerned themselves with the moral sense, with the meaning to the riddle. They were grappling with the imponderables of life. I always felt I had to try to do the same thing. It's always seemed to me that writers should be ambitious, in the deep artistic sense, that they should strive to climb the highest mountain. Faulkner said we should be measured by the splendor of our failures. I'd rather come a cropper on something which mattered than succeed at something precious, something merely to be cuddled and fondled.

Auschwitz, all that it represents, is one of the staggering events in the history of the human race. I wanted to confront it."

IN 1960 PHILIP ROTH'S COLLECTION *of stories,* Goodbye, Columbus, *won the National Book Award for fiction. With his first novel,* Letting Go, *the Club caught up with Roth: that book was reviewed in the* News. *But it wasn't until 1979, with* The Ghost Writer, *that a Roth book became a Club Selection. Too long a wait. Wilfrid Sheed reviewed* The Ghost Writer. *A normally reserved critic, Sheed called Roth "one of our few genuine artist-writers."*

The Ghost Writer by Philip Roth

"LITERARY EVENTS" are forever being announced; but very few of them turn out to be events, and almost none of them are literary.

Philip Roth's latest event, *The Ghost Writer,* is precisely literary; i.e., it runs on words and passion, and not on doomsday plot devices, or veiled references to Henry Kissinger, or any other popular synthetic. To call it Jamesian would probably anger some readers and put others to sleep, so let's just call it an Elysian clash of sensibilities between Henry James and Alexander Portnoy, with the maddened, shallow thrusts of Portnoy baffled and tantalized by the deep reticence and decorum of James. Farfetched, I grant you, but almost legalistically exact as blurb copy goes.

Portnoy/Roth, in all his incarnations, is a divided man anyway, half-satyr and half-librarian, equally besotted by women and literature. In *The Ghost Writer,* his lust for books is on top, but the satyr is still around, giving a desperate itch and vitality to his pendantry.

Young Nathan Zuckerman has come to pay homage to an older writer named E. I. Lonoff, who is an inspired mixture of some American Jewish novelist whose name just escapes you and James himself. Lonoff's typical hero "is more often than not a nobody from nowhere, away from a home where he is not missed, yet to which he must return without delay." And young Nathan is halfway into being a Lonoff hero himself, as he enters the maestro's web on page one.

Because he has just written a story of his own about some less than saintly Jewish relatives, and his family is, as authors' families commonly are, heartbroken. They go so far as to intimate that Nathan's treachery would have given comfort to the German High Command, which seems a bit remote from Newark, New Jersey, but you can't be too careful.

So Nathan is on the run, and what he really wants from the great Lonoff is absolution: the godlike assurance that literature forgives. What he gets instead is a towering lesson in the selfishness of Art which dwarfs his sniffing relatives and their philistine scruples.

Because Lonoff has long since sacrificed *everything*, including life itself, for Art. He has reached a perfect stasis, in which the only movement in the house is Lonoff's pen pushing sentences around and around. His home is as bare of ornament as his prose, his days are nobly empty; and his wife is going crazy, perennially and hopelessly, as she flaps around her cage. If she escapes she will not get far. In short, Nathan might as well seek absolution from the Devil as from Lonoff.

Yet in this stripped-down state, the old writer's intelligence is blindingly, diabolically attractive, and the Good Portnoy is beside himself over it. Unfortunately, the satyr in him is discombobulated by a second acolyte, a haunting young woman named Amy Bellette who is hanging around the house as an archivist, but, who, in view of Lonoff's all-round thrift, must surely be there for something else as well. Mistress, muse, subject? Possibly all three. Lonoff can stretch anything, even his after-dinner brandy, interminably.

Nathan cunningly sleeps over and has an awful night of it. Amy and Lonoff settle in the room directly above, doing whatever they do when they're not archiving. Nathan mustn't allow himself to be jealous of his new hero just yet, so he grimly distracts himself with a Henry James story called "The Middle Years" which could have been left there for him, so close is it to his own master/disciple predicament. Lonoff is teaching him on several levels. Because he has left *himself* in earshot as well, and he and Army proceed to act out a scene of such ambiguity that, between the scene and the James, Nathan has practically become a writer by morning, even while Portnoy writhes.

I won't abridge the scene, because I can't, except to say that Amy has somehow fashioned herself into a character to Lonoff's taste, namely the real Anne Frank, who has miraculously survived and has revealed herself only to Lonoff. Could this possibly be so? And if not, does *she* believe it? Is her passion for Lonoff so much greater even than Nathan's that she can will herself a new past and a new soul to please him? Or are they all, including Nathan, simply props in Lonoff's studio, as he works at his lonely, coquettish art?

Henry James, for all his furbelows, was an explosively passionate writer. Most imitators leave out this one small thing, but Philip Roth leaves out the rest instead, and captures the one small thing beautifully. "Our doubt is our passion, and our passion is our task. The rest is the madness of art," says the dying writer in "The Middle Years." Roth, who is one of our few genuine artist-writers, knows by blood-brother-hood the cost of this madness, in disciples seduced, lovers exploited and paralyzing regret. But he also understands the prize. Lonoff, for all his sterile integrity, *is* somehow godlike; it glows off the page, and one can easily see a woman or disciple paying whatever he asks just for the gift of his company. And any author who can convey that kind of greatness in a short novel has pulled off a trick worthy of the Master himself.

WILFRID SHEED

HOW AN ACCOMPLISHED HISTORIAN *came to write an accomplished work*, Peter the Great.

Robert K. Massie
by David Willis McCullough

SEVERAL years ago, not long after the success of his book *Nicholas and Alexandra*, Robert K. Massie met a man named Tolstoy. Hearing that Massie was at work on a biography of Peter the Great, he congratulated him on his diligence. "My grandfather," he said, "wanted to write a bi-ography of Peter, but it was too difficult. So he wrote *War and Peace* instead."

"It's a good story," Massie said recently as he was editing the final galleys of *Peter the Great* at his home in Irvington, New York, "but it's all wrong. Leo Tolstoy detested Peter for having destroyed old Russia by turning to the West. He had planned to write a novel set in Peter's time, but it never worked out. He dropped it to do *Anna Karenina*."

Massie has spent 12 years with Peter. "I've been asked," he says, "how I could devote so much time to a brute, a barbarian, a man who killed his own son. He did have his son killed, of course, but like every-thing else with Peter it wasn't that simple. He was a brutal man in a brutal age, but he wasn't a sadist. That's an important difference. He and Lenin created modern Russia. Without Peter there never could have been a Pushkin or a Dostoyevsky — or, I suppose, a Lenin."

Massie's study is a wainscoted room in a rambling 1855 Hudson River valley house. His desk is set in a bay window, and from there he can see the bell-shaped roof of an octagon house across the street. The only obviously Russian touch in the room is a ribbon-bedecked portrait of Nicholas II, the last czar, hanging over the fireplace. Massie apologizes for it. "That's a joke," he says, "left over from a party. Usually there's a picture of Falconet's statue of Peter the Great."

Thirteen years ago, when Massie finished his book on Nicholas and Alexandra and the last years of the Romanovs, he was looking for a new subject, and Peter seemed an obvious choice. "Peter," he says, "summoned up the classic Russian questions: old versus new, the West versus not the East but Russia. I knew only the usual clichés about the man, so I spent six months researching him and figured that I'd have a book in three years. Four years later I had 2000 pages of notes, and a book was still years away. Clearly Peter was no one to trifle with."

His research took him from the New York Public Library to the British Museum to three years at the Bibliothèque Nationale in Paris (where the Massies lived in the Marais district, by chance just across the street from a monument to Peter's 1717 visit to the city). He also made trips to Russia to visit sites that figured in Peter's life.

"I speak Russian well enough to get around as a tourist," Massie says, "and I can read it well enough to know when I need help with translation." His wife, Suzanne, can speak Russian fluently. Her mother, who is Swiss, was an *au pair* girl in Russia, teaching European languages to the children in a wealthy household. She was stranded there by World War I and then by the Revolution and didn't return home until 1920. "When Suzanne was growing up," Massie says, "she heard many romantic tales about old Russia and she thinks I've colored my book in favor of progress. She's not convinced that the importation of Western architects and ballet masters was an improvement."

A Yale graduate (class of '50), a Rhodes scholar and a reporter for the old *Saturday Evening Post* and *Newsweek*, Massie was born in Kentucky and raised in Nashville, and although he has lived in the New York area most of his adult life he still associates "home" with Nashville. His interest in prerevolutionary Russia was born in the New York Public Library. When he learned that his young son, Robert, had hemophilia he went to the library to find all that he could about the disease. His discovery that the last czar and czarina also had a hemophilic son led eventually to *Nicholas and Alexandra*.

"With my first book the issues that I raised were all ones of fact," he says. "There were still eyewitnesses alive to satisfy or to refute. With

Peter I'm involved in questions of interpretation. I feel that Peter brought a new sense of meaning to the Russian concept of service. Before him, serfs served the landowners, who served the nobles, who served the czar, who, I suppose, served God. But Peter felt that the czar should also serve the state. Everything he did he did for what he considered the good of the state, even if it involved hanging 1,700 corpses from the Kremlin walls.

"The Soviet government has always been ill at ease in knowing how to regard Peter," Massie says. "He, along with Ivan the Terrible, was popular with Stalin, at least for a while, and since Stalin he has come in and out of official popularity. When I visited the museum at the site of the Battle of Poltava I saw Peter everywhere. His statue was there. He was in all the paintings and dioramas of the battle. But he wasn't mentioned in the captions. If you read them you learn that it was a great victory for the Russian people.

"But he is remembered, especially in Leningrad, which used to be St. Petersburg. When I first visited there, years ago, I went to see where Peter was buried. It's something tourists do, and there, on his tomb, was a little bunch of wildflowers — not some huge, official floral offering, but wildflowers that someone had picked and left there. He's remembered."

THEY CAME LIKE SWALLOWS *by William Maxwell was a Club Selection in 1937. Forty-three years later David Willis McCullough talked about Maxwell's long and distinguished career as writer and editor.*

Eye on Books
by David Willis McCullough

IT HAS been 19 years since William Maxwell's last novel, *The Château,*was published, and it has been four years since he retired as a fiction editor of *The New Yorker*. His new book, *So Long, See You Tomorrow*, is fiction, but it is based on fact, a murder and suicide long ago in Lincoln, Illinois, Maxwell's hometown. The narrator, an old man looking back, says, "This memoir — if that's the right name for it — is a roundabout futile way of making amends."

It is one of the most American novels of the season. American in the sound of its speech, in its small-town setting and in its sense of guilt. "I know evil exists," Maxwell said recently. "I have experienced it internally and externally, but I don't understand it enough to write about it." Instead he has written about good people who ache with loneliness and a feeling of sadness for having left undone what they ought to have done: a boy, for instance, who snubs his only friend after he learns that the boy's father had killed his mother's lover, a neighboring farmer, and then himself.

The friendship between the narrator and the murderer's son is so understated that the boy could almost pass for an imaginary friend. "Alas," Maxwell says, "there was such a boy. If the incident in the high school corridor hadn't happened, if I hadn't passed him without speaking, I went a long way afield to get a story. The incident was true. The facts, as I say in the novel, came from old newspapers I tracked down in the Illinois State Historical Library. The newspaper itself, which is still publishing, had destroyed all its files and back issues. It was the paper I delivered as a boy. I remember that we had to wait outside in the snow for the presses to start running. They were always late. Even in the 1920s the presses were antiques. But reading old newspapers is maddening. They tell you so much you wish they would tell you more. They tell that the murdered man, who was milking a cow when he was shot, was wearing gloves. I wonder why. Maybe he had a skin condition. The papers never mention the name of the murderer's son."

Maxwell says he got over his uneasiness about describing farm life by writing out — and discarding — long accounts of how the farmers in his novel spent their time. "I wrote about them until I felt at ease with them. But that was only for myself. It is nothing for a reader to bother with." He worked as hard on perfecting the sound of Midwestern speech. "As I get older," he says, "the writers I prefer are the ones whose voices I can hear. Writing should seem as natural as speech, and for the best writers it is all one thing."

Maxwell was on *The New Yorker* staff for 40 years. He began in the art department as the person who told cartoonists whether their work had been accepted ("the feeling was that humor was nothing to be sneezed at") and later ("when they taught me to edit") he moved into the fiction department. "I loved working with other people's words," he recalls, "and I had the advantage of working only with very good writers. If I hadn't been an editor I probably would have written more, but not much more."

Over the years he has produced nine novels and short-story collections and a book of family history. He is now at work on a collection of Sylvia Townsend Warner's letters. "I know it is an extravagant thing for a man of my age to be doing, but if I started to write another book now I'd just write the same story again in a different form. I have to wait for the well to fill up."

ANTHONY BURGESS, *the* agent provocateur *of world civilization, has written more than forty books — novels, criticism, plays — and has also composed three symphonies. For his 1981 Selection,* Earthly Powers, *Burgess talked with former* New York Times *writer Israel Shenker about his work, about good and evil, and about "the failure of modern civilization to develop ethical systems."*

Anthony Burgess
by Israel Shenker

HE SPEAKS in short bursts, swallowing words, sometimes whole sentences. Not for him the smooth and measured cadence. Starts and stops, ideas pursued and abandoned, theories advanced and withdrawn, episodes, fragments, debris. A blank page in the typewriter. Write a sentence. Rip out the page. Fresh page. New sentence. Tear it up. Try again. Twenty pages later the chapter is ready to begin.

John Anthony Burgess Wilson is at the keyboard — no, not John Anthony Burgess Wilson. Try again. Anthony Burgess, better name, extricated from the original, self-transformed, new edition, same person, different person. What does he look like? "Ugly," he says. "Old." Not ugly. Interesting, inverted-pyramid face, shrewd expression, eyes burrowed under overhanging brow, flat hair unruly, hanging over brow. Feels younger than his 63 years, wonders how much time he has left.

Born in Manchester, half-Irish, lapsed Catholic, author of about 40 books, novelist, critic, scriptwriter, composer. Yes, composer. Three symphonies. "Hard, physical work. Big score. So I thought it was easier to write a book. I wrote a novel in 1953 and I sent it to Heinemann in London and they liked it and called me in and said, 'We can't publish this as a first novel.' It obviously had the feeling of a second novel. 'Could you write a first novel?' "

Backspace. Went to Manchester University. Studied history of

English language, studied Anglo-Saxon, Old High German, Old Norse. Served abroad during World War II. Worked for colonial services in Malaya, published novel about Malaya. "In 1959, in Borneo, I was told I had a cerebral tumor, which I didn't really have, and was given a year to live. It was necessary to provide money for my widow and I couldn't get a job. So I wrote five novels, five and a half novels in a year and lived, obviously, thereafter, and for a time kept up with the habit of prolificity and have just gone on doing it. I belong to an old tradition, that of H. G. Wells, who never published fewer than four books a year and a number of pamphlets.

"When I'm at home I work every day, including weekends. I'm not a quick writer at all. A dogged writer. Get on with it. Have to. I just drink tea, as all Britishers do. Gallons of tea. Strong tea. And get on with the job. No lunch, because lunch makes you sleepy. I cook dinner for the family in the evening — wife's Italian, a linguist, son is 16. We speak Italian at home."

Backspace. Afternoons, writes articles, book reviews, commissions gratefully accepted. "Reviews take a different kind of energy, a nonfictional energy, a quite genuine relish to discuss someone else's book, and to be rather more sympathetic, especially to a fiction writer, than the average critic is — because you know how difficult it is. I got the award as critic of the year for 1979. Critic of the year. This I didn't like. Novelist of the year would be a different thing."

Backspace. "I'm desperately obsessed with good and evil and the failure of religion in our own age, the failure of modern civilization to develop ethical systems, the violence, the nature of violence — this upsets me terribly. My first wife was the victim of an act of evil." In London, during World War II, she was robbed and beaten up by four American soldiers. "They left her there in her blood, and she was carrying our child at the time, and she lost the child and was very ill and eventually died. I wrote *A Clockwork Orange* — where you see the act of violence — and it helped me work through the event. But I still live with it.

"When I married again I felt the urge to get out, to get out of the country and make a fresh start. So I went to live in Malta, which was pretty well impossible, then I moved to Italy. The difficulties of living in Italy are great — threats of violence, threats of kidnapping — so we moved over the next frontier, which landed us in Monaco."

Backspace. Five years ago he began writing *Earthly Powers*, his first big novel, then stopped. Too many commissions competing for his time. Resumed last year, found he was a different person, started all over again. "The narrator is rather like Somerset Maugham except he's living in Malta, not in France. A homosexual, which I am not, incidentally. I've always been fascinated by Maugham's character because he was so wretched despite his success, his fame. Thin old man, tendons on his neck standing out, cold eyes, elegant, witty, but fundamentally totally disturbed, totally unhappy."

What's left? "I have to write an opera. This must be done. Major opera, chorus, many characters, serious theme, good libretto, interesting music. It'll take a long time. I've been commissioned to write a book on the English language. And a serious, longish book about the Anglo-American novel. The time for writing short novels — which is what we British unfortunately specialize in — is for me past. I must write long novels. This is what the novel's about. That's what Dickens did. Thackeray. This is what I can do — produce three books much the size of this one and regard this as probably all I can hope to do unless I live to a great age."

JOHN KENNETH GALBRAITH *has written widely on economic thought, and he will be particularly remembered for* The Affluent Society, *which William Buckley called "the most influential book on social economics of our generation." That statement was part of a warm-hearted recollection of Galbraith, written by Buckley in connection with the 1981 publication of Galbraith's autobiography. Bill Buckley is not exactly a political bedfellow of Galbraith's, but can there be a warmer friend?*

John Kenneth Galbraith
by William F. Buckley, Jr.

I MET HIM the first time ascending an elevator. Along with Billy Rose, Dorothy Kilgallen and a couple of other savants, we were guests on an innovative program produced by David Susskind, the wrinkle of which was that the public would put its questions into a tiny camera in Grand Central Station so that we would see the face of the questioner while hearing his voice. A little television receiver had been placed in the middle of our round table, designed to rotate toward the person who was being questioned.

"Unhappily," David Susskind explained, "the unions aren't agreed as to which one of us should turn the knob that turns the set, so the only alternative is for me to stall. If the question is, say, for Professor Galbraith, then the person in the chair at which the television set is pointed must get up while I'm talking and Professor Galbraith must run over to the empty chair and answer the question. That way," Susskind beamed, "no one will know anything is wrong."

I wouldn't have thought it possible that during the next two hours seven adults, including a 6'7" titan — who had dictated the price of peanut butter in his 30s; who had written in his 40s the most influential book on social economics of our generation; who wrote speeches for Adlai Stevenson and corrected President Kennedy's policies while presiding over the largest embassy in the world in New Delhi, and who had become the most intellectual economist in the world — would consent, without apparently giving the matter a second thought, to cavorting about a studio as though playing hide-and-seek with his grandchildren, all in deference to the sovereign right of labor unions to disagree with one another at the public expense.

A few months later we met again. He was in Gstaad, where he winters (as I do), and called to suggest that we lunch together. I happily agreed. He asked if he might bring along Jacqueline Kennedy. I told him I had never met Mrs. Kennedy, but that if she could put up with me I could certainly put up with her. The following night JKG instructed David Niven, whom I had not known, to include me in a small party at his house with Mrs. Kennedy. The next day he suggested that we ski together. That was when I first learned the most disconcerting of all his traits, which one runs into again and again in his new and engrossing book. I saw him descending a moderate slope on skis with all the skill of a beginner. Not knowing what exactly to say, I asked: "How long have you been skiing?"

"Thirty years," he replied.

"Oh" — who could have resisted it? — "that's about as long as you've been studying economics?" He told the story on himself all over Europe that spring.

Ten years later, at lunch, I suggested that we discharge a pending obligation to NBC sometime during the first week in June. "During the first week in June," Galbraith said, "I'll be teaching at the University of Moscow."

"Oh," I said, "what do you have left to teach them?" And damned if he didn't spread *that* one all over town. What do you do with someone like that?

Well, for one thing you listen to him, which I have done with rabid pleasure for 15 years, hearing many of the stories he now so skillfully collects in his autobiography. And you read him: for the pleasure that one can take from his prose alone. He is never more instructive than when writing about himself, about adventures shared with his wife, Kitty, about misadventures shared with such of his protégés as Adlai Stevenson, Eugene McCarthy, George McGovern and Edward Kennedy. His capacity for self-appreciation is wonderfully developed, but it is never offensive. And he is a wonderful friend to have, even if he refuses to acknowledge your view of the real world.

In acts of personal generosity he is very nearly unrivaled, both in the spontaneity of the gesture and the adroitness with which he manages to make it appear nothing other than that. The day after a fire burned down our abode in Switzerland he called, not to suggest that he and Kitty vacate their apartment and hand it over to me and my wife, but to *inform* me that he intended to do so. "Kitty and I will go to London," he said. "Got plenty to do there."

In debate he is plenty tough, and he expects you to be plenty tough. He delights in suggesting that what I seek is a world plagued by war, poverty and disease. In fact my ambitions are more modest. I strive for a world in which men will be free to choose — to read Galbraith, and reject Galbraithism. No one who hasn't done it can begin to believe the joys of what Professor Galbraith would call this bimodal approach.

In John Hutchens's *review of Nobel Prize–winner Isaac Bashevis Singer's* Collected Stories, *he writes about Singer the storyteller, this "entertainer of the spirit," and about how Singer reached his homespun eminence.*

The Collected Stories of Isaac Bashevis Singer

A STORYTELLER "must be an entertainer of the spirit," Isaac Bashevis Singer said when he accepted the Nobel Prize in literature in 1978 — an award given for the body of his work including his stories, novels, memoirs and and tales for children. The award came as no surprise to the worldwide admirers of this great storyteller, for they have always known that he is not only a masterful entertainer but a profoundly seri-

ous artist. Here, in this collection of 47 stories that he himself has chosen
from his published output, they will meet him again in all his richness
and variety. Tales that his readers cherished in his previous volumes
will live for them again, like favorite places revisited with the pleasure of
old acquaintance. To readers meeting him more recently or for the first
time he will be seen as an amazing figure for whom "genius" is a fair
word.

Singer's life is itself a remarkable story, to which he turns for much of
his material. One Singer scholar wrote that "his memoirs are fiction and
his fiction memoirs" — to distinguish which is which is one of the delights of reading him. In some tales he is obviously himself. But because
he believes in the supernatural — in spirits and devils and dybbuks —
he also writes frequently as a fantasist. "Ghosts, spirits, premonitions,
telepathy, clairvoyance are actually part of nature," he once told an interviewer. Sometimes in his impish fashion he chooses to appear as
Satan, as in "The Destruction of Kreshev." At other times we see him as
a fairly realistic observer. "Alone," for instance, is a vignette of a bored
tourist in a grimy Miami hotel who rejects the efforts of a crippled
woman — the hotel clerk — to seduce him. It almost appears to be
straight reporting.

Does any other American writer have his virtuosity? None that I can
think of. One important aspect of his career is that he spent a long and
agonizing time reaching his present position. Born in 1904 near Warsaw,
he grew up there and in nearby Jewish ghettos, where he absorbed the
ancient folklore of Jewish Poland. Thus he is a historian as well as a
creator; his memories are an invaluable record of a Yiddish culture and
language that were all but obliterated during World War II.

The son and grandson of rabbis, he grew up in a home where "Jew-
ishness wasn't some diluted formal religion but one that contained all
the flavors, all the vitamins, the entire mysticism of faith." He was a
seminarian for seven years, but the orthodoxy of his family was not for
him, and so in his twenties he began to write for an local newspaper. His
older brother, I. J. Singer, himself a writer of distinction, was a journalist at that time and helped him to get started. Isaac wrote reviews and
stories in Yiddish and, later, a novel.

Meanwhile, other writers were shaping his standards as an artist —
notably, Dostoyevsky, whose *Crime and Punishment* he read at the age
of 10. Other strong influences were Tolstoy, Chekhov, Flaubert, Kafka,
Poe and, as he has amusingly related, Conan Doyle; as a boy the would-
be Sherlock Holmes trailed suspicious-looking characters in the streets

of Warsaw. Doestoyevsky's psychological insight was especially important to him. So was Flaubert's dictum: "When you tell a story, tell a story. Use the words to give information about your characters, but don't talk about them."

In 1935, with Hitler's threat to Poland impending, Singer moved to New York. His first half-dozen years were miserable. He knew no English, couldn't easily adjust to American life and had no appetite for writing. The *Jewish Daily Forward* published some of his old stories, but not until 1945 did he begin to write fiction again. When Saul Bellow translated "Gimpel the Fool" for *Partisan Review* in 1953, Singer was suddenly on the way to acquiring an American public. That story, appropriately, begins this collection.

Unlike most writers, Singer has become more prolific with age, though he continues to throw away much that doesn't please him. A wastepaper basket, he says, is a writer's best friend. In addition to his extraordinary memory of Jewish Poland, he has learned a great deal about New York. (Note "The Cafeteria" and "The Letter Writer.") Mayor Koch has called him "the Homer of the West Side." His neighbors regard him affectionately as a fellow resident — a small and self-effacing man who lives modestly with his wife of more than forty years.

Almost incredibly, for a writer so complex, Singer's style is as simple and direct as conversation. Politics and sociology don't interest him. He simply wants to tell about his characters, their depravity and decency, their tender love and their passions. Critics have sometimes dwelt harshly on the eroticism and sensuality in his work. His reply is that there is much of it in the Bible and in life. As this marvelous collection of stories reminds us, Singer has created an unforgettable panorama of life in two worlds, the old and the new, making them both uniquely his own.

John K. Hutchens

Robert Caro *is busy at work on the second volume of his projected three-volume biography of President Lyndon Johnson. Volume I,* The Path to Power, *won a National Book Award for general nonfiction. His earlier book,* The Power Broker, *a biography of Robert Moses, won the Pulitzer Prize. Caro signed the contract for the Johnson book in 1975, expecting that it would take him ten years to complete. In Mark Singer's*

profile of Caro, you see why the book is behind schedule. Mark Singer is a staff writer for The New Yorker *and the author of* Funny Money, *published in 1985.*

Robert A. Caro
by Mark Singer

IMPLICIT throughout "The Years of Lyndon Johnson" are the years of Robert Caro. Seven years have gone into the first volume, *The Path to Power.* The book raises and answers the extraordinarily complex questions of why and how Johnson acquired power. But another question that it inevitably raises is this: Why did Robert Caro decide to undertake such an exceptionally difficult task?

Caro's apprenticeship for this historic work was a book of equal scope and ambition — *The Power Broker,* a biography of Robert Moses. Published in 1974, it won a Pulitzer Prize and the Francis Parkman Prize, which is awarded annually to the book that "best represents the union of the historian and the artist." It is read in hundreds of college courses — political science, journalism, urban planning, history, even psychology.

What obviously fascinates Caro is the phenomenon of power — its use, its abuse, its magic. Caro graduated from Princeton University in 1957 and went to work as a report for the *New Brunswick* (New Jersey) *Daily Home News.* Two years later he moved to *Newsday,* where he spent seven years, distinguishing himself as an investigative reporter. (Jack Newfield, another distinguished reporter, recently described Caro as "a hero to so many urban writers and reformers.") In 1966, while he was at Harvard as a Nieman Fellow, Caro audited a course in urban planning — a special interest of his at the time. One day he watched a professor sketch on a blackboard an abstract equation that purported to describe how a highway gets built. "I thought, 'Wait. That's not how highways get built,' " Caro recalls. " 'Highways get built because Robert Moses wants to build them.' I knew *why* but I didn't know *how.* And I knew that I couldn't find out within the context of daily newspaper journalism. I had to write a book."

Caro assumed that a book about Moses would take a year. Ultimately the research and writing took seven years, during which he ran out of money and had to sell his house and move with his wife and son into a small apartment. He wrote more than a million words, which he and his editor winnowed to 650,000. In 1975, when Caro was 39, he signed a contract to write a biography of Lyndon Johnson. He told himself that when it was completed in 1985 he would be almost 50. Caro already knows what he would like to write about when he finishes with Johnson. He also knows what he would like to write about after that and after that and after that — time permitting.

To understand how Johnson acquired national power — a prerequisite for understanding how he used it — Caro moved to Austin, near the Texas Hill Country where LBJ grew up. The LBJ library is in Austin. Its stacks have more than 40,000 boxes full of Johnson's papers — 34 million documents in all. For three years Caro studied those documents and conducted almost 1000 interviews.

"The thing that almost defeated me," he says, "was the sheer size of Texas. Every interview was 200 miles from the last one." Later he realized that many people had not been fully forthcoming the first time, and he interviewed hundreds of them again.

"Why didn't you tell me that before?" he would say.

"You never asked me," they replied.

Today Caro works in a small office in midtown Manhattan, convenient to the New York Public Library. He is a trim, fastidious man — gray flannel, regimental tie, button-down collar — who looks younger than his years. He keeps his dark hair carefully combed, he wears horn-rimmed eyeglasses, and he is handsome in a Clark Kentish way. The bookshelves in his office are filled with volumes of political biography, accounts of the New Deal, histories of Texas, books about oil. Maps of Texas are on the walls. There is no electronic data storage equipment, no word processor — only a portable electric typewriter, and he doesn't even use that for first drafts. Robert Caro writes his first drafts in long-hand. Ina Caro, to whom he has been married for 25 years, and who has a Master's degree in history, is his only research assistant.

In the notes from the interviews that Caro conducted while he was living in Texas there is one remark that turns up again and again: "I've been waiting all these years for someone to ask me that." Twenty-one previous biographies of LBJ have been published, but apparently nobody has used a methodology as rigorous as Caro's.

"Early on," he says, "I realized that the truth about Lyndon Johnson had never been told. And I realized that the reason was because this incredibly gifted and cunning and shrewd and energetic man had devoted a great deal of that energy and cunning and shrewdness to guaranteeing that none of it would be known. Everyone thinks that he had such a fascinating career and a fascinating life. Well, he did, but it isn't the career that anyone knows about. This is an unknown president."

No longer.

"He has something that we seem to need and want," writes Clifton Fadiman about Lewis Thomas. Fadiman says that something is "the ability to inform delightfully" and "enlarge our minds" at the same time.

Late Night Thoughts on Listening to Mahler's Ninth Symphony by Lewis Thomas

It is rare when two books come along at the same time by writers who are known for their humanistic approach to the complexities of modern life. In an age that often seems to be dominated by impersonal science and medicine, Lewis Thomas and Norman Cousins keep reminding us that it is the individual mind and spirit that finally sustain us. Their new books are distinctively their own. Yet both of them speak to the same concerns about the world we live in. And both men never cease to marvel at the miracles that are all around us and within us.

With Lewis Thomas we are in the hands of our finest practicing essayist. Especially with his last book, *The Youngest Science*, he has won not merely a devoted but a large body of readers. He has something that we seem to need and want, as other generations needed a T. H. Huxley or an H. G. Wells. The ability to inform delightfully is a rare talent; to go beyond informing — to enlarge our minds with unfailing wit and charm — is more unusual still. Dr. Thomas has the touch.

The 24 essays collected here under a deliberately provocative title range in subject from the playful to the very grave. But, rather than 24 separate subjects, it is a human being that we seem to be ingesting — a person wise without pretentiousness, eager to share rather than to display his knowledge and, above all, a person genuinely fond of the human race.

He writes on music, philology, etymology, medicine; on most of the biological and physical sciences; on the pacemaker that may have saved his life; on dementia and insane asylums; on Clever Hans, the mathematical horse, and why Hans was both dumber and smarter than he

seemed; on the brilliant contributions of alchemy; on the subtly cour-
teous cat that fooled the experimenters; on his theory (based on the lin-
guistics research of Professor Derek Bickerton) that it is children who
are the great creators of language; on smell and the need to preserve leaf
bonfires, "by law if necessary"; on the euglossine bees that became
DDT addicts; on altruism, which he believes is innate in humanity; on
the lie detector and how television would be "abolished as a habitual
felon" if one could be attached to your set.

He pleads for untidying our minds. The slant of his own temperament is revealed in his list of three top priorities for scientific research:
What goes on in the mind of the honeybee? What is music and what
does it do to us? How does hypnosis act on the nervous system? And he
wonders whether stress is not simply "the condition of being human."

Certain themes flow through the book: the excitements, surprises and
errors of science, not the certainties; the need for basic, undifferentiated
science, as opposed to narrow, goal-directed research; the essential unity
of the scientific and humanist temperaments. Glorying in the ambiguity
of science, he remarks that "the poetry of Wallace Stevens is crystal
clear alongside the genetic code."

One major theme is that of the threatened annihilation of the human
race by thermonuclear war. Thomas doesn't indulge in scare-headline
prose, but goes soberly to the heart of the matter: "Human beings cannot fight with such weapons and remain human." The title essay on this
theme, grave and moving, may become a classic for our time.

CLIFTON FADIMAN

ON THE SUBJECT *of John Updike, David Willis McCullough and Peter
Collier, novelist and coauthor of* The Rockefellers *and* The Kennedys,
expressed remarkably similar views. In a 1979 column in the News,
*Collier said that Updike's body of work "if placed in a time capsule
would provide a coherent view of America in the downhill half of the
twentieth century for some future generation." In his 1984 Selection
Report on* The Witches of Eastwick, *McCullough writes that "over the
past 30 years [Updike] has produced a solid four-foot shelf of novels,
short stories, poems, children's books and literary criticism. . . . His
subjects have always been love, death, guilt . . . and the sort of worry
about God that can only be enjoyed by someone who once felt quite familiar with Him."*

The Witches of Eastwick by John Updike

WE ALL KNOW about New England witches. From Nathaniel Hawthorne's *The Scarlet Letter* to Arthur Miller's *The Crucible* we have a
whole literature devoted to those strange and perhaps sinister goings-on
in the woods outside Puritan Salem. Now John Updike, writing in a
mood that ranges from the comic to the diabolic, weighs in with an entirely new look at the sisterhood.

The setting of *The Witches of Eastwick* isn't Massachusetts. It's what
Updike calls the "mysterious crabbed state of Rhode Island," a back-
water that the Puritan fathers left to Quakers, Jews and women to colo-
nize. The time isn't the mist-shrouded 17th century, but the shopworn
and mundane 1960s.

There are three witches to begin with: Jane, Alexandra and Sukie, all
divorced, bored and looking for something to enliven Eastwick. One of
them plays the cello and gives music lessons; another is a successful
amateur sculptor; the third is a writer for the local newspaper, and anyone with a handy dictionary of mythology could see them as blowzy
suburban retreads of the three classical Graces. Not that their lives are
all that graceful. Their frantic love affairs may remind seasoned Updike
readers of the bed-hopping wives in his earlier novel *Couples*, since, as
he puts it here, "being a divorcée in a small town is a little like playing
Monopoly; eventually you land on all the properties."

At first their witchcraft is harmless enough. The weekly meeting of
the "coven" seems more like a boozy kaffeeklatsch, and their magic consists of little more than pranks and practical jokes: a sudden squall is
summoned to clear a beach of rowdies with their transistor radios; the
string on an old bore's pearls breaks to shut her up in mid-harangue; a
tennis ball, during a raucous match on Halloween afternoon, keeps
changing into a bat.

But before events run their course, the real harms begins. There are
even deaths, and for the first time in the living memory of Eastwick the
word "evil" is mentioned in the pulpit of the Unitarian church. "There
is evil in this town," the preacher declares. But by that time the rumors
of witchcraft are so out of hand that the preacher herself is suspected of
being a member of a rival band of witches.

What changes everything for the original three witches is the arrival
of a seductively charming scoundrel who calls himself Van Horne. In
17th-century New England a euphemism for the devil was "the tall man
from Boston." In Updike's 20th-century Rhode Island it could be "the

fat man from Manhattan." The pudgy Van Horne restores a crumbling Victorian mansion, hangs trendy pop art on its walls, installs a hot tub, and beguiles the locals with talk of a new alchemy — the "big interface" between solar energy and electrical energy. He also beguiles the three witches of Eastwick. They have finally met their satanic master — or so they think, at least, as they compete for his favor. A danger game begins: Who is to be the most favored of all — Jane, Alexandra or Sukie?

What is Updike up to with all this marvelous mumbo jumbo about black magic (which has "a tiny burnt odor like a gas jet when first turned on"), the devil and all-too-easily-sold souls? Updike is the most Victorian of America's serious writers. Over the past 30 years he has produced a solid four-foot shelf of novels, short stories, poems, children's books and literary criticism. He never seems to have known failure; he wins all the best prizes. His subjects have always been love, death, guilt (it is guilt that finally brings down the witches of Eastwick) and the sort of worry about God that can only be enjoyed by someone who once felt quite familiar with Him.

In *The Witches of Eastwick* Updike is a master of the deadpan. There is no doubt that witches exist — you can see them having coffee at the diner on Main Street. His descriptions of Rhode Island's marshy seediness are some of the most telling since Roger Williams kept his Colonial diary about the same area. A rococo sermon that Van Horne preaches on Layman Sunday in the Unitarian church is high comedy. The chapter revealing two terrible deaths is Updike at his brilliant best.

Updike's friend John Cheever devoted much of his writing career to stories that celebrated "a world that lies spread out around us like a bewildering and stupendous dream." I think Updike celebrates that same world. Like Cheever, he can see it populated with wonderful beasts and mysterious chimeras which, on closer examination, turn out to be quite ordinary folks like you or me. But he also sees evil and cruelty that, again, turn out to be quite ordinary, even vulgar. Much of the vulgarity lies in the frank sex scenes.

We are all fascinated by witches. We love to read about them. We have an unofficial holiday when we give our children license to be as witchlike as possible. Our mistake might be that we expect things to be back to normal on the morning after Halloween. In setting loose his coven in Eastwick, John Updike has given us a witches' sabbath to remember.

DAVID WILLIS McCULLOUGH

John Updike

by Peter Collier

A COUPLE OF years ago, I began my first literary tour in, of all places, Pittsburgh. I arrived at a local radio station psyched up for what I thought would be a provocative dialogue with a large number of callers-in. A few minutes before air time, the host walked into the studio with a copy of my book *The Rockefellers* under his arm, gestured admiringly and said: "Just read the jacket copy. Powerful stuff here." A red light went on and he introduced me, then sat back reading a paperback on hypnosis while I babbled aimlessly about wealth and power in America for half an hour without a single call lighting the telephone push buttons.

After *Downriver* was recently published I decided that the key to publicizing my novel was to be more urbane. When the first interviewer asked what *Downriver* was about, I framed an answer designed to bounce the ball wittily back into her court. "Sex and violence," I said. "Two subjects about which I have no firsthand knowledge." She looked at me with a kind of irritation and replied: "What are you trying to do, sound like John Updike?"

Isn't it strange that someone who epitomizes a kind of literary success — a fixture at *The New Yorker* since graduating from Harvard; a fixture on the bestseller lists since publishing *Couples* — should cause such a reaction? Now and then one hears that Updike is too cool for his own good, a writer whose unusual talent has kept him from playing the tragic chords of human experience. *Commentary* magazine seems to feel that he is too WASP; John Gardner worries about the morals of his fiction; others suggest that he is too flippant to be regarded seriously.

Most good writers inspire argument. In a time when many novelists are unable to practice their craft without a soapbox, megaphone and suppository, and when a career often consists of the delivery of one book a decade, I believe we owe Updike a kind of debt. For more than twenty years now he has been trying new things, holding onto those that work and leaving behind those that don't — always looking and sometimes finding. The books have appeared with steadying regularity — poems, short stories, novels, a play, children's literature. It is a body of work which if placed in a time capsule would provide a coherent view of America in the downhill half of the twentieth century for some future generation.

In his nonfiction, Updike has always been one of our most thoughtful and sensitive writers. The subjects have had an immense range — from Dostoyevsky to Borges, theology to ethnography. For me some of the most memorable of these picked-up pieces have not always been the portentous ones — the report on Ted Williams' last game at Fenway; the review that made *Fear of Flying* a bestseller.

In his fiction he has been resourceful in his guises: a rabbit; a father and husband; an older, changed rabbit; a literary Jew; a father and husband now anguished by separation and divorce; a defrocked minister. He has been seen most recently in blackface as Ellellou, dictator of the thirsting African nation of Kush in his most exotic book, *The Coup*.

In the stories, which continue to appear in *The New Yorker*, there are little epiphanies about family relationships where heartbreak comes like fine glass breaking. Read nearly fifteen years later, *The Centaur* is still an extraordinarily moving novel. Although slightly old hat in certain ways, *Couples* still contains that flash of precognition about life after the sexual revolution. In *Month of Sundays* and *Marry Me*, there is development of what have become characteristic Updike themes: the need to exercise religious impulse in a world where religion seems to have disappeared; the way profane love and longing become exterior signs of the only salvation possible.

There are plenty of apocalypticians. Updike has a view of things distinctly his own — of generational linkages that have been broken, of relationships filled with sadness and attenuation, of people chronically incomplete. Yet in Updike's stories one also finds hard-won redemption and forgiveness, moments of laughter within the tragic scheme. His people survive. It's not so much "style" that distinguishes this writer as it is a whole way of seeing. He has the quality which T. S. Eliot found in the works of Andrew Marvell: "a tough reasonableness beneath a slight lyric grace."

HELEN HOOVEN SANTMYER *died in February 1986. Three months before that she celebrated her ninetieth birthday. That is, people celebrated around her, for even then she was too ill to take part. The little party was held in Hospitality Home East in Xenia, Ohio, a town like the setting of Santmyer's novel "... And Ladies of the Club." The publication of the book is something of a Cinderella story, although the novel itself does not have a Cinderella theme. It had consumed*

*most of a lifetime of thinking by the author; she had started writing it
when Sinclair Lewis was in full flower. Santmyer's vision of small-
town America was not quite Lewis's, and she wanted to correct his picture. First published by the Ohio State University Press, the novel
found its way to a major publishing house in 1984 and was published
without extravagant expectations. But then wonderful things happened,
among them the Club's decision to make the book a Selection. Santmyer
became front-page news, and the book became a bestseller. It also received many fine reviews. In his report, David Willis McCullough
called it a novel that is "clouded by neither satire nor sentimentality."*

". . . And Ladies of the Club"
by Helen Hooven Santmyer

THE NAMING of a book as a Book-of-the-Month Club Selection hardly
seems like front-page news. But several days after our Editorial Board
chose ". . . *And Ladies of the Club*," news of the choice was a front-page
story in *The New York Times*. HAPPY END FOR NOVELIST'S 50-YEAR EF-
FORT said the headline over a photograph of Helen Hooven Santmyer.
"An 1184-page novel about life in small-town Ohio, begun more than 50
years ago by an author who is now 88 years old and lives in a nursing
home, has been made a Selection of the Book-of-the-Month Club," the
story began. That night the television networks featured the story on
the news, and the weekly newsmagazines followed suit. For all sorts of
obvious human-interest reasons, Helen Santmyer's "sudden" success
was an editor's dream. Probably no other Selection by the Club has
made such a media splash.

But it would be a mistake to patronize Helen Santmyer by classifying
her and her ambitious novel only as endearing oddities. Publication may
have come late in the author's life, but ". . . *And Ladies of the Club*" is
well worth the wait. It's a novel both so enjoyable and so true to a rich
vein of middle America's way of life that it must be taken seriously.
Back in the 1930s, when the first pages of this novel were written, a lot
of energetic young men dreamed of writing something called the Great
American Novel. It was a dream as hopeless as capturing the white
whale, but Santmyer, working quietly away in Xenia, Ohio, has come as
close to realizing a part of that dream as any of her boisterous literary
brothers.

The novel opens in a small town called Waynesboro, Ohio, on graduation day, 1868. The girls of the Waynesboro Female College are addressed by a Civil War hero, and two members of the graduating
class — Anne Alexander and Sally Cochran — are called aside and
asked to join some faculty wives, teachers and a few local grande dames
in organizing a women's club that would meet to read and discuss
papers dealing with literary subjects. The book ends in 1932 with the
death of Anne, the last of the founding members.

In the 64 years between those events, using the women's club as a
framework, Miss Santmyer brings to life a town and its citizens. (Members begin addressing the organization by saying "Madam President
and ladies of the club. . . .") Anne Alexander, the daughter of a doctor,
marries Dr. John Gordon, a veteran of the Union army's medical corps.
Sally marries another veteran, Ludwig Rausch, a German immigrant
who takes over the town's failing rope-and-twine factory and makes it a
success. We see Waynesboro first through their eyes and the eyes of
their fellow club members, and then through the eyes of their children,
grandchildren and great-grandchildren as the ever-widening relationships become more complex and interwoven.

The ladies of the club gossip and dabble in good works, establishing a
public library and organizing a comically inept temperance campaign.
They go through the rituals of 19th-century pregnancy (when confine-
ment was literally that) and mourn all too often the deaths of their children. Beloved teachers grow infirm; teenage children flourish or
disappoint and sometimes leave town, never to return.

A trolley line is built to neighboring towns. There's a new hospital
and new local industries. The economy rises and falls and comes back.
There are weddings and funerals, joyous holiday celebrations, tragic
fires and epidemics. Sons leave to fight the Great War in France. But the
true great war, the one that lingers in the town's memory and remains
the emotional high point of many of the men's lives, is the Civil War.

Husbands are sometimes unfaithful and wives sometimes frigid. The
various shadings of Presbyterian doctrine raise barriers that turn out to
be not as rigid as they seem. A rebellious nephew may indeed marry an
Irish-Catholic girl from the other side of town, but the bride, of course,
will never be a member of the women's club.

It may seem a strange thing to say about a novel as long as ". . . *And
Ladies of the Club,*" but it is written with admirable economy. Scenes
are never padded; everything that's included is included for a purpose.
And if there is more, say, about the workings of the Republican party

than one may want to know, it's clear that the Grand Old Party and its
presidential conventions are every bit as important to the club members
and their husbands as they are to the author.

A simple device that runs through the novel is typical of the author's
economy. Most chapters cover one year, and each chapter begins with a
membership list of the club. In 1868 there are 12 names. A year later
there are still 12, but some members have married and have new sur-
names. By 1872 one name has been dropped to an "In Memoriam" column. And so it goes over the years. New names are added and familiar
ones drop to "In Memoriam" with the natural rhythm of the coming
and going of generations.

The club produces one young member who wants to become a
writer — a young Helen Santmyer, perhaps. First she publishes a book
of recollections based on stories she heard an old soldier tell about fighting Johnny Rebs. Then she decides to write a rebuttal to Sinclair Lewis,
refuting the terrible things she thinks he has been writing about small
Midwestern towns and the people of Main Street. By 1932 the novel still
hasn't been finished.

Whether or not Santmyer's novel stands in that book's place,
". . . And Ladies of the Club" is an effective answer to Sinclair Lewis.
Social satire, of course, is what people remember of Lewis's work. What
is not remembered is that his novels, like *Babbitt*, are as sentimental as
they are satiric. Helen Santmyer's clear-eyed look at small-town
America is clouded by neither satire nor sentimentality. A few truly
dreadful women are members of the club, and she lets us see them for
what they are. She also lets us see the everyday flawed goodness and
uncommon common sense of the best of them.

After several hundred pages of Helen Santmyer's novel I began to
wish I could go to Xenia to see what "Waynesboro" is really like. By the
end I realized that a visit would be pointless. I had come to know the
town better than I ever would by going there.

DAVID WILLIS MCCULLOUGH

MORDECAI RICHLER, *the Club's demon judge from Canada, once again
pounced on a little-known writer — he did the same for Toni Morrison — and helped to introduce John Irving to the reading public.
Richler proclaimed Irving "a large talent that announces itself on
practically every page." And Corby Kummer, an editor of* The Atlan-

tic, *found out why it was that Irving turned to orphans for his much-admired 1985 novel,* The Cider House Rules.

The World According to Garp by John Irving

IT HAS been suggested that novelists, living in chaos like the rest of us, retaliate by composing ordered worlds of their own, proffering them as fictions. If that's the case, John Irving is a brilliant exception. Indeed, he just may inhabit a very ordered world himself, for what he has created in *The World According to Garp* is a loopy novel of inspired anarchy. Some literary lightning, very much to my taste. Something special for admirers of Nathanael West, Terry Southern and Joseph Heller. And yet refreshingly original.

Buckle your seat belts. Garp's world — joltingly absurd, its highways mined with outlandish inventions — is liable to blow up in your face at any time. This savagely comic novel thrives on many levels. It is a flinty satire — long overdue — of the more extreme reaches of the feminist movement. It is also a surprisingly sweet evocation of family life, the paranoia that springs from a man's concern for the safety of his wife and children. Or, put another way, Garp's hilarious but touching attempts to construct a kind of fort for his own family, wherein they can live "unmolested, even untouched by what is called 'the rest of life,' " are conspicuously unsuccessful. Yet for all its nicely calculated shocks, *The World According to Garp* can be savored as a cry of puritan outrage against mindless violence.

Garp is conceived into this world under extraordinary circumstances. His mother, Jenny Fields, a nurse in a Boston hospital in 1942, a hospital swarming with World War II casualties, creates him, as it were, by taking single-minded advantage of a brain-damaged, dying ball turret gunner. "I wanted a baby," she writes in an autobiography that is to become a feminist icon, "but I didn't want to share my body or my life to have one." Jenny moves on from the hospital to become resident nurse in a grand old New England prep school, where Garp is educated, after a fashion, endures many misadventures and falls in love with and marries the wrestling coach's daughter. Garp becomes a novelist. He and Helen have two adorable children. Though they love each other, Garp proves vulnerable to pretty baby sitters, and Helen, an English professor by this time, indulges in a meaningless affair with one of her students. Bizarre incidents proliferate. So does rape. So does murder. So does emasculation for Helen's lover. The truth is I can no more render a coherent outline of the plot of *The World According to Garp* than I could the story line of a vintage Marx Brothers movie; suffice it to say that where the latter leaves off, avoiding real offense, *Garp* merely begins.

Among the novel's more delightful characters is 6′4″ transsexual Roberta Muldoon, formerly Robert Muldoon, once a standout tight end for the Philadelphia Eagles, now denied a job as a sports announcer by decidedy sexist television networks. It is John Irving's achievement to render this character more than a joke, but uncannily real, even lovable.

Not so lovable are the girls of the Ellen James Society.

Ellen James was raped when she was 11 years old, and her attackers cut her tongue out so she wouldn't be able to tell anyone what they looked like. Members of the Ellen James Society have also had their tongues cut out, in sympathy with the girl. They call themselves Ellen Jamesians and, introduced to a stranger, promptly present him with a card:

> Hello, I'm Martha. I'm an Ellen Jamesian.
> Do you know what an Ellen Jamesian is?

If the stranger doesn't know, he is handed another card. With details.

The World According to Garp is a novel that will offend some and infuriate others, and even though it would have benefited from some pruning here and there, it delighted me. Garp, after he becomes a successful novelist, writes to a disgruntled reader, "I have nothing but sympathy for how people behave — and nothing but laughter to console them with. Laughter is my religion. In the manner of most religions, I admit that my laughter is pretty desperate." Yes, and abusive as well, but redeemed by a disarming tenderness and a large talent that announces itself on practically every page.

MORDECAI RICHLER

John Irving
by Corby Kummer

JOHN IRVING knew that orphans would be the subject of his new book before he knew anything else about it. For one thing, he had been reading Dickens, and, as he points out, orphans are a favorite subject of novelists — families don't have to be invented for them and the reader's sympathy can be counted on. But the reasons go much deeper — into Irving's own life.

He grew up at Phillips Exeter Academy, a privileged boarding school in New Hampshire, where his stepfather taught history. "The students at Exeter might as well have been orphans, for all the care the parents took to make them a part of their lives," Irving recalls. His mother worked with abused families at a community services center, and his real father was a mystery.

"My mother remarried when I was six," Irving says, "and I liked — loved — the man she married so well that I resented it when people referred to him as my stepfather. To do much prying might have hurt their feelings. I thought that the past was none of my business. It was for me to imagine, not to ask."

Many years later, when he was in his 30s, Irving moved to a town in Vermont. There he found himself going, again and again, to the local orphanage. He had a natural sympathy for children who didn't know who their parents were, and he thought of them as "rich territory," a universal subject. "Anyone who is ultra-sensitive or who has been injured in any way can think of himself as an orphan," Irving says. "It used to amuse me when people said that the orphanage looked just like a boarding school. There's a big difference. When you pull into the driveway of a boarding school and get out of the car, no one looks at you or cares who are you are. Park your car at an orphanage and everybody looks at you and wonders why you're there."

At about the same time, Irving's mother showed him some letters that his real father, a flier in the air force, had written to her in 1942, soon after Irving was born. The letters told of being shot down over Burma. The flier survived the war, but Irving doesn't know whether he is still alive today. Those wartime letters, along with one of several versions of his father that Irving has imagined, went into the character of Wally in *The Cider House Rules.*

One member of the family that the author didn't have to imagine was his maternal grandfather, an obstetrician named Frederick Irving (John Irving took his mother's name), who wrote several books that Irving used as research for his remarkably detailed accounts of American medicine at the turn of the century. He also found a doctor at Yale, Dr. Sherwin B. Nuland, who filled him in on countless facts that he couldn't find in his grandfather's books and who led him to other sources. "Those early doctors kept massive journals, as if they were trying to create a history for places that didn't have one," Irving says. He had decided to make the director of the orphanage a doctor because he didn't know what an orphanage director would do all day.

After writing 150 pages Irving realized that any doctor who was practicing medicine almost a century ago would have been taught by men who remembered when the decision to abort was between them and their patients (abortion was still legal in some states until 1860) and that the usefulness of abortions would occur to any doctor who was running an orphanage.

"I feel that I came to the subject clean," Irving says. Still, having stumbled on it, he didn't want it to take over his book, which, like all his novels, he plotted elaborately before starting to write. Though he is eloquent on the subject of illegal abortion, he doesn't think abortion should be a political subject. In fact, he doesn't think *The Cider House Rules* is more political than any of his other books. By setting it in the past he feels that he made it less of an "issue" novel and more of a historical document. "I wanted it to seem like something that really happened, not like something I invented. My goal is to be the medium, the vehicle — just a storyteller."

For the sections that take place in an apple orchard, Irving relied on his memory — as a teenager he spent five autumns picking apples, along with black migrant workers, in an orchard in New Hampshire. Ironically, memory turned out to be a faulty research tool. "When I showed my manuscript to medical experts," he says, "they found only two mistakes, which were excessive doses of anesthesia. But when I showed it to the children of the man I worked for in the apple orchard they found a list of errors so long that they lectured at me for two hours.

"With something that you've actually lived you assume you know what you're talking about," Irving says. Having discovered that this isn't necessarily true, he thinks there's much to be said for conjuring. "You have to believe that it's somehow better to imagine a story completely than to experience it. The amount of imagining that I've done about my natural father has been healthy for me — quite possibly healthier and happier than finding him. What would that tell me? Maybe better not to have the encounter and to just think it out."

THE BOOK-OF-THE-MONTH CLUB *started paying attention to Anne Tyler in 1974 with a review of* Celestial Navigation, *her fifth novel. The Club was moving slowly. With her most recent three books,* Morgan's Passing, Dinner at the Homesick Restaurant, *and* The Accidental Tourist, *the Club's interest in Tyler deepened as she deepened as an artist. It is as Wilfrid Sheed says in his opening paragraph on* The Accidental

Tourist: *"Anne Tyler has slipped into the front rank of American writers as unobtrusively as someone taking her shoes off to enter a temple."*

The Accidental Tourist by Anne Tyler

ANNE TYLER has slipped into the front rank of American writers as unobtrusively as someone taking her shoes off to enter a temple. A gem here and a minor masterpiece there, and pretty soon (in Senator Dirksen's immortal phrase about a billion here and a billion there) it adds up to real money — or, in this case, a body of work to reckon with.

Ms. Tyler is a master of the sad-funny story — the novel that won't let you off with a single, uncluttered emotion. If such a thing can exist as a kindhearted satirist, that's Tyler. Her latest novel, *The Accidental Tourist*, is by far her funniest book: which means, in some ways, her most compassionate, because she never creates a character who is just amusing.

In framework it is a classic comedy of manners, in which *Pygmalion* (is there really any other story?) gets stood on its head and the professor is brought to life by the flower girl. Except that this time the professor is a whole family, a miniature social caste of four. The Learys are Baltimore gentlefolk on the way down. The three brothers and one sister that remain of the family are so ingrown that, as a kind of keep-out sign, they have evolved a preposterous card game that only they can play. Against this game, called "Vaccination," wives dash themselves in vain. There is no way they can enter it — and indeed they can barely even enter the conversation, which is another Leary game, as elaborately private and pointless as everything else about them.

But if other people can't get in, the Learys also can't get out. Whenever one of them attempts the mildest of escapes he comes limping back, baffled (and relieved) to hunker down once more with his siblings in the family "bomb shelter."

There they seem to be holding an interminable town meeting, discussing from every conceivable angle whether or not to leave the windows open at night, and precisely how much or whether one *must* have turkey for Thanksgiving whether one likes it or not. The dead air is filled with fuss. The social class they come from once controlled estates and industries, but now it is down to controlling somewhat smaller matters such as menus and grammar. At one point our hero, Macon

Leary, in a twitch of liberation, attempts a reconciliation with his wife, but finds himself uncontrollably correcting her usage of English. Fuss-budgetry can go no further.

Fortunately for Macon, he has found a way to turn his family's awe-some sterility to some small use. He writes guide books for "accidental tourists" — people like himself who find traveling a miserable business and who regret leaving home even before they've done so. "Generally, food in England is not as jarring as in other countries," he consoles. On his own cautious journeys he compiles lists of absolutely unmenacing hotels, and samples dozens and dozens of breakfasts, that least alarming of meals. The ideal is to carry your own home with you on your back, so you can crawl in safely wherever you are.

However, no plan is safe enough for a Leary. One evening Macon is unexpectedly assailed by acrophobia at the top of "an impossibly tall building." Tottering to a phone, he calls his brother Charles, who, by chance, suffers from claustrophobia and is trapped in the pantry by Macon's slightly mad dog, Edward — a fairly typical Leary impasse.

This same dog (who walks "as if he had sand in his bathing suit") turns out to be the *deus ex machina* who introduces us to one of the most satisfying characters in recent literature — Muriel Pritchett, a dog trainer and anything else that needs doing. Muriel embodies everything guaranteed to make a Leary flinch, including bad taste, unpredictability and life. But she sets her outrageous thrift-shop cap for Macon anyway, thus initiating a heartbreakingly funny one-way courtship.

Along the way we learn that Macon — and perhaps his class — can still be mighty effective when it has something useful to do, and that a hustler like Muriel can be as much a perfectionist in her own way as any Leary. Of Anne Tyler we learn, if we didn't already know it, that her fertility in inventing characters is apparently inexhaustible — every time the doorbell rings, the reader wants to answer it himself — and that her visual gifts are in turn comic and lyrical and, always, exact. "A tan vinyl suitcase with rounded edges reminded Macon of a partly chewed caramel" is an image that will stay with me forever.

Finally, special thanks are due to any satirist (though Tyler is much more than that, of course) who is not content to work the same 20 blocks of Manhattan or one of our New England college towns. Her subject is simply the indoor and outdoor of everywhere. The scope of the phrase "accidental tourist" gradually broadens until it no longer refers to just the tired businessman in the safe hotel, but to everyone anywhere who steps out of his house, out of his clan, and into the infinitely surprising street — in short, to everyone who has ever had the good luck to be born.

Not a small subject. Not a small writer.

WILFRID SHEED

JOHN LE CARRÉ'S *last five novels, including* A Perfect Spy, *have been Club Selections, and before that the Club used all but one of his other novels. "Novel" is the operative word because although le Carré writes thrillers about the secret subterranean wars that go on between countries, he is, always, the novelist first. For* A Perfect Spy *we thought it best to let le Carré himself explain how he came to write this novel about another kind of secret war, that between father and son.*

John le Carré on *A Perfect Spy*

IT IS HARD for me to talk sensibly about the writing of *A Perfect Spy*, either about how the book came to life, or about what it contains, and I strongly advise you not to trust me on the subject. In the first place, the notion of the novel has been with me in one form or another since long before I began writing professionally. I scribbled and plotted, wrote myself little messages about it, *samizdats* (secret letters) against the secret régimes around me. I grew my hair long, cut it short, but no book came.

And when my other novels did begin to flow, each in one way or another seemed to be the surrogate for the one I had still failed to write. Until gradually a gloomy ritual developed. As soon as a novel was finished, I returned in despair to the mountain I was still unable to scale.

Father-son books are perilous documents at the best of times. Seeking analogies to guide me, I dipped into a bunch of them and found few I liked. Even such good good writers as Joe Ackerley and Edmond Gosse seemed to affect a kind of weary cultural superiority over their subjects, as if the sheer effort of living in the parental shadow had left them exquisitely drained. I did not need their tone, and I did not believe in their feigned objectivity. The monsters of our childhood do not fade away, neither are they ever wholly monstrous. But neither, in my experience, do we ever reach a plane of detachment regarding our parents, however wise and old we may become. To pretend otherwise is to cheat.

Another lesson I discovered as I continued my explorations was that books that set out deliberately to destroy one character to the advantage of another, whether in fact or in fiction, have an unnerving way of producing the contrary effect. Halfway through them, the reader suddenly finds the current of his sympathy flowing in the wrong direction. The intended victim, with his wicked ways, becomes the hero, while the narrator who is busy getting his own back becomes the whimpering turncoat we cannot like. "I went through worse than that myself," the reader snorts impatiently. "And look what *I* became."

These were some of the pitfalls I spotted as I tapped my way along. Usually I had fallen into them by the time I woke to them, so it was back to other projects without the option.

But I began to learn. In a shoot-out between father and son, for example, there had to be a balance of culpability on both sides. There had to be love in the midst of revulsion; and pity in the midst of revenge. The son's fight for identity should never cease while he had breath. But the reader must know, and so must the son, that there would never be any hope that he could one day fight himself free of his genetic snares. It is not distance but proximity that makes wars. It is not victory but failure that makes us keep on fighting.

And this war, I decided, would be a secret one, waged in the back alleys of their relationship, until one or both dropped dead, and its chief weapon would be love. Secrecy had always been the father's natural element. It should become the son's also. Young Pym should take refuge in the secret world as in a new father. His failed gods should be the discarded absolutes that he has embraced and thrown away in his search for a better father image. He should take to the secret world as to a cloister, and give himself to his country as a means of taking himself away from his father. . . .

There my apologia ceases. To ask me what is "true" in this novel and what is "imagined" is to address the least reliable of sources. There is not a writer on earth I would trust to tell me the time of day when it comes to separating fact from fiction, and John le Carré is no exception. For anyone who has ever been near to the creative process, the argument is anyway sterile: good for the literary bureaucrats, misleading for readers, irrelevant for writers. A novelist's job is to make fables from his own life. His tools are his wit, his eyes and ears, and the marks upon his own soul.

INDEX

Accidental Tourist, The (Tyler), review of, 321–323

Act of Faith and Other Stories (Shaw), review of, 82–83

Affluent Society, The (Galbraith), 301

Agee, James: *A Death in the Family*, review of, 145

All the King's Men (Warren), xviii; review of, 87–88

All the President's Men (Bernstein and Woodward), 224–226

Allen, Fred: essay by, on Herman Wouk, 99–100

Alternate, BOMC, xviii

American Heritage (publishers): *A Sense of History*, xxi

Americans, The: The Democratic Experience (Boorstin), 208

—*And I Worked at the Writer's Trade* (Cowley), 267

". . . *And Ladies of the Club*" (Santmyer), 313–314; review of, 314–316

Animal Farm (Orwell), xviii, 88; BOMC president's statement on, 89; review of, 89–91

Appointment in Samarra (O'Hara), review of, 37–38

Armies of the Night (Mailer), review of, 183–184

Aurora Dawn (Wouk), 99

Autobiography of Malcolm X, The, review of, 177–178

Babe Ruth Story, The (Ruth), review of, 111

Baldwin, James: *The Fire Next Time*, review of, 160–161; *Nobody Knows My Name*, review of, 160

Barbato, Joseph, 268; essay by, on James Michener, 272–274

Bellow, Saul, 305; essay on, 241–243; *Henderson the Rain King*, review of, 239–240; *Herzog*, review of, 240–241; *Humboldt's Gift*, 239, 242

Benét, Rosemary C.: review by, of *Stuart Little* (E. B. White), 83–84

Benét, William Rose: review by, of *The Postman Always Rings Twice* (Cain), 20–21

Bernstein, Carl, and Bob Woodward: *All the President's Men*, 224–226; interview of, 224–226

Big Sky, The (Guthrie), 117, 119

Birds Fall Down, The (West), 176, 177

Black Boy (Wright), xviii, 67

Blixen, Baroness Karen. *See* Dinesen, Isak

Book of the Month, selection process for, xvii–xviii, 11–12, 25

Book-of-the-Month Club (BOMC): Editorial Board of, xvi–xviii, xix–xx; first novels in, 106–108; founder of, xiii, xiv, xv–xvii, xviii; history of, xi–xx; monthly offerings of, xviii–xix; prominent au-

Book-of-the-Month Club (BOMC)
(*continued*)
thors of, xii–xiii, 3–9; reactions to,
xv, 32; selection process of, for
Book of the Month, xvii–xviii,
11–12, 25
Boorstin, Daniel, 207–208; *The
Americans: The Democratic Expe-
rience*, 208; essay on, 208–210
Bourne Conspiracy, The (Ludlum),
283
Boys of Summer, The (Kahn), 111
Brave Men (Pyle), 63
Bread and Wine (Silone), 54
Breit, Harvey, 49; essay by, on John
Steinbeck, 52–53
Brideshead Revisited (Waugh), 80;
review of, 76–79
Bridge Too Far, A (Ryan), 226, 229
Brighton Rock (Greene), review of,
215–216
Broun, Heywood, xvii
Brown, Dee: *Bury My Heart at
Wounded Knee*, review of,
199–200
Brown, John Mason, xix; obituary
by, for Henry Seidel Canby,
98–99
Buck, Pearl S.: *The Good Earth*, re-
view of, 25–28
Buckley, William F., Jr., essay by, on
John Kenneth Galbraith, 301–303
Burgess, Anthony: *Earthly Powers*,
299; essay on, 299–301
Burnett, W. R.: *Little Caesar*, review
of, 19
Burr (Vidal), author's piece on,
210–215
Bury My Heart at Wounded Knee
(Brown), review of, 199–200

Cain, James M.: *The Postman Al-
ways Rings Twice*, review of,
20–21
Caine Mutiny, The (Wouk), xviii
Canby, Henry Seidel, xiii, 93;
American Memoir, xvii, 25, 43,
49; and BOMC selection process,
xvii, 25; on *Catcher in the Rye*
(Salinger), 127; on *Elmer Gantry*
(Lewis), 17; on *Gone with the
Wind* (Mitchell), 43; on *Lolly

Willowes, or The Loving Hunts-
man* (Warner), 11; obituary for,
by BOMC Editorial Board, 98–99;
support by, for *The Grapes of
Wrath* (Steinbeck), xvii, 49; on
Thomas Wolfe, 56. Essays by: on
Herbert Hoover and Maj. Laban J.
Miles, 29–31; on George Orwell,
91–92. Reviews by: *All the King's
Men* (Warren), 87–88; *Charlotte's
Web* (E. B. White), 84; *The Com-
plete Sherlock Holmes* (Doyle),
22–24; *For Whom the Bell Tolls*
(Hemingway), 3, 5–7; *Gone with
the Wind* (Mitchell), 43–45; *The
Good Earth* (Buck), 25–28; *The
Grapes of Wrath* (Steinbeck),
51–52; *I, Claudius* (Graves),
31–32; *Light in August*
(Faulkner), 28–29; *Man's Fate*
(Malraux), 34–35; *Of Time and
the River* (Wolfe), 56–57; *Tender
Is the Night* (Fitzgerald), 74–75;
The Web and the Rock (Wolfe),
57–58; *You Can't Go Home Again*
(Wolfe), 58–59
Canfield, Dorothy, 37, 93; on *The
Good Earth* (Buck), 27; letter to
reader by, 94–97; obituary for, by
Robert Frost, 97–98; standards of,
in book selection, xvii. Reviews by:
Appointment in Samarra
(O'Hara), 37–38; *The Heart Is a
Lonely Hunter* (McCullers), 59–60
Capote, Truman: essay on, 178–180;
In Cold Blood, 178–180; *Other
Voices, Other Rooms*, review of,
108
Caputo, Philip, 258–259; essay on,
260–262; *A Rumor of War*,
261–262; review of, 259–260
Caro, Robert A., 305–306; essay on,
306–308; *The Path to Power*, 305,
306, 307–308
Carson, Rachel: *Silent Spring*, 163;
review of, 164–167
Catcher in the Rye (Salinger), xviii,
129; review of, 125–127
Catch-22 (Heller), 162; review of,
163
Cather, Willa, xi; essay on, 100–
101

Catton, Bruce, xxi; essay on, 131–134; *A Stillness at Appomattox*, 133; review of, 131; *This Hallowed Ground*, 131

Cerf, Bennett, 64; essay by, on Richard Tregaskis, 65–67; on Harry Scherman, xvi

Charlotte's Web (E. B. White), 83; review of, 84

Cheever, John: *The Stories of John Cheever*, 278; reviews of, 281–283; *The Wapshot Chronicle*, review of, 278–279; *The World of Apples*, 278; review of, 279–281

Chesapeake (Michener): author's note on, 270–272; review of, 268–270

Churchill, Randolph: essay by, on Evelyn Waugh, 79–81

Churchill, Winston: *The Gathering Storm*, review of, 113–114

Cider House Rules, The (Irving), 317, 318–320

Clark, Marsh, 259; essay by, on Philip Caputo, 260–262

Collapse of the Third Republic, The (Shirer), 147

Collected Stories of Isaac Bashevis Singer, The, review of, 303–305

Collier, Peter, 309; essay by, on John Updike, 312–313

Colum, Padraic: essay by, on Robert Frost, 41–43

Confessions of Nat Turner, The (Styron), 285, 289, 290

Cousins, Norman: essay by, on John Hersey, 120–123

Cowley, Malcolm: —*And I Worked at the Writer's Trade*, 267; essay on, 266–268

Crack-Up, The (Fitzgerald), review of, 75–76

Crusade in Europe (Eisenhower), xviii

Daniel Martin (Fowles), 264–265

Darkness at Noon (Koestler), xviii; review of, 60–62

Davenport, Basil, xvi; obituary by, on Henry Seidel Canby, 98–99

David, Gwenda, 175–176; essay by, on Rebecca West, 176–177

Day, Clarence: essay on, 38–41; *Life with Father*, 38

Day of the Jackal, The (Forsyth): author's note on, 202–205; review of, 200–202

Days of Wrath (Malraux), 34

De Voto, Bernard, essay by, on A. B. Guthrie, Jr., 117–119

De Vries, Peter: essay on, 143–144; *The Tents of Wickedness*, review of, 141–143

Death Be Not Proud (Gunther), review of, 103

Death in the Family, A (Agee), 145

Death of a Salesman (Miller), 114, 116–117

Deindorfer, Robert G: essay by, on Robert Ludlum, 283–285

Detective fiction (1930s), 18, 21

Dinesen, Isak (Baroness Karen Blixen), 153; essay on, 154–155

Doctorow, E. L.: essay on, 235–237; *Ragtime*, 235–237

Doubleday, Nelson, essay by, on A. P. Herbert, 32–34

Douglas, William O., 163; review by, of *Silent Spring* (Carson), 164–167

Doyle, Sir Arthur Conan: *The Complete Sherlock Holmes*, review of, 21–25

Durant, Ariel, xii, 13; essay on, 15–17

Durant, Will, xii, 13; essay on, 15–17; *The Story of Civilization*, xii, 13, 16; *Our Oriental Heritage*, review of, 14–15; *The Story of Philosophy*, xii, 13, 15, 16; review of, 13–14

Earthly Powers (Burgess), 299

Easton, Elizabeth, 215; interview by, of Graham Greene, 218–222

Eco, Umberto: *The Name of the Rose*, Fadiman on, xx

Eighth Day, The (Wilder), 181

Eisenhower, Dwight D: *Crusade in Europe*, xviii

Elements of Style, The (Strunk and White), 145; review of, 146

Ellison, Ralph, 218; *Invisible Man*, review of, 130

Elmer Gantry (Lewis), review of, 17

European Discovery of America, The: The Northern Voyages (Morison), 205

Fadiman, Clifton, xix–xx; on American readers, xvi; on Dorothy Canfield, 93; on *Daniel Martin* (Fowles), 265; essay by, on Will and Ariel Durant, 15–17; on *The Name of the Rose* (Eco), xx; obituary by, on Henry Seidel Canby, 98–99; on Harry Scherman, xvi; on *Voyage: A Novel of 1896* (Hayden), 251. Reviews by: *Catcher in the Rye* (Salinger), 125–127; *The Day of the Jackal* (Forsyth), 200–202; *The Fire Next Time* (Baldwin), 160–161; *The Heart of the Matter* (Greene), 216–218; *Herzog* (Bellow), 240–241; *Late Night Thoughts on Listening to Mahler's Ninth Symphony* (Thomas), 308–309; *The Making of the President 1960* (T. H. White), 155–157; *A New Age Now Begins* (Smith), 245–248; *Something of Value* (Ruark), 134–137; *The Stories of John Cheever*, 281; *The Thurber Carnival* (Thurber), 71–74; *The Wapshot Chronicle* (Cheever), 278–279; *The Young Lions* (Shaw), 107

Fairfield, Cicily Isabel. See West, Rebecca

Farewell to Arms, A (Hemingway), 3, 8

Faulkner, William: *Light in August*, review of, 28–29; *The Reivers*, xviii, 28

Fay, Martha, 239; on *Song of Solomon* (Morrison), 263. Essays by: on Saul Bellow, 241–243; on Sterling Hayden, 251–254

Ferber, Edna: *Show Boat*, xii

Fincher, Jack, 245; essay by, on Page Smith, 248–250

Fire Next Time, The (Baldwin), 160–161

Fischer, Louis: essay by, on Arthur Koestler, 62–63

Fisher, Dorothy Canfield. *See* Canfield, Dorothy

Fitzgerald, F. Scott, xi, 74; *The Crack-Up*, review of, 75–76; *Tender Is the Night*, review of, 74–75

Flowering Judas (Porter), 169

Foley, Martha: essay by, on Ignazio Silone, 54–56

Fools Die (Puzo), 184, 186–189

For Whom the Bell Tolls (Hemingway), 3; review of, 5–7

Forsyth, Frederick: *The Day of the Jackal*, author's note on, 202–205; review of, 200–202

Fortunate Pilgrim (Puzo), 184; review of, 185

Fowles, John, 264–265; biographical sketch on, 265–266; *Daniel Martin*, 264–265

Friedman, Bruce Jay: essay by, on Mario Puzo, 186–189

Frost, Robert: essay on, 41–43; *A Further Range*, 41; obituary by, for Dorothy Canfield, 97–98

Further Range, A (Frost), 41

Galbraith, John Kenneth, xxi; *The Affluent Society*, 301; essay on, 301–303

Galsworthy, John: *The Silver Spoon*, xii

Gammack, Gordon, 63; essay by, on Ernie Pyle, 64–65

Garden of Eden, The (Hemingway), xii, 3–4

Gathering Storm, The (Churchill), review of, 113–114

George (Williams), 167, 169

Ghost Writer, The (Roth), review of, 293–295

Gibbs, Wolcott, 83; essay by, on E. B. White, 85–87

Glass Key (Hammett), review of, 19–20

Godfather, The (Puzo), review of, 185–186

Gone with the Wind (Mitchell), xiv–xv; review of, 43–45

Good Earth, The (Buck), review of, 25–28

Goodbye Darkness (Manchester), 277–278; review of, 274–276

Goodman, Walter: essay by, on Daniel Boorstin, 208–210; interview by, of Carl Bernstein and Bob Woodward, 224–226

Grapes of Wrath, The (Steinbeck), 49, 53; Canby's support for, xvii, 49; review of, 51–52

Graves, Robert: *I, Claudius*, review of, 31–32

Greene, Graham: interview of, 218–222. Works: *Brighton Rock*, review of, 215–216; *The Heart of the Matter*, review of, 216–218; *The Honorary Consul*, 215, 219, 220, 221, 222

Greenwich Village, essay on, 112–113

Group, The (McCarthy), review of, 174–175

Guadalcanal Diary (Tregaskis), 63, 66–67

Gulag Archipelago, The (Solzhenitsyn), review of, 230–234

Guns of August, The (Tuchman), 190, 191–192

Gunther, John, 102; *Death Be Not Proud*, review of, 103; essay on, 103–106; *Inside U.S.A.*, 102, 105; note on death of son of, by Bernardine Kielty, 102; review by, of *The Rise and Fall of the Third Reich* (Shirer), 147–150

Guthrie, A. B., Jr.: *The Big Sky*, 117, 119; essay on, 117–119; *The Way West*, 117, 119

Haas, Robert K., 153; essay by, on Isak Dinesen, 154–155

Hammett, Dashiell: *Glass Key*, review of, 19–20; *The Thin Man*, review of, 20

Hayden, Sterling: essay on, 251–254; *Voyage: A Novel of 1896*, 251, 252, 253

Heart Is a Lonely Hunter, The (McCullers), review of, 59–60

Heart of the Country (Matthews), judges' support for, xvii

Heart of the Matter, The (Greene), review of, 216–218

Heaven's My Destination (Wilder), 181

Heilbroner, Robert, xxi

Heller, Joseph: *Catch-22*, 162; review of, 163

Hemingway, Ernest, xi, xii–xiii, 3–4; essay on, 7–9; *A Farewell to Arms*, 3, 8; *For Whom the Bell Tolls*, 3; review of, 5–7; *The Garden of Eden*, xii, 3–4; *The Sun Also Rises*, xii, 3; review of, 4

Henderson the Rain King (Bellow), review of, 239–240

Herbert, A. P.: essay on, 32–34; *Holy Deadlock*, 32

Here Is New York (E. B. White), 83

Hersey, John, 119–120; essay by, on Theodore H. White, 158–159; essay on, 120–123; *Hiroshima*, 119–122; *The Wall*, 120, 123

Herzog (Bellow), review of, 240–241

Highet, Gilbert, xix, 192; obituary by, on Henry Seidel Canby, 98–99. Reviews by: *The Elements of Style* (Strunk and White), 146; *The Group* (McCarthy), 174–175; *Henderson the Rain King* (Bellow), 239–240; *The Last of the Just* (Schwarz-Bart), 153; *The New English Bible*, 192–199; *A Rumor of War* (Caputo), 259–260

Hiroshima (Hersey), 119–122

Historical romances (1947), 101

Holden, Raymond: review by, of *A Stillness at Appomattox* (Catton), 131

Holy Deadlock (Herbert), 32

Honorary Consul, The (Greene), 215, 219, 220, 221, 222

Hoover, Herbert, 29–31

Horgan, Paul, xix; essay by, on Thornton Wilder, 181–183

Humboldt's Gift (Bellow), 239, 242

Hutchens, John K., xix; on the Lost Generation, xi; on *The Path Between the Seas* (McCullough), 256; support by, for *Heart of the Country* (Matthews), xvii. Reviews by: *Bury My Heart at*

Hutchens, John K. (*continued*)
Wounded Knee (Brown),
199–200; *Chesapeake* (Michener),
268–270; *The Collected Stories of
Isaac Bashevis Singer*, 303–305;
Fortunate Pilgrim (Puzo), 185;
Goodbye Darkness (Manchester),
274–276; *The Stories of John
Cheever*, 281–282

I, Claudius (Graves), review of,
31–32
Ides of March, The (Wilder), 181
In Cold Blood (Capote), 178–180
Inside U.S.A. (Gunther), 102, 105
Invisible Man (Ellison), review of,
130
Irving, John, 316–317; *The Cider
House Rules*, 317, 318–320; essay
on, 318–320; *The World Accord-
ing to Garp*, xviii; review of,
317–318
*Is Sex Necessary? Or Why You Feel
the Way You Do* (Thurber and
E. B. White), review of, 18

Janeway, Elizabeth: essay by, on
Barbara Tuchman, 190–192
John Adams (Smith), 245
Johnson, Lucy: review by, of *Catch-
22* (Heller), 163

Kahn, Roger: *The Boys of Summer*,
111
Kanin, Garson: essay by, on Emlyn
Williams, 167–169
Kazin, Alfred: essay by, on Mark
Schorer, 161–162
Kent, Edward Allen: review by, of
The Autobiography of Malcolm X,
177–178
Kielty, Bernardine: on *Act of Faith
and Other Stories* (Shaw), 82; on
death of John Gunther's son, 102;
obituary for, by David Willis
McCullough, 234; on undeliverable
mail, 119; on *Williwaw* (Vidal),
82. Essays by: on Willa Cather,
100–101; on Greenwich Village,
112–113. Reviews by: *Act of Faith
and Other Stories* (Shaw), 82–83;
The Crack-Up (Fitzgerald), 75–76

Koestler, Arthur: *Darkness at Noon*,
xviii; review of, 60–62; essay on,
62–63
Kummer, Corby, 316; essay by, on
John Irving, 318–320

La Farge, Christopher: *The Sudden
Guest*, 89
Lancelot (Percy), 254, 256
Last Hurrah, The (O'Connor), 138,
139
Last of the Just, The (Schwarz-
Bart), review of, 153
*Late Night Thoughts on Listening to
Mahler's Ninth Symphony*
(Thomas), review of, 308–309
Latham, H. S.: essay by, on Mar-
garet Mitchell, 46–48
le Carré, John: *A Perfect Spy*, au-
thor's note on, 323–324
Lee, Harper: essay by, on Truman
Capote, 178–180
Leonard, Elmore, xii–xiii
Letting Go (Roth), 293
Lewis, Sinclair: biography of
(Schorer), 161–162; *Elmer Gan-
try*, review of, 17; vs. Helen Hoo-
ven Santmyer, 314, 316
Lie Down in Darkness (Styron),
285, 287, 292
Life with Father (Day), 38
Light in August (Faulkner), review
of, 28–29
Little Caesar (Burnett), review of,
19
*Lolly Willowes, or The Loving
Huntsman* (Warner), xiii–xiv; re-
view of, 11–13
Loveman, Amy, xvi; on *Catcher in
the Rye* (Salinger), 127; dissent
by, to *Something of Value*
(Ruark), 137; review by, of
Death Be Not Proud (Gunther),
103
Lowry, Malcolm: *Under the Vol-
cano*, xviii; review of, 101–102
Ludlum, Robert: *The Bourne Con-
spiracy*, 283; essay on, 283–285;
The Matarese Circle, 283, 284

McCarthy, Mary: *The Group*, review of, 174–175

McCormick, Ken, 108; essay by, on W. Somerset Maugham, 108–111

McCullers, Carson: *The Heart Is a Lonely Hunter*, review of, 59–60

McCullough, David (historian), xxi, 256; essay on, 257–258; *The Path Between the Seas*, 256, 258

McCullough, David Willis, xvi, xix, 11; obituary by, for Bernardine Kielty, 234; support by, for *Heart of the Country* (Matthews), xvii. Essays by: on Malcolm Cowley, 266–268; on Peter De Vries, 143–144; on Robert K. Massie, 295–297; on William Maxwell, 297–299; on S. J. Perelman, 243–245; on William Zinsser, 237–239. Reviews by: "... *And Ladies of the Club*" (Santmyer), 314–316; *Armies of the Night* (Mailer), 183–184; *Slaughterhouse Five* (Vonnegut), 189; *The Witches of Eastwick* (Updike), 310–311; *The World of Apples* (Cheever), 279–281

Mailer, Norman: *Armies of the Night*, review of, 183–184; *The Naked and the Dead*, review of, 106–107

Making of the President 1960, The (T. H. White), review of, 155–157

Malraux, André: *Days of Wrath*, 34; essay on, 35–37; *Man's Fate*, xviii; review of, 34–35

Manchester, William, 274; essay on, 277–278; *Goodbye Darkness*, 277–278; review of, 274–276

Mandelbaum, Helene: review by, *The Godfather* (Puzo), 185–186

Man's Fate (Malraux), xviii; review of, 34–35

Marquand, John P., xix; on *Catcher in the Rye* (Salinger), 127. Reviews by: *The Naked and the Dead* (Mailer), 106–107; *The Tents of Wickedness* (De Vries), 141–143

Massie, Robert K.: essay on, 295–297; *Peter the Great*, 295–297

Matarese Circle, The (Ludlum), 283, 284

Mathews, John Joseph, 29, 31; *Wah'Kon-Tah*, 29, 30

Matthews, Greg: *Heart of the Country*, judges' support for, xvii

Maugham, W. Somerset: essay on, 108–111; *Of Human Bondage*, 109; Mario Puzo on, 188

Maxwell, William, 125; essay by, on J. D. Salinger, 128–130; essay on, 297–299; *They Came Like Swallows*, 297

Michener, James, 268; essay on, 272–274. *Chesapeake*: author's note on, 270–272; review of, 268–270

Miles, Maj. Laban J., 29–31

Miller, Arthur: *Death of a Salesman*, 114, 116–117; essay on, 114–117

Mitchell, Margaret: essay on, 46–48; *Gone with the Wind*, xiv–xv; review of, 43–45

Mitford, Nancy: essay on, 123–125

Morison, Samuel Eliot: essay on, 205–207; *The European Discovery of America: The Northern Voyages*, 205

Morley, Christopher, xvii; on *Catcher in the Rye* (Salinger), 127. Reviews by: *Animal Farm* (Orwell), 89–91; *Brideshead Revisited* (Waugh), 76–79; *Brighton Rock* (Greene), 215–216; *Darkness at Noon* (Koestler), 60–62; *Of Mice and Men* (Steinbeck), 49–51; *The Thin Man* (Hammett), 20

Morris, Willie, 285; essay by, on William Styron, 289–293

Morrison, Toni, 316; *Song of Solomon*, xviii, 262; review of, 263–264

Naked and the Dead, The (Mailer), review of, 106–107

Name of the Rose, The (Eco), Fadiman on, xx

Native Son (Wright), xviii, 70–71; review of, 67–69

Nevins, Allan: on Henry Seidel Canby, 93, 99; essay by, on Bruce Catton, 131–134

New Age Now Begins, A (Smith), review of, 245–248

New English Bible, The, review of,
    192–199
New Meaning of Treason, The
    (West), 177
Newcombe, Jack: essays by: on
    David McCullough, 257–258; on
    Walker Percy, 254–256
1984 (Orwell), xviii; review of,
    91–92
Nobody Knows My Name (Bald-
    win), review of, 160
Norris, Gloria, xvi, xix, xx, 283

O'Connor, Edwin: essay on,
    138–139; *The Last Hurrah* 138,
    139
Of Human Bondage (Maugham),
    109
Of Mice and Men (Steinbeck), re-
    view of, 49–51
Of Time and the River (Wolfe),
    8–9; review of, 56–57
O'Hara, John: *Appointment in Sa-
    marra*, review of, 37–38
On Writing Well (Zinsser), 237
Orwell, George: *Animal Farm*, xviii,
    88; BOMC president's statement
    on, 89; review of, 89–91; essay on,
    91–92; *1984*, xviii; review of, 91–92
Other Voices, Other Rooms (Ca-
    pote), review of, 108

Path Between the Seas, The (McCul-
    lough), 256, 258
Path to Power, The (Caro), 305,
    306, 307–308
Percy, Walker: essay on, 254–256;
    Lancelot, 254, 256
Perelman, S. J.: essay on, 243–245;
    Vinegar Puss, 243, 244
Perfect Spy, A (le Carré), author's
    note on, 323–324
Perkins, Maxwell, xii, 3; essay by, on
    Ernest Hemingway, 7–9
Peter the Great (Massie), 295–297
Porter, Katherine Anne: essay on,
    170–174; *Flowering Judas*, 169;
    Ship of Fools, review of, 169–170
Postman Always Rings Twice, The
    (Cain), review of, 20–21
Proud Tower, The (Tuchman), 190,
    191

Puzo, Mario, 184; essay on, 186–189;
    Fools Die, 184, 186–189; *Fortunate
    Pilgrim*, 184; review of, 185; *The
    Godfather*, review of, 185–186;
    The Sicilian, 184
Pyle, Ernie, 63; essay on, 64–65;
    Brave Men, 63

Ragtime (Doctorow), 235–237
Reivers, The (Faulkner), xviii, 28
Richler, Mordecai, xix; promotion
    by, of John Irving, 316; promotion
    by, of Toni Morrison, 316. Re-
    views by: *Song of Solomon* (Mor-
    rison), 262, 263–264; *The Stories
    of John Cheever*, 282; *The World
    According to Garp* (Irving),
    317–318
*Rise and Fall of the Third Reich,
    The* (Shirer), 146–147; review of,
    147–150
Rosenthal, Lucy, xvi; review by, of
    The Stories of John Cheever, 282
Rosen, Axel, xxii
Rosin, Katharine S.: essay by, on
    Arthur Miller, 114–117
Roth, Philip: *The Ghost Writer*, re-
    view of, 293–295; *Letting Go*, 293
Royko, Mike; essay by, on Studs
    Terkel, 222–224
Ruark, Robert: essay on, 137. *Some-
    thing of Value*: dissent to, 137; re-
    view of, 134–137
Rumor of War, A (Caputo),
    261–262; review of, 259–260
Ruth, Babe: *The Babe Ruth Story*,
    review of, 111
Ryan, Cornelius: *A Bridge Too Far*,
    226, 229; essay on, 227–229

Salinger, J. D.: *Catcher in the Rye*,
    xviii, 129; review of, 125–127;
    essay on, 128–130
Salisbury, Harrison: review by, of
    The Gulag Archipelago (Solzhen-
    itsyn), 230–234
Santmyer, Helen Hooven: "… *And
    Ladies of the Club*," 313–314; re-
    view of, 314–316
Savago, Joe, xxi
Scherman, Bernardine Kielty. *See*
    Kielty, Bernardine

Scherman, Harry, xiii, xiv, xv–xvii, xviii; on *Animal Farm* (Orwell), 89; on the BOMC, 93; review by, of *The Gathering Storm* (Churchill), 113–114; on *The Rise and Fall of the Third Reich* (Shirer), 147; and *Thunder Out of China* (T. H. White), 155

Schorer, Mark, essay on, 161–162

Schwarz-Bart, André: *The Last of the Just*, review of, 153

Seabrook, William: essay by, on André Malraux, 35–37

Seaver, Edwin, 67; essay by, on Richard Wright, 69–71. Reviews by: *Other Voices, Other Rooms* (Capote), 108; *Under the Volcano* (Lowry), 101–102

Selection, BOMC. *See* Book of the Month

Sense of History, A (American Heritage), xxi

Shapiro, Larry, xxi

Shaw, Irwin: *Act of Faith and Other Stories*, review of, 82–83; *The Young Lions*, review of, 107

Sheed, Wilfrid, xix. Reviews by: *The Accidental Tourist* (Tyler), 321–323; *The Ghost Writer* (Roth), 293–295; *The Stories of John Cheever*, 282–283

Shenker, Israel, 299; essay by, on Anthony Burgess, 299–301

Ship of Fools (Porter), review of, 169–170

Shirer, William L.: essay by, on John Gunther, 103–106; essay on, 150–152; *The Collapse of the Third Republic*, 147; *The Rise and Fall of the Third Reich*, 146–147; review of, 147–150

Show Boat (Ferber), xii

Sicilian, The (Puzo), 184

Silberman, James H.: essay by, on E. L. Doctorow, 235–237

Silent Spring (Carson), 163; review of, 164–167

Silone, Ignazio: *Bread and Wine*, 54; essay on, 54–56

Silver Spoon, The (Galsworthy), xii

Silverman, Al, xx–xxiii

Singer, Isaac Bashevis: *The Collected Stories of Isaac Bashevis Singer*, review of, 303–305

Singer, Mark, 306; essay by, on Robert A. Caro, 306–308

Slaughterhouse Five: Or, The Children's Crusade (Vonnegut), review of, 189

Slavitt, D. R.: review by, of *Nobody Knows My Name* (Baldwin), 160

Smith, Page, 245; essay by, on Samuel Eliot Morison, 205–207; essay on, 248–250; *John Adams*, 245; *A New Age Now Begins*, review of, 245–248

Something of Value (Ruark): dissent to, 137; review of, 134–137

Song of Solomon (Morrison), xviii, 262; review of, 263–264

Solzhenitsyn, Aleksandr, 229–230; *The Gulag Archipelago*, review of, 230–234

Sophie's Choice (Styron), 289–293

Soskin, William: review by, of *Invisible Man* (Ellison), 130

Steinbeck, John: essay on, 52–53; Works: *The Grapes of Wrath*, 53; Canby's support for, xvii, 49; review of, 51–52; *Of Mice and Men*, review of, 49–51; *The Wayward Bus*, 49, 53

Stillness at Appomattox, A (Catton), 133; review of, 131

Stilwell and the American Experience in China (Tuchman), 190, 192

Stories of John Cheever, The, 278; reviews of, 281–283

Story of Civilization, The (Durant and Durant), xii, 13, 16; *Our Oriental Heritage*, review of, 14–15

Story of Philosophy, The (W. Durant), xii, 13, 15, 16; review of, 13–14

Strunk, William, Jr.: *The Elements of Style*, review of, 146

Stuart Little (E. B. White), review of, 83–84

Styron, William: essays on, 285–293. Works: *The Confessions of Nat Turner*, 285, 289, 290; *Lie Down in Darkness*, 285, 287, 292; *Sophie's Choice*, 289–293

Sudden Guest, The (La Farge), 89
Sun Also Rises, The (Hemingway),
  xii, 3; review of, 4

Tender Is the Night (Fitzgerald), re-
  view of, 74–75
Tents of Wickedness, The (De
  Vries), review of, 141–143
Terkel, Studs: essay on, 222–224;
  Working, 222–224
They Came Like Swallows (Max-
  well), 297
Thin Man, The (Hammett), review
  of, 20
This Hallowed Ground (Catton),
  131
Thomas, Lewis: *Late Night
  Thoughts on Listening to Mahler's
  Ninth Symphony,* review of,
  308–309
Thompson, Ralph, 144–145; review
  by, of *A Death in the Family*
  (Agee), 145
Thurber, James, 18; *Is Sex Neces-
  sary? Or Why You Feel the Way
  You Do,* review of, 18; *The
  Thurber Carnival,* review of,
  71–74
Thurber Carnival, The (Thurber),
  review of, 71–74
Tregaskis, Richard, 64; essay on,
  65–67; *Guadalcanal Diary,* 63,
  66–67
Tuchman, Barbara, xxi; essay by, on
  William L. Shirer, 150–152; essay
  on, 190–192; *The Guns of August,*
  190, 191–192; *The Proud Tower,*
  190, 191; *Stilwell and the American Experience in China,* 190,
  192
Tyler, Anne, 320–321; *The Accidental Tourist,* review of, 321–323

Under the Volcano (Lowry), xviii;
  review of, 101–102
Updike, John: essay on, 312–313;
  The Witches of Eastwick, review
  of, 310–311

Van Doren, Carl, xv
Vidal, Gore: *Burr,* author's piece on,
  210–215; *Williwaw,* 82

Vinegar Puss (Perelman), 243, 244
Vonnegut, Kurt, Jr.: *Slaughterhouse
  Five: Or, The Children's Crusade,*
  review of, 189
Voyage: A Novel of 1896 (Hayden),
  251, 252, 253

Wah'Kon-Tah (Mathews), 29, 30
Wall, The (Hersey), 120, 123
Wapshot Chronicle, The (Cheever),
  review of, 278–279
Warner, Sylvia Townsend: *Lolly
  Willowes, or The Loving Hunts-
  man,* xiii–xiv; review of, 11–13
Warren, Robert Penn: *All the King's
  Men,* xviii; review of, 87–88; essay
  by, on William Styron, 285–289
Waugh, Evelyn: *Brideshead Re-
  visited,* 80; review of, 76–79; essay
  by, on Nancy Mitford, 123–125;
  essay on, 79–81
Way West, The (Guthrie), 117, 119
Wayward Bus, The (Steinbeck), 49,
  53
Web and the Rock, The (Wolfe), re-
  view of, 57–58
Weeks, Edward, 138; essay by, on
  Edwin O'Connor, 138–139
Wescott, Glenway, 169; essay by, on
  Katherine Anne Porter, 170–174
West, Rebecca (Cicily Isabel Fair-
  field): *The Birds Fall Down,* 176,
  177; essay on, 176–177; *The New
  Meaning of Treason,* 177
White, E. B.: essay by, on Clarence
  Day, 38–41; essay on, 85–87.
  Works: *Charlotte's Web,* 83; re-
  view of, 84; *The Elements of Style,*
  145; review of, 146; *Here Is New
  York,* 83; *Is Sex Necessary? Or
  Why You Feel the Way You Do,*
  review of, 18; *Stuart Little,* review
  of, 83–84
White, Theodore H., 155; essay by,
  on Cornelius Ryan, 227–229; essay
  on, 158–159; *The Making of the
  President 1960,* review of, 155–
  157
White, William Allen, xvii
Whitman, Alden, 274; essay by, on
  William Manchester, 277–278
Wilder, Thornton: essay on,

181-183. Works: *The Eighth Day*, 181; *Heaven's My Destination*, 181; *The Ides of March*, 181
Williams, Emlyn: essay on, 167-169; George, 167, 169
Williwaw (Vidal), 82
Wind, Herbert Warren: review by, of *The Babe Ruth Story* (Ruth), 111
Witches of Eastwick, The (Updike), review of, 310-311
Wolfe, Thomas, 56; *Of Time and the River*, review of, 56-57; *The Web and the Rock*, review of, 57-58; *You Can't Go Home Again*, review of, 58-59
Woodward, Bob, and Carl Bernstein: *All the President's Men*, 224-226; interview of, 224-226
Working (Terkel), 222-224
World According to Garp, The (Irving), xviii; review of, 317-318

World of Apples, The (Cheever), 278; review of, 279-281
World War II: nonfiction on, 63-64, 274-276; novels about, 106-107, 162, 163
Wouk, Herman: *Aurora Dawn*, 99; *The Caine Mutiny*, xviii; essay on, 99-100
Wright, Richard: *Black Boy*, xviii, 67; essay on, 69-71; *Native Son*, xviii, 70-71; review of, 67-69

X, Malcolm: *The Autobiography of Malcolm X*, review of, 177-178

You Can't Go Home Again (Wolfe), review of, 58-59
Young Lions, The (Shaw), review of, 107

Zinsser, William: essay on, 237-239; *On Writing Well*, 237